PowerPoint® 2013

onDemand

Steve Johnson

Perspection, Inc.

que® Que Publishing, 800 East 96th Street, Incianapolis, IN 46240 USA

PowerPoint® 2013 on Demand

Library of Congress Cataloging-in-Publication Data is on file

ISBN-13: 978-0-7897-4856-0
ISBN-10: 0-7897-4856-8

Printed and bound in the United States of America
First Printing: April 2013
16 15 14 13   4 3 2 1

Que Publishing offers excellent discounts on this book when ordered in quantity for bulk purchases or special sales.

For information, please contact: U.S. Corporate and Government Sales

    1-800-382-3419 or corpsales@pearsontechgroup.com

For sales outside the U.S., please contact: International Sales

    1-317-428-3341 or International@pearsontechgroup.com

Trademarks
All terms mentioned in this book that are known to be trademarks or service marks have been appropriately capitalized. Que cannot attest to the accuracy of this information. Use of a term in this book should not be regarded as affecting the validity of any trademark or service mark.

Microsoft and the Microsoft Office logo are registered trademarks of Microsoft Corporation in the United States and/or other countries.

Warning and Disclaimer
Every effort has been made to make this book as complete and as accurate as possible, but no warranty or fitness is implied. The authors and the publishers shall have neither liability nor responsibility to any person or entity with respect to any loss or damage arising from the information contained in this book.

Publisher
Paul Boger

Associate Publisher
Greg Wiegand

Executive Editor
Loretta Yates

Managing Editor
Steve Johnson

Author
Steve Johnson

Page Layout
James Teyler

Interior Designers
Steve Johnson
Marian Hartsough

Photographs
Tracy Teyler

Indexer
Katherine Stimson

Proofreader
Beth Teyler

Team Coordinator
Cindy Teeters

Acknowledgments

Perspection, Inc.

PowerPoint 2013 on Demand has been created by the professional trainers and writers at Perspection, Inc. to the standards you've come to expect from Que publishing. Together, we are pleased to present this training book.

Perspection, Inc. is a software training company committed to providing information and training to help people use software more effectively in order to communicate, make decisions, and solve problems. Perspection writes and produces software training books, and develops multimedia and web-based training. Since 1991, we have written more than 130 computer books, with several bestsellers to our credit, and sold over 5 million books.

This book incorporates Perspection's training expertise to ensure that you'll receive the maximum return on your time. You'll focus on the tasks and skills that increase productivity while working at your own pace and convenience.

We invite you to visit the Perspection web site at:

www.perspection.com

Acknowledgments

The task of creating any book requires the talents of many hard-working people pulling together to meet impossible deadlines and untold stresses. We'd like to thank the outstanding team responsible for making this book possible: the writer, Steve Johnson; the production editor, James Teyler; the editor and proofreader, Beth Teyler; and the indexer, Katherine Stimson.

At Que publishing, we'd like to thank Greg Wiegand and Loretta Yates for the opportunity to undertake this project, Cindy Teeters for administrative support, and Lori Lyons for your production expertise and support.

Perspection

About the Author

Steve Johnson has written more than 80 books on a variety of computer software, including Adobe Edge Animate, Adobe Photoshop CS6, Adobe Dreamweaver CS6, Adobe InDesign CS6, Adobe Illustrator CS6, Adobe Flash Professional CS5, Microsoft Windows 8, Microsoft Office 2013 and 2010, Microsoft Office 2008 for the Macintosh, and Apple OS X Mountain Lion. In 1991, after working for Apple Computer and Microsoft, Steve founded Perspection, Inc., which writes and produces software training. When he is not staying up late writing, he enjoys coaching baseball, playing golf, gardening, and spending time with his wife, Holly, and three children, JP, Brett, and Hannah. Steve and his family live in Northern California, but can also be found visiting family all over the western United States.

We Want to Hear from You!

As the reader of this book, *you* are our most important critic and commentator. We value your opinion and want to know what we're doing right, what we could do better, what areas you'd like to see us publish in, and any other words of wisdom you're willing to pass our way.

I welcome your comments. You can email or write to let me know what you did or didn't like about this book—as well as what we can do to make our books better.

Please note that I cannot help you with technical problems related to the topic of this book.

When you write, please be sure to include this book's title and author as well as your name, email address, and phone number. I will carefully review your comments and share them with the author and editors who worked on the book.

Email: feedback@quepublishing.com

Mail: Que Publishing
        ATTN: Reader Feedback
        800 East 96th Street
        Indianapolis, IN 46240 USA

For more information about this book or another Que title, visit our web site at *www.quepublishing.com*. Type the ISBN (excluding hyphens) or the title of a book in the Search field to find the page you're looking for.

Contents

Introduction

i

Welcome to *PowerPoint 2013 on Demand*, a visual quick reference book that shows you how to work efficiently with Microsoft PowerPoint. This book provides complete coverage of basic to advanced PowerPoint skills.

How This Book Works

You don't have to read this book in any particular order. We've designed the book so that you can jump in, get the information you need, and jump out. However, the book does follow a logical progression from simple tasks to more complex ones. Each task is presented on no more than two facing pages, which lets you focus on a single task without having to turn the page. To find the information that you need, just look up the task in the table of contents or index, and turn to the page listed. Read the task introduction, follow the step-by-step instructions in the left column along with screen illustrations in the right column, and you're done.

What's New

If you're searching for what's new in PowerPoint 2013, just look for the icon: **New!**. The new icon appears in the table of contents and throughout this book so you can quickly and easily identify a new or improved feature in PowerPoint 2013. A complete description of each new feature appears in the New Features guide in the back of this book.

Keyboard Shortcuts

Most menu commands have a keyboard equivalent, such as Ctrl+P, as a quicker alternative to using the mouse. A complete list of keyboard shortcuts is available on the web at *www.queondemand.com* or *www.perspection.com*.

How You'll Learn

How This Book Works

What's New

Keyboard Shortcuts

Step-by-Step Instructions

Real World Examples

Workshops

Microsoft Office Specialist

Get More on the Web

Step-by-Step Instructions

This book provides concise step-by-step instructions that show you "how" to accomplish a task. Each set of instructions includes illustrations that directly correspond to the easy-to-read steps. Also included in the text are time-savers, tables, and sidebars to help you work more efficiently or to teach you more in-depth information. A "Did You Know?" provides tips and techniques to help you work smarter, while a "See Also" leads you to other parts of the book containing related information about the task.

Real World Examples

This book uses real world examples files to give you a context in which to use the task. By using the example files, you won't waste time looking for or creating sample files. You get a start file and a result file, so you can compare your work. Not every topic needs an example file, such as changing options, so we provide a complete list of the example files used through out the book. The example files that you need for project tasks along with a complete file list are available on the web at *www.queondemand.com* or *www.perspection.com*.

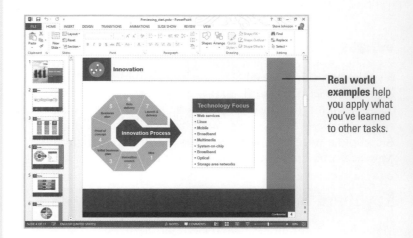

Easy-to-follow introductions focus on a single concept.

Illustrations match the numbered steps.

Numbered steps guide you through each task.

See Also points you to related information in the book.

Did You Know? alerts you to tips, techniques and related information.

Real world examples help you apply what you've learned to other tasks.

Workshops

This book shows you how to put together the individual step-by-step tasks into in-depth projects with the Workshops. You start each project with a sample file, work through the steps, and then compare your results with a project results file at the end. The Workshop projects and associated files are available on the web at *www.queondemand.com* or *www.perspection.com*.

Workshops

Introduction

The Workshops are all about being creative and thinking outside of the box. These workshops will help your right-brain soar, while excising your left-brain happy, by explaining why things work the way they do. Exploring possibilities is great fun; however, always stay grounded with knowledge of how things work.

Getting and Using the Project Files

Each project in the Workshop includes a start file to help you get started with the project, and a final file to provide you with the results of the project so you can see how well you accomplished the project.

Before you can use the project files, you need to download them from the web. You can access the files at *www.perspection.com* in the software downloads area. After you download the files from the web, uncompress the files into a folder on your hard drive where you'll have easy access from Microsoft PowerPoint.

Project 1: Optimizing Presentations

Skills and Tools: PowerPoint options

PowerPoint comes with a variety of features that allow you to create different kinds of presentations. However, not all features are created equal. Some features, such as hardware graphics acceleration, give you a little extra speed when you have the right hardware on your computer, but it also causes some movies not to display properly on the screen. Other features, like AutoFormat, are great when you want PowerPoint to automatically resize title or body text, but can be frustrating when you don't want text size to automatically change. If you take your presentations on the road, not having the right fonts installed on the presentation computer, missing linked movies and sounds, or showing a slow presentation can create big problems.

The Project

In this project, you'll learn how to set options to optimize PowerPoint and presentations for typical usage on any computer.

The **Workshops** walks you through in-depth projects to help you put Microsoft PowerPoint to work.

Microsoft Office Specialist

This book prepares you for the Microsoft Office Specialist (MOS) exam for Microsoft PowerPoint 2013. Each MOS certification exam has a set of objectives, which are organized into broader skill sets. To prepare for the MOS certification exam, you should review and perform each task identified with a MOS objective to confirm that you can meet the requirements for the exam. Information about the MOS program is available in the back of this book. The MOS objectives and the specific pages that cover them are available on the web at *www.queondemand.com* or *www.perspection.com*.

Microsoft Office Specialist

About the MOS Program

The Microsoft Office Specialist (MOS) certification is the globally recognized standard for validating expertise with the Microsoft Office suite of business productivity programs. Earning an MOS certificate acknowledges you have the expertise to work with Microsoft Office programs. To earn the MOS certification, you must pass a certification exam for the Microsoft Office desktop applications of Microsoft Word, Excel, PowerPoint, Outlook, Access, OneNote, SharePoint, or Office 365. (The availability of Microsoft Office Specialist certification exams varies by program, program version, and language. Visit *www.microsoft.com* and search on *MOS* or *Microsoft Office Specialist* for exam availability, and more information about the program.) The Microsoft Office Specialist program is the only Microsoft-approved program in the world for certifying proficiency with Microsoft Office programs.

What Does This Logo Mean?

It means this book has been approved by the Microsoft Office Specialist program to be certified courseware for learning Microsoft PowerPoint 2013 and preparing for the certification exam. This book will prepare you for the Microsoft Office Specialist exam for Microsoft PowerPoint 2013. Each certification level, either Core or Expert, has a set of objectives, which are organized into broader skill sets. Content that pertains to a Microsoft Office Specialist objective is identified with the following objective number and the specific pages throughout this book:

 PP13C-1.1
PP13C-2.2

Get More on the Web

In addition to the information in this book, you can also get more information on the web to help you get up to speed faster with PowerPoint 2013. Some of the information includes:

Transition Helpers

◆ **Only New Features.** Download and print the new feature tasks as a quick and easy guide.

Productivity Tools

◆ **Keyboard Shortcuts.** Download a list of keyboard shortcuts to learn faster ways to get the job done.

More Content

◆ **Photographs.** Download photographs and other graphics to use in your Office documents.

◆ **More Content.** Download new content developed after publication. For example, you can download a chapter on SharePoint server and Office 365.

You can access these additional resources on the web at *www.perspection.com*.

Keyboard Shortcuts

k

Microsoft PowerPoint 2013

If a command on the ribbon or a menu includes a keyboard reference, known as a **keyboard shortcut**, in a ScreenTip or next to the command name, you can perform the action by pressing and holding the first key, and then pressing the second key to perform the command quickly. In some cases, a keyboard shortcut uses three keys. Simply press and hold the first two keys, and then press the third key. For keyboard shortcuts in which you press one key immediately followed by another key, the keys to press are separated by a comma (,). Keyboard shortcuts provide an alternative to using the mouse and make it easy to perform repetitive commands.

Finding a Keyboard Shortcut

To help you find the keyboard shortcut you're looking for, the shortcuts are organized in categories and listed with page numbers.

Common Tasks

Broadcast, 7
Copy/Cut and Paste, 5
Dialog Boxes: Open and Save As, 2
File, 2
Find and Replace, 4
Font and Format, 4
Grids and Guides, 6
Help, 2
Media in Slide Show, 7

Move Between Panes, 3
Ribbon, 3
Slide Show, 6
Text, 3
Text in an Outline, 3
Text in Tables, 4
Undo and Redo, 5
Work with Objects, 5
Work with SmartArt Graphics, 5

Function Keys

Alt+Function, 8
Function, 7
Ctrl+Function, 8
Ctrl+Alt+Function, 8

Alt+Shift+Function, 8
Shift+Function, 7
Ctrl+Shift+Function, 8

If you're searching for new keyboard shortcuts in Microsoft PowerPoint 2013, just look for the letter: N. The N appears in the Keyboard Shortcuts table so you can quickly and easily identify new or changed shortcuts.

k

1

Additional content is available on the web. You can download keyboard shortcuts.

Getting Started with PowerPoint

Introduction

Whether you need to put together a quick presentation of sales figures for your management team or create a polished slide show for your company's stockholders, Microsoft PowerPoint 2013 can help you present your information efficiently and professionally.

PowerPoint is a **presentation graphics program**—software that helps you create a slide show presentation and supplements, such as handouts and speaker's notes. A slide show presentation is made up of a series of slides that can contain charts, diagrams, pictures, bulleted lists, eye-catching text, multimedia, and more. PowerPoint is set up with a tab-based Ribbon and dialog boxes that provide you with the tools you need when you need them to get tasks done. The customizable Quick Access Toolbar gives you easy access to commonly-used commands, such as Save, Undo, and Redo.

PowerPoint provides a variety of professionally designed templates, themes, and style galleries to help you create great-looking presentations. When it comes time to develop your presentation, PowerPoint offers a selection of views and panes—Normal view, Outline view, Slide Sorter view, Notes Page view, Reading view, and Slide Show view. Normal view is helpful for working on individual slides and notes, while Outline view helps you work with content. Slide Sorter view helps you organize all of your slides and add transition elements. If you need to write extensive notes, Notes Page view provides the additional space you need. Reading and Slide Show view pulls it all together, allowing you to view your presentation for fine tuning.

When you complete your presentation, you can save it in a more efficient PowerPoint XML format or as a PDF or XPS document, send it through e-mail for review, package it on a disc for clients, or even collaborate and share it with co-workers using a SkyDrive or SharePoint site.

What You'll Do

Start PowerPoint

View the PowerPoint Window

Use the Ribbon and Status Bar

Choose Commands

Work with the Ribbon and Toolbars

Choose Dialog Box Options

Create a Blank Presentation

Create a Presentation Using a Template

Create a Presentation from an Existing One

Arrange Windows

Use Task Panes and Window Panes

Understand PowerPoint Views

Browse a Presentation

Convert an Existing Presentation

Get Help While You Work

Save a Presentation

Work with Accounts

Recover a Presentation

Close a Presentation and Exit PowerPoint

Starting PowerPoint

The two quickest ways to start Microsoft PowerPoint are to select it on the Start screen (Win 8) (**New!**) or on the Start menu (Win 7). PowerPoint lets you work the way you like and start programs with a click of a button. When you start PowerPoint, a program window opens, displaying the Start screen (**New!**) where you can create or open a presentation in order to quickly get started.

Start PowerPoint

1. Start Windows, if necessary, and then use the method for your Windows version.

   ◆ **Windows 8.** Display the Start screen; click or tap the **Start** button on the Charm bar.

   ◆ **Windows 7.** Click **Start** on the taskbar, point to **All Programs** (which changes to Back), and then point to **Microsoft Office**.

2. Click **PowerPoint 2013**.

   If Office asks you to activate the program, follow the instructions enter an account or product key. to complete the process.

   TIMESAVER *To change the accounts, click the File tab, click Account, and then click the Switch Account link.*

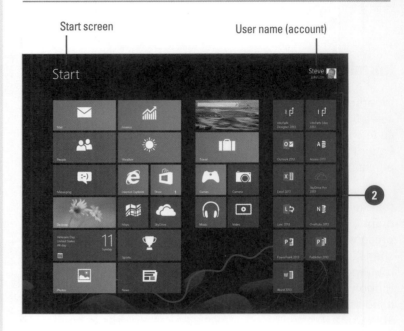

Start screen · User name (account)

Did You Know?

You can create a program shortcut from the Start menu to the desktop. Right-click the Microsoft PowerPoint 2013 program on the Start menu or screen. For Win 8, click the Pin To Taskbar button on the App bar. For Win 7, point to Send To, and then click Desktop (Create Shortcut).

You can start PowerPoint and open a presentation from an Explorer window. Double-clicking any PowerPoint file icon in an Explorer window opens that file and PowerPoint.

PowerPoint 2013 System Requirements

Hardware/Software	Minimum (Recommended)
Computer Processor	1 gigahertz (Ghz) or faster x86 (32 bit) or x64 (64 bit) processor with SSE2
Operating System	Windows 7, Windows 8, Windows Server 2008 R2, or Windows Server 2012
Available RAM	1 GB (32 bit), 2 GB (64 bit)
Hard Drive	3 GB of available space
Monitor Resolution	1024 x 576
Video Card	Graphics hardware acceleration requires a DirectX10 graphics card
Browser	Microsoft IE 8, 9, or 10; Firefox 10.x or later; Apple Safari 5; or Google Chrome 17.x
.NET version	3.5, 4.0, or 4.5

Viewing the PowerPoint Window

File tab
Click to access Office PowerPoint file commands.

Quick Access Toolbar
Click to access commands on this customizable toolbar.

Tabs
Click to access tools and commands.

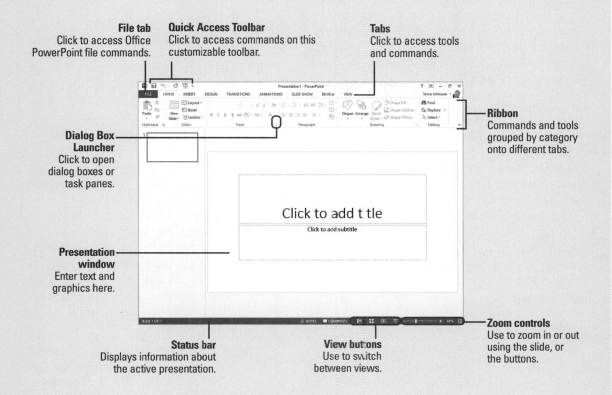

Dialog Box Launcher
Click to open dialog boxes or task panes.

Ribbon
Commands and tools grouped by category onto different tabs.

Presentation window
Enter text and graphics here.

Status bar
Displays information about the active presentation.

View buttons
Use to switch between views.

Zoom controls
Use to zoom in or out using the slide, or the buttons.

Using the Ribbon

The **Ribbon** is a results oriented way of working in PowerPoint 2013. The Ribbon is located at the top of the presentation window and is comprised of **tabs** that are organized by task or objects. The controls on each tab are organized into **groups**, or subtasks. The controls, or **command buttons**, in each group execute a command, or display a menu of commands or a drop-down gallery. Controls in each group provide a visual way to quickly make presentation changes. The File tab displays Backstage view, where you can access file-related commands.

If you prefer using the keyboard instead of the mouse to access commands, PowerPoint provides easy to use shortcuts. Simply press and release the Alt or F10 key to display **KeyTips** over each feature in the current view, and then continue to press the letter shown in the KeyTip until you press the one that you want to use. To cancel an action and hide the KeyTips, press and release the Alt or F10 key again. If you prefer using the keyboard shortcuts, such as Ctrl+P (for Print), all the keyboard shortcuts and keyboard accelerators work exactly the same in PowerPoint 2013.

Tabs

PowerPoint provides three types of tabs on the Ribbon. The first type is called a **standard** tab—such as File, Home, Insert, Design, Transitions, animations Slide Show, Review, and View—that you see whenever you start PowerPoint. The second type is called a **contextual** tab—such as Picture Tools, Drawing Tools, or Table Tools—that appears only when they are needed based on the type of task you are doing. PowerPoint recognizes what you're doing and provides the right set of tabs and tools to use when you need them. The third type is called a **program** tab that replaces the standard set of tabs when you switch to certain views or modes.

Live Preview

When you point to a gallery option, such as Quick Styles, on the Ribbon, PowerPoint displays a **live preview** of the option so that you can see what your change will look like before selecting it. The Paste Options button also displays a live preview for pasted content.

Display Options

If you want more display screen, you can collapse and expand the Ribbon as you need it. Click the Ribbon Display Options button (**New!**) to select an option: Auto-hide Ribbon, Show Tabs, or Show Tabs and Commands. Auto-hide Ribbon collapses the Ribbon until you click the top of the program. Show Tabs displays only tabs until you click a tab to show it. Show Tabs and Commands displays the Ribbon all the time.

> **TIMESAVER** *To collapse the Ribbon, click the Collapse the Ribbon button (Ctrl+F1) or double-click the current tab. Click a tab to auto display it (Ribbon remains collapsed). To expand the Ribbon, press Ctrl+F1 or double-click a tab.*

Key Tip   Standard tabs   Contextual tab   Ribbon Display Options

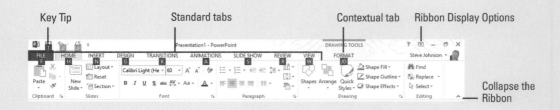

Collapse the Ribbon

Choosing Commands

PowerPoint commands are organized in groups on the Ribbon, Quick Access Toolbar, and Min -Toolbar. Commands are available as buttons or options on the Ribbon, or as menus on button or option arrows or the File tab. The Quick Access Toolbar and Mini-Toolbar (**New!**) display frequently used buttons that you may be already familiar with from previous versions of PowerPoint, while the File tab on the Ribbon displays file related menu commands to exit the File tab, click the Back button (**New!**). In addition to the File tab, you can also open a **shortcut menu** with a group of related commands by right-clicking a program element.

Choose a Menu Command Using the File Tab

1. Click the **File** tab on the Ribbon.

2. Click the command you want.

    TIMESAVER *You can use a shortcut key to choose a command. Press and hold down the first key and then press the second key. For example, press and hold the Ctrl key and then press S (or Ctrl+S) to select the Save command.*

3. To return to the program window, click the **Back** button (**New!**).

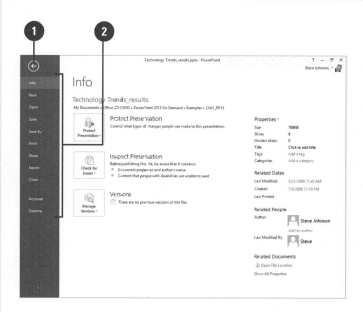

Choose a Command from a Shortcut Menu

1. Right-click an object (text or graphic element).

    TIMESAVER *Press Shift+F10 to display the shortcut menu for a selected command.*

2. Click a command on the shortcut menu or the Mini-Toolbar (**New!**). If the command is followed by an arrow, point to the command to see a list of related options, and then click the option you want.

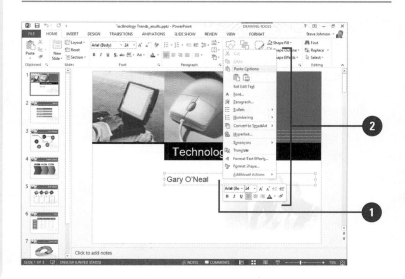

Working with the Ribbon and Toolbars

PowerPoint includes its most common commands, such as Save and Undo, on the **Quick Access Toolbar**. Click a toolbar button to choose a command. If you are not sure what a toolbar button does, point to it to display a ScreenTip. When PowerPoint starts, the Quick Access Toolbar appears at the top of the window, unless you've changed your settings. You can customize the Quick Access Toolbar or Ribbon by adding command buttons or groups to it. You can also move the toolbar below or above the Ribbon so it's right where you need it. In addition to the Quick Access Toolbar, PowerPoint also displays the Mini-Toolbar when you point to selected text. The **Mini-Toolbar** appears above the selected text and provides quick access to formatting tools.

Choose a Command Using a Toolbar or Ribbon

◆ **Get command help**. If you're not sure what a button does, point to it to display a ScreenTip. If the ScreenTip includes *Press F1 for more help*, press F1.

◆ **Choose a command**. Click the button, or button arrow, and then click a command or option.

ScreenTip

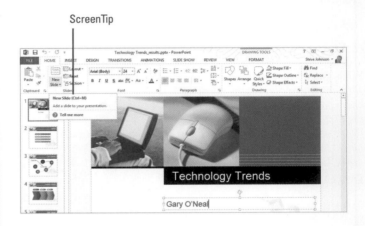

Add or Remove Items from the Quick Access Toolbar

◆ **Add or remove a common button**. Click the **Customize Quick Access Toolbar list arrow**, and then click a button name (checked item appears on the toolbar).

◆ **Add a Ribbon button or group**. Right-click the button or group name on the Ribbon, and then click **Add to Quick Access Toolbar**.

◆ **Remove a button or group**. Right-click the button or group name on the Quick Access Toolbar, and then click **Remove from Quick Access Toolbar**.

Customize Quick Access Toolbar list arrow   Click to add or remove frequently used buttons

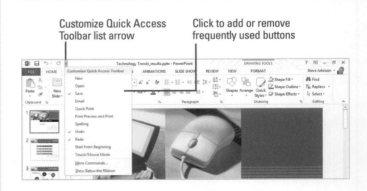

Right-click to add a button or group

Customize the Ribbon or Quick Access Toolbar

① Click the **File** tab, and then click **Options**.

② Click the **Customize Ribbon** or **Quick Access Toolbar**.

③ Click the **Choose commands from** list arrow, and then click **All Commands** or a specific Ribbon.

④ Click the list arrow (right column), and then select the tabs or toolbar you want to change.

⑤ For the Ribbon, click **New Tab** to create a new tab, or click **New Group** to create a new group on the selected tab (right column).

⑥ To import or export a customized Ribbon or Quick Access Toolbar, click the **Import/Export** list arrow, select a command, and then select an import file or create an export file.

⑦ Click the command you want to add (left column) or remove (right column), and then click **Add** or **Remove**.

◆ To insert a separator line between buttons in the Quick Access Toolbar, click **<Separator>**, and then click **Add**.

⑧ Click the **Move Up** and **Move Down** arrow buttons to arrange the order.

⑨ To reset the Ribbon or Quick Access Toolbar, click the **Reset** list arrow, and then select a reset option.

⑩ Click **OK**.

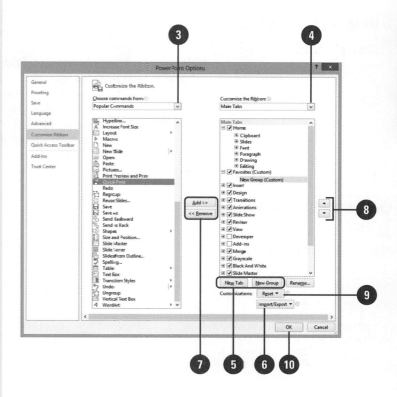

For Your Information

Moving Toolbars and the Ribbon

You can move the Quick Access Toolbar to another location. Click the Customize Quick Access Toolbar list arrow, and then click Show Below The Ribbon or Show Above The Ribbon. You can minimize the Ribbon. Click the Minimize The Ribbon (Ctrl+F1) button on the right side of the Ribbon (to the left of the Help button). Click the Expand The Ribbon button to maximize it. When the Ribbon is minimized, you can click a tab to auto maximize it. When you click an option or in the presentation, the Ribbon minimizes again. Just like an auto-hide option.

Changing ScreenTips

You can turn off or change ScreenTips. Click the File tab, click Options, click General, click the ScreenTip Style list arrow, click Don't Show Feature Descriptions In ScreenTips or Don't Show ScreenTips, and then click OK.

Choosing Dialog Box Options

A **dialog box** is a window that opens when you click a Dialog Box Launcher. **Dialog Box Launchers** are small icons that appear at the bottom corner of some groups. When you point to a Dialog Box Launcher, a ScreenTip with a thumbnail of the dialog box appears to show you which dialog box opens. A dialog box allows you to supply more information before the program carries out the command you selected. After you enter information or make selections in a dialog box, click the OK button to complete the command. Click the Cancel button to close the dialog box without issuing the command. In many dialog boxes, you can also click an Apply button to apply your changes without closing the dialog box.

Choose Dialog Box Options

All dialog boxes contain the same types of options, including the following:

- ◆ **Tabs**. Click a tab to display its options. Each tab groups a related set of options.

- ◆ **Option buttons**. Click an option button to select it. You can usually select only one.

- ◆ **Up and down arrows**. Click the up or down arrow to increase or decrease the number, or type a number in the box.

- ◆ **Check box**. Click the box to turn on or off the option. A checked box means the option is selected; a cleared box means it's not.

- ◆ **List box**. Click the list arrow to display a list of options, and then click the option you want.

- ◆ **Text box**. Click in the box and type the requested information.

- ◆ **Button**. Click a button to perform a specific action or command. A button name followed by an ellipsis (...) opens another dialog box.

- ◆ **Preview box**. Many dialog boxes show an image that reflects the options you select.

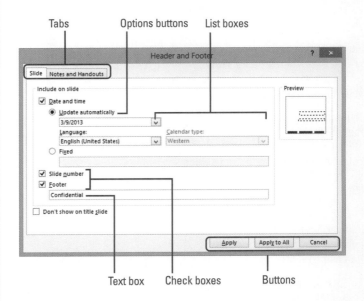

For Your Information

Navigating a Dialog Box

Rather than clicking to move around a dialog box, you can press the Tab key to move from one box or button to the next. You can also use Shift+Tab to move backward, or Ctrl+Tab and Ctrl+Shift+Tab to move between dialog box tabs.

Using the Status Bar

The **Status bar** appears across the bottom of your screen and displays presentation information—slide number, Office theme name, and current slide display zoom percentage—and some PowerPoint controls, such as view shortcut buttons, zoom slider, and Fit To Window button. With the click of the mouse, you can quickly customize exactly what you see on the Status bar. In addition to displaying information, the Status bar also allows you to check the on/off status of certain features or add/remove options, including Notes (**New!**), Comments (**New!**), and Languages. You can click an item on the Status bar to open or enable a command.

Add or Remove Items from the Status Bar

◆ **Add Item**. Right-click the Status bar, and then click an unchecked item.

The following items are turned on by default:

- ◆ View Indicator
- ◆ Spell Check
- ◆ Language
- ◆ Notes (**New!**)
- ◆ Comments (**New!**)
- ◆ View Shortcuts
- ◆ Zoom Slider
- ◆ Zoom
- ◆ Zoom Fit

You can click an item on the Status bar to open or enable a command.

◆ **Remove Item**. Right-click the Status bar, and then click a checked item.

> ### See Also
>
> *See "Adding a Digital Signature" on page 382 or "Simplifying Tasks with Macros" on page 436 for information on changing the status of items on the Status bar.*

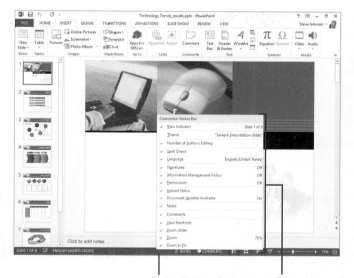

Right-click the Status bar   Status information

Creating a Blank Presentation

When you start PowerPoint, the program opens by default with the Start screen (**New!**) on the Backstage, where you can open a new presentation so that you can begin working in it. If you're already working in PowerPoint, you can use the New command (**New!**) on the File tab to create a new presentation. Each new presentation displays a default name—such as "Presentation1," "Presentation2" and so on—numbered according to how many new presentations you have started during the work session until you save it with a more meaningful name. The presentation name appears on the title bar and taskbar buttons.

Start a Blank Presentation

1. Start a blank PowerPoint presentation from either of the following:

   ◆ **Start Screen.** Start PowerPoint 2013 from Windows (**New!**).

   ◆ **New Screen.** Click the **File** tab, and then click **New** (**New!**).

   TIMESAVER *To create a blank PowerPoint presentation without the New screen, press Ctrl+N.*

2. Click **Blank Presentation** under Featured.

   A new blank presentation appears in the PowerPoint program window.

Did You Know?

You can start PowerPoint and not show the Start screen. Click the File tab, click Options, clear the Show The Start Screen When This Application Starts check box (**New!**), and then click OK.

You can remove an item from a recent presentations or folders list or clear unpinned items. In the Start, Open, or Save As screen, right-click an item in the list, and then click Remove From List (**New!**) or Clear Unpinned Presentations (**New!**).

Back button   2   New screen

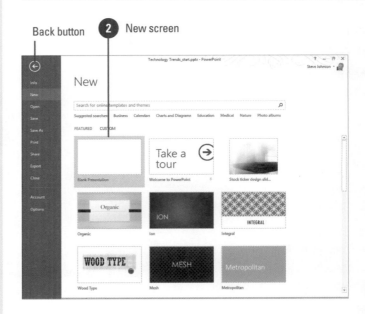

Use to open presentations   2   Start screen

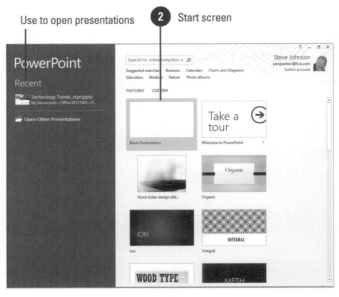

Creating a Presentation Using a Template

PowerPoint provides a collection of professionally designed templates that you can use to help you create presentations. Start with a template when you have a good idea of your content but want to take advantage of a template's professional look. A **template** is a file that provides you with an unified design, which includes themes, so you only need to add text and graphics. In the Start or New screen (**New!**), you can choose a template from those already installed with PowerPoint or from the library on the Microsoft Office Online web site. If you frequently use a template, you can pin it (**New!**) to the Start or New screen.

Start a Presentation with a Template

1. Start a PowerPoint presentation from either of the following:
   - **Start Screen.** Start PowerPoint 2013 from Windows (**New!**).
   - **New Screen.** Click the **File** tab, and then click **New** (**New!**).

2. Use one of the following (**New!**):
   - **Featured or Custom.** Click a template.
   - **Suggested searches.** Click a search option, click a category, and then click a template.
   - **Search for online templates.** Type criteria in the Search box, click the **Search** button or press Enter, click a category, and then click a template.

3. To pin a template to the New screen, point to a template, and then click the **Pin to List** button (**New!**). To unpin a template, click the **Pin from List** (**New!**).

4. To navigate, click the **Home** button.

5. Click **Create**.

Did You Know?

You can download templates on the web. Go to *www.microsoft.com*, click the Office link, and then search for Office Templates.

New on the File tab

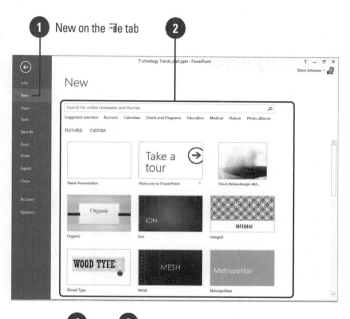

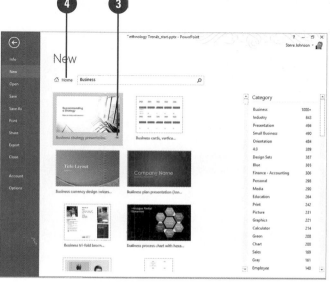

Creating a Presentation from an Existing One

Instead of creating a presentation from scratch, you can also create a presentation from an existing presentation you already have. If you have a presentation that is close to what you want to create, you can select it from the Start or New screen to create an untitled presentation with the contents of an existing presentation. When you place a presentation or template in the default personal templates location (**New!**) specified in the PowerPoint Options dialog box under Save, you can select the presentation or template from the Custom tab within the template folder in the Start or New screen to create a new presentation from an existing one. If you have saved a document theme (.thmx) in the default folder location with the look and feel you want, you can create a new presentation from the custom theme (**New!**). You can select the custom theme from the Custom tab within the Document Themes folder.

Create a Presentation from an Existing Presentation

1. Start a PowerPoint presentation from either of the following:
   - ◆ **Start Screen.** Start PowerPoint 2013 from Windows (**New!**).
   - ◆ **New Screen.** Click the **File** tab, and then click **New** (**New!**).

2. Click **Custom** (**New!**).

   TROUBLE? *If Custom is not available, you need to specify a default personal templates location in PowerPoint options.*

3. Click the **My Templates** folder or the folder you specified in Default personal templates location in the PowerPoint Options under Save.

   Personal Templates. C:\Users\ *user name*\My Templates; your location might differ, or C:\Users\ *user name*\Documents\Custom Office Templates (default).

4. Select the presentation or template file you want to use.

5. Click **Create**.

   A new presentation appears in the PowerPoint window.

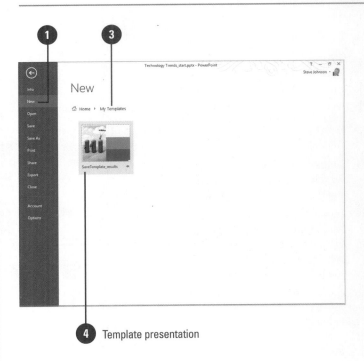

4 Template presentation

Create a New Presentation From a Document Theme

1. Start a PowerPoint presentation from either of the following:
   - ◆ **Start Screen.** Start PowerPoint 2013 from Windows (**New!**).
   - ◆ **New Screen.** Click the **File** tab, and then click **New** (**New!**).
2. Click **Custom** (**New!**).
3. Click the **Document Themes** folder.

   Document Themes Folder. C:\Users*user name*\AppData\Roaming\Microsoft\Templates\Document Themes; typical Office location, yours can differ.

4. Select the document theme you want to use.
5. Click **Create**.

   A new presentation appears in the PowerPoint window.

See Also

See "Creating a Custom Theme" on page 104 or "Creating a Personal Templates" on page 111 for more information on creating custom themes or templates.

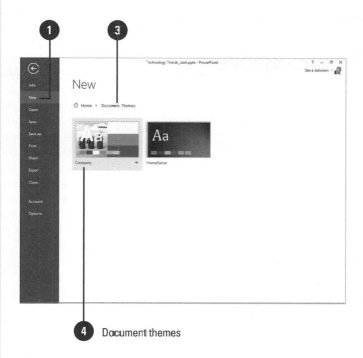

4 Document themes

Default Office themes location

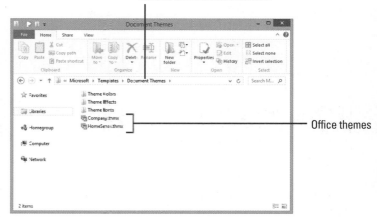

Office themes

Opening an Existing Presentation

You can open an existing presentation from the Start screen (**New!**) when the PowerPoint program starts or Open screen by using the File tab. On the Open screen, you can choose a recently used presentation, locate and select the presentation on your SkyDrive, SharePoint, or computer. SkyDrive (**New!**) is a cloud-based online personal storage system, which requires a Microsoft account to access, while SharePoint server (**New!**) is a cloud-based online organizational storage and management system. When you open a presentation from PowerPoint 97-2003, PowerPoint 2013 goes into compatibility mode—indicated on the title bar—where it disables new features that cannot be displayed or converted well by previous versions. The presentation stays in compatibility mode until you convert it to the PowerPoint 2013 file format. The Open screen allows you to pin recently used presentations or folders (**New!**) that you want to remain accessible regardless of recent use. The Pin icon to the right of the file name on the File tab makes it easy to pin or unpin as needed.

Open a Presentation from the Program Window

1. Click the **File** tab, and then click **Open**.

2. Click **Computer**.

3. Click **Browse** or a recent folder.

4. If you want to open a specific file type, click the **Files of type** list arrow, and then click a file type.

   - **Strict Open XML Presentation.** You can also open presentations in the Strict Open XML format (**New!**) to resolve leap year issues with 1900.

5. Navigate to the location where you want to open the file, and then select the file.

6. Click **Open**, or click the **Open** button arrow, and then click one of the following options:

   - **Open Read-Only.**
   - **Open as Copy.**
   - **Open in Browser.**
   - **Open in Protected View.**
   - **Open and Repair.**

Access SharePoint   Access SkyDrive   Recent folder locations

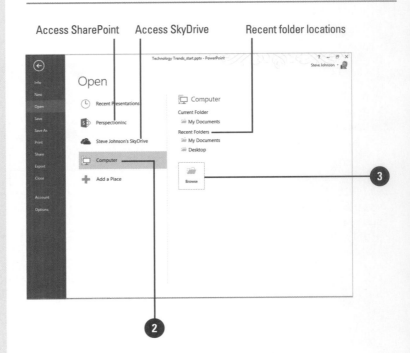

Open a Recently Opened Presentation or Folder

1 Click the **File** tab, and then click **Open**.

TIMESAVER *In the Start screen* (**New!**), *click a recent presentation.*

2 Click **Recent Presentations** or **Computer** (**New!**).

3 To pin or unpin a presentation or folder, point to a presentation or folder (displays the pin):

◆ **Pin a presentation or folder.** Click the **Pin** icon on the Recent Presentations or Recent Folders list.

◆ **Unpin a presentation or folder.** Click the **Unpin** icon to display a pin on the Recent Presentations or Recent Folders list.

4 Click the presentation or folder you want to open.

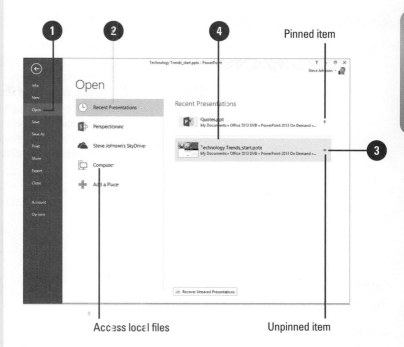

Pinned item

Access local files   Unpinned item

Open recent presentations on the Start screen

Click to open a presentation from the Open dialog box

Did You Know?

You can add recently used presentations to the File tab. Click the File tab, click Options, click Advanced, select the Quickly Access This Number Of Recent Presentations check box, specify the number of presentations you want to display, and then click OK.

You can change the number of recently opened files that appear on the File tab. Click the File tab, click Options, click Advanced, change the Show This Number Of Recent Presentations list, and then click OK.

You can change the default file location of the Open dialog box. Click the File tab, click Options, click Save, enter a new location in the Default File Location box, and then click OK.

Arranging Windows

Each presentation opens inside a separate PowerPoint window, which contains its own title bar, Ribbon, and a work area (**New!**). Most often, you'll probably fill the entire screen with one window. But when you want to move or copy information between programs or presentations, it's easier to display several windows at once. You can arrange two or more windows from one program or from different programs at the same time. However, you must make the window active to work in it. You can use window commands on the View tab to arrange or switch between presentation windows. You can also click the PowerPoint buttons on the taskbar to switch between open presentations.

Resize and Move a Window

◆ **Maximize button**. Click to make a window fill the entire screen.

◆ **Restore Down button**. Click to reduce a maximized window to a reduced size.

◆ **Minimize button**. Click to shrink a window to a taskbar button. To restore the window to its previous size, click the taskbar button.

◆ **Close button**. Click to shut a window.

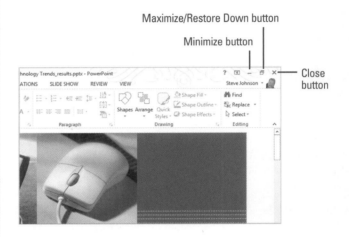

Maximize/Restore Down button

Minimize button

Close button

Arrange or Switch Between Windows

1. Open the presentations you want to arrange or switch between.

2. Click the **View** tab.

3. In the Window group, click:

   ◆ **Switch Windows**, and then click the presentation name you want.

   ◆ **Arrange All** to fit the windows on the screen.

   ◆ **Cascade** to arrange windows diagonally.

   ◆ **Move Split** to resize panes with Arrow keys; press Enter to exit.

   ◆ **New Window** to open a new window containing a view of the current presentation.

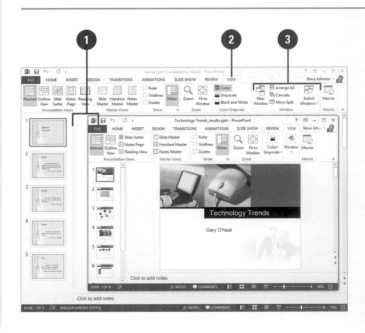

Using Task and Window Panes

Task panes are separate windows that appear when you need them, such as Navigation or Format Picture pane, or when you click a Dialog Box Launcher icon, such as Clipboard. A task pane displays various options that relate to the current task. Many task panes are organized into categories and groups of options (**New!**), which you can display by clicking a tab (if available), clicking a category icon button (like a tab) at the top, and expanding a group below. Task panes function differently depending on the type. **Window panes** are sections of a window, such as a split window. If you need a larger work area, you can use the Close button in the upper-right corner of the pane to close a task or window pane, or move a border edge (for task panes) or **splitter** (for window panes) to resize it.

Work with Task and Window Panes

◆ **Open a Task Pane.** It appears when you need it or when you click a **Dialog Box Launcher** icon.

◆ **Close a Task or Window Pane.** Click the **Close** button in upper-right corner of the pane.

◆ **Resize a Task Pane.** Point to the Task Pane border edge until the pointer changes to double arrows, then drag the edge to resize it.

◆ **Resize a Window Pane.** Point to the window pane border bar until the pointer changes to a double bar with arrows, then drag the edge to resize it.

◆ **Display Options in a Pane.** Click a tab (if available), click a category icon button (like a tab) at the top of the pane (**New!**), click to expand a category, and then select the options you want.

Did You Know?

You can resize window panes. Click the View tab, click the Move Split button, and then use Arrow keys to size, and then press Enter.

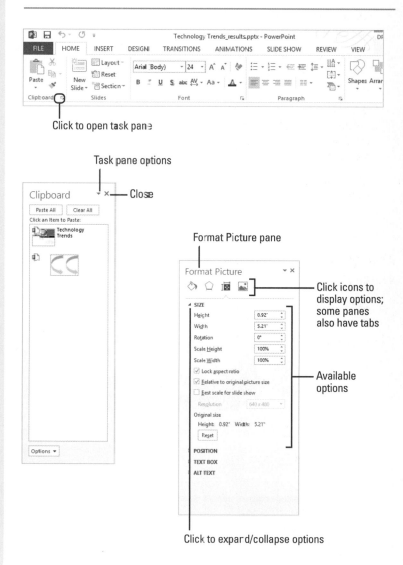

Click to open task pane

Task pane options

Close

Format Picture pane

Click icons to display options; some panes also have tabs

Available options

Click to expand/collapse options

Understanding PowerPoint Views

To help you during all phases of developing a presentation, PowerPoint provides three different views: Normal, Slide Sorter, Reading and Slide Show. You can switch from one view to another by clicking a view button located on the Status bar or by using the buttons in the Presentation Views group on the View tab. In any view, you can use the Zoom feature on the Status bar to increase and decrease the page view size and display the slide to fit the screen.

Normal view

Use the Normal view to work with the three underlying elements of a presentation—the outline, slide, and notes—each in its own pane. These panes provide an overview of your presentation and let you work on all of its parts. You can adjust the size of the panes by dragging the pane borders. You can switch between the Slides and Outline panes by clicking the Normal view button (**New!**) on the Status bar or use the Normal or Outline View buttons on the View tab. You can use the Outline pane to develop and organize your

presentation's content. Use the Slides pane to add text, graphics, movies, sounds, and hyperlinks to individual slides, and the Notes pane to add speaker notes or notes you want to share with your audience. To show or hide the Notes pane, click the Notes button (**New!**) on the View tab.

Outline pane

Use the Outline pane in Normal view to develop your presentation's content. Individual slides are numbered and a slide icon appears for each slide.

Slides pane

Use the Slides pane in Normal view to preview each slide. Click the slide you want to view. You can also move through your slides using the scroll bars or the Previous Slide and Next Slide buttons. When you drag the scroll box up or down on the vertical scroll bar, a label appears that indicates which slide will be displayed if you release the mouse button.

Reading view

Reading view presents your slides in a slide show one at a time in a separate window. Use this view when you're ready to rehearse your presentation. This view is especially useful when you want to show two presentations in a slide show in separate windows at the same time.

Slide Sorter view

Use the Slide Sorter view to organize your slides, add actions between slides—called slide transitions—and apply other effects to your slide show. The Transitions tab helps you add slide transitions and control your presentation. When you add a slide transition, you see an icon that indicates an action will take place as one slide replaces another during a show. If you hide a slide, you see an icon that indicates the slide will not be shown during the presentation.

Slide Show view

Slide Show view presents your slides one at a time. Use this view when you're ready to rehearse or give your presentation. To move through the slides, click the screen, or press Enter to move through the show.

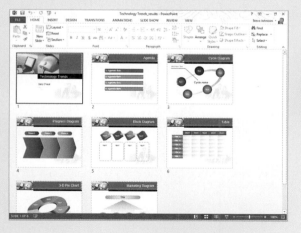

Browsing a Presentation

You might want to browse through a completed presentation to view the contents and design of each slide and to evaluate the types of slides in a presentation in several ways. When a slide doesn't fit the screen, you can change the presentation view size, or click the scroll arrows to scroll line by line or click above or below the scroll box to scroll window by window and move to another slide. To move immediately to a specific slide, you can drag the scroll box. In Slides pane, you can click the Next Slide and Previous Slide buttons, which are located at the bottom of the vertical scroll bar, to switch between slides in a presentation. If you're working with PowerPoint on a touch screen device, all you need is your finger to make gestures (**New!**). You can swipe, tap, scroll, zoom, and pan within any PowerPoint view to navigate between and work with slides. You can select an object or range of text to edit it, swipe right or left to switch slides, or pinch/stretch to zoom in or out.

Browse Through a Presentation

◆ Click the **Up** scroll arrow or **Down** scroll arrow to scroll line by line.

   When you scroll to the top or bottom of a slide, you automatically move to the previous or next page.

◆ Click above or below the **Scroll** box to scroll window by window.

◆ Drag the **Scroll** box to move immediately to a specific slide.

   As you drag, a slide indicator box appears, telling you the slide number and title.

◆ Click the **Previous Slide** or **Next Slide** button.

◆ On a touch screen (**New!**), swipe up and down on the slide to scroll or swipe right or left to switch slides.

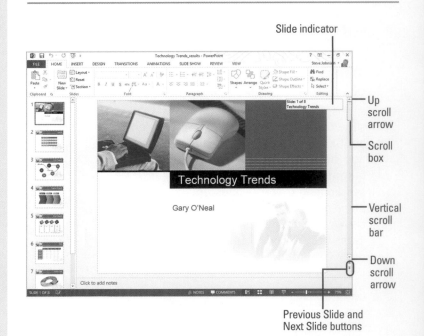

Slide indicator

Up scroll arrow

Scroll box

Vertical scroll bar

Down scroll arrow

Previous Slide and Next Slide buttons

Did You Know?

You can use the keyboard to browse slides. Press the Page Up or Page Down key to switch between slides. If you use these keys, the slides in the Slides pane will change also.

Browse Through Slides or an Outline

1. In Normal view, click the **Normal View** button (**New!**) on the Status bar or buttons on the View tab to switch between the Outline or Slides pane.

   ◆ Click the **Up** scroll arrow or **Down** scroll arrow to scroll line by line.

   The slide doesn't change as you scroll.

   ◆ Click a slide icon or slide miniature to display the slide.

   ◆ On a touch screen (**New!**), swipe right or left to switch slides.

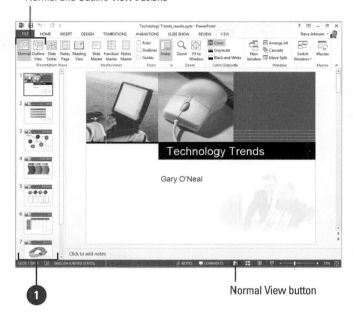

Normal and Outline View buttons

Normal View button

Change Presentation View Size

◆ Click the zoom percentage on the Status bar, click the option size you want, and then click **OK**.

◆ Click the **Zoom In** (+) or **Zoom Out** (-) buttons on the Status bar.

◆ Drag the **Zoom** slider on the Status bar.

◆ Click the **Fit To Window** button to resize the slide to the current window.

◆ On a touch screen (**New!**), pinch (zoom out) or stretch (zoom in) two fingers.

Zoom controls

See Also

See "Navigating a Slide Show with Touch" on page 344 or "Working with Touch Screens" on page 346 for more information on using gestures in PowerPoint.

Documenting Properties

PowerPoint automatically documents properties while you work—such as file size, save dates, and various statistics—and allows you to document other properties, such as title, author, subject, keywords, category, and status. You can view or edit standard document properties or create advanced custom properties by using the **Document Information Panel**, which is an XML-based Microsoft InfoPath form hosted in the Office program. You can use document properties—also known as **metadata**—to help you manage and track files; search tools can use the metadata to find a document based on your search criteria. If you associate a document property to an item in the document, the document property updates when you change the item.

View and Edit Document Properties

1. Click the **File** tab, and then click **Info**.

2. To display other properties, click the **Properties** button, and then select an option:

   ◆ **Show Document Panel.** Shows Document panel in the presentation.

   ◆ **Advanced Properties.** Displays the Properties dialog box.

3. Enter the standard properties, such as author, title, subject, keywords, category, status, and comments.

   ◆ **Show All Properties.** Click the link to displays more options.

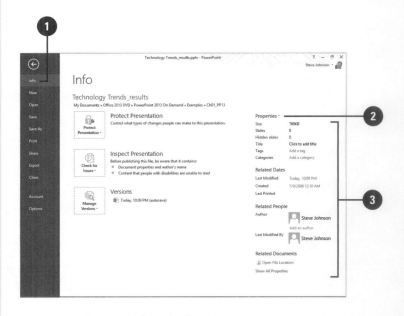

Document Information Panel

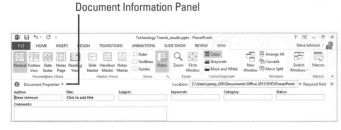

Did You Know?

You can view or change presentation properties when you open or save a file. In the Open or Save As dialog box, select the presentation you want, click the arrow next to the Views, and then click Details to view file size and last changed date, or click Properties to view all information. If you want to insert or change author names or keywords, click the Authors box or Tags box, and then type what you want.

Converting an Existing Presentation

When you open a presentation from PowerPoint 97-2003, PowerPoint 2013 goes into compatibility mode—indicated on the title bar—where it disables new features that cannot be displayed or converted well by previous versions. When you save a presentation, PowerPoint 2013 saves PowerPoint 97-2003 files in their older format using compatibility mode. The presentation stays in compatibility mode until you convert it to the PowerPoint 2013 file format. PowerPoint 2007-2013 use the same file extensions, however there may be feature differences between the versions.

Convert a PowerPoint 97-2003 Presentation to PowerPoint 2013

1. Open the PowerPoint presentation 97-2003 you want to convert to the PowerPoint 2013 file format.

   The PowerPoint presentation opens in compatibility mode.

2. Click the **File** tab, and then click **Info**.

3. Click **Convert**.

4. Click **OK** to convert the file to the PowerPoint 2013 format.

   PowerPoint exits compatibility mode, which is only turned on when a previous version is in use.

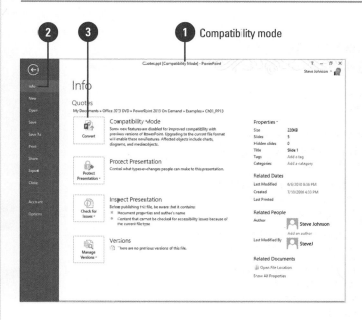

Compatibility mode

Did You Know?

You can display extensions in the Save and Open dialog boxes and Recent Presentations list. Changing the Windows option also changes PowerPoint. In the Folder Options dialog box on the View tab, clear the Hide Extensions For Known File Types check box, and then click OK.

Getting Help While You Work

At some time, everyone has a question or two about the program they are using. The Office Help Viewer provides the answers and resources you need, including feature help, articles, tips, templates, training, and downloads. By connecting to Office.com on the Microsoft web site, you not only have access to standard product help information, but you also have access to updated information over the web without leaving the Help Viewer. The web browser-like Help Viewer allows you to browse a catalog of topics to locate information (**New!**), use popular searches (**New!**), or enter your own phrases to search for information. When you use any of these help options, a list of possible answers is shown to you with the most likely answer or most frequently-used at the top of the list.

Use the Help Viewer to Get Answers

1 Click the **Help** button on the Ribbon.

  TIMESAVER *Press F1.*

2 Locate the Help topic you want.

  ◆ **Popular searches.** Click a popular search (**New!**).

  ◆ **Help topic.** Click a topic tile on the home page (**New!**).

3 Read the topic, and then click any links to get Help information.

4 Click the **Back**, **Forward**, and **Home** buttons on the toolbar to move around in the Help Viewer.

5 If you want to print the topic, click the **Print** button on the toolbar.

6 To keep the Help Viewer window (not maximized) on top or behind, click to toggle the **Keep Help On Top** button (pin pushed in) and **Don't Keep Help On Top** button (pin not pushed in) on the toolbar.

  TIMESAVER *Press Ctrl+T to toggle Help On Top (**New!**).*

7 When you're done, click the **Close** button.

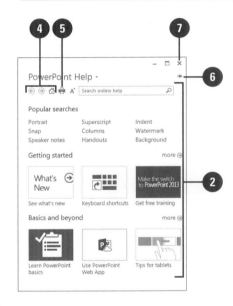

Click to change the topic font size

Topic

Search for Help

1. Click the **Help** button on the Ribbon.

2. To use a popular search, click one of the popular searches (**New!**).

3. Type one or more keywords in the Search For box, and then click the **Search** button to display results.

   ◆ **Prev or Next.** Scroll to the bottom, and then click **Prev** or **Next** to view more results.

4. Click a topic.

5. Read the topic, and then click any links to get information on related topics or definitions.

6. When you're done, click the **Close** button.

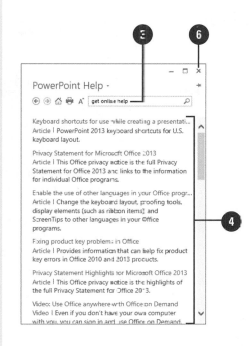

Use Local or Online Help

1. Click the **Help** button on the Ribbon.

2. Click the **Help** list arrow at the top of the Help Viewer.

3. Click the option where you want to get help information:

   ◆ **Help from Office.com** to get product help from this computer and the internet (online).

   ◆ **Help from your computer** to get product help from this computer only (offline).

4. When you're done, click the **Close** button.

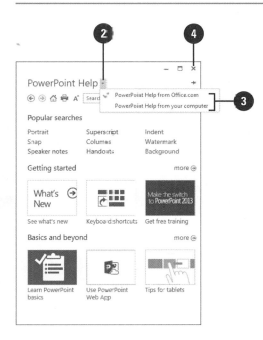

Saving a Presentation

After you create a PowerPoint presentation, you can save it to your computer, SkyDrive (**New!**) cloud-based online storage system, or Office 365 SharePoint service (**New!**). When you save a presentation for the first time or if you want to save a copy of a file, use the Save As command. When you want to save an open presentation, use the Save button on the Quick Access Toolbar. When you save a presentation, PowerPoint 2013 saves 97-2003 files in an older format using compatibility mode and 2007-2013 files in an XML (Extensible Markup Language) based file format. The XML format significantly reduces file sizes, provides enhanced file recovery, and allows for increased compatibility, sharing, reuse, and transportability. If you have issues with leap year dates for 1900, you can use the Strict Open XML Presentation format (**New!**) with ISO8601. A PowerPoint 97-2003 presentation stays in compatibility mode—indicated on the title bar—until you convert it to the 2013 file format. Compatibility mode disables new features that cannot be displayed or converted well by previous versions.

Save a Presentation for PowerPoint 2013

1. Click the **File** tab, and then click **Save As**.

2. Click **Computer**.

3. Click **Browse** or a recent folder.

4. Click the **Save in** list arrow, and then select the location where you want to save the file.

5. Type a presentation file name.

6. Click the **Save as type** list arrow, and then click **PowerPoint Presentation (*.pptx)**.

7. To enter document properties, click the **Authors** or **Tags** box, and then enter the text you want.

8. Click **Save**.

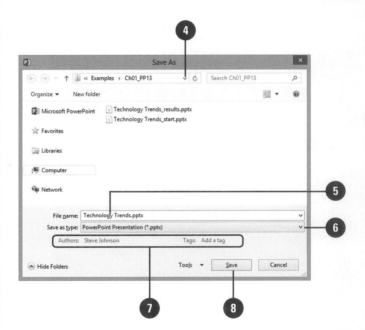

Did You Know?

You can access options from the Save dialog box. In the Save dialog box, click Tools, and then click the command option you want: Save Options, General Options, or Compress Pictures.

Save a PowerPoint 97-2003 Presentation in Compatibility Mode

1. Open the PowerPoint 97-2003 presentation you want to continue to save in the original format.

   The PowerPoint presentation opens in compatibility mode.

2. Click the **Save** button on the Quick Access Toolbar, or click the **File** tab, and then click **Save**.

   PowerPoint stays in compatibility mode.

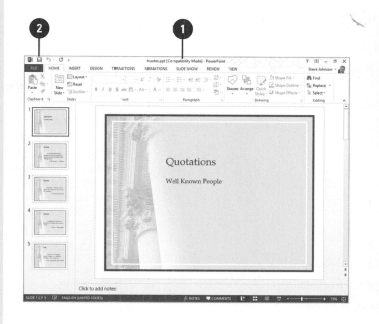

Set Save Options

1. Click the **File** tab, and then click **Options**.

2. In the left pane, click **Save**.

3. Set the save options you want:

   ◆ **Default Save Format.** Click the **Save files in this format** list arrow, and then click the default format you want.

   ◆ **Don't show the Backstage when opening or saving files.** Select to enable (**New!**).

   ◆ **Show additional places for saving, even if sign-in may be required.** Select to enable (**New!**).

   ◆ **Save to Computer by default.** Select to enable (**New!**).

   ◆ **Default local file location.** Specify the complete path to the folder where you want to save your presentations.

4. Click **OK**.

Saving a Presentation with Different Formats

PowerPoint is a versatile suite of programs that allow you to save your presentations in a variety of different formats—see the table on the following page for a complete list and description. For example, you might want to save your presentation as a web page that you can view in a web browser or save your presentation in the OpenPresentation format for use in the OpenOffice program. Or you can save a presentation in an earlier 97-2003 version in case the people you work with have not upgraded to PowerPoint 2013. If you save a presentation to 97-2003, some new features and formatting are converted to uneditable pictures or not retained. The format is compatible with versions before 2003 with a software patch. However, for best results, if you're creating a presentation for someone with PowerPoint 97 to PowerPoint 2003, it's better to save it with the .doc file format. If you have issues with leap year dates for 1900, you can use the Strict Open XML Presentation format (**New!**) with ISO8601.

Save a Presentation with Another Format

1. Click the **File** tab, and then click **Export**.

2. Click **Change File Type**.

3. Click the file type you want.

4. Click the **Save As** button.

    The Save As dialog box opens with the selected file type.

    ◆ You can also click the **File** tab, click **Save As**, click **Computer**, click **Browse**, and then select a file format.

5. Navigate to the location where you want to save the file.

6. Type a presentation file name.

7. Click **Save**.

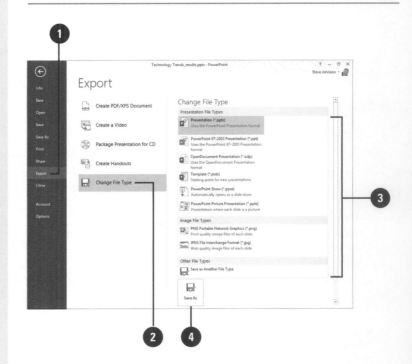

Did You Know?

You can access options from the Save dialog box. In the Save dialog box, click Tools, and then click the option you want, either General Options, Web Options, or Compress Pictures.

PowerPoint 2013 Supported File Formats

Save As file type	Extension	Used to save
PowerPoint Presentation	.pptx	PowerPoint 2013 presentation
PowerPoint Macro-Enabled Presentation	.pptm	PowerPoint 2013 presentation that contains Visual Basic for Applications (VBA) code
PowerPoint 97-2003	.ppt	PowerPoint 97 to PowerPoint 2003 presentation
PDF	.pdf	Fixed-layout electronic file format that preserves document formatting developed by Adobe Systems
XPS Document	.xps	Fixed-layout electronic file format that preserves document formatting developed by Microsoft
PowerPoint Template	.potx	PowerPoint 2013 template
PowerPoint Macro-Enabled Template	.potm	PowerPoint 2013 template that includes preapproved macros
PowerPoint 97-2003 Template	.pot	PowerPoint 97 to PowerPoint 2003 template
Office Theme	.thmx	Style sheet that include theme definitions
PowerPoint Show	.pps; .ppsx	PowerPoint 2013 presentation that opens in Slide Show view
PowerPoint Macro-Enabled Show	.ppsm	PowerPoint 2013 show that includes preapproved macros
PowerPoint 97-2003 Show	.ppt	PowerPoint 97-2003 presentation that opens in Slide Show view
PowerPoint Add-In	.ppam	PowerPoint 2013 add-in that stores specialized functionality, such as VBA code
PowerPoint 97-2003 Add-in	.ppa	PowerPoint 97-2003 add-in that stores specialized functionality, such as VBA code
PowerPoint XML Presentation	.xml	XML (Extensible Markup Language) based file with the presentation content
Windows Media Video	.wmv	Movie video file that plays in Windows Media Player and other players
GIF, JPEG, PNG, TIFF, Device Independent Windows Metafile, Enhanced Windows Metafile	.gif, .jpg, .png .tif, .wmf, .emf	Various graphics formats that open in other programs
Outline/RTF	.rtf	Presentation outline as a text-only document
Strict Open XML Presentation (**New!**)	.pptx	PowerPoint 2013 presentation format to resolve leap year issues with 1900
OpenDocument Presentation	.odt	OpenDocument presentation; a file created from the OpenOffice program

Saving a Presentation to Online Services

PowerPoint 2013 is integrated to work with online services (**New!**) to make it easier to save and open presentations on other devices and share them with others. With a Microsoft or SharePoint account, you can save presentations directly to a SkyDrive (**New!**), a personal cloud-based online storage system, or Office 365 SharePoint (**New!**), a customized Microsoft web site with SharePoint services. With your presentations on a SkyDrive or SharePoint site, you can do a lot of things. You can sync the files from the SkyDrive or SharePoint site to other desktops or devices, such as a tablet or mobile phone for easy access from anywhere. You can view or edit presentations online from the desktop PowerPoint program or browser-based PowerPoint Web App. You can share a presentation with other people using e-mail or social networks (**New!**) and even work on the same presentation at the same time with more than one person (**New!**).

Save a Presentation to Online Storage

1. Click the **File** tab, and then click **Save As**.

2. To add a shortcut place for easy access later, click **Add a Place**, click **Office 365 SharePoint** or **SkyDrive**, and then follow the on-screen connection instructions.

3. Click the SkyDrive or SharePoint name.

4. Click **Browse** or a recent folder.

5. Navigate to the location where you want to save the file.

6. Type a presentation file name.

7. Click the **Save as type** list arrow, and then click **PowerPoint Presentation (*.pptx)**.

8. Click **Save**.

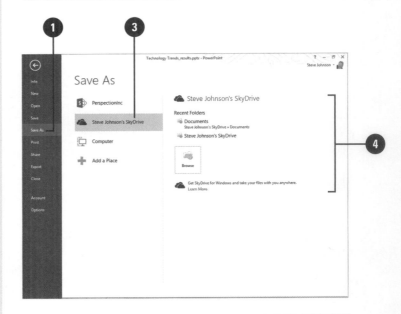

Add a Place

Working with Accounts

When you set up PowerPoint 2013 or Office 2013, it requests a Microsoft account to work with online services, such as SkyDrive or SharePoint. You can add, switch, or modify accounts or sign out entirely. You can also use to other online services (**New!**), such as Flickr and YouTube for images and video, and Facebook, LinkedIn, and Twitter for sharing. Before you can use the services, you need to add them to PowerPoint, which requires an established account with a user name and password.

Work with Online Accounts

① Click the **File** tab, and then click **Account** (**New!**).

> **TIMESAVER** *Click the User Account list arrow, and then click an account option.*

② Click any of the following links:

- ◆ **Change photo.** Click to open your account profile.

- ◆ **About me.** Click to open your account profile.

- ◆ **Sign out.** Click to sign out of your account.

- ◆ **Switch Account.** Click to switch or add accounts.

③ Click the **Back** button to exit the File tab.

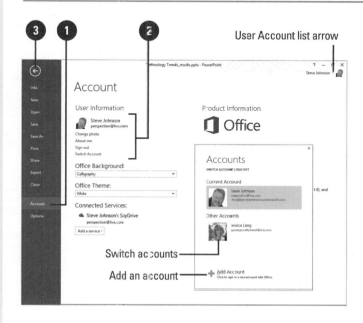

Add Online Services

① Click the **File** tab, and then click **Account** (**New!**).

② Click **Add a service** (**New!**), point to a service type (options vary):

- ◆ **Images & Videos**, and then click **Flickr** or **YouTube**.

- ◆ **Storage**, and then click **Office 365 SharePoint** or **SkyDrive**.

- ◆ **Sharing**, and then click **Facebook**, **LinkedIn**, or **Twitter**.

③ Follow the on-screen instructions to add the service.

④ Click the **Back** button to exit the File tab.

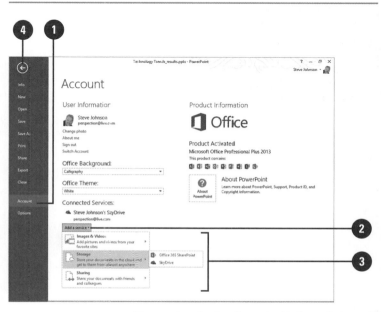

Recovering a Presentation

If PowerPoint encounters a problem and stops responding, the program automatically tries to recover the file. The recovered files are stored and managed by PowerPoint. You can use the Manage Versions button on the Info screen under the File tab to open any available recovered unsaved files. If you have a lot of recovered files, you can also delete all file versions to save disk space. To use the AutoRecover option, you need to enable it in the Save category of the Options dialog box. You can set AutoRecover options to periodically save a temporary copy of your current file, which ensures proper recovery of the file and allows you to revert to an earlier version of a file. In addition, if you didn't save your changes when you closed a presentation, you can select an AutoRecover option to save your work as a safe guard.

Recover or Revert a Presentation

1. Click the **File** tab, and then click **Info**.

2. To open a recovered or previous version, click a file from the available list.

3. Click the **Manage Versions** button, and then click **Recover Unsaved Presentations**.

    TIMESAVER *Click the File tab, click Recent, and then click Recover Unsaved Presentations folder icon.*

4. Select the file version you want to recover.

5. Click **Open**.

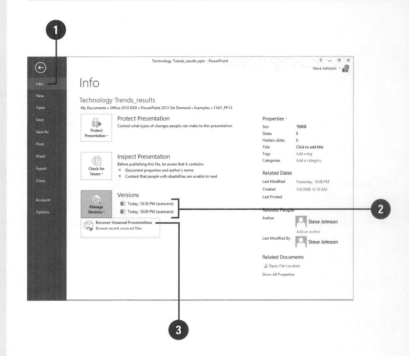

Did You Know?

You can delete all draft versions of unsaved files. Click the File tab, click Info, click the Manage Versions button, click Delete All Unsaved Presentations, and then click Yes to confirm the deletions.

Open an Unsaved Files

1. Click the **File** tab, and then click **Open**.

2. Click the **Recover Unsaved Presentations** button.

3. Select the unsaved file you want to open from the Unsaved Files folder in the Office folder.

4. Click **Open**.

Use AutoRecover

1. Click the **File** tab, and then click **Options**.

2. In the left pane, click **Save**.

3. Select the **Save AutoRecover information every _x_ minutes** check box.

4. Enter the number of minutes, or click the **Up** and **Down** arrows to adjust the minutes.

5. Select the **Keep the last autosaved version if I close without saving** check box as a safe guard to save your work if you don't save it.

6. Specify the complete path to the folder location where you want to save your AutoRecover file.

7. Click **OK**.

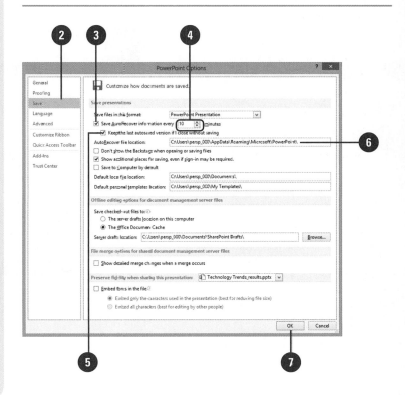

Closing a Presentation and Exiting PowerPoint

After you finish working on a presentation, you can close it. Closing a presentation frees up more computer memory for other activities. Closing a presentation is different from exiting, or quitting, PowerPoint; after you close a presentation, PowerPoint is still running. You close a presentation by using the Close command on the File tab (**New!**), which keeps the PowerPoint program window open. Since each presentation opens in its own program window (**New!**), you don't need an Exit command, so you exit PowerPoint by using the Close button on the program window. To protect your files, always save your presentations and exit before turning off the computer.

Close a Presentation

1. Click the **File** tab, and then click **Close**.

   TIMESAVER *Press Ctrl+W.*

2. If you have made changes to any open files since last saving them, a dialog box opens, asking if you want to save changes. Click **Save** to save any changes, or click **Don't Save** to ignore your changes.

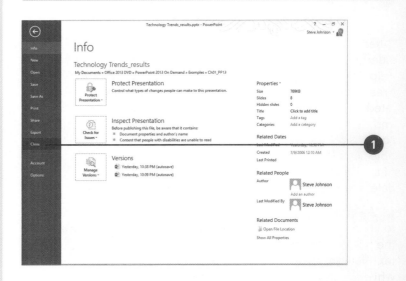

Exit PowerPoint

1. Click the **Close** button on the PowerPoint program window.

   ◆ **Close All**. Right-click the PowerPoint icon on the taskbar, and then click **Close all windows**.

   TIMESAVER *To create an Exit button, add the Exit command to the Quick Access Toolbar.*

2. If you have made changes to any open files since last saving them, a dialog box opens asking if you want to save changes. Click **Save** to save any changes, or click **Don't Save** to ignore your changes.

Developing Presentation Content

2

Introduction

When creating a new presentation, there are things to consider as you develop your content. Microsoft PowerPoint can help you with this process. There are various elements to a presentation that make looking at your slides interesting: bulleted lists, clip art, charts and diagrams, organization charts and tables, and media clips or pictures. All of these items are considered graphic objects, and are separate from the text objects that you enter. Objects can be moved from one part of a presentation to another. You can also resize, move, and delete them.

As you develop your presentation, there are a few things to keep in mind—keep the text easy to read and straight to the point, make sure it isn't too wordy, and have a balance of text and graphics. Too much text can lose your audience while too many graphics can distract their focus.

PowerPoint offers many tools to help develop your text. Using the AutoCorrect feature, text is corrected as you type. A built-in Thesaurus is always a few keystrokes away, as is a research option that allows you to look for information is available in PowerPoint or has links to the Web.

Once you've begun to enter your text, you can adjust the spacing, change the alignment, set tabs, and change indents. You can also format your text by changing the font style or its attributes such as adding color to your text. If you decide to enter text in outline form, PowerPoint offers you the Outline pane to jot down your thoughts and notes. If bulleted or numbered lists are your preference, you can enter your ideas in this format. Should you need to rearrange your slides, you can do this in various PowerPoint views.

What You'll Do

Create New and Consistent Slides

Work with Objects

Develop and Modify Text

Set Editing Options

Correct and Resize Text While Typing

Insert Information the Smart Way

Insert and Develop an Outline

Move and Indent Text

Set Tabs

Change Text Alignment and Spacing

Change Character Spacing and Direction

Format Text

Modify a Bulleted and Numbered List

AutoFormat Text While Typing

Apply a Format Style

Create a Text Box and Columns

Find and Replace Text

Rearrange Slides

Organize Slides into Sections

Use Slides from Other Presentations

Creating New and Consistent Slides

Creating consistent looking slides makes it easier for your audience to follow and understand your presentation. PowerPoint provides a gallery of slide layouts to help you position and format slides in a consistent manner. A slide layout contains **placeholders**, such as text, chart, table, or SmartArt graphic, where you can enter text or insert elements. When you create a new slide, you can apply a standard layout or a custom layout of your own design. You can also apply a layout to an existing slide at any time. When you change a slide's layout, PowerPoint keeps the existing information and applies the new look.

Insert a New Slide

1. Click the **Home** tab.

2. Click the **New Slide** button arrow.

   TIMESAVER *To insert a slide quickly without using the gallery, click the Add Slide button (icon).*

3. In the Slide Layout gallery, click the slide layout you want to use.

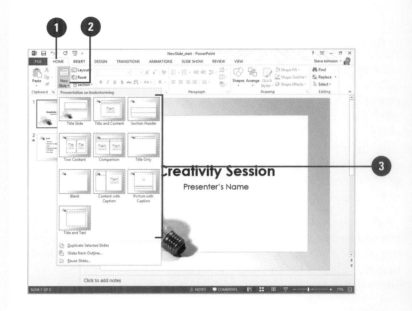

Apply a Layout to an Existing Slide

1. In Normal view, display the slide you want to change.

2. Click the **Home** tab.

3. Click the **Layout** button, and then click the slide layout you want.

See Also

See "Using Slides from Other Presentations" on page 80 for information on adding slides from other presentations.

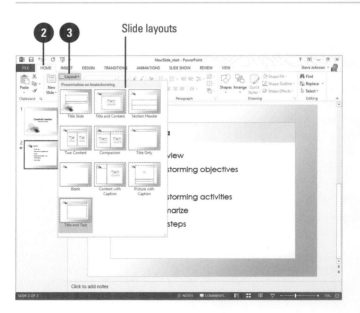

Slide layouts

Enter Information in a Placeholder

◆ For text placeholders, click the placeholder, and then type the text.

◆ For other objects, click the icon in the placeholder, and then work with the accessory that PowerPoint starts.

Did You Know?

You can duplicate a slide. In Outline or Slides pane or Slide Sorter view, select the slide you want to duplicate, click the Home tab, click the Add Slide button arrow in the Slides group, and then click Duplicate Selected Slides.

You can quickly delete a slide. In Outline or Slides pane or Slide Sorter view, select the slide you want to delete, and then press Delete or click the Delete button in the Slides group on the Home tab.

You can reset a placeholder position back to the default location. In Outline or Slides pane or Slide Sorter view, select the slide you want to reset, click the Home tab, and then click the Reset button in the Slides group.

Layout Placeholder

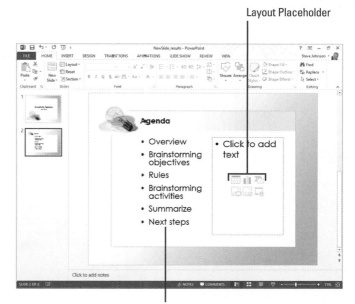

A placeholder is a border that defines the size and location of an object.

Slide Layout Placeholders

Placeholder	Description
Title	Enter title text
Bulleted	Enter bulleted list
Table	Inserts a table
Chart	Inserts a chart
SmartArt	Inserts a diagram, chart, or other graphics
Online Picture (**New!**)	Inserts a picture from Office.com
Picture	Inserts a picture from a file
Video	Inserts a video clip

Working with Objects

Once you create a slide, you can modify any of its objects, even those added by a slide layout. To manipulate objects, use Normal view. To perform any action on an object, you first need to select it. When you select an object, such as text or graphic, the object is surrounded by a solid-lined rectangle, called a **selection box**, with sizing handles (small white circles at the corners and small white squares on the sides) around it. You can resize, move, delete, and format selected objects.

Select and Deselect an Object

◆ To select an object, move the pointer (which changes to a four-headed arrow) over the object or edge, and then click to select.

◆ To select multiple objects, press and hold Shift as you click each object or drag to enclose the objects you want to select in the selection box. Press Ctrl+A to select all objects on a slide.

◆ To deselect an object, click outside its border.

◆ To deselect one of a group of objects, press and hold Shift, and then click the object.

Selection box

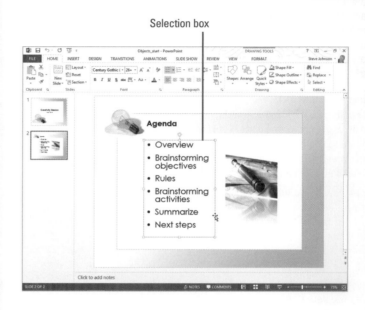

Resize an Object

1 Move the pointer over a sizing handle.

2 Drag the sizing handle until the object is the size you want.

A live layout preview (**New!**) appears for the objects.

TIMESAVER *Use the Shift and Ctrl keys while you drag. The Shift key constrains an edge; the Ctrl key maintains a proportional edge; and the Shift and Ctrl keys together maintains a proportional object.*

Sizing handle

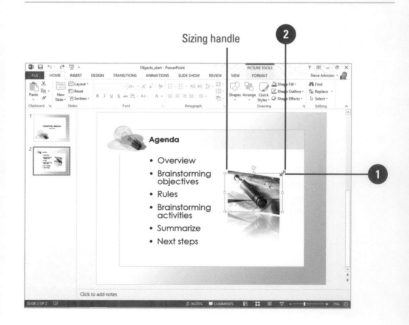

Move or Copy an Object

◆ **Using the mouse**. To copy, press and hold Ctrl while you drag. Move the pointer (which changes to a four-headed arrow) over the object, and then drag it to the new location. For unfilled objects, drag the border. You can move or copy an object in a straight line by pressing Shift as you drag the object. As you drag, a live layout preview (**New!**) appears for the objects.

◆ **Using the keyboard**. To move, click the object, and then press the arrow keys to move the object in the direction you want.

◆ **Using the keyboard shortcuts**. To cut an object from a slide, select the object and then press Ctrl+X. To copy an object, select the object, and then press Ctrl+C. To paste an object on a slide, press Ctrl+V.

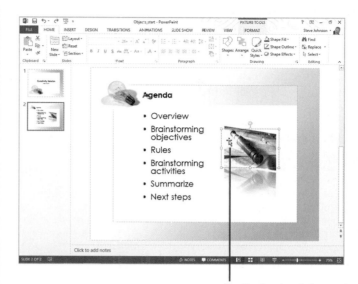

Use the four-headed arrow to drag the object to a new location.

Delete an Object

1 Click the object you want to delete.

2 Press Delete or click the **Cut** button on the Home tab.

Did You Know?

You can use the Tab key to select hard-to-click objects. If you are having trouble selecting an object that is close to other objects, click a different object and then press Tab until you select the object you want. *See "Selecting Objects Using the Selection Pane" on page 157 for more information on selecting hard-to-click objects.*

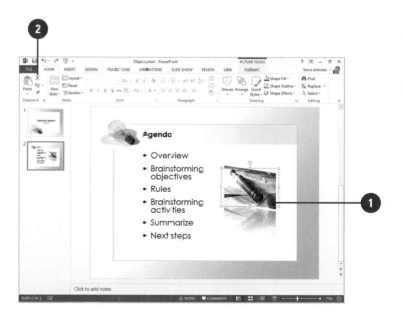

Developing Text

Your presentation's text lays the foundation for the presentation. Keep these basic presentation rules in mind when developing your text.

- ◆ Keep it simple.

- ◆ If you plan to present your slides to a large group, think about the people at the back of the room and what they can see.

- ◆ Keep the text to a minimum with no more than five bullets per slide and no more than five words per bullet.

- ◆ If you find a graphic that illustrates your point in a memorable way, use it instead of a lot of text.

PowerPoint provides several views that can help you organize your text. You can work with text and other objects one slide at a time in Normal view or you can work with all the presentation text on all slides at once in the Outline pane.

PowerPoint also offers many text formatting features traditionally associated with word processing software. You can apply fonts and text attributes to create the look you want. You can set tabs, indents, and alignment. Finally, you can edit and correct your text using several handy tools, including style, grammar, and spelling checkers.

PowerPoint includes three types of text objects.

- ◆ **Title text objects**. Presized rectangular boxes that appear at the top of each slide—used for slide titles and, if appropriate, subtitles.

- ◆ **Bulleted list objects**. Boxes that accommodate bulleted or numbered lists.

- ◆ **Text box objects**. Boxes that contain non-title text that you don't want to format in bulleted or numbered lists—often used for captions.

The first slide in a presentation typically contains title and text and a subtitle. Other slides often start with a title and then list major points in a bulleted list. Use text boxes only occasionally—when you need to include annotations or minor points that don't belong in a list.

When to Enter Text on a Slide

Use the Slides pane of Normal view to enter text when you are focusing on the text or objects of one slide at a time.

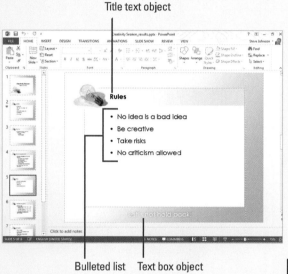

Title text object

Bulleted list   Text box object

When to Enter Text in an Outline

If you are concentrating on developing presentation content, but not on how the text looks or interacts with other objects on the slide, use the Outline pane in Normal view. This view lets you see the titles, subtitles, and bulleted text on all your slides at a single glance.

The Outline pane in Normal view is particularly useful for reorganizing the content of your presentation and ensuring that topics flow well from one to the next. You can easily move presentation topics up and down the outline.

You can switch between the Slides pane and Outline pane by clicking the Normal View button (**New!**) on the Status bar while in Normal view, or clicking the Normal View or Outline View button on the View tab.

Title text in the Outline pane appears next to the slide number and slide icon.

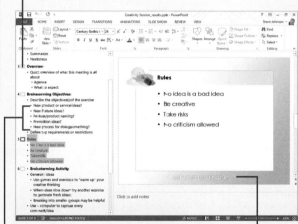

Bulleted lists appear in the list format with the different levels indented.

Text boxes do not appear in the Outline pane.

Entering Text

In Normal view, you can type text directly into the text placeholders. A **text placeholder** is an empty text box. If you type more text than fits in the placeholder, the text is automatically resized to fit on the slide. You can also manually increase or decrease the line spacing or font size of the text. The insertion point (the blinking vertical line) indicates where text will appear when you type. To place the insertion point into your text, move the pointer over the text. The pointer changes to an I-beam to indicate that you can click and then type. When a selection box of dashed lines appears, your changes affect only the selected text. When a solid-lined selection box appears, changes apply to the entire text object.

Enter Text into a Placeholder

1. In Normal view, click the text placeholder if it isn't already selected.

2. Type the text you want to enter.

3. Click outside the text object to deselect it.

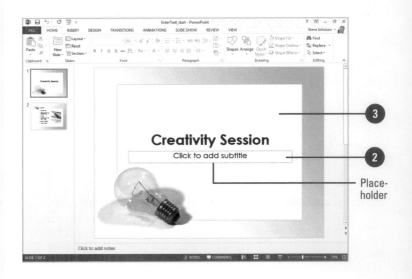

Insert Text

1. Click to place the insertion point where you want to insert the text.

2. Type the text.

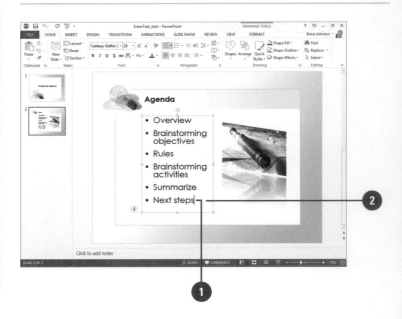

Enter Text in a Bulleted or Numbered List

1. In Normal view, click the bulleted text placeholder.

2. To switch to a numbered list, click the **Home** tab, if necessary, and then click the **Numbering** button.

3. Type the first item.

4. Press Enter.

   ◆ To increase the list level, press Tab or click the **Increase List Level** button on the Home tab.

   ◆ To decrease the list level, press Shift+Tab, or click the **Decrease List Level** button on the Home tab.

5. Type the next item.

6. Repeat steps 4 and 5 until you complete the list.

See Also

See "Moving and Indenting Text" on page 56 or "Modifying a Bulleted and Numbered List" on page 66 for information on changing text in a bulleted list.

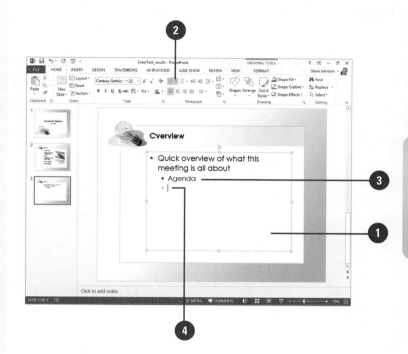

Editing Text

If you are familiar with word processing programs, you probably already know how to perform most text editing tasks in PowerPoint. You can move (cut and paste), copy (copy and paste), or delete existing text; replace it with new text; and undo any changes you just made. Some of the editing methods require that you select the text first. When you select text, the text is surrounded by a rectangle of gray dashed lines, indicating you can now edit the text.

Select and Modify Text

1. Position the mouse pointer to the left of the text you want to highlight.

2. Drag the pointer over the text—just a few words, a few lines, or entire paragraphs, and then release the mouse button.

3. To select discontinuous text, press Ctrl, and then drag the pointer over text.

4. Modify the text the way you want.

   ◆ To delete text, press Delete.

   ◆ To replace text, type your new text.

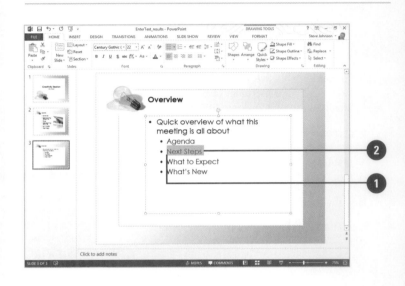

Move or Copy Text

1. Select the text you want to move or copy.

2. Use any of the following methods:

   ◆ To move text short distances in the Outline pane or on a slide, drag the text. To copy text, press and hold the Ctrl key as you drag the text.

   ◆ To move or copy text between slides, click the **Cut** or **Copy** button on the Home tab, click where you want to insert the text, and then click the **Paste** button, or click the **Paste** button arrow and click a paste option: **Use Destination Theme**, **Keep Source Formatting**, **Picture**, or **Keep Text Only**.

Paste button and Paste button arrow

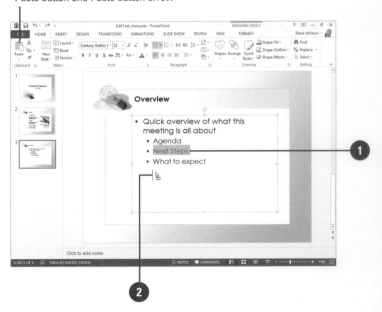

Setting Editing Options

If you spend a lot of time modifying documents, you can set editing options in PowerPoint to customize the way you work. You can set options to automatically select entire words, allow text to be dragged and dropped, automatically switch the keyboard to match the language of the surrounding text, specify the maximum number of undos, and don't automatically hyperlink screen shots (**New!**). You can also set cutting, copying, and pasting options to specify preferences when you paste text and graphics with Smart Cut and Paste and Show Paste Options button when they are needed.

Set Editing Options

1. Click the **File** tab, and then click **Options**.

2. In the left pane, click **Advanced**.

3. Select or deselect the check box options you want turned on or off:

   ◆ **When selecting, automatically select entire word** (default on). Select to select the entire word when you click a word.

   ◆ **Allow text to be dragged and dropped** (default on). Select to move or copy text by dragging.

   ◆ **Automatically switch keyboard to match language of surrounding text** (default off). Select to have PowerPoint switch keyboard to match the language (only available with multiple keyboard languages).

   ◆ **Maximum number of undos** (default 20). Enter the number of undos to track.

   ◆ **Do not automatically hyperlink screenshot** (default off). Select to not hyperlink pasted screenshots (**New!**).

   ◆ **Use smart cut and paste** (default on). Select to adjust the spacing of words and objects.

   ◆ **Show Paste Options button when content is pasted** (default on). Select to show the Paste Options button after you paste.

4. Click **OK**.

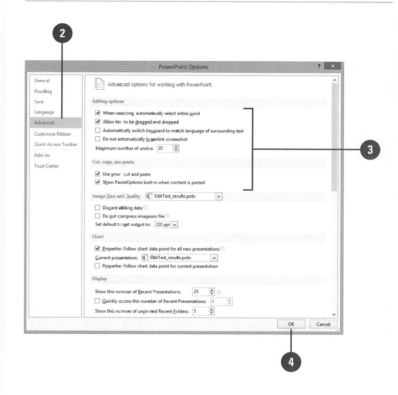

Correcting Text While Typing

With AutoCorrect, PowerPoint corrects common capitalization and spelling errors as you type. For example, if you accidentally type two capital letters or forget to capitalize the first letter of a sentence or table cell, AutoCorrect will fix it for you. You can customize AutoCorrect to recognize or ignore routine misspellings you make or to ignore specific text that you do not want AutoCorrect to change. If you use math symbols in your work, you can use Math AutoCorrect to make it easier to insert them. It works just like AutoCorrect. When you point to a word that AutoCorrect changed, a small blue box appears under the first letter. When you point to the small blue box, the AutoCorrect Options button appears, which gives you control over whether you want to correct the text. You can change text back to its original spelling, stop AutoCorrect from correcting text, or change AutoCorrect settings.

Set AutoCorrect Options

1. Click the **File** tab, and then click **Options**.

2. Click **Proofing**, and then click **AutoCorrect Options**.

3. Click the **AutoCorrect** tab.

4. Select the **Show AutoCorrect Options buttons** check box to display the button to change AutoCorrect options.

5. Select the capitalization and correction check boxes you want.

6. Select the **Replace text as you type** check box.

7. To change AutoCorrect exceptions, click **Exceptions**, click the **First Letter** or **INitial CAps** tab, make the changes you want, and then click **OK**.

8. To add an AutoCorrect entry, type Replace text, type the With text, and then click **Add**.

9. To use Math AutoCorrect, click the **Math AutoCorrect** tab, and then select the **Use Math AutoCorrect rules outside of math regions** check box.

10. Click **OK**, and then click **OK** again.

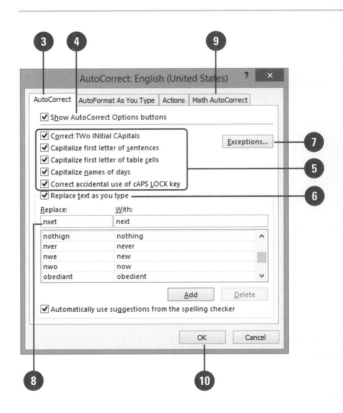

Correcting Text as You Type

1 If you misspell a word that PowerPoint recognizes, it will correct it and the AutoCorrect button will appear.

2 Point to the small blue box under the corrected word, and then click the **AutoCorrect Options** button list arrow to view your options.

3 Click an option, or click a blank area of the slide to deselect the AutoCorrect Options menu.

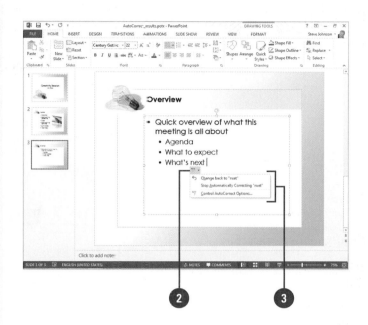

Examples of AutoCorrect Changes

Type of Correction	If You Type	AutoCorrect Inserts
Capitalization	cAP LOCK	Cap Lock
Capitalization	TWo INitial CAps	Two Initial Caps
Capitalization	thursday	Thursday
Common typos	can;t	can't
Common typos	windoes	windows
Superscript ordinals	2nd	2nd
Stacked fractions	1/2	½
Smart quotes	" "	" "
Em dashes	Madison--a small city in Wisconsin--is a nice place to live.	Madison—a small city in Wisconsin— is a nice place to live.
Symbols	(c)	©
Symbols	(r)	®

Undoing and Redoing an Action

You may realize you've made a mistake shortly after completing an action. The Undo feature lets you "take back" one or more previous actions, including text you typed, edits you made, or commands you selected. For example, if you were to enter a title in a presentation, and then decide you don't like it, you could undo it instead of selecting the text and deleting it. If you decide the text you deleted was alright, you can use the Redo feature to restore it or the Repeat feature to repeat the last action.

Undo an Action

1. Click the **Undo** button on the Quick Access Toolbar to undo the last action you completed.

    TIMESAVER *Press Ctrl+Z.*

2. Click the **Undo** button arrow on the Quick Access Toolbar to see recent actions that can be undone.

3. Click an action. Word reverses the selected action and all actions above it.

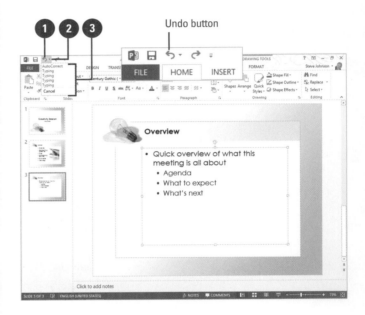

Undo button

Redo or Repeat an Action

1. Click the **Redo** button on the Quick Access Toolbar to restore your last undone action or click the **Repeat** button on the Quick Access Toolbar to repeat the last action.

   TIMESAVER *Press Ctrl+Y.*

   TROUBLE? *If the Redo button is not available on the Quick Access Toolbar, click the Customize Quick Access Toolbar list arrow, and then click Redo.*

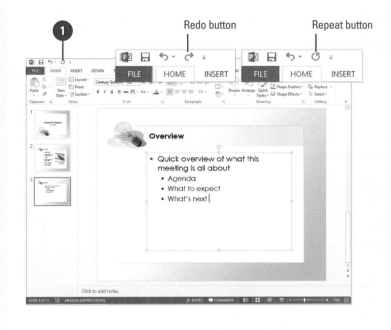

Set Undo Options

1. Click the **File** tab, and then click **Options**.

2. In the left pane, click **Advanced**.

3. Enter the maximum number of undos you want PowerPoint to track (default 20).

4. Click **OK**.

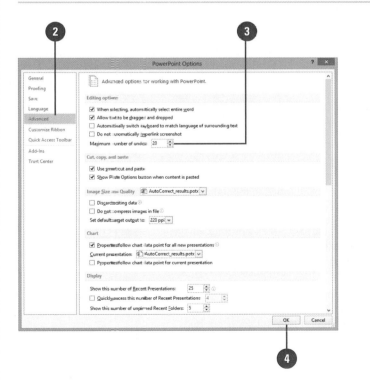

Resizing Text While Typing

If you type text in a placeholder, PowerPoint uses AutoFit to resize the text, if necessary, to fit into the placeholder. The AutoFit Text feature changes the line spacing—or paragraph spacing—between lines of text and then changes the font size to make the text fit. The AutoFit Options button, which appears near your text the first time that it is resized, gives you control over whether you want the text to be resized. The AutoFit Options button displays a menu with options for controlling how the option works. You can also display the AutoCorrect dialog box and change the AutoFit settings so that text doesn't resize automatically.

Resize Text as You Type

1. If the AutoFit Options box appears while you type, click the **AutoFit Options** button to select an option, or continue typing and PowerPoint will automatically adjust your text to fit.

2. If you click the AutoFit Options button, click the option you want to fit the text on the slide.

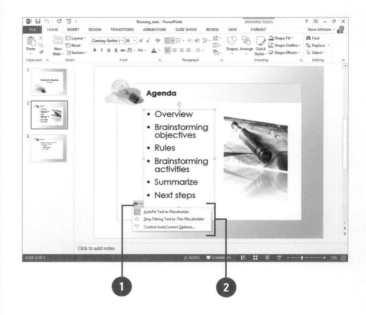

Turn Off AutoFit

1. Click the **File** tab, and then click **Options**.

2. In the left pane, click **Proofing**, and then click **AutoCorrect Options**.

3. Click the **AutoFormat As You Type** tab.

4. Clear the **AutoFit Title Text To Placeholder** and **AutoFit Body Text To Placeholder** check boxes.

5. Click **OK**.

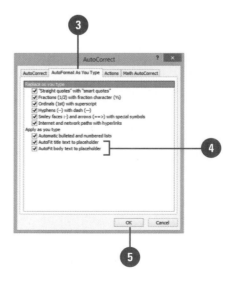

Change AutoFit Options for a Specific Object

1. Right-click the object with text you want to change, and then click **Format Shape**.

2. In the Format Shape pane, click **Text Options**.

3. Click the **Text Box** icon, and then expand **Text Box**, if needed.

4. Click the Autofit option you want.

   ◆ **Do not AutoFit.** To turn off AutoFit for the selected object.

   ◆ **Shrink text on overflow.** To resize text to fit in the selected object (default).

   ◆ **Resize shape to fit text.** To change the size of the shape to fit the text.

5. Click the **Close** button in the pane.

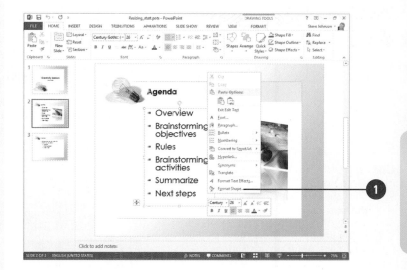

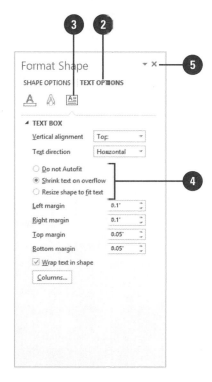

Inserting Information the Smart Way

Actions, a replacement for smart tags, help you integrate actions typically performed in other programs directly in PowerPoint. For example, you can insert a financial symbol to get a stock quote, add a person's name and address in a presentation to the contacts list in Microsoft Outlook, or copy and paste information with added control. PowerPoint analyzes the data you type and recognizes certain types that it marks with actions. The types of actions you can take depend on the type of data with the action. To use an action, you right-click an item to view any custom actions associated with it.

Change Options for Actions

1. Click the **File** tab, and then click **Options**.

2. In the left pane, click **Proofing**, and then click **AutoCorrect Options**.

3. Click the **Actions** tab.

4. Select the **Enable additional actions in the right-click menu** check box.

5. Select the check boxes with the actions you want.

6. To get properties about an action, select the action, and then click **Properties**.

7. To add more actions, click **More Actions**, and then follow the online instructions.

8. Click **OK**.

9. Click **OK** again.

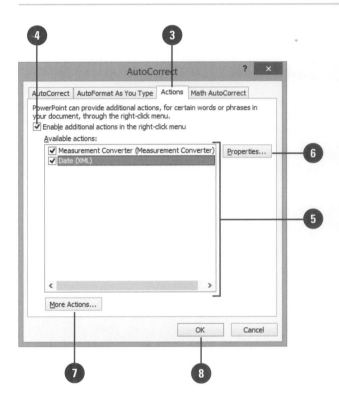

Insert Information Using an Action

① Click to select an item, such as a text box, where you want to insert an action.

② Type the information needed for the action, such as the date, a recognized financial symbol in capital letters, or a person's name from your contacts list, and then press Spacebar.

③ Right-click the item, and then point to **Additional Actions** (name varies depending on item).

④ Click the action option you want; options vary depending on the action. For example, click Show my Calendar or Schedule a Meeting.

Did You Know?

You can remove an action from text or item. Select text or item, and then press Delete to remove it.

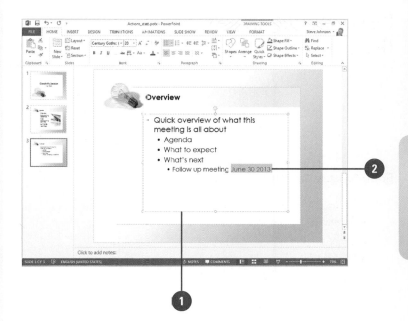

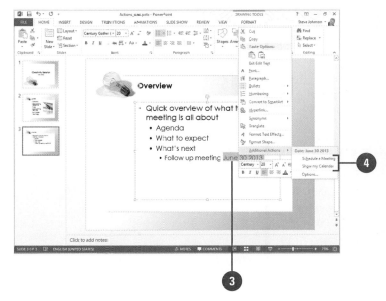

Inserting and Developing an Outline

Outlining your content is a great way to create a presentation. You can outline and organize your thoughts right in PowerPoint or insert an outline you created in another program, such as Microsoft Word. If you prefer to develop your own outline, you can create a blank presentation, and then type your outline in the Outline pane of Normal view. As you develop an outline, you can add new slides or duplicate existing ones. If you have an outline, make sure the document containing the outline is set up using outline heading styles. When you insert the outline, it creates slide titles, subtitles, and bulleted lists based on those styles.

Enter Text in the Outline Pane

1. In Normal view, click the **Normal View** button on the Status bar to switch to the Outline pane.

2. In the Outline pane of Normal view, click to place the insertion point where you want the text to appear.

3. Type the title text you want, pressing Enter after each line.

   To indent right a level for bullet text, press Tab before you type. Press Shift+Tab to indent left a level.

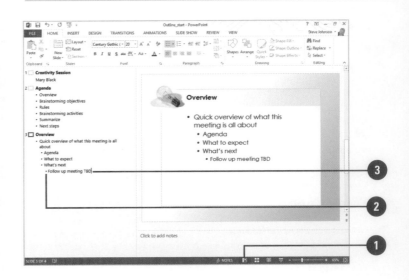

Add a Slide in the Outline Pane

1. In the Outline pane of Normal view, click at the end of the slide text where you want to insert a new slide.

2. Press Ctrl+Enter, or click the **Home** tab, click the **New Slide** button arrow, and then click a layout.

Did You Know?

You can delete a slide. In the Outline or Slides pane or in Slide Sorter view, select the slide you want to delete. Press Delete, or click the Delete button in the Slides group on the Home tab.

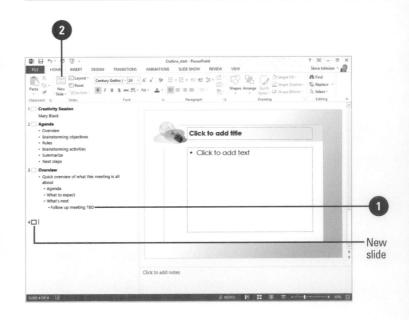

New slide

Duplicate a Slide

1. In the Outline pane of Normal view, click the slide you want to duplicate.

   TIMESAVER *To select slides in a sequence, click the first slide, hold down the Shift key, and then click the last slide. To select multiple slides, use the Ctrl key.*

2. Click the **Home** tab.

3. Click the **New Slide** button arrow.

4. Click **Duplicate Selected Slides**.

   The new slide appears directly after the slide duplicated.

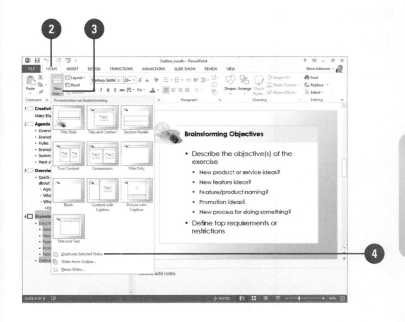

Insert an Outline from Another Program

1. In the Outline pane of Normal view, click the slide after which you want to insert an outline.

2. Click the **Home** tab.

3. Click the **New Slide** button arrow, and then click **Slides from Outline**.

4. Locate and select the file containing the outline you want to insert.

5. Click **Insert**.

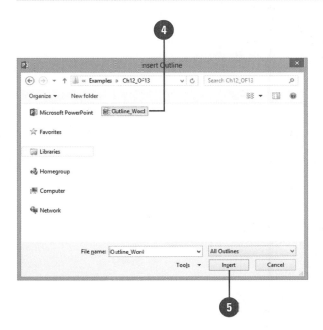

Did You Know?

You can open an outline from another program in PowerPoint. Click the File tab, click Open, click Computer, click Browse, click the Files Of Type list arrow, click All Outlines, and then double-click the outline file to open it.

Moving and Indenting Text

Body text on a slide typically contains bulleted text, which you can indent to create levels. You can indent paragraphs of body text up to five levels using the Increase List Level and Decrease List Level buttons. In an outline, these tools let you demote text from a title, for example, to bulleted text. You can view and change the locations of the indent markers within an object with text using the ruler. In PowerPoint, pressing Enter within an object with text creates a paragraph. You can set different indent markers for each paragraph in an object.

Change the Indent Level

1. In Normal view (Outline pane or slide), click the paragraph text or select the lines of text you want to indent.

2. Click the **Home** tab.

3. Click the indent level option you want:

   ◆ Click the **Increase List Level** button to move the line up one level (to the left).

   ◆ Click the **Decrease List Level** button to move the line down one level (to the right).

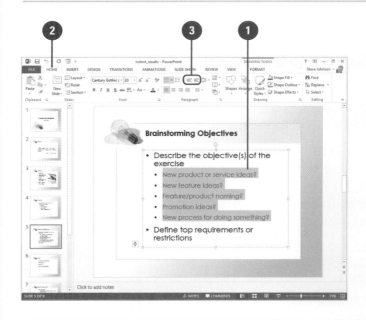

Display or Hide the Ruler

1. In Normal view, click the **View** tab.

2. Select the **Ruler** check box to display it, or clear the **Ruler** check box to hide it.

Did You Know?

You can use the Ruler with shape text. When you select a text object and then view the ruler, the ruler runs the length of just that text object, and the origin (zero point) of the ruler is at the box borders, starting with the upper left.

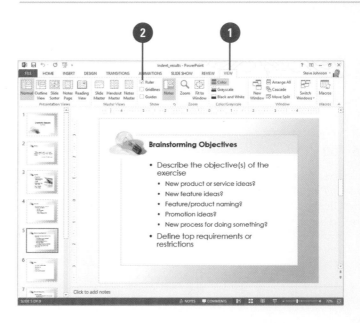

Change the Indent

1. Display the ruler.

2. Select the text for which you want to change the indentation.

3. Change the indent level the way you want.

   ◆ To change the indent for the first line of a paragraph, drag the first-line indent marker.

   ◆ To change the indent for the rest of the paragraph, drag the left indent marker.

   ◆ To change the distance between the indents and the left margin, but maintain the relative distance between the first-line and left indent markers, drag the rectangle below the left indent marker.

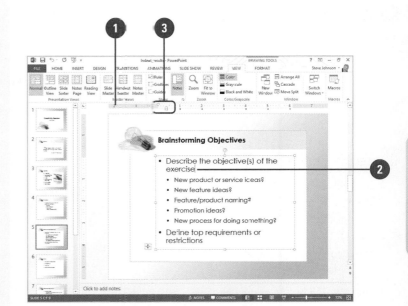

Did You Know?

You can use the mouse to increase or decrease list level text. Move the mouse pointer over the bullet you want to increase or decrease, and then when it changes to a four-headed arrow, drag the text to the left to increase the level or to the right to decrease the level.

You can show or hide formatting in Outline pane. In Outline pane, right-click a slide icon, and then click Show Text Formatting. Turning off formatting is useful for viewing more slides.

Setting Tabs

PowerPoint includes default tab stops at every inch; when you press the Tab key, the text moves to the next tab stop. You can control the location of the tab stops using the ruler. When you set a tab, tab markers appear on the ruler. Tabs apply to an entire paragraph, not a single line within that paragraph. You can also clear a tab by removing it from the ruler.

Set a Tab

1. Click the paragraph or select the paragraphs whose tabs you want to modify. You can also select a text object to change the tabs for all paragraphs in that object.

2. If necessary, click the **View** tab, and then select the **Ruler** check box to display the ruler.

3. Click the **Tab** button at the left of the horizontal ruler until you see the type of tab you want.

4. Click the ruler where you want to set the tab.

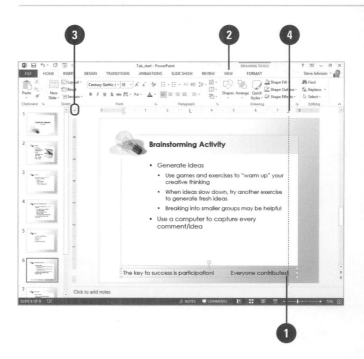

Did You Know?

You can use the Tabs dialog box to make multiple changes at one time. On the Home tab, click the Paragraph Dialog Box Launcher, click Tabs, select the tab stop you want to change, click Clear or make a change and click Set, and then click OK.

You must use caution when you change a default tab. When you drag a default tab marker to a new location, the spaces between all the tab markers change proportionally.

Tab Button Alignments

Tab Button	Aligns Text with
⌞	Left edge of text
⊥	Center of text
⌟	Right edge of text
⊥•	Decimal points in text

Change the Distance Between Default Tab Stops

① Select the text object in which you want to change the default tab stops.

② If necessary, click the **View** tab, and then select the **Ruler** check box to display the ruler.

③ Drag any default tab stop marker to a new position.

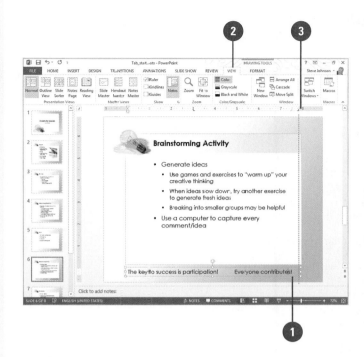

Clear a Tab

① Select the text object in which you want to clear tab stops.

② If necessary, click the **View** tab, and then select the **Ruler** check box to display the ruler.

③ Drag the tab marker off the ruler.

Tab cleared

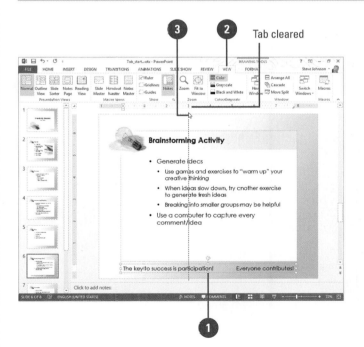

Changing Text Alignment and Spacing

PowerPoint enables you to control the way text lines up on the slide. You can align text horizontally to the left or right, to the center, or to both left and right (justify) in a text object. You can also align text vertically to the top, middle, or bottom within a text object. In addition to vertical text alignment in a text object, you can also adjust the vertical space between selected lines and the space before and after paragraphs. You set specific line spacing settings before and after paragraphs in points. A **point** is equal to about 1/72 of an inch (or .0138 inches) and is used to measure the height of characters. Points are typically used in graphics and desktop publishing programs.

Adjust Line Spacing Quickly

1. Select the text box.

2. Click the **Home** tab.

3. Click the **Line Spacing** button, and then click **1.0 - 3.0**.

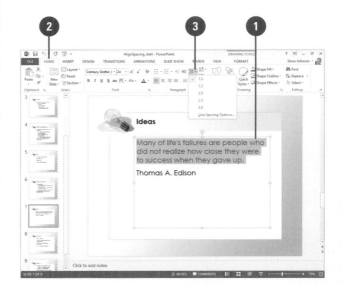

Adjust Line Spacing Exactly

1. Select the text box.

2. Click the **Home** tab.

3. Click the **Line Spacing** button, and then click **Line Spacing Options**.

4. Click the **Before Spacing** or **After Spacing** up or down arrows to specify a setting.

5. Click the **Line Spacing** list arrow, and then select a setting.

   If you select Exactly or Multiple, specify at what spacing you want.

6. Click **OK**.

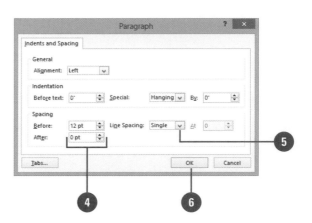

Change Text Alignment Horizontally

1. Select the text box.

2. Click the **Home** tab.

3. Click an alignment button:

   ◆ **Align Left** to align text evenly along the left edge and is useful for paragraph text.

   ◆ **Center** to align text in the middle and is useful for titles and headings.

   ◆ **Align Right** to align text evenly along the right edge and is useful for text labels.

   ◆ **Justify** to align both left and right and is useful for column text.

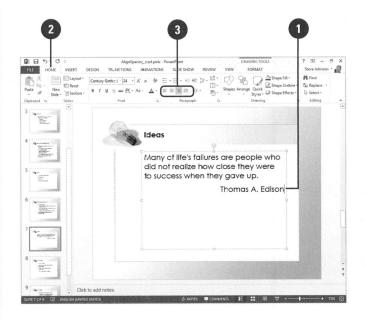

Change Text Alignment Vertically

1. Select the text box.

2. Click the **Home** tab.

3. Click the **Align Text** button, and then click one of the following:

   ◆ **Top**, **Middle**, or **Bottom** to quickly align text within a text box.

   ◆ **More Options** to select from additional alignment options in the Format Shape pane, including Top Centered, Middle Centered, and Bottom Centered.

4. If you selected More Options, click the **Vertical Alignment** list arrow, and then select an align option.

5. If you selected More Options, click the **Close** button in the pane.

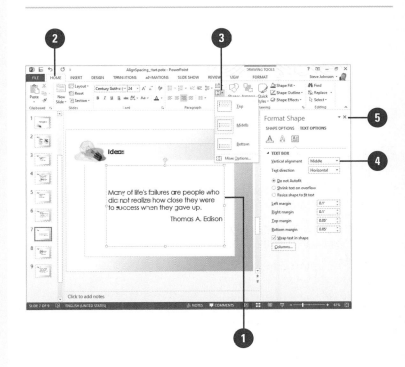

Changing Character Spacing

Kerning is the amount of space between each individual character that you type. Sometimes the space between two characters is larger than others, which makes the word look uneven. Kerning works only with TrueType or Adobe Type Manager fonts. You can expand or condense the character spacing to create a special effect for a title, or realign the position of characters to the bottom edge of the text—this is helpful for positioning the copyright or trademark symbols.

Change Character Spacing Quickly

1. Select the text you want to format.

2. Click the **Home** tab.

3. Click the **Character Spacing** button, and then click **Very Tight**, **Tight**, **Normal**, **Loose**, or **Very Loose**.

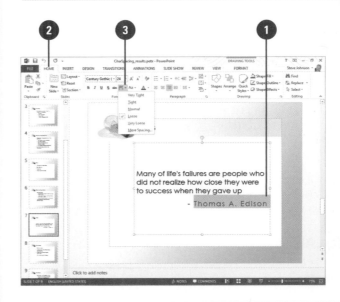

Change Character Spacing Exactly

1. Select the text you want to format.

2. Click the **Home** tab.

3. Click the **Character Spacing** button, and then click **More Spacing**.

4. Click the **Spacing** list arrow, and then select **Normal**, **Expanded**, or **Condensed**.

5. If you want, click the **By** up and down arrows to set the spacing distance (in points).

6. To apply conditional kerning, select the **Kerning for fonts** check box, and then specify a font point size.

7. Click **OK**.

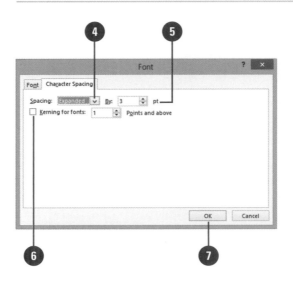

Changing Character Direction

Sometimes changing the direction of text on a slide creates a unique or special effect that causes the audience to remember it. In PowerPoint, you can rotate all text in an object 90 and 270 degrees or stack letters on top of one another to create the look you want. For a more exact rotation, which you cannot achieve in 90 or 270 degree increments, you can drag the green rotate lever at the top of an object to rotate it to any position. This is useful when you want to change the orientation of an object, such as the direction of an arrow.

Change Character Direction Quickly

1. Select the text you want to format.

2. Click the **Home** tab.

3. Click the **Character Direction** button, and then click one of the following:

   ◆ **Horizontal** to align text normally across the slide from left to right.

   ◆ **Rotate all text 90°** to align text vertically down the slide from top to bottom.

   ◆ **Rotate all text 270°** to align text vertically down the slide from bottom to top.

   ◆ **Stacked** to align text vertically down the slide one letter on top of another.

   ◆ **More Options** to select additional options, such as alignment, direction or resize shape to fit text.

4. If you selected More Options, select the character direction options you want.

5. If you selected More Options, click the **Close** button in the pane.

6. If necessary, resize text box.

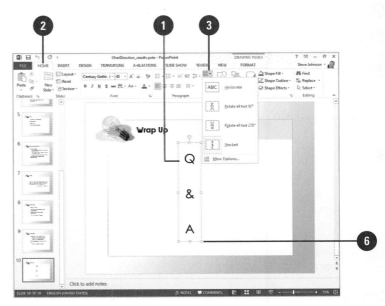

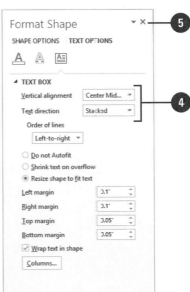

Formatting Text

Although PowerPoint's layouts and themes provide preformatted styles for text, you can change the formatting or add extra emphasis to a word or text object. You can format a single letter, a word, a phrase, or all the text in a text object. The basic formats you apply to text are available on the Home tab in the Font group or in the Font dialog box. Some of the formats include strikethrough or double strike-through, all caps or small caps, and double or color underline. If you no longer like your text formatting, you can quickly remove it.

Change the Font Using the Ribbon

1. Select the text or text object whose font you want to change.

2. Click the **Home** tab, click the **Font** list arrow, and then point for a live preview, or click the font you want, either a theme font or any available fonts.

3. Click one to change the font size:

   ◆ Click the **Font Size** list arrow on the Home tab, and then click the font size you want.

   ◆ Click the **Increase Font Size** button or **Decrease Font Size** button on the Home tab.

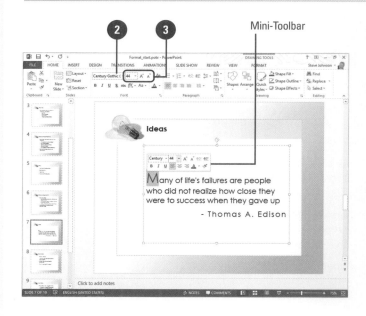

Format or Unformat Text Using the Ribbon

1. Select the text you want to format, or click the selection box of a text object to format all the text in the box.

2. Click one or more of the formatting buttons on the Home tab in the Font group: **Bold**, **Italic**, **Underline**, **Shadow**, **Strikethrough**, or **Font Color**.

3. To clear all formatting and return to default text style, click the **Clear All Formatting** button on the Home tab.

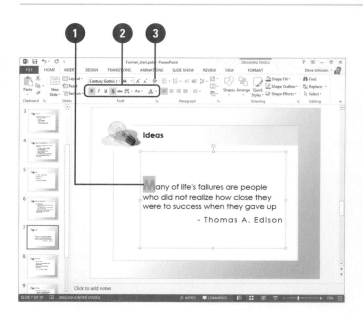

Format the Text Font

① Select the text you want to format, or click the selection box of a text object to format all the text in the box.

② Click the **Home** tab.

③ Click the **Font Dialog Box Launcher**.

④ Make any changes you want to the Font, Font Style, and Size.

⑤ Select or clear the effects you want or don't want: **Strikethrough, Double Strikethrough, Superscript, Subscript, Small Caps, All Caps,** and **Equalize Character Height**.

⑥ If you want, click **Font Color**, and then click a color.

⑦ If you want, click **Underline Style list arrow**, and then click a style. If you want to add an underline style, click **Underline Color**, and then click a color.

⑧ Click **OK**.

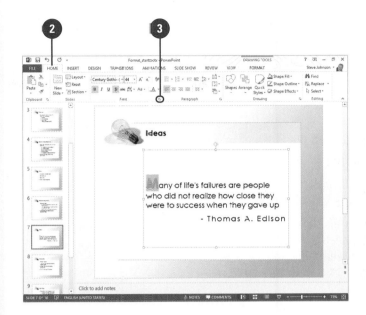

Did You Know?

You can replace fonts for an entire presentation. Click the Home tab, click the Replace button arrow, and then click Replace Fonts. Click the Replace list arrow, select the font in which you want to replace, click the With list arrow, select the font in which you want to replace it with, and then click Replace.

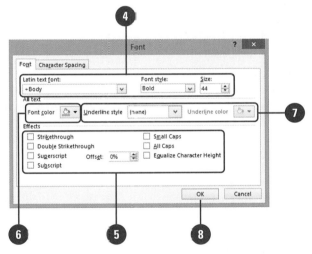

For Your Information

Quick Formatting with the Mini-Toolbar

When you point to selected text, PowerPoint displays the Mini-Toolbar above it. The Mini-Toolbar provides easy access to common formatting toolbar buttons, such as font, font size, increase and decrease font size, format painter, bold, italic, left align, center, right align, font color, increase and decrease list level, and bullets. If you don't want to display the Mini-Toolbar, you can use PowerPoint Options to turn it off.

Modifying a Bulleted and Numbered List

When you create a new slide, you can choose the bulleted list slide layout to include a bulleted list placeholder. You can customize the appearance of your bulleted list in several ways, including symbols or numbering. You also have control over the appearance of your bullets, including size and color. You can change the bullets to numbers or pictures. You can also adjust the distance between a bullet and its text using the PowerPoint ruler.

Add and Remove Bullets or Numbering from Text

1 Select the text in the paragraphs in which you want to add a bullet.

2 Click the **Bullets** or **Numbering** button arrow on the Home tab, and then select the style you want.

> **TIMESAVER** *Click the Bullets or Numbering button (not the arrow) on the Home tab to turn it on with the default setting.*

3 To remove the bullet or numbering, select the text, and then click the **Bullets** or **Numbering** button on the Home tab.

Select a style

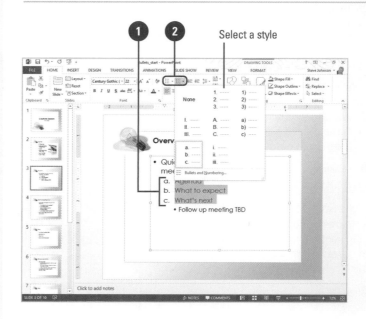

Change the Distance Between Bullets and Text

1 Select the text you want to indent.

2 If the ruler isn't visible, click the **View** tab, and then select the Ruler check box.

3 Drag the indent markers on the ruler.

◆ **First-line Indent.** The top upside down triangle marker indents the first line.

◆ **Hanging Indent.** The middle triangle marker indent second line and later.

◆ **Left Indent.** The bottom square marker indent entire line.

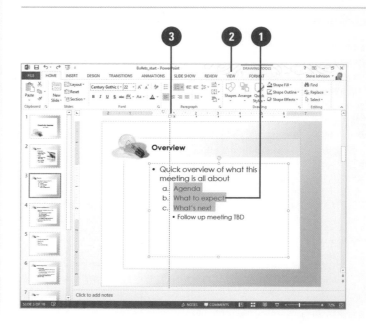

Change the Bullet or Number Character

1. Select the text or text object whose bullet character you want to change.

2. Click the **Bullets** or **Numbering** button arrow on the Home tab, and then click **Bullets and Numbering**.

3. Click the **Bulleted** or **Numbered** tab.

4. Click one of the predefined styles or do one of the following:

   ◆ Click **Customize**, and then click the character you want to use for your bullet character.

   ◆ Click **Picture**, and then click the picture you want to use for your bullet character.

5. To change the bullet or number's color, click the **Color** arrow, and then select the color you want.

6. To change the bullet or number's size, enter a percentage in the Size box.

7. Click **OK**.

Did You Know?

You can select bulleted or numbered text. Position the mouse pointer over the bullet or number next to the text you want to select; when the pointer changes to the four-headed arrow, click the bullet.

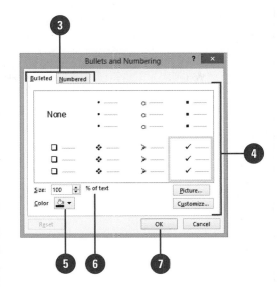

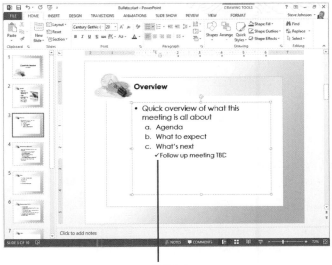

Bullet change

AutoFormatting Text While Typing

PowerPoint recognizes ordinals, fractions, em-dashes and en-dashes, formatted AutoCorrect entries and smart quotes followed by a number, and formats them as you type. For example, if you type 1/2, PowerPoint replaces it with ½. You can also automatically number a list. PowerPoint recognizes your intent; when you enter a number followed by a period and a space, PowerPoint will format the entry and the subsequent entries as a numbered list. If you insert a new line in the middle of the numbered list, PowerPoint automatically adjusts the numbers.

AutoFormat Text as You Type

① In Normal view, click to place the insertion point in the text where you want to type.

② Type text you can AutoFormat, such as 1/2, and then press the Spacebar or Enter.

PowerPoint recognizes this as a fraction and changes it to ½.

You can also type and replace any of the following:

◆ Straight quotes with "smart quotes".

◆ Ordinals (1st) with superscript.

◆ Hyphens (--) with dash (—).

◆ Smiley faces :-) and arrows (==>) with special symbols.

◆ Internet and network paths with hyperlinks.

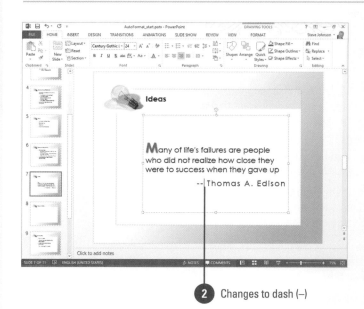

② Changes to dash (–)

Did You Know?

You can use the AutoCorrect Options button to undo automatic numbering or fractions. Click the AutoCorrect Options button that appears when AutoCorrect makes a change, and then click the Undo Automatic *x* command. If you want to stop AutoCorrect from making a change, click Stop Automatically *x* command.

AutoNumber a List as You Type

1. In Normal view, click to place the insertion point in the text at the beginning of a blank line where you want to begin a numbered list.

2. Type 1., press the Spacebar, type text, and then press Enter.

   PowerPoint recognizes this as a numbered list and displays the next number in the list in gray.

3. Type text, and continue until you complete the list.

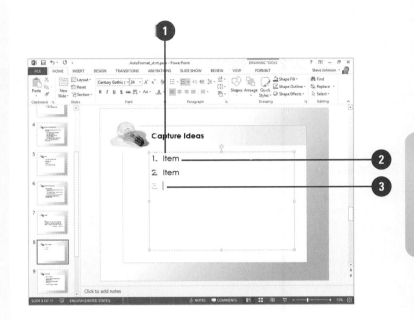

Change AutoFormat Options

1. Click the **File** tab, and then click **Options**.

2. Click **Proofing**, and then click **AutoCorrect Options**.

3. Click the **AutoFormat As You Type** tab.

4. Select or clear any of the following check boxes:

   ◆ Straight quotes with "smart quotes".

   ◆ Fractions (1/2) with fraction character (½).

   ◆ Ordinals (1st) with superscript.

   ◆ Hyphens (--) with dash (—).

   ◆ Smiley faces :-) and arrows (==>) with special symbols.

   ◆ Internet and network paths with hyperlinks.

5. Click **OK**.

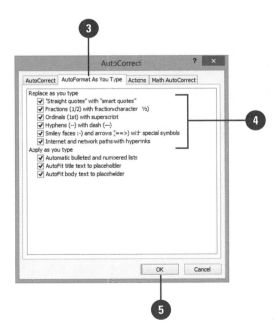

Applying a Format Style

The Format Painter lets you "pick up" the style of one section of text or object and apply, or "paint," it to another. The Format Painter is useful for quickly applying formatting styles to one or more text or shape objects. To apply a text or shape style to more than one item, double-click the Format Painter button on the Home tab instead of a single-click. The double-click keeps the Format Painter active until you want to press Esc to disable it, so you can apply formatting styles to any text or object you want in your presentation.

Apply a Format Style Using the Format Painter

1. Select the word or object whose format you want to pick up.

2. Click the **Home** tab.

3. Click the **Format Painter** button.

    If you want to apply the format to more than one item, double-click the Format Painter button.

4. Drag to select the text or click the object to which you want to apply the format.

5. If you double-clicked the Format Painter button, drag to select the text or click the object to which you want to apply the format, and then press Esc when you're done.

See Also

See Chapter 4, "Drawing and Modifying Shapes," on page 113 for information on formatting text boxes by applying Quick Styles, fills, outline borders, and effects.

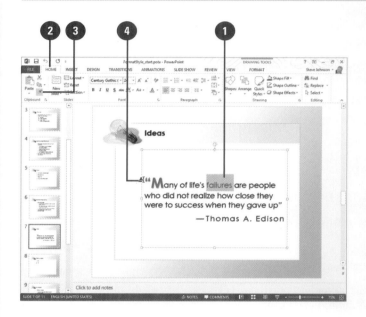

Apply new Format

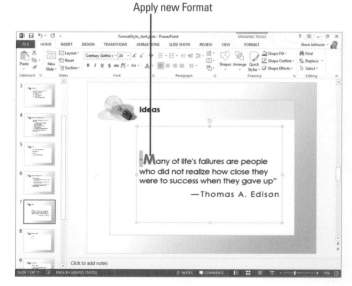

Inserting Symbols

PowerPoint comes with a host of symbols for every need. Insert just the right one to keep from compromising a presentation's professional appearance with a hand-drawn arrow («) or missing mathematical symbol (å). In the Symbol dialog box, you use the Recently used symbols list to quickly insert a symbol that you want to insert again. If you don't see the symbol you want, use the Font list to look at the available symbols for other fonts installed on your computer.

Insert Symbols and Special Characters

1. Click the presentation where you want to insert a symbol or character.

2. Click the **Insert** tab, and then click the **Symbol** button.

3. To see other symbols, click the **Font** list arrow, and then click a new font.

4. Click a symbol or character.

    You can use the Recently used symbols list to use a symbol you've already used.

5. Click **Insert**.

Did You Know?

You can insert a symbol using a character code. When the From box displays ASCII (decimal), you can use the number shown in the Character Code box to insert a character or symbol. Place your insertion point where you want the character on the slide, make sure Num Lock is on, hold down the Alt key, and then use the numeric keypad to type 0 (zero) followed by the character code. Then release the Alt key. The code applies to the current code page only, so some characters may not be available this way.

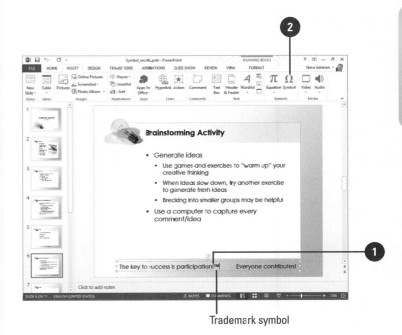

Trademark symbol

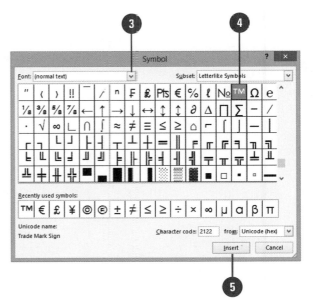

Creating a Text Box

Usually you use the title, subtitle, and bulleted list placeholders to place text on a slide. However, when you want to add text outside one of the standard placeholders, such as for an annotation to a slide or shape text, you can create a text box. Text boxes appear in all views and panes. In Outline pane, PowerPoint labels slides with multiple text boxes in numbered order. Your text box doesn't have to be rectangular—you can also use one of PowerPoint's shapes, a collection of shapes that range from rectangles and circles to arrows and stars. When you place text in a shape, the text becomes part of object. You can format and change the object using Font options, as well as Shape and WordArt styles. You can also adjust the text margins with a text box or a shape to create the look you want.

Create a Text Box

1. In Normal view, click the **Insert** tab.

2. Click the **Text Box** button.

3. Perform one of the following:

   ◆ To add text that wraps, drag to create a box, and then start typing.

   ◆ To add text that doesn't wrap, click and then start typing.

4. To delete a text box, select it, and then press Delete.

5. Click outside the selection box to deselect the text box.

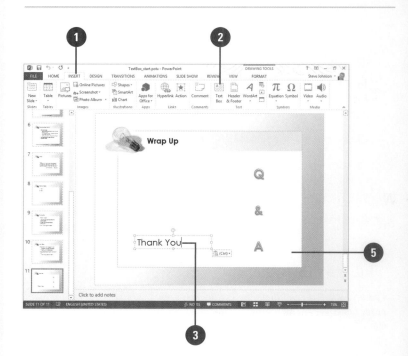

Did You Know?

You can use the sizing handles to adjust text boxes. If you create a text box without word wrapping and then find that the text spills over the edge of your slide, use the sizing handles to resize the text box so it fits on your slide. The text then wraps to the size of the box.

You can edit a text box. Click the text box, and then select the text you want to edit. Edit the text, and then click outside the text box to deselect it.

Add Text to a Shape

1. Click the **Home** or **Insert** tab.

2. Click the **Shapes** button to display a complete list of shapes.

3. Click the shape you want.

4. Drag to draw the shape on your slide.

5. Type your text.

Did You Know?

You can apply a Quick Style to a text box. Just like a shape, you can apply a quick style to a text box. Select the text box, click the Home tab, click the Quick Styles button, and then click a style.

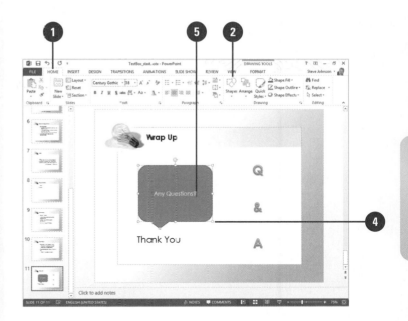

Wrap and Adjust Text Margins

1. Select an object with text.

2. Click the **Home** tab.

3. Click the **Drawing Dialog Box Launcher**.

4. In the Format Shape pane (**New!**), click **Text Options**.

5. Click the **Text Box** icon, and then expand **Text Box**, if needed.

6. Select the **Wrap text in shape** check box.

7. Use the margin **up** and **down** arrows to change the left, right, top, and bottom slides of the shape.

8. Click the **Close** button in the pane.

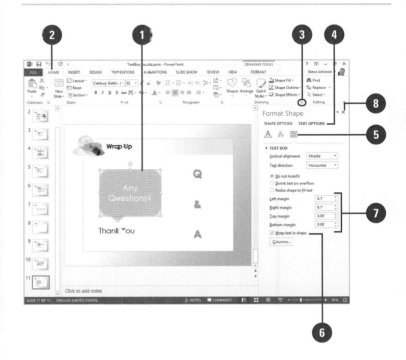

Creating Text Columns

Like Microsoft Word, PowerPoint can now create text columns within a text box. You can quickly transform a long list of text into a two, three, or more columns. After you create text columns, you can change the spacing between them to create the exact look you want. If you want to return columns back to a single column, simply change a text box to one column.

Create Text Columns

1. Select the text box.

2. Click the **Home** tab.

3. Click the **Columns** button, and then click one of the following:

   ◆ **One**, **Two**, or **Three** to quickly create text columns.

   ◆ **More Columns** to create larger text columns and change columns spacing.

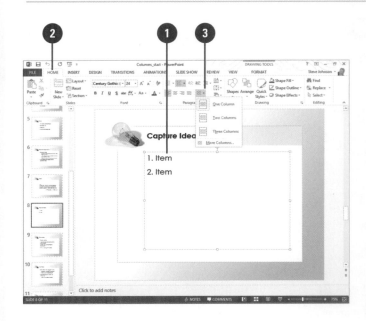

Adjust Column Spacing

1. Select the text box with the columns.

2. Click the **Home** tab.

3. Click the **Columns** button, and then click **More Columns**.

4. Click the **Spacing up** and **down** arrows, or enter a specific size.

5. Click **OK**.

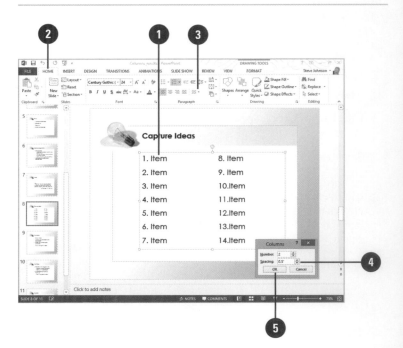

Finding and Replacing Text

The Find and Replace commands on the Home tab allow you to locate and change specific text in a presentation. Find helps you locate each occurrence of a specific word or set of characters, while Replace locates every occurrence of a specific word or set of characters and replaces it with a different one. You can change every occurrence of specific text all at once, or you can individually accept or reject each change.

Find and Replace Text

1. Click the **Home** tab.

2. Click the **Replace** button.

3. Click the **Find What** box, and then type the text you want to replace.

4. Click in the **Replace With** box, and then type the replacement text.

5. Click one of the following buttons.

   - **Match Case.** Select to find text with the same upper and lower case.

   - **Find whole words only.** Select to find entire text as a word.

6. Click one of the following buttons.

   - **Find Next.** Click to find the next occurrence of the text.

   - **Replace.** Click to find and replace this occurrence of the text.

   - **Replace All.** Click to find and replace all occurrences of the text.

7. Click **OK** when you reach the end of the presentation, and then click **Close**.

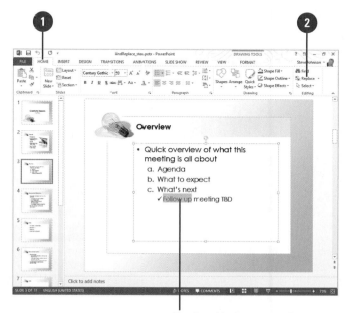

Text found in the presentation

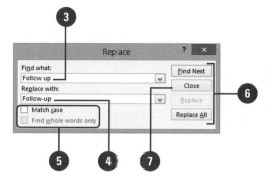

Did You Know?

You can use the Find command to search for text. To find text in your presentation, click the Home tab, click the Find button, type what you want to find, and then click Find Next.

Rearranging Slides

You can instantly rearrange slides in Outline or Slides pane in Normal view or in Slide Sorter view. You can use the drag-and-drop method or the Cut and Paste buttons to move slides to a new location. In the Outline pane, you can also collapse the outline to its major points (titles) so you can more easily see its structure and rearrange slides, and then expand it back.

Rearrange a Slide in Slides Pane or Slide Sorter View

1. In the Slides pane in Normal view or click the **Slide Sorter View** button.

2. Select the slide(s) you want to move.

3. Drag the selected slide to a new location.

   A vertical bar appears where the slide(s) will be moved when you release the mouse button.

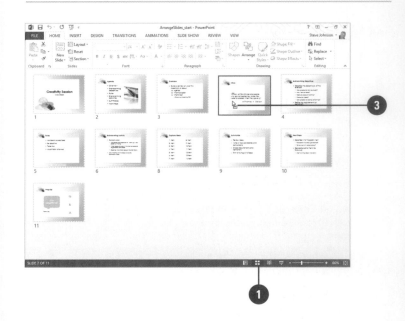

Move a Slide Using Cut and Paste

1. In the Outline or Slides pane or in Slide Sorter view, select the slide(s) you want to move.

2. Click the **Cut** button on the Home tab.

   The Clipboard pane might open, displaying items you have cut or copied.

3. Click the new location.

4. Click the **Paste** button on the Home tab.

Rearrange a Slide in the Outline Pane

1 In the Outline pane in Normal view (click the **Outline View** button on the View tab), select the slide(s) icons you want to move.

TIMESAVER *To select slides in a sequence, click the first slide, hold down the Shift key, and then click the last slide. To select multiple slides, use the Ctrl key.*

2 Drag the selected slide up or down to move it in Outline pane to a new location.

A vertical bar appears where the slide(s) will be moved when you release the mouse button.

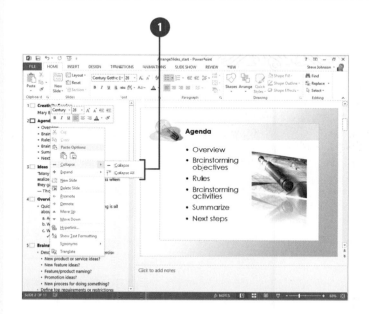

Collapse and Expand Slides in the Outline Pane

1 In the Outline pane in Normal view (click the **Outline View** button on the View tab), select the slide text you want to work with, and then:

◆ To collapse selected or all slides, right-click the slides, point to **Collapse**, and then click **Collapse**, or **Collapse All**.

A horizontal line appears below a collapsed slide in Outline view.

◆ To expand selected or all slides, right-click the slides, point to **Expand**, and then click **Expand**, or **Expand All**.

TIMESAVER *Double-click a slide icon in the Outline pane to collapse or expand it.*

Organizing Slides into Sections

When you're working on large presentations or collaborating on a presentation with others, organizing slides into sections can make the workflow process easier. After you create a section of slides in a presentation, you can rename the untitled section. When you rename a section, you can include a name assignment to make it easier for others working the presentation to know which slides to modify. When you no longer need a section, you can remove individual sections, or quickly remove them all.

Organize Slides into Sections

1. Click the **Home** tab.

2. In the Slides pane in Normal view or click the **Slide Sorter View** button.

3. Click to place the insertion point where you want to insert a new selection or select the slide(s) you want to place into a section.

4. Click the **Section** button, and then click **Add Section**.

Did You Know?

You can print sections. Click the File tab, click Print, click the Print Range list arrow, select the section name, and then click Print.

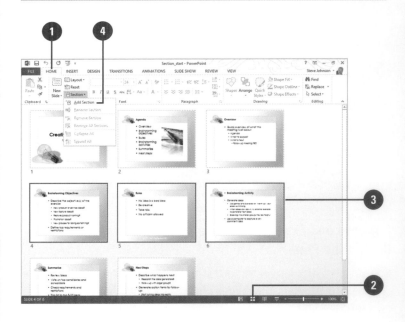

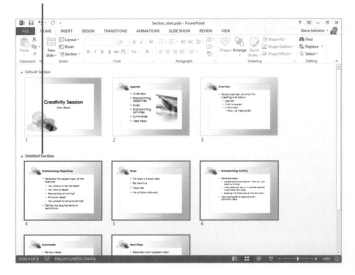

New section

Work with Sections

1. Click the **Home** tab.

2. In the Slides pane in Normal view or click the **Slide Sorter View** button.

3. Select the section you want to change.

4. To collapse or expand a section, click the **Collapse** or **Expand** arrow in the section name.

5. To rename a section, click the **Section** button, click **Rename Section**, type a name, and then click **OK**.

    ◆ To assign a name to a section, type it in when you rename a section.

6. To remove a section, click the **Section** button, click **Remove Section** or **Remove All Sections**.

7. To move slides in a section, drag them to another location.

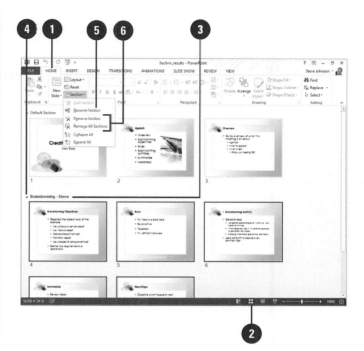

Slides pane in Normal view

Using Slides from Other Presentations

To insert slides from other presentations, you can open the presentation and copy and paste the slides you want, or you can use the Reuse Slides pane. With the Reuse Slides pane, you don't have to open the presentation first; instead, you can view a miniature of each slide in a presentation and then insert only the ones you select. If you only want to reuse the theme from another presentation, the Reuse Slides pane can do that too.

Insert Slides from Another Presentation

① Click the **Home** tab.

② Click the **New Slide** button arrow, and then click **Reuse Slides**.

③ If the presentation you want is not available, click **Browse**, click **Browse File**, locate and select the file you want, and then click **Open**.

④ Select the slides you want to insert.

◆ To display a larger preview, point to the slide.

◆ To insert a slide, click the slide.

◆ To insert all slides, right-click a slide, and then click **Insert All Slides**.

◆ To insert only the theme for all slides, right-click a slide, and then click **Apply Theme to All Slides**.

◆ To insert only the theme for the selected slides, right-click a slide, and then click **Apply Theme to Selected Slides**.

⑤ Click the **Close** button in the pane.

See Also

See "Publishing Slides to a SharePoint Library" on page 462 for information on using SharePoint.

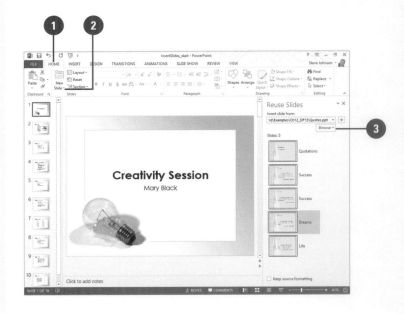

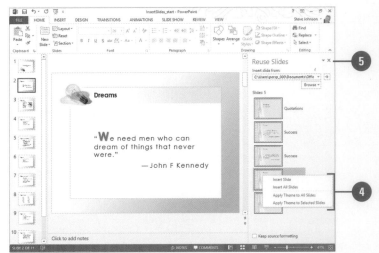

Designing a Look

Introduction

As you develop your presentation, an important element needs to be considered: the look of your slides. The design of your presentation is just as important as the information that it contains. A poorly designed presentation without the eye-catching design elements will lose your audience, and then what your presentation has to say won't really matter.

Microsoft PowerPoint comes with professionally designed templates to help you create a consistent presentation look. A template is a presentation file that consists of one or more slide masters. A **slide master** is the part of a template that contains all of the properties of your PowerPoint presentation—slide layouts, themes, effects, animation, backgrounds, text font style and color, date and time, and graphic placement. Each slide master contains one or more slide layouts, which defines the positioning and formatting of content on a slide. Layouts contain placeholders, which hold and format future text and other slide content, such as slide numbers, date, time, and headers and footers.

Besides the text and graphics that you place on your slides, another important part of a presentation is the use of color. Not everyone has an eye for color, and pulling it all together can be daunting, so PowerPoint provides you with professionally designed color themes, which you can apply to any slide master. A **theme** is a set of unified design elements that provides a consistent look for a presentation by using color themes, fonts, and effects, such as shadows, shading, and animations.

Once you've set up your masters and themes to be exactly the way you want them, you can save it as a design template. Company specific styles, logos, colors themes and other elements, can now become a new template to be used with other presentations in the future.

What You'll Do

Make Your Presentation Look Consistent

View Masters

Control Slide Appearance with Masters

Control a Slide Layout with Masters

Modify Placeholders

Control a Slide Background with Masters

Add a Header and Footer

Insert Slide Numbers

Insert the Date and Time

View and Apply a Theme

Understand and Create Color Themes

Choose Theme Effects and Font

Create a Custom Theme

Add Colors to a Presentation

Add and Modify a Background Style

Set Up for Personal Templates

Create a Personal Template

Open a Template

Making Your Presentation Look Consistent

Each PowerPoint presentation comes with a set of **masters**: slide, notes, and handout. A master controls the properties of each corresponding slide or page in a presentation. For example, when you make a change on a slide master, the change affects every slide. If you place your company logo, other artwork, the date and time, or slide number on the slide master, the element will appear on every slide.

Each master contains placeholders and a theme to help you create a consistent looking presentation. A placeholder provides a consistent place on a slide or page to store text and

information. A theme provides a consistent look, which incorporates a color theme, effects, fonts, and slide background style. Placeholders appear on the layouts associated with the master. The notes and handout masters use one layout while the slide master uses multiple layouts. Each master includes a different set of placeholders, which you can show or hide at any time. For example, the slide master includes master title and text placeholders, which control the text format for every slide in a presentation, while the handout master includes header, footer, date, page number, and body placeholders. You can modify and arrange placeholders on all of the

Slide Master view

Slide master

Slide layouts

Slide Title layout

master views to include the information and design you want.

You can also view and make changes to a master—either slide, notes, or handout—in one of the master views, which you can access using the View tab. When you view a master, the Ribbon adds a Program tab that correspond to the master. For example, when you switch to Slide Master view, the Slide Master tab appears. The Ribbon on each master view also includes a Close Master View button, which returns you to the view you were in before you opened the master.

The Ribbon for each master view also includes commands specific to the type of master. For example, the Slide Master tab contains several buttons to insert, delete, rename, duplicate, and preserve slide masters. You can insert one or more slide masters into a presentation, which is useful for creating separate sections within the same presentation. When you preserve a slide master, you protect it from being deleted. As you work with slide masters in Slide Master view, you can create custom slide layouts and insert placeholders.

Edit master slides

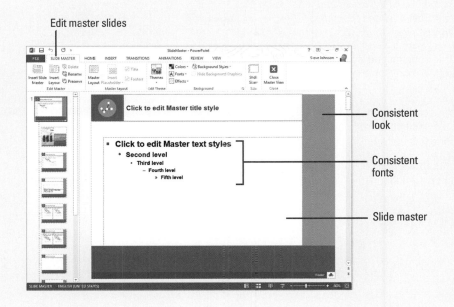

Consistent look

Consistent fonts

Slide master

Viewing Masters

If you want to change the appearance of each instance of a slide element, like all the title fonts or all the bullet characters, you don't have to change every slide individually. Instead, you can change them all at once using a slide master. PowerPoint updates the existing slides, and then applies your settings to any slides you add. Each PowerPoint presentation contains three masters: slide, notes, and handout. Which master you open depends on what part of your presentation you want to change. The slide master controls all the presentation slides, while the **notes master** and **handout master** controls the appearance of all speaker notes pages, and handout pages, respectively.

View the Slide Master

1. Click the **View** tab.

2. Click the **Slide Master** button.

    The slide master appears in the left pane as a larger slide miniature with a number next to it and the slides layouts associated with it appear below it.

    TIMESAVER *You can view the slide master quickly. Press and hold the Shift key, and then click the Normal view button.*

3. Click the slide master or slide layout to display it in the slide master view.

    Use the scroll bar in the left pane to display additional slide masters and slide layouts.

4. Click the **Close Master View** button on the Ribbon.

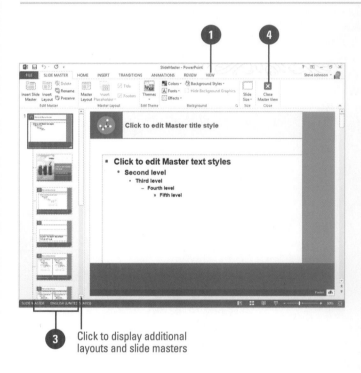

Click to display additional layouts and slide masters

View the Notes Master

1. Click the **View** tab.

2. Click the **Notes Master** button.

   The Notes Master controls the look of your notes pages.

3. Click the **Close Master View** button on the Ribbon.

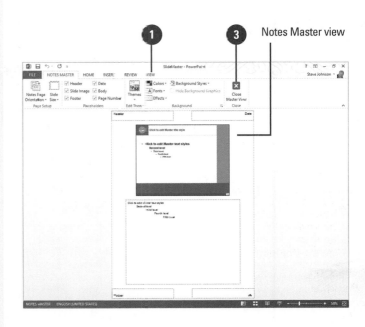

Notes Master view

View the Handout Master

1. Click the **View** tab.

2. Click the **Handout Master** button.

   TIMESAVER *You can view the handout master quickly. Press and hold the Shift key, and then click the Slide Sorter view button.*

   The Handout Master controls the look of your handouts.

3. Click the **Slides-per-page** button, and then use one of the following:

   ◆ Click the number of slides you want on your handout pages: **1**, **2**, **3**, **4**, **6**, or **9**.

   ◆ Click **Show Slide Outline** to show the slide outline, click the Slides-per-page button.

   The item you select in steps 2 or 3

4. Click the **Close Master View** button on the Ribbon.

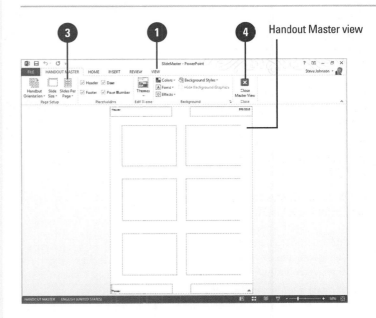

Handout Master view

Controlling Slide Appearance with Masters

If you want an object, such as a company logo or clip art, to appear on every slide in your presentation, place it on the **Slide Master**. All of the characteristics of the Slide Master (background color, text color, font, and font size) appear on every slide. However, if you want an object to appear on a certain slide type, place it on a slide layout in Slide Master view. The Slide Master tab contains several buttons to insert, delete, rename, duplicate, and preserve masters. You can create unique slides that don't follow the format of the masters. When you preserve a master, you protect (lock) it from being deleted. You can also arrange the placeholders the way you want them.

Include an Object on Every Slide or Only Specific Slides

1. Click the **View** tab, and then click the **Slide Master** button.

2. Add the objects you want to a slide master or slide layout, and then modify its size and placement.

   ◆ **Slide master.** Includes object on every slide.

   Slide master is the top slide miniature in the left column.

   ◆ **Slide layout.** Includes object only on the specific layout.

3. Click the **Close Master View** button on the Ribbon.

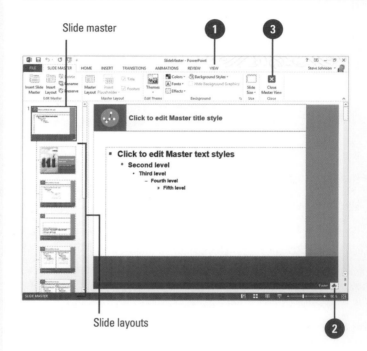

Slide master

Slide layouts

Did You Know?

You can delete a slide master. Click the View tab, click the Slide Master button, select the slide master you want to delete, click the Delete button in the Edit Master group, and then click the Close Master View button.

You can rename a slide master. Click the View tab, click the Slide Master button, select the slide master you want to rename, click the Rename button in the Edit Master group, type a new name, click Rename, and then click the Close Master View button.

Insert a New Slide Master

1 Click the **View** tab, and then click the **Slide Master** button.

2 Click the **Insert Slide Master** button.

The new slide master appears at the bottom of the left pane with a push pin indicating the new master is preserved.

3 Click the **Close Master View** button on the Ribbon.

The new slide master and associated layouts appears in the Add Slide and Layout galleries at the bottom (scroll down if necessary).

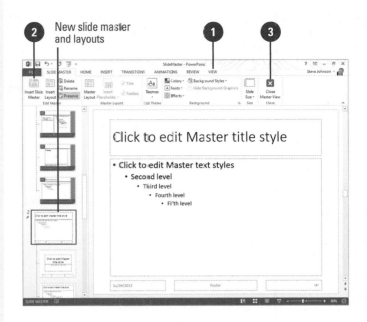

New slide master and layouts

Preserve or Not Preserve a Slide Master

1 Click the **View** tab, and then click the **Slide Master** button.

2 Click the master that you want to preserve or not preserve.

A push pin appears under the slide master number to indicate the master is currently preserved.

3 Use the Preserve button to toggle it on (highlighted) and off (not highlighted).

◆ **Preserve.** Click the **Preserve** button to lock the master (highlighted).

◆ **Not preserve.** Click the **Preserve** button to unlock the master (not highlighted), and then click **Yes** or **No** to delete the master (if not used).

4 Click the **Close Master View** button on the Ribbon.

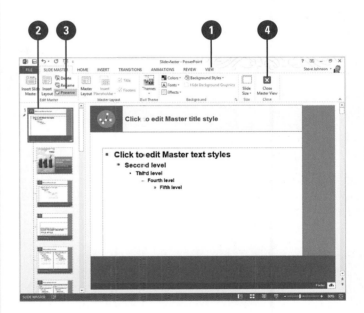

Controlling a Slide Layout with Masters

Each slide master includes a standard set of slide layouts. If the standard layouts don't meet your specific needs, you can modify one to create a new custom slide layout, or insert and create a new custom slide layout from scratch. You can use the Ribbon in Slide Master view to help you create a custom slide layout. In the Master Layout group, you can show and hide available placeholders or insert different types of placeholders, such as Content, Text, Picture, Chart, Table, Diagram, Media, and Clip Art.

Insert a New Slide Layout

1. Click the **View** tab, and then click the **Slide Master** button.

2. Select the slide master in the left pane in which you want to associate a new layout.

3. Click the **Insert Layout** button.

   The new slide layout appears at the end of the current slide layouts for the slide master.

4. Click the **Close Master View** button on the Ribbon.

See Also

See "Modifying Placeholders" on page 90 for information on showing, hiding, and formatting placeholders.

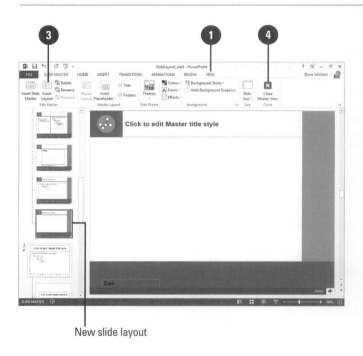

New slide layout

Create a New Slide Layout from an Existing One

1. Click the **View** tab, and then click the **Slide Master** button.

2. Right-click the slide layout you want to use, and then click **Duplicate Layout**.

   The duplicate layout appears below the original one.

3. Click the **Rename** button.

4. Type a new layout name.

5. Click **Rename**.

6. Click the **Close Master View** button on the Ribbon.

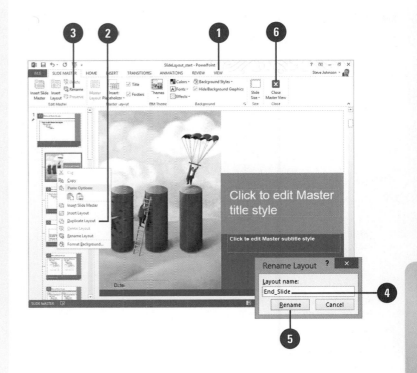

Insert a Placeholder

1. Click the **View** tab, and then click the **Slide Master** button.

2. Select the slide layout to which you want to insert a placeholder.

3. Click the **Insert Placeholder** button arrow, and then click the placeholder you want to insert.

   TIMESAVER *Click the Insert Placeholder button to insert a placeholder used to hold any kind of content.*

4. On the slide, drag to create a placeholder the size you want on the slide layout.

5. Click the **Close Master View** button on the Ribbon.

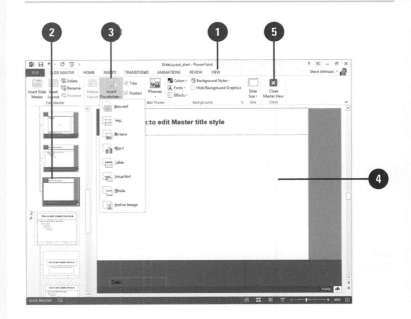

Modifying Placeholders

Each PowerPoint master comes with a different set of standard placeholders. The slide master comes with Title and Footer placeholder, while the handouts master comes with Header, Footer, Date, and Page Number placeholders. If a master doesn't contain the information you need, you can modify it by showing or hiding placeholders. After you display the placeholders you want, you can insert content—such as header or footer text—and format it like any other text box with the look you want. For example, you can format placeholder text using WordArt styles and Font and Paragraphs tools on the Home tab.

Show or Hide a Placeholder

1. Click the **View** tab, and then click the master view (**Slide Master**, **Handout Master**, or **Notes Master**) button with the master you want to change.

2. If you're in Slide Master view, select the slide master or slide layout you want to change.

3. Select or clear the check box for the placeholder you want to show or hide.

   ◆ **Slide Master.** Select or clear the Title or Footers check boxes.

   ◆ **Handout Master.** Select or clear the Header, Footer, Date, or Page Number check boxes.

   ◆ **Notes Master.** Select or clear the Header, Slide Image, Footer, Date, Body, or Page Number check boxes.

4. Click the **Close Master View** button on the Ribbon.

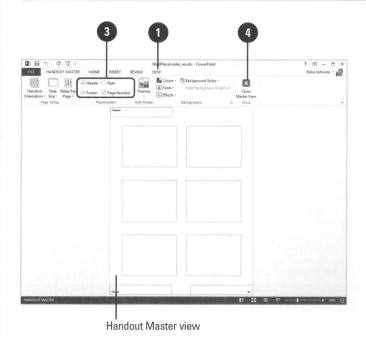

Handout Master view

See Also

See "Controlling a Slide Layout with Masters" on page 88 for information on inserting placeholders on a slide master or slide layout.

Modify and Format Placeholders

1 Click the **View** tab, and then click the master view (**Slide Master**, **Handout Master**, or **Notes Master**) button with the master you want to change.

2 If you're in Slide Master view, select the slide master or slide layout you want to change.

3 Select the placeholder you want to change.

4 To add information to a place-holder, such as a header or footer, click the text box to insert the I-beam, and then type the text you want.

5 To format the placeholder, click the **Home** and **Format** (under Drawing Tools) tabs, and then use the formatting tools on the Ribbon.

◆ Use the WordArt Styles to apply Quick Styles from the Style gallery.

◆ Use tools in the Font and Paragraph groups to modify the placeholder.

6 To delete the placeholder, press the Delete key.

7 Click the **Close Master View** button on the Ribbon.

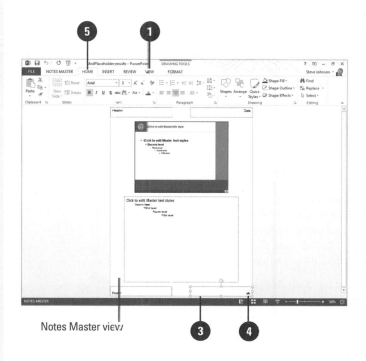

Notes Master view

Did You Know?

You can change the slide master layout. If you delete an item from the slide master, you can reshow it again. Select the slide master in Slide Master view, click the Slide Layout button, select the placeholder check boxes you want, and then click OK.

For Your Information

Using Objects on the Notes Master

Why don't the objects on the Notes master appear in the Notes pane in Normal view? The objects that you add to the Notes master will appear when you print the notes pages. They do not appear in the Notes pane of Normal view or when you save your presentation as a web page.

Controlling a Slide Background with Masters

You may want to place an object onto most slides, but not every slide. Placing the object on the slide master saves you time. Use the Insert tab to help you insert objects. Once an object is placed on the slide master, you can hide the object in any slide you want. You can even choose to hide the object on every slide or only on specific ones. If you select the slide master in Slide Master view, you can hide background graphics on all slides. If you select a slide layout, you can hide them on the selected layout.

Hide Master Background Objects on a Slide

1. Click the **View** tab, click the **Slide Master** button, and then select the slide master (for all slides) or slide layout (for specific slides) you want to hide background objects.

2. Select the **Hide Background Graphics** check box.

   ◆ To hide a background object on a single slide, display the slide in Normal view, click the **Design** tab, and then select the **Hide Background Graphics** check box.

3. Click the **Close Master View** button on the Ribbon.

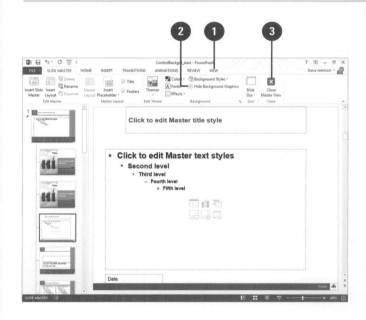

Add Background Graphics

1. Click the **View** tab, and then click the master view (**Slide Master**, **Handout Master**, or **Notes Master**) button with the master you want to change.

2. Click the **Insert** tab, click the **Insert Picture** button, locate and select the picture you want, and then click **Insert**.

3. Click the **Close Master View** button on the Ribbon.

Inserted graphic

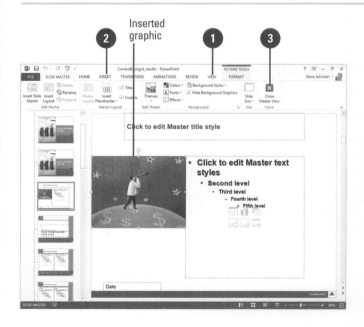

Adding a Header and Footer

Headers and footers appear on every slide. You can choose to not have them appear on the title slide. They often include information such as the presentation title, slide number, date, and name of the presenter. Use the masters to place header and footer information on your slides, handouts, or notes pages. Make sure your header and footer don't make your presentation look cluttered. The default font size is usually small enough to minimize distraction, but you can experiment by changing their font size and placement to make sure.

Add a Header and Footer

1. Click the **Insert** tab, and then click the **Header & Footer** button.

2. Click the **Slide** or **Notes and Handouts** tab.

3. Enter or select the information you want to include on your slide or your notes and handouts.

4. To not include a header and footer on the title slide, select the **Don't show on title slide** check box.

5. Click **Apply** to apply your selections to the current slide (if available), or click **Apply to All** to apply the selections to all slides.

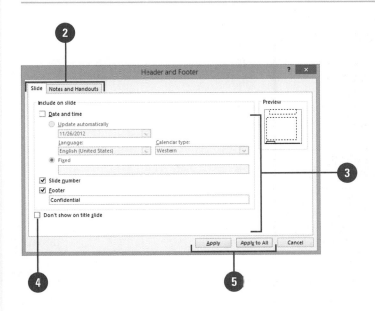

Change the Look of a Header or Footer

1. Click the **View** tab, and then click the master view (**Slide Master**, **Handout Master**, or **Notes Master**) button with the master you want to change.

2. Make the necessary changes to the header and footer like any other text box. You can move or resize them or change their text attributes using the Home tab.

3. Click the **Close Master View** button on the Ribbon.

Make changes to the footer

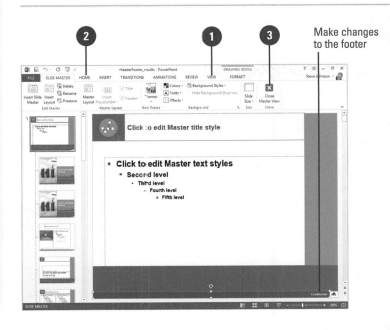

Inserting Slide Numbers

You can insert slide numbers into the text of your presentation. When you insert slide numbers, PowerPoint keeps track of your slide numbers for you. You can insert slide numbers on every slide or only on a specific slide. To insert a slide number on every page, you place it in a placeholder on the slide master. In the Slide Master view, PowerPoint inserts a code <#> for the slide number. When you view slides in other views, the slide number is shown. To insert a slide number only on a specific page, you insert it in a text box on the slide you want. You can even start numbering with a page number other than one. This is useful when your slides are a part of a larger presentation.

Insert Slide Numbering on Slides, Notes, and Handouts

1. Click the **View** tab, and then click the master view (**Slide Master, Handout Master,** or **Notes Master**) button with the master you want to change.

2. Select the master or layout in which you want to insert a slide number, if available.

3. Click to place the insertion point in the text object where you want to insert the current slide number.

4. Click the **Insert** tab.

5. Click the **Insert Slide Number** button.

   The <#> symbol appears in the text.

6. Click the **Slide Master** tab, and then click the **Close Master View** button on the Ribbon.

Did You Know?

Insert slide numbers on slides, notes, and handout using the default placeholder. Click the Insert tab, click the Slide or Notes And Handouts tab, click the Date & Time button, select the Slide Number check box, and then click Apply or Apply To All.

Insert Slide Numbering on a Specific Slide

1. Click to place the insertion point in the text object where you want to insert the current slide number.

2. Click the **Insert** tab.

3. Click the **Insert Slide Number** button.

   The current slide number is inserted into the text box.

   TROUBLE? *If you don't place the insertion point, the Header and Footer dialog opens.*

Start Numbering with a Different Number

1. Insert the slide number if you need one on the slide or slide master.

2. Click the **View** tab, and then click the master view (**Slide Master**, **Handout Master**, or **Notes Master**) button with the master you want to change.

3. Click the **Slide Size** button, and then click **Custom Slide Size**.

4. Click the **Number slides from** up or down arrow to set the number you want.

5. Click **OK**.

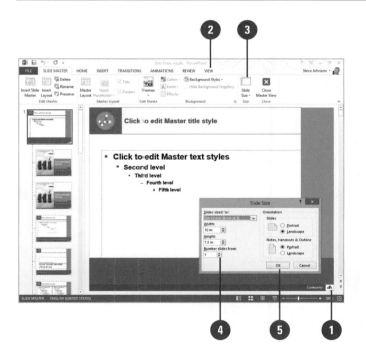

Inserting the Date and Time

You can insert the date and time into your presentation. For example, you might want today's date to appear in a stock market quote. You can insert the date and time on every slide, notes page or handout, or only on a specific slide. To insert the date and time on every page, you place it in a placeholder on the slide master. To insert the date and time only on a specific page, you insert it in a text box on the slide you want. You can set the date and time to automatically update to your system clock or stay fixed until you change it.

Insert the Date and Time on a Specific Slide

① Click to place the insertion point in the text object where you want to insert the date and time.

② Click the **Insert** tab.

③ Click the **Date & Time** button.

④ Click the date or time format you want.

⑤ To have the date and time automatically update, select the **Update Automatically** check box.

⑥ To change the default date and time format, click **Default**, and then click **Yes** to confirm.

⑦ Click **OK**.

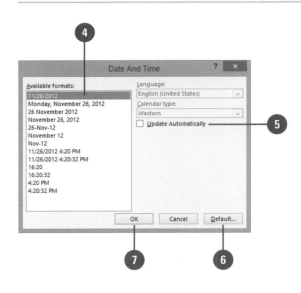

Insert the Date and Time on Slides, Notes, and Handouts

① Click the **Insert** tab.

② Click the **Date & Time** button.

③ Click the **Slide** or **Notes and Handouts** tab.

④ Click the **Date and time** check box.

⑤ Click the **Update automatically** or **Fixed** option, and then specify or select the format you want.

⑥ Click **Apply** to apply your selections to the current slide, or click **Apply to All** to apply the selections to all slides.

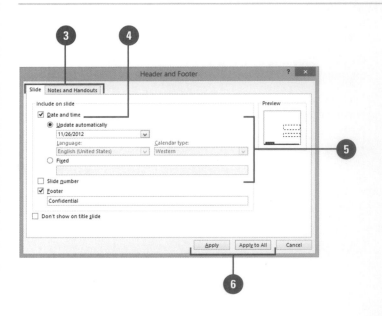

Understanding Color Themes

Every presentation has at least one color theme. A presentation with more than one set of slide masters can have more than one color theme. A color theme helps you create professional-looking presentations that use an appropriate balance of color for your presentation content. You can use a default color theme or create a custom one.

Color themes in PowerPoint are made up of a palette of twelve colors. These colors appear on color palettes when you click the Shape Fill and Outline Color or Font Color button arrow on the Home and Format tabs.

These twelve colors correspond to the following elements in a presentation:

Four Text and Background. The two background colors (light and dark combinations) are the canvas, or drawing area, color of the slide. The two text colors (light and dark combinations) are for typing text and drawing lines, and contrast with the background colors.

Six Accent. These colors are designed to work as a complementary color palette for objects, such as shadows and fills. These colors contrast with both the background and text colors.

One hyperlink. This color is designed to work as a complementary color for objects and hyperlinks.

One followed hyperlink. This color is designed to work as a complementary color for objects and visited hyperlinks.

The first four colors in the Theme Colors list represent the presentation text and background colors (light and dark for each). The remaining colors represent the six accent and two hyperlink colors for the theme. When you apply another theme or change any of these colors to create a new theme, the colors shown in the Theme Colors dialog box and color palettes change to match the current colors.

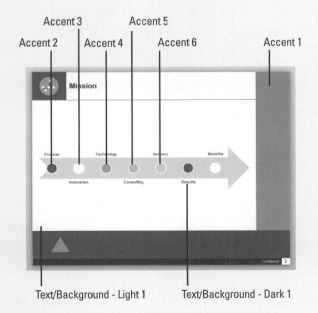

Accent 3
Accent 5
Accent 2
Accent 4
Accent 6
Accent 1

Text/Background - Light 1
Text/Background - Dark 1

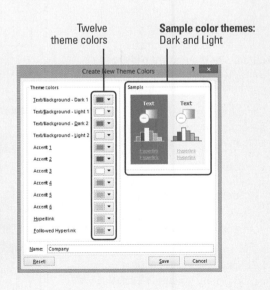

Twelve theme colors
Sample color themes: Dark and Light

Viewing and Applying a Theme

A presentation theme consists of theme colors, fonts, and effects. You can quickly format an entire presentation with a professional look by applying a theme. If a theme is not exactly what you want, you can apply a theme variation to give you more options (**New!**). To quickly see if you like a theme, point to one on the Design tab to display a ScreenTip with name and information about it, and a live preview of it in the current slide. If you like it, you can apply it. When you apply a theme, the background, text, graphics, charts, and tables all change to reflect the theme. You can apply a theme to a matching slide, selected slides or all slides in a presentation. You can choose from one or more standard themes. When you add new content, the slide elements change to match the theme ensuring all of your material will look consistent. You can even use the same theme in other Microsoft Office programs, such as Word and Excel, so all your work matches. Can't find a theme you like? Search Microsoft Office.com on the web.

View and Apply a Theme

1. Select the slide with the slide master you want to change.

2. Click the **Design** tab.

3. Click the scroll up or down arrow, or click the **More** list arrow in the Themes gallery to see additional themes.

   The current theme appears highlighted in the gallery.

4. Point to a theme.

   A live preview of the theme appears in the current slide, and a ScreenTip with the theme name and how many slides use it.

5. Click the theme you want from the gallery to apply it to the selected slide master (and all its slides).

   ◆ To apply the theme to matching slides, all slides, or selected slides, right-click the theme from the gallery, and then click the option you want.

   ◆ To set a theme as default, right-click the theme you want from the gallery, and then click **Set as Default Theme**.

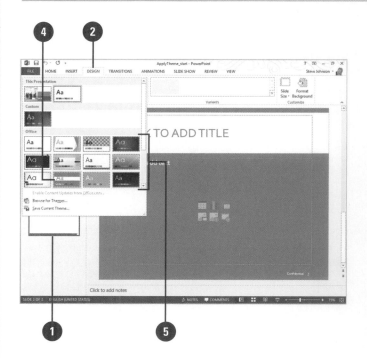

For Your Information

Getting Theme Updates from Office.com

If you want to get theme updates from Office.com, you can enable updates. Select the slide with the slide master you want to change, click the Design tab, click the More list arrow in the Themes gallery, and then click Enable Content Updates From Office.com.

Apply a Theme Variation

1. Select the slide with the slide master you want to change.

2. Click the **Design** tab.

3. Click the scroll up or down arrow, or click the **More** list arrow in the Variants gallery (**New!**) to see variations on the current theme.

4. Point to a theme variation.

   A live preview of the theme variation appears in the current slide, and a ScreenTip with the theme name and how many slides use it.

5. Click the theme variation you want from the gallery to apply it to the selected slide master (and all its slides).

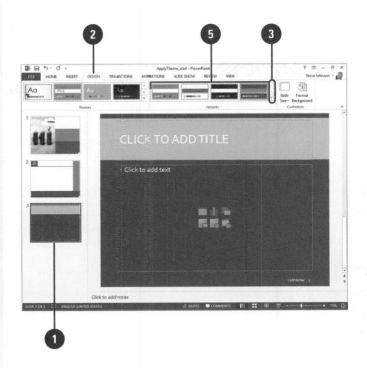

Apply the Theme of One Slide to Another

1. Click the **Normal View** or **Slide Sorter View** button.

2. Click the **Home** tab.

3. Click the slide with the color theme you want to apply.

4. Click the **Format Painter** button on the Home tab to apply the color theme to one slide, or double-click the button to apply the color theme to multiple slides.

5. Click the slides to which you want to apply the color theme.

6. If you are applying the theme to more than one slide, press Esc to cancel the Format Painter. If you are applying the theme to only one slide, the Format Painter is canceled automatically.

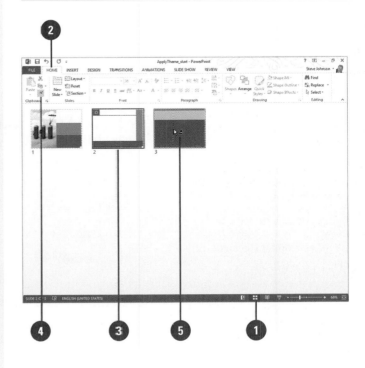

Creating a Color Theme

You may like a certain color theme except for one or two colors. You can change an existing color theme and apply your changes to the entire presentation or to just a few slides. You can add other custom colors to your theme by using RGB (Red, Green, and Blue) or HSL (Hues, Saturation, and Luminosity) color modes. The RGB color mode is probably the most widely used of all the color modes. You can accomplish this by using sliders, dragging on a color-space, or entering a numeric value that corresponds to a specific color. Once you create this new color theme, you can add it to your collection of color themes so that you can make it available to any slide in the presentation.

Change a Color in a Standard Color Theme

1. Click the **Design** tab.

2. Click the **More** list arrow in the Variants gallery, point to **Colors**, and then click **Customize Colors**.

3. Click the Theme Colors buttons (Text/Background, Accent, or Hyperlink, etc.) for the colors you want to change.

4. Click a new color, or click **More Colors** to select a color from the **Standard** or **Custom** tab, and then click **OK**.

   ◆ To select a custom color, drag across the palette until the pointer is over the color you want, or choose a Color Model, and then enter the Hue, Sat, Lum, or Red, Green, and Blue values.

5. If you don't like your color choices, click the **Reset** button to return all color changes to their original colors.

6. Type a new name for the color theme.

7. Click **Save**.

   ◆ To apply theme colors to a presentation, click the **More** list arrow in the Variants gallery, point to **Colors**, and then click a color theme.

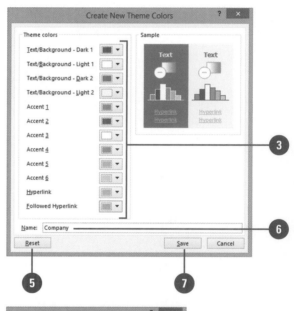

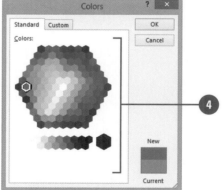

Select Custom Colors

1. Select a text box.

2. Click the **Font Color** button on the Home tab, and then click **More Colors**.

   This is one method. You can also use other color menus to access the Colors dialog box.

3. Click the **Custom** tab.

4. Click the **Color model** list arrow, and then click **RGB** or **HSL**.

5. Select a custom color using one of the following methods:

   ◆ If you know the color values, enter them, either Hue, Sat, Lum, or Red, Green, and Blue.

   ◆ Drag across the palette until the pointer is over the color you want. Drag the black arrow to adjust the amount of black and white in the color.

   The new color appears above the current color at the bottom right.

6. Click **OK**.

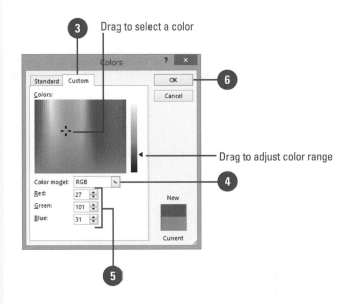

Drag to select a color

Drag to adjust color range

Did You Know?

You can edit a custom color theme.
On the Design tab, click the Theme Colors button, right-click the custom color theme you want to edit, click Edit, make changes, and then click Save.

You can delete a custom color theme.
On the Design tab, click the Theme Colors button, right-click the custom color theme you want to delete, click Delete, and then click Yes.

The Properties of Color	
Characteristic	**Description**
Hue	The color itself; every color is identified by a number, determined by the number of colors available on your monitor.
Saturation	The intensity of the color. The higher the number, the more vivid the color.
Luminosity	The brightness of the color, or how close the color is to black or white. The larger the number, the lighter the color.
Red, Green, Blue	Primary colors of the visible light spectrum. RGB generates color using three 8-bit channels: 1 red, 1 green, and 1 blue. RGB is an additive color system, which means that color is added to a black background. The additive process mixes various amounts of red, green and blue light to produce other colors.

Choosing Theme Fonts

A presentation theme consists of theme colors, fonts, and effects. Theme fonts include heading and body text fonts. Each presentation uses a set of theme fonts. When you click the Theme Fonts button on the Design tab, the name of the current heading and body text font appear highlighted in the gallery menu. You can apply a set of theme fonts to another theme or create your own set of theme fonts.

View and Apply Theme Fonts

1. Select the slide with the slide master you want to change.

2. Click the **Design** tab.

3. Click the **More** list arrow in the Variants gallery, and then point to **Fonts**.

   The current theme fonts appear highlighted in the menu.

   TIMESAVER *Point to the Fonts button to display a ScreenTip with the current theme fonts.*

4. Click the theme fonts you want from the gallery menu.

   ◆ To apply the theme fonts to matching slides or all slides, right-click the theme fonts name on the menu, and then click the option you want.

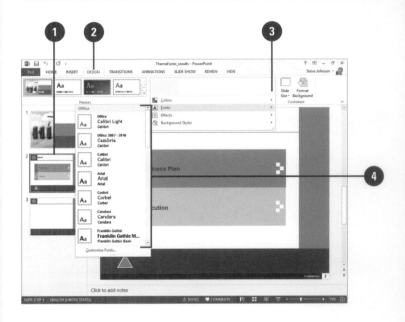

Create Theme Fonts

1. Click the **Design** tab.

2. Click the **More** list arrow in the Variants gallery, point to **Fonts**, and then click **Customize Fonts**.

3. Click the **Heading font** list arrow, and then select a font.

4. Click the **Body font** list arrow, and then select a font.

5. Type a name for the custom theme fonts.

6. Click **Save**.

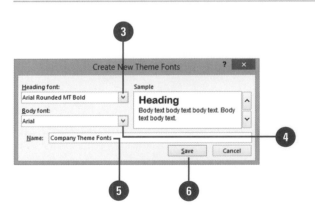

Choosing Theme Effects

A presentation theme consists of theme colors, fonts, and effects. Theme effects are sets of lines, fills, and special effects styles for shapes, graphics, charts. SmartArt, and other design elements. By combining the lines, fills, and special effects styles with different formatting levels (subtle, moderate, and intense), PowerPoint provides a variety of visual theme effects. Each presentation uses a set of theme effects. Some are more basic while others are more elaborate. When you click the Theme Effects button on the Design tab, the name of the current theme effects appears highlighted in the gallery menu. While you can apply a set of theme effects to another theme, you cannot create your own set of theme effects at this time.

View and Apply Theme Effects

1. Select the slide with the slide master you want to change.

2. Click the **Design** tab.

3. Click the **More** list arrow in the Variants gallery, and then point to **Effects**.

   The current theme effects appear highlighted in the menu.

   TIMESAVER *Point to the Effects button to display a ScreenTip with the current theme effects name.*

4. Click the theme effects you want from the menu.

   ◆ To apply the theme effects to matching slides or all slides, right-click the theme effects name on the menu, and then click the option you want.

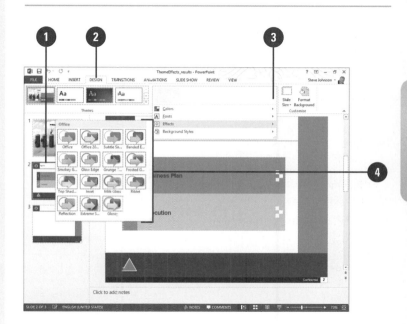

Did You Know?

You can edit or delete a custom theme fonts. On the Design tab, click the More list arrow in the Variants gallery, point to Fonts, and then right-click the theme you want to edit or delete. To edit it, click Edit, change it, and then click Save. To delete it, click Delete, and then click Yes.

Creating a Custom Theme

If you have special needs for specific colors, fonts, and effects, such as a company sales or marketing presentation, you can create your own theme by customizing theme colors, theme fonts, and theme effects, and saving them as a theme file (.thmx), which you can reuse. You can apply the saved theme to other presentations and slides. When you save a custom theme, the file is automatically saved in the Document Themes folder and added to the list of custom themes used by PowerPoint and other Office programs. When you no longer need a custom theme, you can delete it.

Create a Custom Theme

1. Click the **Design** tab, and then create a theme by customizing theme colors, theme fonts, and theme effects.

2. Click the **More** list arrow in the Themes gallery, and then click **Save Current Theme**.

   Document Themes Folder. C:\Users*user name*\AppData\ Roaming\Microsoft\Templates\ Document Themes; typical Office location, yours can differ.

3. Type a name for the theme file.

4. Click **Save**.

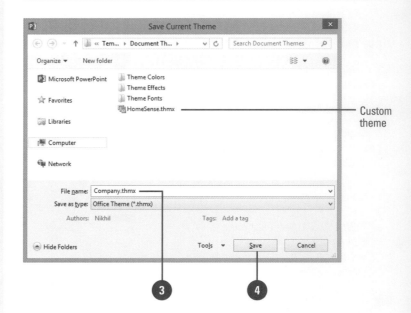

Choose a Custom Theme

1. Click the **Design** tab.

2. Click the scroll up or down arrow, or click the **More** list arrow in the Themes gallery to see additional themes.

3. Point to the custom theme you want to display a live preview and a ScreenTip with the theme name.

4. Click the custom theme you want from the gallery to apply it to the selected slide master (and all its slides).

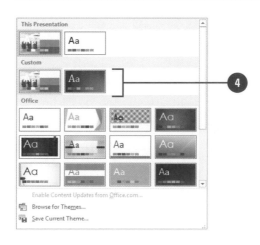

Apply a Custom Theme From a File

1. Select the slide with the slide master you want to change.

2. Click the **Design** tab.

3. Click the **More** list arrow in the Themes gallery, and then click **Browse for Themes**.

4. If you want to open a specific file type, click the **Files of type** list arrow, and then click a file type.

   - Office Themes and Themed Documents.

   - Office Themes.

   - Office Themes and PowerPoint Templates.

5. If the file is located in another folder, click the **Look in** list arrow, and then navigate to the file.

   Document Themes Folder. C:\Users*user name*\AppData\Roaming\Microsoft\Templates\Document Themes; typical Office location, yours can differ.

6. Click the theme file you want.

7. Click **Apply**.

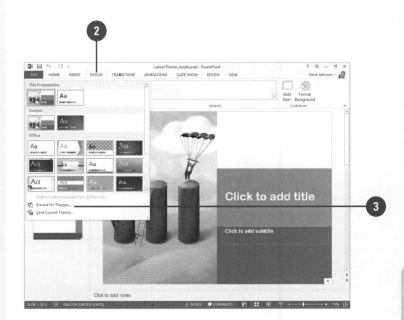

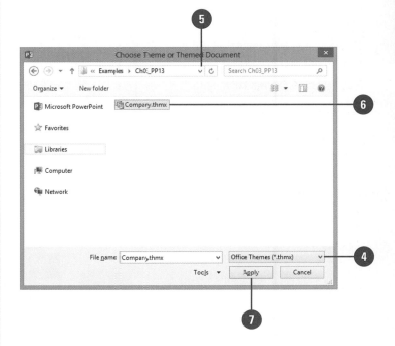

Did You Know?

You can remove a custom theme from the gallery menu. Simply move the theme file from the Document Themes folder into another folder. You can also right-click a theme in the Themes gallery, click Delete, and then click Yes.

Adding Colors to a Presentation

In addition to the twelve color theme colors, PowerPoint allows you to add more colors to your presentation. These additional colors are available on each color button palette on the Ribbon or in a dialog box, such as the Font Color button. These colors are useful when you want to change the color of an object to a specific color, but the presentation color theme does not have that color. Colors that you add to a presentation appear in all color palettes and remain in the palette even if the color theme changes. PowerPoint "remembers" up to ten colors that you've added. If you add an eleventh, it appears first on the palette, replacing the oldest.

Add a Color to the Menus

1. Click the object whose color you want to change, and then click the **Format** tab under Drawing Tools.

2. Click the **Shape Fill Color**, **Shape Outline Color**, or **Font Color** button arrow on the Home or Format tabs to change an object's color, and then click **More Fill Colors**, **More Outline Colors**, or **More Colors**.

3. Select a color from the **Standard** or **Custom** tab.

   ◆ To select a custom color, drag across the palette until the pointer is over the color you want, or choose a Color Model, and then enter the Hue, Sat, Lum, or Red, Green, and Blue values.

4. To adjust transparency, drag the **Transparency** slider or enter a value.

5. Click **OK**.

   The current selection is changed to the new color, plus the new color is added to the Recent Colors section of the menu and is now available to use throughout the presentation.

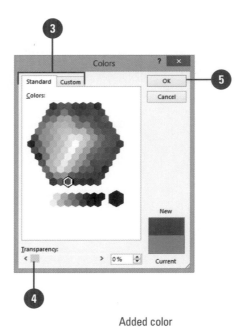

Added color

Adding a Background Style

In PowerPoint, you can add a background style to your presentation. A **background style** is a background fill made up of different combinations of theme colors. When you change a presentation theme, the background styles change to reflect the new theme colors and backgrounds. To quickly see if you like a background style, you can point to one in the Background Styles gallery to display a live preview of it with the current slide. If you like it, you can apply it.

Add a Background Style

1 Click the **Design** tab to change the background of the selected slide, or click the **View** tab, and then click the **Slide Master View** tab to change the background of the selected slide master or slide layout.

2 Click the **More** list arrow under Variants point to **Background Styles** (Design tab), or click the **Background Styles** button (Slide Master View).

3 Point to a style to display a live preview of the style.

4 Click the style you want from the gallery to apply it to the selected slide, slide master (and all its slides), or slide layout.

◆ To apply the style to matching slides, all slides, selected slides, or slide master, right-click the style from the gallery, and then click an option.

5 To set options, click the **More** list arrow under Variants point to **Background Styles** (Design tab), or click the **Background Styles** button (Slide Master View), and then click an option.

◆ **Options.** Click **Format Background**, select options in the pane (**New!**), and then click **Apply to All**.

◆ **Reset.** Click **Reset Slide Background**.

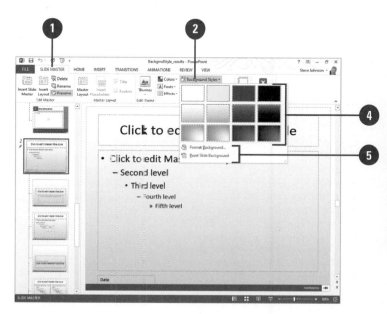

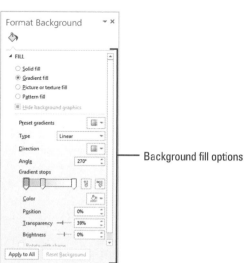

Background fill options

Modifying a Background Style

In PowerPoint, you can create a background style by adding a solid, a gradient, a texture, a pattern, or even a picture. A gradient background is a visual effect in which a solid color gradually changes from light to dark or dark to light. PowerPoint offers one-color and two-color gradient backgrounds with six styles: horizontal, vertical, diagonal up, diagonal down, from corner, and from title. For a one-color gradient background, the shading color can be adjusted lighter or darker, depending on your needs. You can also choose one of 24 professionally designed backgrounds in which the color gradient changes direction according to the shading style selected. In addition to a shaded background, you can also have a background with a texture, a pattern, or a picture. PowerPoint has several different textures, patterns, and pictures that you can apply to a presentation.

Create a Picture or Texture Background Style

1. Click the **Design** tab to change the selected slide background, or click the **View** tab, and then click the **Slide Master View** tab to change the selected slide master or slide layout background.

2. Click the **Background Styles** button, and then click **Format Background**.

3. Click the **Picture or texture fill** option to display the available fill effects.

4. Click the **Texture** button, and select a texture, or click **File**, **Clipboard**, or **Online**, and select a picture.

5. To tile the background, select the **Tile picture as texture** check box, and then specify the offset x and y, scale x and y, alignment, and mirror type you want. If you clear the check box, specify the stretch background options you want.

6. Drag the **Transparency** slider to specify a percentage.

7. Click **Apply to All** to apply the fill effect to all slides, or click the **Close** button in the pane to apply only to the selected slide or slide master.

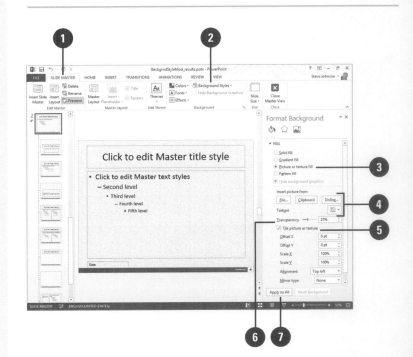

Create a Gradient Background Style

1. Click the **Design** tab to change the selected slide background, or click the **View** tab, and then click the **Slide Master View** tab to change the selected slide master or slide layout background.

2. Click the **Background Styles** button, and then click **Format Background**.

3. Click the **Gradient fill** option to display the available fill effects.

4. Click the **Preset Colors** button, and then select a color style.

5. Click the **Type** list arrow, and then click a type: Linear, Radial, Rectangle, or Path.

6. Click the **Direction** list arrow, select a direction, and then specify an angle.

7. Add or remove gradient stops, select a color, and then drag the **Stop position** slider to specify a percentage.

8. Drag the **Transparency** slider to specify a percentage.

9. Select or clear the **Rotate with shape** check boxes as desired.

10. Click **Apply to All** to apply the fill effect to all slides, or click the **Close** button in the pane to apply only to the selected slide or slide master.

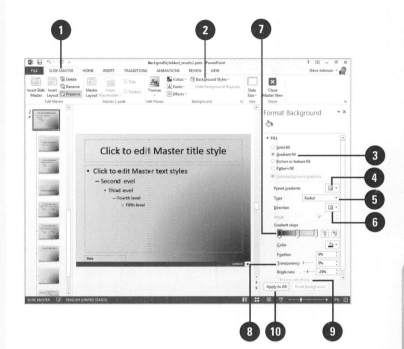

Setting Up for Personal Templates

If you want to create your own custom personal templates and access them from the Start or New screen, you should create a My Templates folder (**New!**)—such as C:\Users*user name*\My Templates—and then specify the folder as the default for your personal templates (**New!**). If you don't create a folder, Microsoft creates one named Custom Office Templates in the C:\Users*user name*\Documents folder. You can specify your default personal templates folder in the Options dialog box under Save. After you set up your personal templates folder, you can access them from the Start or New screen under Custom (**New!**).

Set Up for Personal Templates

① In Windows Explorer, navigate to the location where you want to store your personal templates, and then create a folder named My Templates.

◆ **Personal Templates Folder.** C:\Users*user name*\My Templates; typical location, yours can differ.

② Click the **File** tab, and then click **Options**.

③ In the left pane, click **Save**.

④ In the Default personal templates location box, enter the path to a personal templates folder.

My Templates Folder. C:\Users*user name*\My Templates; typical location, yours can differ.

Custom Office Templates Folder. C:\Users*user name*\Documents\ Custom Office Templates.

⑤ Click **OK**.

See Also

See "Creating a Personal Template" on page 112 for more information on creating a custom template for use in the My Templates folder.

Creating a Personal Template

You can create your own personal template as easily as you create a presentation. Like those that come with PowerPoint, custom templates can save you time. Perhaps each month you create a presentation in which you enter repetitive information; all that changes is the actual data. By creating your own template, you can have a custom form that is ready for completion each time you take inventory. A template file (.potx) saves all the customization you made to reuse in other documents. You can store your template anywhere you want; however, you may find it handy to store it in a My Templates folder (**New!**), or the default Custom Office Templates folder (**New!**). When you set up the default personal templates folder in the Options dialog box under Save, your personal templates appear under Custom in the Start or New screen.

Create a Personal Template

1. Enter all the necessary information in a presentation—including text, graphics, and formatting.

2. Click the **File** tab, and then click **Save As**.

3. Click **Computer**, and then click **Browse**.

4. Click the **Save as type** list arrow, and then select a template format.

   ◆ **PowerPoint Template**. Creates a template for PowerPoint 2007-2013.

   ◆ **PowerPoint Macro-Enabled Template**. Creates a template for PowerPoint 2007-2013 with macros.

   ◆ **PowerPoint 97-2003 Template**. Creates a template for PowerPoint 97-2003.

5. Navigate to your personal templates folder.

   My Templates. C:\Users\ *user name*\My Templates; your location might differ.

   Custom Office Templates. C:\Users*user name*\Documents\ Custom Office Templates.

6. Type a name for your template.

7. Click **Save**.

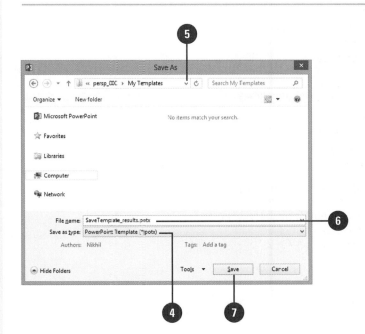

Opening a Template

You may not realize it, but every presentation you create is based on a template. When you start a new presentation without specifying a template, PowerPoint creates a new presentation based on the default template file. When you specify a particular template in the Start or New screen (**New!**), whether it's one supplied by PowerPoint or one you created yourself, PowerPoint starts a new presentation that contains the text, graphics, and formatting contained in that template. The template itself does not change when you enter data in the new presentation, because you are working on a new file, not with the template file.

Open a Template

1. Click the **File** tab, and then click **Open**.

2. Click **Computer**, and then click **Browse**.

3. Click the **Files of type** list arrow, and then click **Templates**.

4. Click the **Look in** list arrow, and then select the folder that contain the template you want to open.

   Personal Templates. C:\Users\ *user name*\My Templates; your location might differ, or C:\Users\ *user name*\Documents\Custom Office Templates (default).

   Office Templates. C:\Program Files\Microsoft Office\ Templates\1033

5. Click the file name of the template you want to open.

6. Click **Open**.

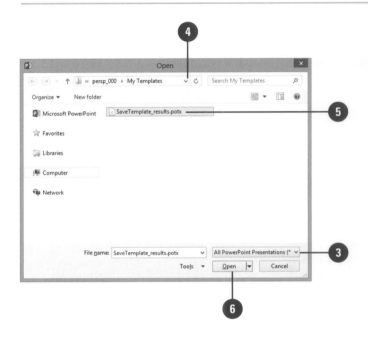

See Also

See "Setting Up for Personal Templates" on page 110 for more information on creating a My Templates folder and setting the default personal templates folder.

For Your Information

Changing a Template

Office has a selection of premade PowerPoint templates designed for you to use. These templates are available in the Start or New screen under Featured (**New!**). If you like one of these templates, you can use it as the basis of your own template. To customize one, open the template, make the changes you want, and then save it. If you save the original template back in the same location with the same name as the original, you create a new default template. The original one is replaced by the newly saved template. If you don't want to change the original, save the template in your My Templates or Custom Office Templates folder.

Drawing and Modifying Shapes

4

Introduction

When you want to add objects to your presentations, you can use Microsoft PowerPoint as a drawing package. PowerPoint offers a wide range of predesigned shapes, line options or freeform tools that allow you to draw, size, and format your own shapes and forms.

You can add three types of drawing objects to your PowerPoint presentations—shapes, lines, and freeforms. **Shapes** are preset objects, such as stars, circles, or ovals. **Lines** are simply the straight or curved lines (arcs) that can connect two points or are used as arrows. **Freeforms** are irregular curves or polygons that you can create as a free-hand drawing.

Once you create a drawing object, you can move, resize, nudge, copy or delete it on your slides. You can also change its style, by adding color, creating a fill pattern, rotating it, applying a shadow, or 3-D effect. Take a simple shape and by the time you are done adding various effects, it could become an attractive piece of graphic art for your presentation. You can also take multiple shapes and merge them together to create a new object.

Object placement on your slides is a key factor to all of your hard work. Multiple objects should be grouped if they are to be considered one larger object. Grouping helps you make changes later on, or copy your objects to another slide. PowerPoint has the ability to line up your objects with precision—rulers and guides are part of the alignment process to help you. By grouping and aligning, you are assured that your drawing objects will be accurately placed.

Drawing and Resizing Shapes

PowerPoint supplies ready-made shapes, ranging from hearts to lightning bolts to stars. The ready-made shapes are available directly on the Shapes gallery on the Insert and Format tabs. Once you have placed a shape on a slide, you can resize it using the sizing handles. Many shapes have an **adjustment handle**, a yellow square located near a resize handle that you can drag to alter the shape. When you resize or move objects, a live layout preview (**New!**) with your changes appear on the page. For precision when resizing, use the Size Dialog Box Launcher to specify the new size of the shape.

Draw a Shape

1 Click the **Home** or **Insert** tab.

2 Click the **Shapes** button.

3 Click the shape you want to draw.

4 Drag the pointer on the slide where you want to place the shape until the drawing object is the shape and size that you want.

The shape you draw uses the line and fill color defined by the presentation's theme.

TIMESAVER *To draw a proportional shape, hold down Shift as you drag the pointer.*

Did You Know?

You can quickly delete a shape. Click the shape to select it, and then press Delete.

You can draw a perfect circle or square. To draw a perfect circle or square, click the Oval or Rectangle button on the Shapes gallery, and then press and hold Shift as you drag.

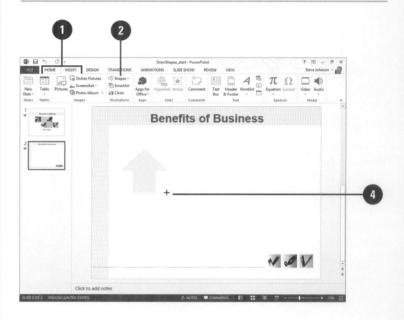

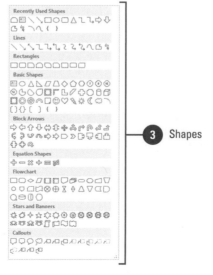

3 Shapes

Resize a Shape

1. Click the object you want to resize.

2. Drag one of the sizing handles.

   ◆ To resize the object in the vertical or horizontal direction, drag a sizing handle on the side of the selection box.

   ◆ To resize the object in both the vertical and horizontal directions, drag a sizing handle on the corner of the selection box.

   ◆ To resize the object with precise measurements, click the **Format** tab under Drawing Tools, and then specify exact height and width settings in the Size group.

   A live layout preview (**New!**) appears for the objects.

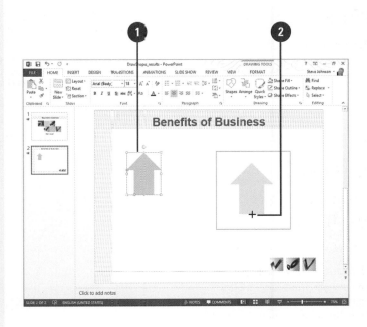

Adjust a Shape

1. Click the shape you want to adjust.

2. Click one of the adjustment handles (yellow squares), and then drag the handle to alter the form of the shape.

Did You Know?

You can replace a shape. Replace one shape with another, while retaining the size, color, and orientation of the shape. Click the shape you want to replace, click the Format tab, click the Edit Shape button, point to Change Shape, and then click the new shape you want.

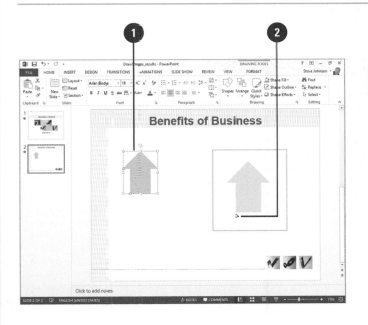

Inserting Multiple Shapes

If you need to draw the same shape several times on one or more slides in your presentation, you can use PowerPoint's Lock Drawing Mode to draw as many of the same shapes as you want without having to reselect it from the Shapes gallery. This can be a timesaver and save you extra mouse clicks. PowerPoint stays in Lock Drawing Mode until you press Esc. If a shape doesn't look the way you want, you can change the shape instead of redrawing it.

Insert Multiple Shapes

1. Click the **Home** or **Insert** tab.

2. Click the **Shapes** button.

3. Right-click the shape you want to add, and then click **Lock Drawing Mode**.

4. Drag the pointer on the slide where you want to place the shape until the drawing object is the shape and size that you want. Continue to draw shapes as you want in your presentation.

5. When you're done, press Esc.

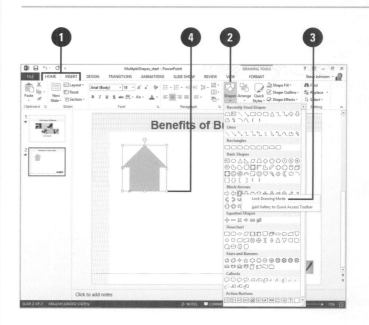

Change a Shape to Another Shape

1. Select the shape you want to modify.

2. Click the **Format tab** under Drawing Tools.

3. Click the **Edit Shape** button, and then point to **Change Shape**.

4. Click the shape you want to use from the Shapes gallery.

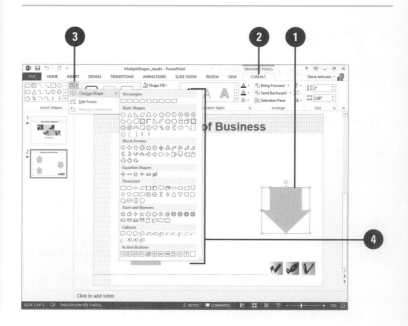

Adding Text to a Shape

You can add text to a shape in the same way you add text to a text box. Simply, select the shape object, and then start typing. After you add text to a shape, you can select and change it to bullets or numbering. The text you add becomes part of the shape. If you rotate or flip the shape, the text rotates or flips too. You can use tools, such as an alignment button or Font Style, on the Mini-toolbar and Home tab to format the text in a shape like the text in a text box.

Add Text to a Shape

1. Click the shape in which you want to add text.

2. Type the text you want.

3. To edit the text in a shape, click the text to place the insertion point, and then edit the text.

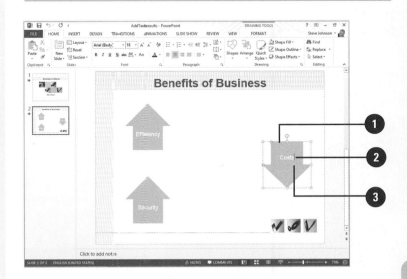

Add a Bulleted or Numbered List to a Shape

1. Click the text in the shape in which you want to add bullets or numbering to.

2. Click the **Home** tab.

3. Click the **Bullets** or **Numbering** button arrow, and then select the style you want.

   ◆ To select additional bullets and numbering options, click the **Bullets and Numbering** button arrow on the Mini-toolbar, and then click **Bullets and Numbering**.

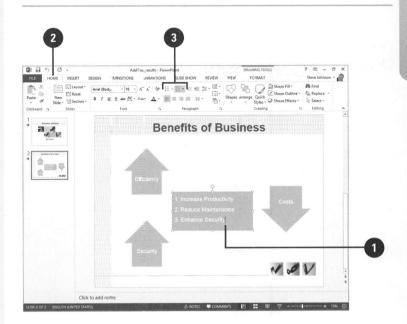

Drawing Lines and Arrows

The most basic drawing objects you can create on your slides are lines and arrows. Use the Line shape to create line segments or the Arrow shape to create arrows that emphasize key features of your presentation. You can quickly add multiple formatting to a line or arrow using Shape Quick Styles or change individual formatting—solid, dashed, or a combination—using the Shape Outline button and the Format Shape pane (**New!**). The Shape Outline button lets you change the type of line or arrow. You can add arrowheads to any lines on your slide.

Draw a Straight Line or Arrow

1. Click the **Home** or **Insert** tab.

2. Click the **Shapes** button, and then click a Line or Arrow shape in the Shapes gallery.

3. Drag the pointer to draw a line. The endpoints of the line or arrow are where you start and finish dragging.

4. Release the mouse button when the line or arrow is the correct length. Sizing handles appear at both ends of the line. Use these handles to resize your line or move an endpoint.

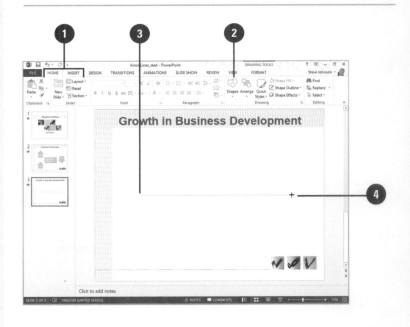

Add a Quick Style to a Line

1. Click the shape you want to apply a new or different Quick Style.

2. Click the **Home** tab.

3. Click the **Quick Styles** button.

   ◆ You can also click the Format tab under Drawing Tools, and then select a shape style.

4. Point to a style.

   A live preview of the style appears in the current shape.

5. Click the style you want from the gallery to apply it to the selected line.

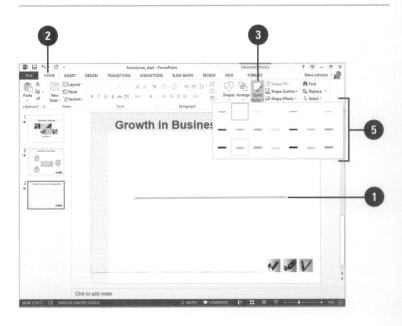

Edit a Line or Arrow

1. Click the line or arrow you want to edit.

2. Click the **Home** or **Format** tab under Drawing Tools.

3. Click the **Shape Outline** button to select a line or arrow style or thickness.

4. Click a color, or point to **Weight**, **Dashes**, or **Arrows**, and then select a style.

5. Drag a sizing handle to change the size or angle of the line or arrow.

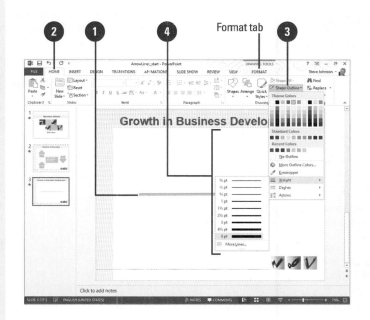

Modify a Line or Arrow

1. Click the line or arrow you want to edit.

2. Click the **Home** or **Format** tab under Drawing Tools.

3. Click the **Shape Outline** button, point to **Weight**, **Dashes**, or **Arrows**, and then click **More Lines** or **More Arrows**.

4. In the Format Shape pane (**New!**) under Line & Fill, expand **Line**.

5. For line and arrow select a color, transparency, width, compound type (double or triple lines), dash type, cap type—end of line style (square, round, or flat end), or join type—style used to connect two lines (round, bevel, or miter).

6. For an arrow, select a begin type, end type, begin size, and end size.

7. Click the **Close** button in the pane.

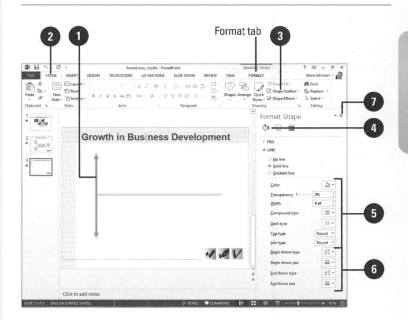

Creating and Editing Freeforms

When you need to create a customized shape, use the PowerPoint freeform tools. Choose a freeform tool from the Lines category in the list of shapes. Freeforms are like the drawings you make with a pen and paper, except that you use a mouse for your pen and a slide for your paper. A freeform shape can either be an open curve or a closed curve. You can edit a freeform by using the Edit Points command to alter the vertices that create the shape.

Draw a Freeform Polygon

1. Click the **Home** or **Insert** tab.

2. Click the **Shapes** button and then **Freeform** in the Shapes gallery under Lines.

3. Click the slide where you want to place the first vertex of the polygon.

4. Move the pointer, and then click to place the second point of the polygon. A line joins the two points.

   ◆ To draw a line with curves, drag a line instead of clicking in steps 3 and 4.

5. Continue moving the mouse pointer and clicking to create additional sides of your polygon.

6. Finish the polygon. For a closed polygon, click near the starting point. For an open polygon, double-click the last point in the polygon.

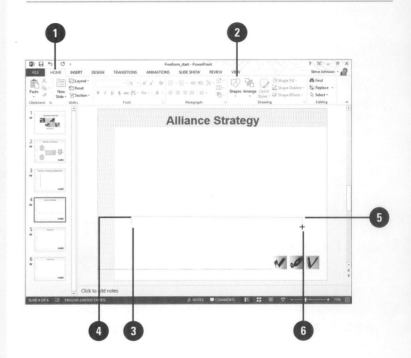

Draw a Curve

1. Click the **Home** or **Insert** tab.

2. Click the **Shapes** button and then **Curve** in the Shapes gallery.

3. Click the slide where you want to place the curve's starting point.

4. Click where you want your curve to bend. Repeat this step as often as you need to create bends.

5. Finish the curve. For a closed curve, click near the starting point. For an open curve, double-click the last point in the curve.

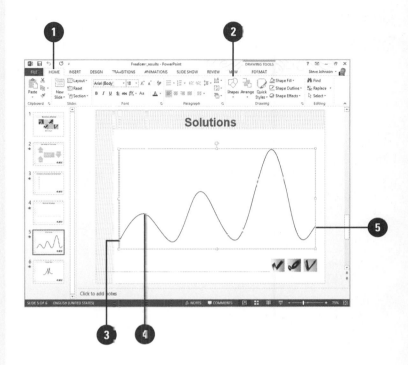

Scribble

1. Click the **Home** or **Insert** tab.

2. Click the **Shapes** button and then **Scribble** in the Shapes gallery.

3. Drag the pointer across the screen to draw freehand.

Did You Know?

You can format freeforms and curves.
Enhance freeforms and curves just as you can enhance other shapes. For example, you can add color or a pattern, change the line style, flip or rotate them, and add shadow or 3-D effects.

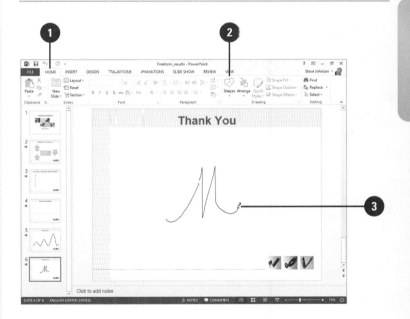

Modifying a Freeform

Each **vertex** indicated by a black dot (a corner in an irregular polygon and a bend in a curve) has two attributes: its position, and the angle at which the curve enters and leaves it. You can move the position of each vertex and control the corner or bend angles. You can also add or delete vertices as you like. When you delete a vertex, PowerPoint recalculates the freeform and smooths it among the remaining points. Similarly, if you add a new vertex, PowerPoint adds a corner or bend in your freeform.

Move a Vertex in a Freeform

1. Click the freeform object you want to edit.

2. Click the **Format** tab under Drawing Tools.

3. Click the **Edit Shape** button, and then click **Edit Points**.

4. Drag one of the freeform vertices to a new location.

5. Click outside the freeform to set the new shape.

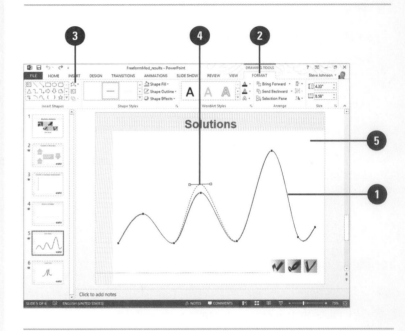

Insert a Freeform Vertex

1. Click the freeform object in which you want to insert a vertex.

2. Click the **Format** tab under Drawing Tools.

3. Click the **Edit Shape** button, and then click **Edit Points**.

4. Position the pointer on the curve or polygon border (not on a vertex), and then drag in the direction you want the new vertex, or right-click the curve, and then click **Add Point**.

5. Click outside the freeform to set the new shape.

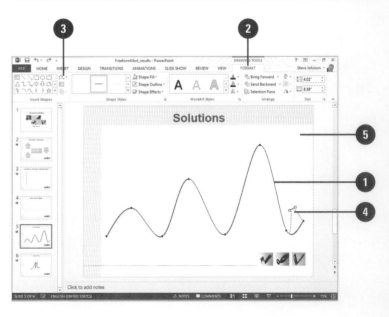

Delete a Freeform Vertex

1. Click the freeform object you want to edit.

2. Click the **Format** tab under Drawing Tools.

3. Click the **Edit Shape** button, and then click **Edit Points**.

4. Right-click the vertex and then click **Delete Point**.

5. Click outside the freeform to set the new shape.

Did You Know?

You can make it easier to work with freeforms. Select the freeform, and then increase the view magnification on the Status bar. You can also set your mouse pointer to the slowest speed, available in the Control Panel, to gain more drawing control.

Modify a Vertex Angle

1. Click the freeform object.

2. Click the **Format** tab under Drawing Tools.

3. Click the **Edit Shape** button, and then click **Edit Points**.

4. Right-click a vertex and click **Open Path, Close Path, Smooth Point, Straight Point**, or **Corner Point**. Angle handles appear.

5. Drag one or both of the angle handles to modify the shape of the line segments going into and out of the vertex.

6. Click outside the freeform to set the new shape.

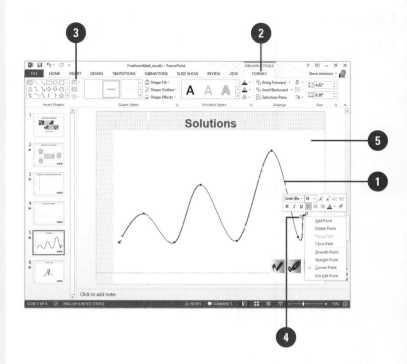

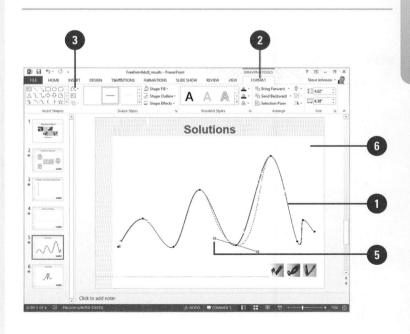

Copying and Moving Objects

After you create a drawing object, you can copy or move it. You can quickly move objects using the mouse, or if you want precise control over the object's new position, use the Format Shape pane (**New!**) under Size & Properties to specify the location of the object. You can copy a selected object or multiple objects to the Office Clipboard and then paste the objects in other parts of the presentation. When you copy multiple items, the Office Clipboard pane appears and shows all of the items stored there. You can paste these items of information into PowerPoint, either individually or all at once. You can also copy an object to another location in a single movement by using the Ctrl key.

Copy or Move an Object in One Step

1. Hold down the Ctrl key, and then drag the object to copy it, or simply drag the object to move it.

   Make sure you aren't dragging a sizing handle or adjustment handle. If you are working with a freeform and you are in Edit Points mode, drag the interior of the object, not the border, or you will end up resizing or reshaping the object, not moving it.

   A live layout preview (**New!**) appears for the objects.

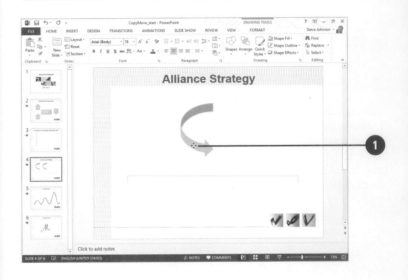

Copy or Move an Object

1. Select the object you want to copy or move.

2. Click the **Home** tab.

3. Click the **Copy** button (to copy) or click the **Cut** button (to move).

4. Display the slide on which you want to paste the object.

5. Click the **Paste** button.

   The Paste Options button appears, providing additional ways to adjust the paste results.

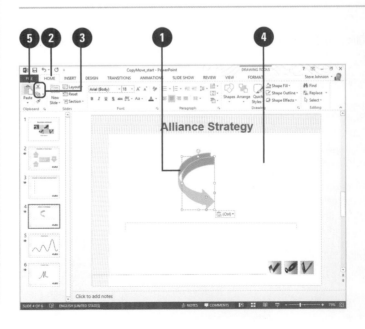

Move an Object with Precision

1. Select the object you want to move.

2. Click the **Format** tab under Drawing Tools.

3. Click the **Size Dialog Box Launcher**.

4. In the Format Shape pane (**New!**), expand **Size** or **Position**, and then change the height and width or horizontal and vertical settings.

5. Click the **Close** button in the pane.

Did You Know?

You can use the keyboard to nudge a drawing object. Click the object you want to nudge, and then press the Up, Down, Left or Right arrow key.

Copy Multiple Objects Using the Office Clipboard Pane

1. Select the multiple objects you want to copy.

2. Click the **Home** tab.

3. Click the **Copy** button.

4. Click the **Clipboard Dialog Box Launcher**.

5. Display the slide on which you want to paste the object(s).

6. In the Clipboard pane, click an item to paste it on the slide.

   ◆ **Clipboard Options.** In the Clipboard pane, click the **Options** button and then turn on or off your preferences.

7. Click the **Close** button in the pane.

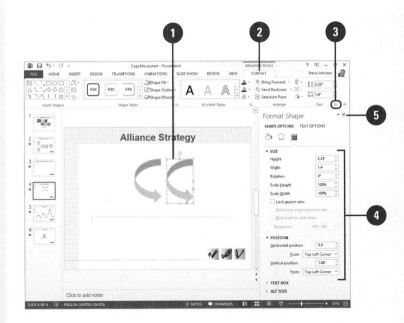

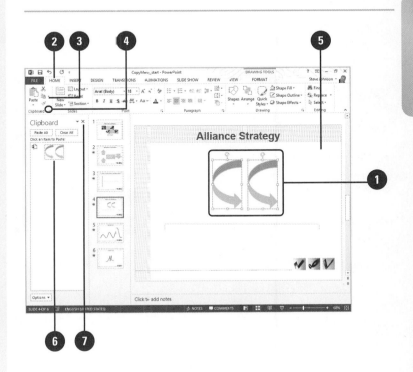

Adding a Quick Style to a Shape

Instead of changing individual attributes of a shape—such as shape fill, shape outline, and shape effects—you can quickly add them all at once with the Shape Quick Style gallery. The Shape Quick Style gallery provides a variety of different formatting combinations. To quickly see if you like a Shape Quick Style, point to a thumbnail in the gallery to display a live preview of it in the selected shape. If you like it, you can apply it.

Add a Quick Style to a Shape

1. Click the shape you want to apply a new or different Quick Style.

2. Click the **Format** tab under Drawing Tools.

3. Click the scroll up or down arrow, or click the **More** list arrow in the Shapes Styles group to see additional styles.

   The current style appears highlighted in the gallery.

4. Point to a style.

   A live preview of the style appears in the current shape.

5. Click the style you want from the gallery to apply it to the selected shape.

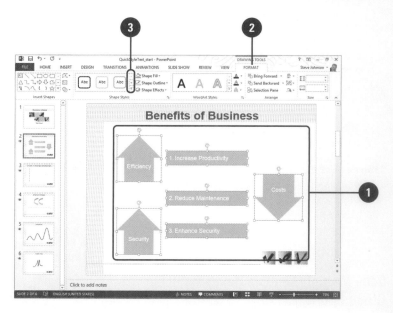

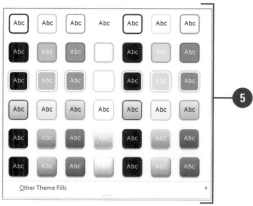

Did You Know?

You can add a Quick Style to a text box. A shape is a text box without a fill and outline (border), so you can apply a Quick Style to a text box using the same steps.

You can use a Mini-Toolbar to apply styles, fills, and outlines. Right-click the object you want to modify, click the Style, Fill, or Outline button (**New!**), and then select an option.

Adding a Quick Style to Shape Text

Instead of changing individual attributes of text in a shape, such as text fill, text outline, and text effects, you can quickly add them all at once with the WordArt Quick Style gallery. The WordArt Quick Style gallery provides a variety of different formatting combinations. To quickly see if you like a WordArt Quick Style, point to a thumbnail in the gallery to display a live preview of t in the selected shape. If you like it, you can apply it.

Add a Quick Style to Shape Text

1. Click the shapes with the text you want to apply a new or different Quick Style.

2. Click the **Format** tab under Drawing Tools.

3. Click the scroll up or down arrow, or click the **More** list arrow in the WordArt Styles group to see additional styles.

   The current style appears highlighted in the gallery.

4. Point to a style.

   A live preview of the style appears in the current shape text.

5. Click the style you want from the gallery to apply it to the selected shape.

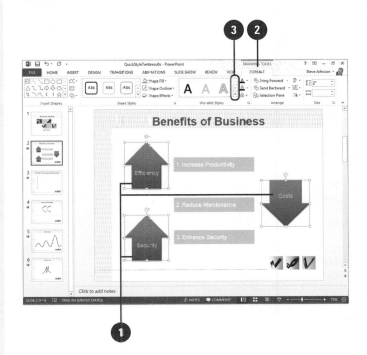

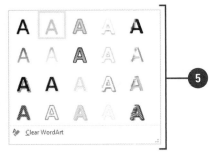

Did You Know?

You can arrange shapes in a SmartArt graphic. Select the shape in the SmartArt graphic, click the Format tab under SmartArt Tools, click the Arrange button, and then use any of the arrange button options: Bring To Front, Send To Back, Align, Group, or Rotate.

You can edit a SmartArt graphic shape in 2-D. Select the SmartArt graphic with the 3-D style, click the Format tab under SmartArt Tools, and then click the Edit In 2-D button.

Applying Color Fills

When you create a closed drawing object such as a square, it applies the Shape Fill color to the inside of the shape, and the Shape Outline color to the edge, or border, of the shape. A line drawing object uses the Shape Outline color. You can set the Shape Fill to be a solid, gradient, texture or picture, and the Shape Outline can be a solid or gradient along with a thickness (weight) and style (dashes). If you want to use a color from another element on the screen, you can use the eyedropper (**New!**) to select it. If you want to make multiple changes to a shape at the same time, the Format Shape pane (**New!**) allows you to do everything in one place. If the solid color appears too dark, you can make the color fill more transparent. If you no longer want to apply a shape fill to an object, you can remove it.

Apply a Color Fill to a Shape

1. Click the drawing object whose fill color you want to change.

2. Click the **Format** tab under Drawing Tools.

3. Click the **Shape Fill** button.

4. Select the fill color option you want.

   ◆ **Select a Color from the Screen.** Click **Eyedropper** (**New!**), point to a color on the screen, and then click to apply it to the selection. To cancel the eyedropper, press Esc.

5. To remove a color fill, click the **Shape Fill** button, and then click **No Fill**.

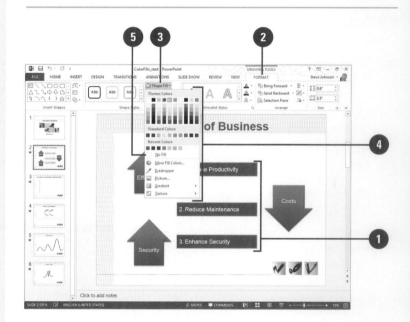

Did You Know?

You can use the presentation background as the fill for a shape. Right-click the object, click Format Shape. In the Format Shape pane (**New!**), expand Fill, click the Fill icon, click the Background option, and then click the Close button in the pane.

Apply a Shape Color Fill with a Transparency

1. Right-click the drawing object you want to modify, and then click **Format Shape**.

2. Click the **Fill & Line** button (**New!**), and then expand **Fill**.

3. Click the **Solid fill** option.

4. Click the **Color** button, and then select the fill color you want.

5. Drag the **Transparency** slider or enter a number from 0 (fully opaque) to 100 (fully transparent).

   All your changes are instantly applied to the shape.

6. Click the **Close** button in the pane.

   TROUBLE? *To cancel changes in the Format Shape pane, click the Undo button on the Quick Access Toolbar.*

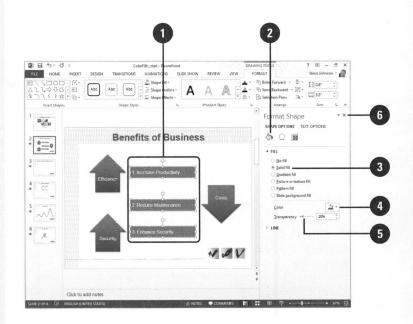

Apply a Color Outline to a Shape

1. Click the drawing object whose fill color you want to change.

2. Click the **Format** tab under Drawing Tools.

3. Click the **Shape Outline** button.

4. Select the outline color you want.

   ◆ To change the outline thickness or style, point to **Weight**, or **Dashes**, and then select a style, or click **More Lines** to select multiple options.

5. To remove an outline color, click the **Shape Outline** button, and then click **No Outline**.

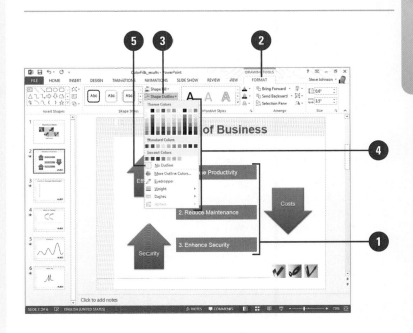

Applying Picture Fills

Applying a shape fill to a drawing object can add emphasis or create a point of interest in your presentation. You can insert a picture or clip art into a shape. You can insert a picture from a file, clip art on Office .com (**New!**), Bing Image Search (**New!**), online service (**New!**), such as Flickr, SkyDrive (**New!**), or Office 365 SharePoint (**New!**). Stretch a picture to fit across the selected shape or repeatedly tile it horizontally and vertically to fill the shape. When you stretch an image, you can also set offsets, which determine how much to scale an image to fit a shape relative to the edges. A positive offset number moves the image edge toward the center of the shape, while a negative offset number moves the image edge away from the shape. If the image appears too dark, you can make the picture more transparent.

Apply a Picture Fill to a Shape

1. Select the drawing object you want to modify.

2. Click the **Format** tab under Drawing Tools.

3. Click the **Shape Fill** button, and then click **Picture**.

   TIMESAVER *To apply a picture fill, right-click the shape, click Fill button, and then click Picture.*

4. Browse and select a picture file using any of the following:

   ◆ **From a file.** Click **Browse**, select a file on your computer or network.

   ◆ **Office.com Clip Art.** Search, and then select an online clip art image (**New!**).

   ◆ **Bing Image Search.** Search and then select an online image (**New!**).

   ◆ **SkyDrive or SharePoint.** Click **Browse**, and then select a file on your SkyDrive (**New!**) or SharePoint site (**New!**).

   ◆ **Online service.** Select a file from a service, such as Flickr (**New!**).

5. Click **Insert**.

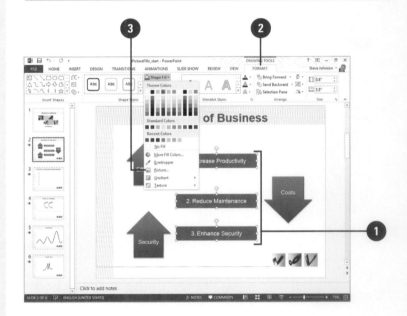

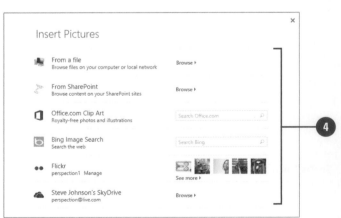

Apply a Custom Picture Fill

1. Right-click the drawing object you want to modify, and then click **Format Shape**.

2. Click the **Fill & Line** button (**New!**), and then expand **Fill**.

3. Click the **Picture or texture fill** option.

4. Click one of the following buttons:

   ◆ **File** to insert a picture from a file.

   ◆ **Clipboard** to paste a picture from the Office Clipboard or another program. Copy the picture to the clipboard before you click this button.

   ◆ **Online** (**New!**) to open the Insert Pictures dialog box, where you can find the online clip art and images you want, and then click to insert it.

5. Clear the **Tile picture as texture** check box.

6. Specify the **Offset X** & **Y**, **Scale X** & **Y**, and **Alignment** settings for the picture.

   Positive numbers move the picture edge toward the center and negative numbers move the edge away from the shape.

7. Drag the **Transparency** slider or enter a number from 0 (fully opaque) to 100 (fully transparent).

8. Select the **Rotate with shape** check box to rotate the picture with the shape's rotation.

9. Click the **Close** button in the pane.

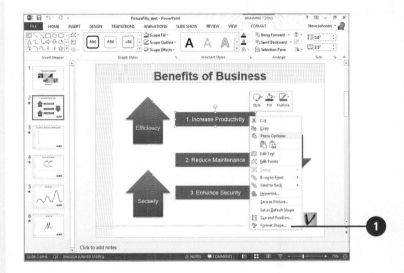

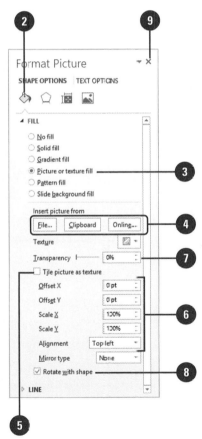

Applying Texture Fills

You can quickly apply a texture fill to a shape by using the Texture gallery or using the Format Shape pane to select custom options. Stretch a texture to fit across the selected shape or repeatedly tile the texture horizontally and vertically to fill the shape. If you tile a texture, you can also set offset, scale, alignment, and mirror options to determine the appearance of the texture in the selected shape. The offset x and y options determine how much to scale a texture to fit a shape relative to the edges, while scale x and y options determine horizontal and vertical scaling. If you want to play with the tile look, you can change the mirror type to determine whether the alternating tiles display a mirror or flip image with every other tile. If the texture doesn't provide enough contrast in the shape, you can make the texture more transparent.

Apply a Texture Fill to a Shape

1. Click the drawing object whose fill you want to change.

2. Click the **Format** tab under Drawing Tools.

3. Click the **Shape Fill** button.

4. Point to **Texture**, and then select a texture from the gallery.

Did You Know?

You can undo changes made in the Format Shape pane. Since changes made in the Format Shape pane are instantly applied to the shape, it is not possible to Cancel it. To remove changes, you can click the Undo button on the Quick Access Toolbar.

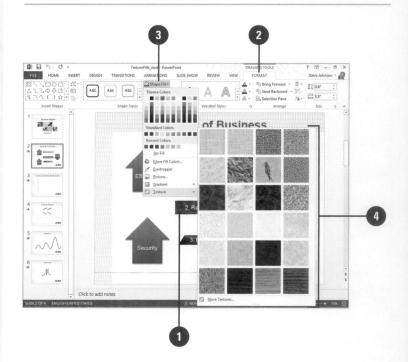

Apply a Custom Texture Fill

① Right-click the drawing object you want to modify, and then click **Format Shape** or **Format Picture**.

② Click the **Fill & Line** button (**New!**), and then expand **Fill**.

③ Click the **Picture or texture fill** option.

④ Click the **Texture** button arrow, and then select a texture.

⑤ Select the **Tile picture as texture** check box.

⑥ Specify the following tiling options:

 ◆ **Offset x and y.** For offset x, enter a negative number to shift left and a positive number to shift right. For offset y, enter a negative number to shift up and a positive number to shift down.

 ◆ **Scale x and y.** For scale x, enter a percentage for horizontal scaling. For scale y, enter a percentage for vertical scaling.

 ◆ **Alignment.** Select an anchor position where the picture begins to tile.

 ◆ **Mirror type.** Specify an option to alternate the horizontal or vertical tile to display a mirror or flip image with every other tile.

⑦ Drag the **Transparency** slider or enter a number from 0 (fully opaque) to 100 (fully transparent).

⑧ Select the **Rotate with shape** check box to rotate the texture with the shape's rotation.

 All your changes are instantly applied to the shape.

⑨ Click the **Close** button in the pane.

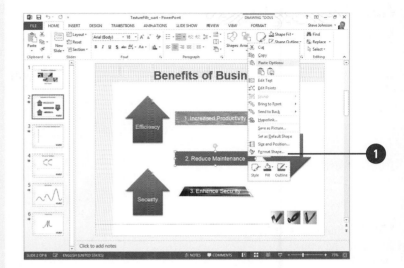

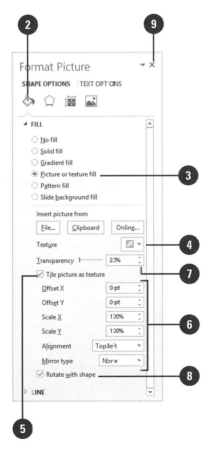

Applying Gradient Fills

Gradients are made up of two or more colors that gradually fade into each other. They can be used to give depth to a shape or create realistic shadows. Apply a gradient fill to a shape—now including lines—by using a gallery or presets for quick results, or by using the Format Shape pane (**New!**) for custom results. A gradient is made up of several gradient stops, which are used to create non-linear gradients. If you want to create a gradient that starts blue and goes to green, add two gradient stops, one for each color. Gradient stops consist of a position, a color, brightness, and a transparency percentage.

Apply a Gradient Fill to a Shape

1. Select the drawing object you want to modify.

2. Click the **Format** tab under Drawing Tools.

3. Click the **Shape Fill** button.

4. Point to **Gradient**, and then select a gradient from the gallery.

   Four gradient modes are available: linear (parallel bands), radial (radiate from center), rectangle (radiate from corners), and path (radiate along path).

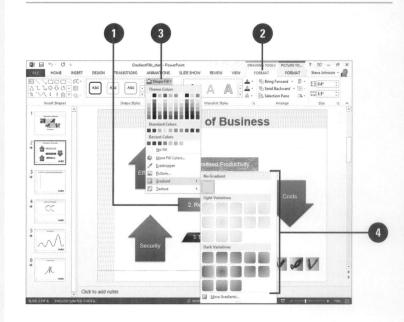

Apply a Gradient Fill Preset

1. Right-click the drawing object you want to modify, and then click **Format Shape**.

2. Click the **Fill & Lines** button under Shape Options (**New!**), and then expand **Fill**.

3. Click the **Gradient fill** option.

4. Click the **Preset colors** button arrow, and then select the built-in gradient fill you want.

   All your changes are instantly applied to the shape.

5. Click the **Close** button in the pane.

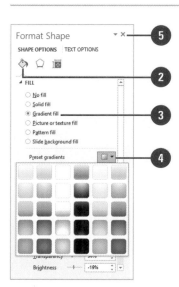

Apply a Custom Gradient Fill

1. Right-click the drawing object you want to modify, and then click **Format Shape**.

2. Click the **Fill & Lines** button under Shape Options (**New!**), and then expand **Fill**.

3. Click the **Gradient fill** option.

4. Click the **Preset colors** button arrow, and then select the built-in gradient fill you want.

5. Click the **Type** list arrow, and then select a gradient direction.

6. Click the **Direction** list arrow, and then select a shading progression; options vary depending on the gradient type.

7. If you selected the Linear type, specify the angle (in degrees) the gradient is rotated in the shape.

8. Specify the following tiling options:

   ◆ **Add.** Click the **Add** button, and then set the gradient stop options you want.

   ◆ **Remove.** Select a gradient stop, and then click the **Remove** button.

   ◆ **Position.** Specify a location for the color and transparency change in the gradient fill.

   ◆ **Color.** Click the **Color** button, and then select a color for the gradient stop.

   ◆ **Brightness.** Drag the slider to adjust the brightness color contrast.

   ◆ **Transparency.** Drag the slider or enter a number from 0 (fully opaque) to 100 (full transparent) for the selected stop position.

9. Select the **Rotate with shape** check box to rotate the gradient with the shape's rotation.

10. Click **Close** button in the pane.

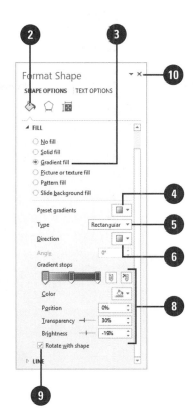

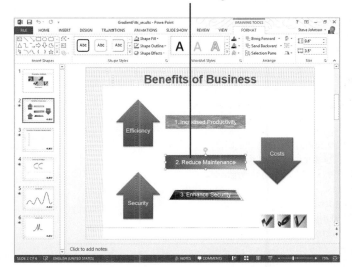

Custom gradient fill

Applying Shape Effects

You can change the look of a shape by applying effects, like shadows, reflections, glow, soft edges, bevels, and 3-D rotations. Apply effects to a shape by using the Shape Effects gallery for quick results, or by using the Format Shape pane for custom results. From the Shape Effects gallery you can apply a built-in combination of 3-D effects or individual effects to a shape. To quickly see if you like a shape effect, point to a thumbnail in the Shape Effects gallery to display a live preview of it in the selected shape. If you like it, you can apply it. If you no longer want to apply a shape effect to an object, you can remove it. Simply select the shape, point to the effect type in the Shape Effects gallery, and then select the No effect type option.

Add a Preset Effect to a Shape

1. Click the shape you want to apply a new or different shape effect.

2. Click the **Format** tab under Drawing Tools.

3. Click the **Shape Effects** button, and then point to **Preset**.

    The current effect appears highlighted in the gallery.

4. Point to an effect.

    A live preview of the style appears in the current shape.

5. Click the effect you want from the gallery to apply it to the selected shape.

6. To remove the preset effect, click the **Shape Effects** button, point to **Preset**, and then click **No Presets**.

7. To set more options, click an option command on the Shape Effects submenu or right-click the shape, and then click **Format Shape**. Expand an effect category (**Shadow**, **Reflection**, **Glow and Soft Edges**, **3-D Format**, or **3-D Rotation**), select the options you want, and then click the **Close** button in the pane.

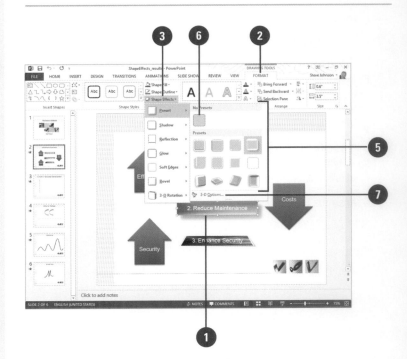

Add Individual Effects to a Shape

1. Click the shape you want to apply a new or different shape effect.

2. Click the **Format** tab under Drawing Tools.

3. Click the **Shape Effects** button, and then point to one of the following:

   ◆ **Shadow** to select No Shadow, one of the shadow types, or Shadows Options.

   ◆ **Reflection** to select No Reflection, one of the Reflection Variations, or Reflection Options.

   ◆ **Glow** to select No Glow, one of the Glow Variations, or Glow Options.

   ◆ **Soft Edges** to select No Soft Edges, or a point size to determine the soft edge amount, or Soft Edges Options.

   ◆ **Bevel** to select No Bevel, one of the bevel variations, or 3-D Options.

   ◆ **3-D Rotation** to select No Rotation, one of the rotation types (Parallel, Perspective, or Oblique), or 3-D Rotation Options.

   When you point to an effect, a live preview of the style appears in the current shape.

4. Click the effect you want to apply to the selected shape.

Did You Know?

3-D effects take precedence. If you add a 3-D effect, such as a bevel or 3-D rotation, to a shape and then add soft edges, the soft edge effect doesn't appear in the shape until you delete the 3-D effect.

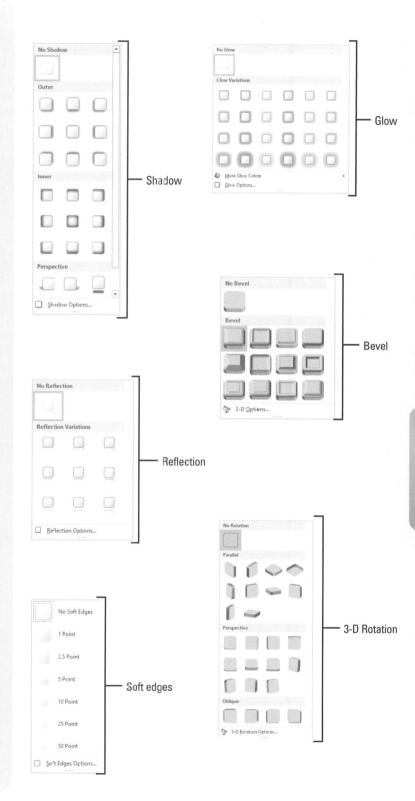

Shadow

Glow

Bevel

Reflection

Soft edges

3-D Rotation

Creating Shadows

You can give objects on your slides the illusion of depth by adding shadows. PowerPoint provides several preset shadowing options, or you can create your own by specifying color, transparency, size, blur, angle, and distance. You can change all these shadow options at the same time in the Format Shape pane. Instead of starting from scratch, you can select a preset shadow in the Format Shape pane, and then customize it.

Add a Preset Shadow to a Shape

1. Click the shape you want to apply a new or different shape effect.

2. Click the **Format** tab under Drawing Tools.

3. Click the **Shape Effects** button, and then point to **Shadow**.

   The current effect appears highlighted in the gallery.

4. Point to an effect.

   A live preview of the style appears in the current shape.

5. Click the effect you want from the gallery to apply it to the selected shape.

6. To remove the shadow, click the **Shape Effects** button, point to **Shadow**, and then click **No Shadow**.

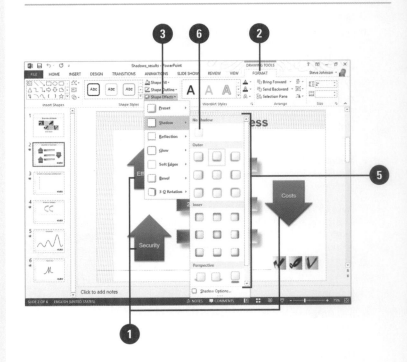

Add a Custom Shadow to a Shape

1. Click the shape you want to apply a new or different shape effect.

2. Click the **Format** tab under Drawing Tools.

3. Click the **Shape Effects** button, point to **Shadow**, and then click **Shadows Options**.

4. To customize a preset shadow, click the **Presets** button arrow, and then select a starting shadow.

5. Specify the following custom options:

   ◆ **Color.** Select the color of the shadow.

   ◆ **Transparency.** Drag the slider or enter a number from 0 (fully opaque) to 100 (fully transparent).

   ◆ **Size.** Drag the slider or enter a number from 1 to 200 to set the shadow size relative to the original shape.

   ◆ **Blur.** Drag the slider or enter a number from 0 (no blur) to 25 (full blur) points to set the radius of the blur.

   ◆ **Angle.** Drag the slider or enter a number from 0 to 359 degrees to set the angle the shadow is drawn.

   ◆ **Distance.** Drag the slider or enter a number from 0 (no blur) to 25 (full blur) points to set the distance the shadow is drawn.

   All your changes are instantly applied to the shape.

6. Click the **Close** button in the pane.

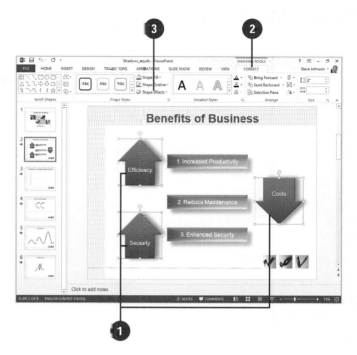

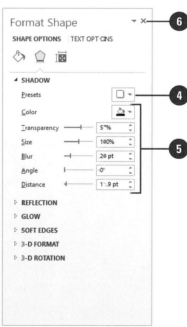

Adding 3-D Effects to a Shape

You can add the illusion of depth to your slides by adding a 3-D effect to a shape. Create a 3-D effect by using one of the preset 3-D styles, or use the 3-D format tools to customize your own 3-D style. The settings you can control with the customization tools include the bevel (a 3-D top or bottom edge effect), the shape depth (distance of shape from its surface), the contour (raised border), the surface material and lighting. You can apply interesting surfaces—matte, plastic, metal, wire frame, soft or dark edges, flat, translucent, and clear—to a 3-D shape. In addition, you can change the type of lighting—neutral, warm, cool, flat, glow, and bright room—applied to a 3-D shape. Each lighting type defines one or more lights that illuminate a 3-D scene, not just for the shape. Each light contains a position, intensity, and color.

Add a 3-D Effect to a Shape

1. Click the shape you want to apply a new or different shape effect.

2. Click the **Format** tab under Drawing Tools.

3. Click the **Shape Effects** button, and then point to **Preset** or **Bevel**.

    The current effect appears highlighted in the gallery.

4. Point to an effect.

    A live preview of the style appears in the current shape.

5. Click the effect you want from the gallery to apply it to the selected shape.

6. To remove the 3-D effect, click the **Shape Effects** button, point to **Preset** or **Bevel**, and then click **No Preset** or **No Bevel**.

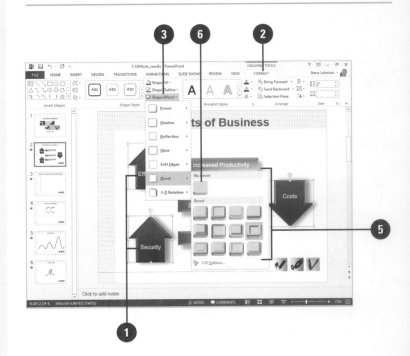

Add a Custom 3-D Effect to a Shape

1. Click the shape you want to apply a new or different shape effect.

2. Click the **Format** tab under Drawing Tools.

3. Click the **Shape Effects** button, point to **Preset** or **Bevel**, and then click **3-D Options**.

4. Click the **Effects** button under Shape Options (**New!**), and then expand **3-D Format**.

5. Specify the following custom options:

   ◆ **Bevel.** Click **Top** or **Bottom** to apply a raised edge to the top or bottom of a shape. The corresponding width and height numbers appear.

   ◆ **Depth.** Click the **Color** button to select a depth color, and then enter a depth number.

   ◆ **Contour.** Click the **Color** button to select a contour color, and then enter a size.

   ◆ **Surface.** Click **Material** to select a surface, and then click **Lighting** to specify the way light illuminates the 3-D shape.

   To rotate all of the lights around the front face of a shape, enter an angle.

   All your changes are instantly applied to the shape.

6. To remove 3-D formatting and restore default setting, click **Reset**.

7. Click **Close** button in the pane.

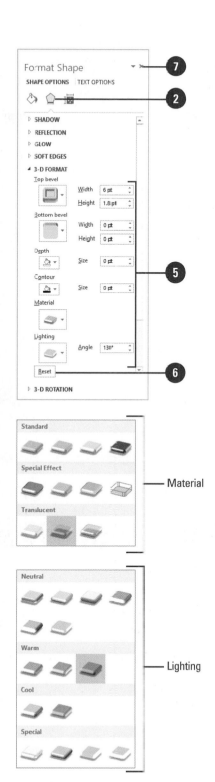

Material

Lighting

Adding 3-D Rotation Effects to a Shape

After you create a 3-D or even a 2-D shape, you can use 3-D rotation options to change the orientation and perspective of the shape. You can also create a 3-D rotation effect using one of the preset 3-D rotation styles, or you can use the 3-D rotation tools to create your own 3-D effect. The settings control with the customization tools include the 3-D rotation (x, y, and z axis), text rotation, and object position (distance from ground).

Add a 3-D Rotation Effect to a Shape

1. Click the shape you want to apply a new or different shape effect.

2. Click the **Format** tab under Drawing Tools.

3. Click the **Shape Effects** button, and then point to **3-D Rotation**.

    The current effect appears highlighted in the gallery.

4. Point to an effect.

    A live preview of the style appears in the current shape.

5. Click the effect you want from the gallery to apply it to the selected shape.

6. To remove the 3-D rotation effect, click the **Shape Effects** button, point to **3-D Rotation**, and then click **No Rotation**.

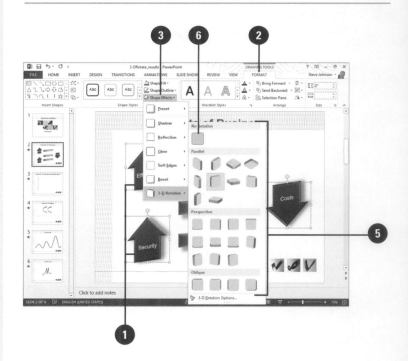

Add a Custom 3-D Rotation Effect to a Shape

1. Click the shape you want to apply a new or different shape effect.

2. Click the **Format** tab under Drawing Tools.

3. Click the **Shape Effects** button, point to **3-D Rotation**, and then click **3-D Rotation Options**.

4. Specify the following custom options:

   - **Rotation x and y.** Change the orientation of the x (horizontal axis) and y (vertical axis). Use the arrow buttons to nudge the position left, right, up, and down.

   - **Rotation z.** Change the position higher or lower than the shape. Use the arrow buttons to nudge the position clockwise or counter-clockwise.

   - **Perspective.** Change the field of view. Enter a number from 0 (parallel camera) to 120 (wide-angle camera). Use the arrow buttons to narrow or widen the view.

   - **Text.** Select the **Keep Text Flat** check box to prevent text in a shape from rotating (always stays on top).

   - **Distance from ground.** Enter a distance from ground number to move the shape backward or forward in 3-D space.

   All your changes are instantly applied to the shape.

5. To remove 3-D formatting and restore default setting, click **Reset**.

6. Click the **Close** button in the pane.

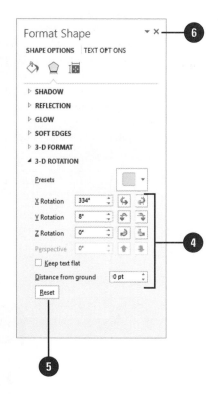

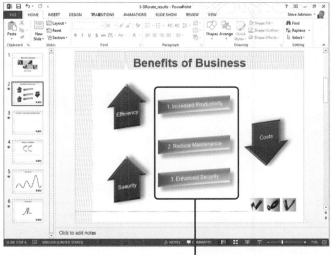

Custom 3-D rotation effect

Aligning Objects to Gridlines and Guides

PowerPoint guides can align an individual object or a group of objects to a vertical or horizontal guide. For quick alignment, Smart Guides (**New!**) automatically appear as you draw or move objects. Turning on the visible grid or visible guides option makes it easier to create, modify, and align a shape. Within the Grid and Guides dialog box, you can select from a variety of options, such as snapping objects to the grid and displaying drawing and smart guides on-screen. To align several objects to a guide, you first turn the guides on. Then you adjust the guides and drag the objects to align them to the guide.

Show, Hide, and Set Options for Gridlines or Guides

1. Click the **View** tab.

2. To show or hide gridlines and guides, do any of the following:

   - **Gridlines.** Select or clear the check box for gridlines.

   - **Guides.** Select or clear the check box for guide lines.

3. To set Grid and Guides options, click the **Show Dialog Box Launcher**.

   TIMESAVER *To open the Grid and Guides dialog box, right-click a blank area of the slide, and then click Grid and Guides.*

4. To set options for gridlines and guides, do any of the following:

   - **Snap objects to grid.** Select or clear the check box to snap objects to a gridline.

   - **Display grid on screen.** Select or clear the check box to show or hide gridlines.

   - **Display drawing guides on screen.** Select or clear the check box to show or hide guides as you draw.

   - **Display smart guides when shapes are aligned.** Select or clear the check box to smart guides as you align shapes.

5. Click **OK**.

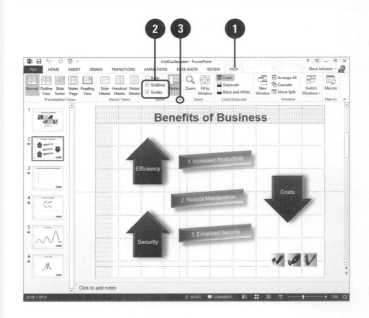

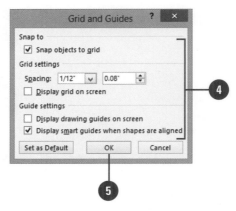

Add, Move, or Remove a Guide

◆ To move a guide, drag it.

◆ To add a new guide, press and hold the Ctrl key, and then drag the line to the new location. You can place a guide anywhere on the slide.

◆ To remove a guide, drag the guide off the slide. You cannot remove the original guides, they must be turned off.

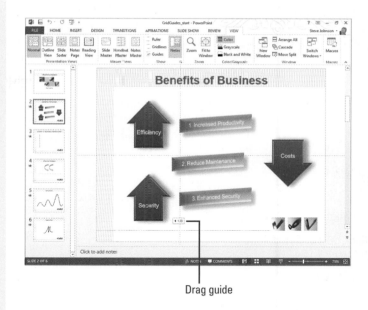

Drag guide

Align an Object to a Guide

① If you want, display guides on the screen (horizontal and vertical) or enable Smart Guides.

② Drag the object's center or edge near the guide. PowerPoint aligns the center or edge to the guide.

Did You Know?

You can align objects using Smart Guides. When Smart Guides are enabled, alignment and spacing guides automatically appear (**New!**) as you draw or move objects on the slide. To turn on or off, right-click a blank area of the slide, point to Grid and Guides, and then click Smart Guides.

You can use the keyboard to override grid settings. To temporarily override settings for the grids and guides, press and hold the Alt key as you drag an object.

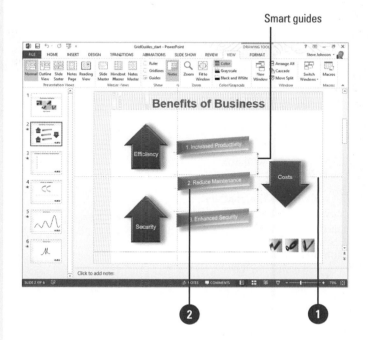

Smart guides

Aligning and Distributing Objects

In addition to using grids and guides to align objects to a specific point, you can align a group of objects to each other. The Align commands make it easy to align two or more objects relative to each other vertically to the left, center, or right, or horizontally from the top, middle, or bottom. To align several objects to each other evenly across the slide, either horizontally or vertically, you select them and then choose a distribution option. Before you select an align command, specify how you want PowerPoint to align the objects. You can align the objects in relation to the slide or to the selected objects.

Distribute Objects

1. Select the objects you want to distribute.

2. Click the **Format** tab under Drawing Tools.

3. Click the **Align** button.

   ◆ You can also click the **Home** tab, click the **Arrange** button, and then point to **Align**.

4. On the Align menu, click the alignment method you want.

   ◆ Click **Align to Slide** if you want the objects to align relative to the slide.

   ◆ Click **Align Selected Objects** if you want the objects to align relative to each other.

5. On the Align menu, click the distribution command you want.

   ◆ Click **Distribute Horizontally** to evenly distribute the objects horizontally.

   ◆ Click **Distribute Vertically** to evenly distribute the objects vertically.

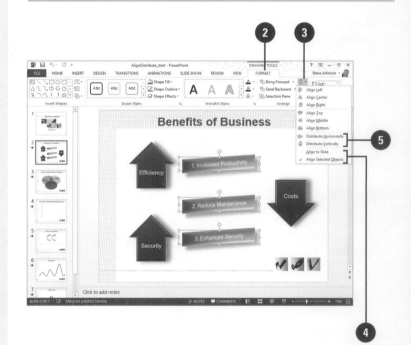

Align Objects with Other Objects

1. Select the objects you want to align.

2. Click the **Format** tab under Drawing Tools.

3. Click the **Align** button.

   ◆ You can also click the **Home** tab, click the **Arrange** button, and then point to **Align**.

4. On the Align menu, click the alignment method you want.

   ◆ Click **Align to Slide** if you want the objects to align relative to the slide.

   ◆ Click **Align Selected Objects** if you want the objects to align relative to each other.

5. On the Align menu, click the alignment command you want.

   ◆ Click **Align Left** to line up the objects with the left edge of the selection or slide.

   ◆ Click **Align Center** to line up the objects with the center of the selection or slide.

   ◆ Click **Align Right** to line up the objects with the right edge of the selection or slide.

   ◆ Click **Align Top** to line up the objects with the top edge of the selection or slide.

   ◆ Click **Align Middle** to line up the objects vertically with the middle of the selection or slide.

   ◆ Click **Align Bottom** to line up the objects with the bottom of the selection or slide.

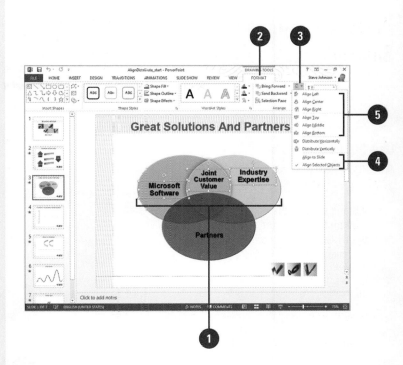

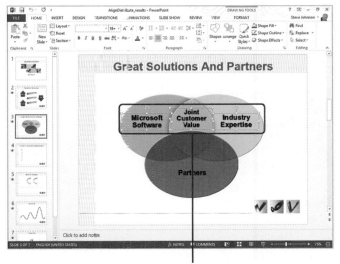

Arrange objects

Aligning Objects with Smart Guides

PowerPoint gives you the ability to use Smart Guides (**New!**) to help align shapes and objects as you draw or move them. They appear automatically (**New!**) as you draw or move a shape, and then disappear after the shape is drawn or moved. They enable you to visually space or line up one object to another with a minimum of effort. Smart Guides are automatically turned on by default. However, you can turn them on and off using context menu or the Grid and Guides dialog box.

Use Smart Guides to Automatically Space Objects

1. To enable smart guides, right-click a blank area of the slide, point to **Grid and Guides**, and then click **Smart Guides** to select it (checkmark).

2. Select the objects you want to align.

3. Drag the objects.

   As you drag, alignment guides appear on the slide indicating spacing and alignment.

4. Release the mouse button when the objects are placed where you want.

See Also

See "Aligning Objects to Gridlines and Guides" on page 144 for more information on turning Smart Guides on and off.

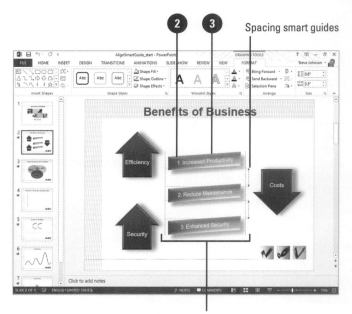

Spacing smart guides

Alignment smart guides

Changing Stacking Order

Multiple objects on a slide appear in a stacking order, like layers of transparencies. Stacking is the placement of objects one on top of another. In other words, the first object that you draw is on the bottom and the last object that you draw is on top. You can change the order of this stack of objects by using Bring to Front, Send to Back, Bring Forward, and Send Backward commands on the Format tab under Drawing or Picture Tools.

Arrange a Stack of Objects

1. Select the object or objects you want to arrange.

2. Click the **Format** tab under Drawing or Picture Tools.

3. Click the stacking option you want.

   ◆ Click the **Bring Forward** button arrow, and then click **Bring to Front** or **Bring Forward** to move a drawing to the top of the stack or up one location in the stack.

   ◆ Click the **Send Backward** button arrow, and then click **Send to Back** or **Send Backward** to move a drawing to the bottom of the stack or back one location in the stack.

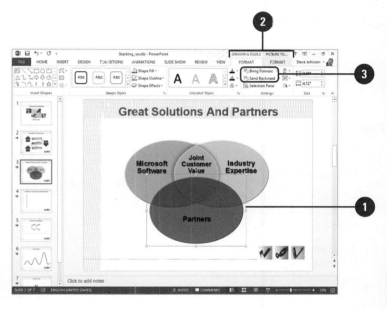

Did You Know?

You can view a hidden object in a stack. Press the Tab key or Shift+Tab to cycle forward or backward through the objects until you select the object you want.

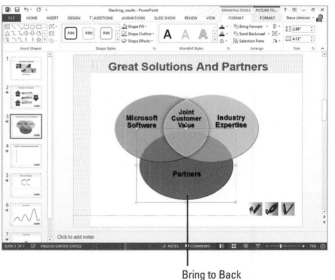

Bring to Back

Connecting Shapes

PowerPoint makes it easy to draw and modify flow charts and diagrams. Flow charts and diagrams consist of shapes connected together to indicate a sequence of events. With PowerPoint, you can join two objects with a connecting line. There are three types of connector lines: straight, elbow, and curved. Once two objects are joined, the connecting line moves when you move either object. The connecting line touches special connection points on the objects. When you position the pointer over an object, small red handles, known as connection sites, appear, and the pointer changes to a small box, called the connection pointer. You can drag a connection end point to another connection point to change the line or drag the adjustment handle (yellow diamond) to change the shape of the connection line. After you're done connecting shapes, you can format connector lines in the same way you format others lines in PowerPoint, including the use of Shape Quick Styles.

Connect Two Objects

1. Click the **Home** or **Insert** tab.

2. Click the **Shapes** button, and then click a connector (located in the Lines category) in the Shapes gallery.

   ◆ To draw multiple connector lines, right-click the connector in the Shapes gallery, and then click Lock Drawing Mode.

   TIMESAVER *In the Shapes gallery, point to shapes in the Lines category to display ScreenTips to locate a connector.*

3. Position the pointer over an object handle (turns red).

4. Drag the connector to the object handle (turns red) on another object.

   TIMESAVER *To constrain the line at 15-degree angles from its starting point, hold down Shift while you drag.*

   An attached connector point appears as red circles, while an unattached connector point appears as light blue (almost transparent).

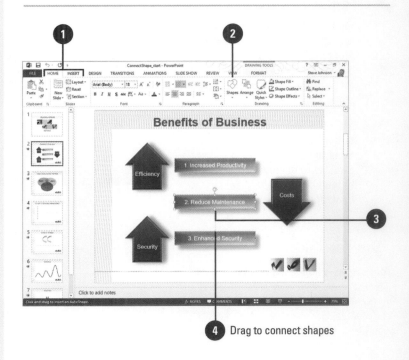

4 Drag to connect shapes

Change a Connector Line

1. Click on the connector line you want to modify to select it.

2. Use any of the following methods to change a connector line:

   ◆ Drag the adjustment handle (yellow diamond) to change the shape of the connector line.

   ◆ Drag a connection point (red circle) to another object handle to change a connection site, or right-click a connector line, and then click **Reroute Connectors**.

   ◆ Right-click a connector line, point to **Connector Types**, and then click the connector type to which you want change.

   ◆ Press Delete to remove it.

Format a Connector Line

1. Click on the connector line you want to modify to select it.

   To select more than one line, hold down Shift, and then click all the connector lines you want to modify.

2. Click the **Format** tab under Drawing Tools.

3. Use any of the following formatting options:

   ◆ Click the **More** list arrow in the Shapes Styles group, point to a Quick Style, and then click the one you want.

   ◆ Click the **Shape Outline** button, and then select the options you want, such as color, weight, dashes, and arrows.

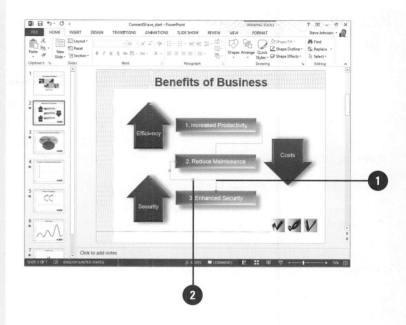

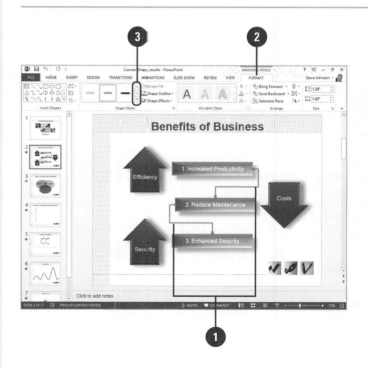

Rotating and Flipping a Shape

After you create an object, you can change its orientation on the slide by rotating or flipping it. Rotating turns an object 90 degrees to the right or left; flipping turns an object 180 degrees horizontally or vertically. For a more freeform rotation, which you cannot achieve in 90 or 180 degree increments, drag the circle arrow rotate lever at the top of an object. You can also rotate and flip any type of picture—including bitmaps—in a presentation. This is useful when you want to change the orientation of an object or image, such as changing the direction of an arrow.

Rotate an Object to any Angle

1. Click the object you want to rotate.

2. Position the pointer (which changes to the Free Rotate pointer) over the circle arrow rotate lever at the top of the object.

3. Drag to rotate the object.

4. Click outside the object to set the rotation.

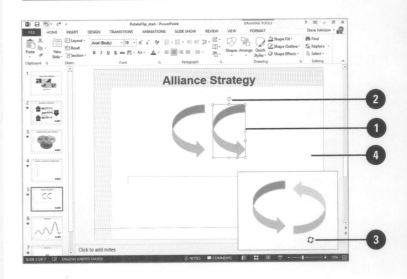

Rotate or Flip an Object Using Preset Increments

1. Click the object you want to rotate or flip.

2. Click the **Format** tab under Drawing or Picture Tools.

3. Click the **Rotate** button, and then click the option you want.

   ◆ **Rotate.** Click **Rotate Right 90°** or **Rotate Left 90°**.

   ◆ **Flip.** Click **Flip Vertical** or **Flip Horizontal**.

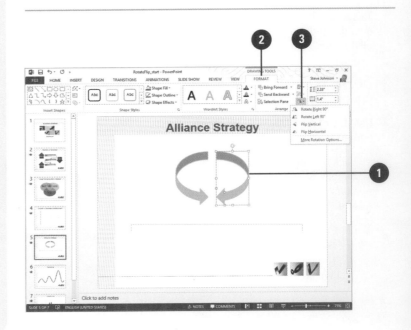

Precisely Rotate an Object

1. Click the object you want to rotate.

2. Click the **Format** tab under Drawing or Picture Tools.

3. Click the **Rotate** button, and then click **More Rotation Options**.

4. In the Format Shape pane, enter the angle of rotation, or click the up or down arrows.

5. Click the **Close** button in the pane.

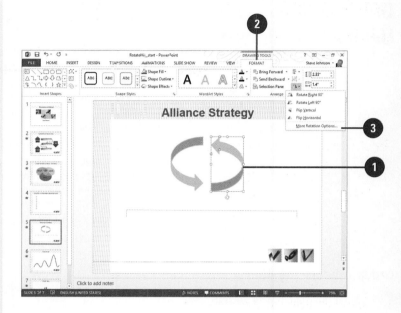

Did You Know?

You can constrain the rotation to 15-degree increments. Press and hold Shift when you rotate the object.

You cannot rotate or flip some imported objects. Not all imported objects can be rotated or flipped. By ungrouping the imported object and then regrouping its components, you might be able to rotate or flip it.

Grouping and Ungrouping Shapes

Objects can be grouped, ungrouped, and regrouped to make editing and moving them easier. Rather than moving several objects one at a time, you can group the objects and move them all together. Grouped objects appear as one object, but each object in the group maintains its individual attributes. You can change an individual object within a group without ungrouping. This is useful when you need to make only a small change to a group, such as changing the color of a single shape in the group. You can also format specific shapes, drawings, or pictures within a group without ungrouping. Simply select the object within the group, change the object or edit text within the object, and then deselect the object. However, if you need to move an object in a group, you need to first ungroup the objects, move it, and then group the objects together again. After you ungroup a set of objects, PowerPoint remembers each object in the group and regroups those objects in one step when you use the Regroup command. Before you regroup a set of objects, make sure that at least one of the grouped objects is selected.

Group Objects Together

1. Select the objects you want to group together.

2. Click the **Format** tab under Drawing or Picture Tools.

3. Click the **Group** button, and then click **Group**.

Did You Know?

You can use the Tab key to select objects in order. Move between the drawing objects on your slide (even those hidden behind other objects) by pressing the Tab key.

You can use the shortcut menu to select Group related commands. Right-click the objects you want to group, point to Group, and then make your selections.

You can no longer ungroup tables. Due to the increased table size and theme functionality, tables can no longer be ungrouped.

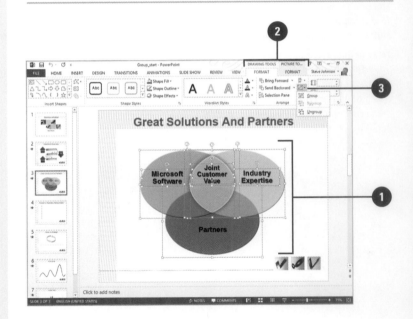

Ungroup a Drawing

1. Select the grouped object you want to ungroup.

2. Click the **Format** tab under Drawing or Picture Tools.

3. Click the **Group** button, and then click **Ungroup**.

See Also

See "Selecting Objects Using the Selection Pane" on page 157 for information on selecting "hard-to-select" objects.

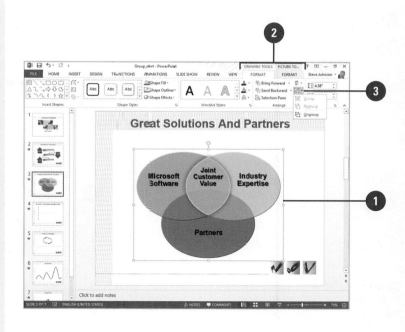

Regroup a Drawing

1. Select one of the objects in the group of objects you want to regroup.

2. Click the **Format** tab under Drawing or Picture Tools.

3. Click the **Group** button, and then click **Regroup**.

Did You Know?

You can troubleshoot the arrangement of objects. If you have trouble selecting an object because another object is in the way, you can use the Selection pane to help you select it.

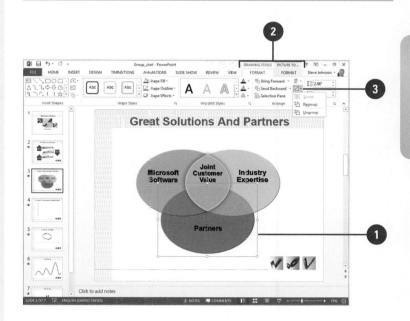

Merging Shapes Together

Instead of grouping shapes together, you can merge (**New!**) two or more shapes to create new shapes. The Merge command allows you to specify how you want to combine shapes together. You can select Union, Combine, Fragment, Intersect or Subtract. Union brings together all areas into one; Combine cuts out the overlapping area; Fragment cuts out intersecting lines to divide it; Intersect cuts out the non-intersecting areas; and Subtract cuts out the overlapping area and the non primary shapes (the first selection). The best way to figure out how these work is to experiment with overlapping objects. Have fun!

Merge Objects

1. Select the objects you want to merge.

2. Click the **Format** tab under Drawing Tools.

3. Click the **Merge** button (**New!**), and then click an option:

   ◆ **Union.** Brings together all areas into one.

   ◆ **Combine.** Cuts out the overlapping area.

   ◆ **Fragment.** Cuts out intersecting lines to divide it.

   ◆ **Intersect.** Cuts out the non-intersecting areas.

   ◆ **Subtract.** Cuts out the overlapping area and the non primary shapes (the first selection).

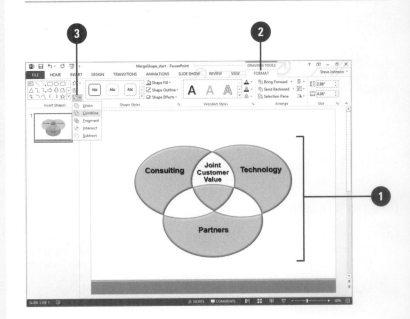

Selecting Objects Using the Selection Pane

Sometimes it's hard to select an object when it is behind another one. With the Selection pane, you can now select individual objects and change their order and visibility. When you open the Selection pane, it lists each shape in the current presentation by name (in terms of object type). You can click a shape title to select a "hard-to-select" object on a slide, use the Re-order buttons to change the stacking order on a slide, or click the eye icon next to a shape title to show or hide "hard-to-see" individual objects.

Select Objects Using the Selection Pane

1. Select any object you want to work with in the Selection pane.

2. Click the **Format** tab under Drawing or Picture Tools.

3. Click the **Selection Pane** button.

   ◆ You can also click the **Home** tab, click the **Select** button, and then click **Selection Pane**.

   Titles for all the shapes on the current slide appear in the pane.

   ◆ **Rename Objects.** Click the object name in the Selection pane, click the name again to edit it, rename the object, and then press Enter.

4. To select an object, click the title in the pane.

   To select more than one object, hold down the Ctrl key while you click object titles.

5. To change the order of the objects, select an object, and then click the Re-order **Move Up** or **Move Down** buttons in the pane.

6. To show or hide individual objects, click the eye icon in the pane.

7. When you're done, click the **Close** button in the pane.

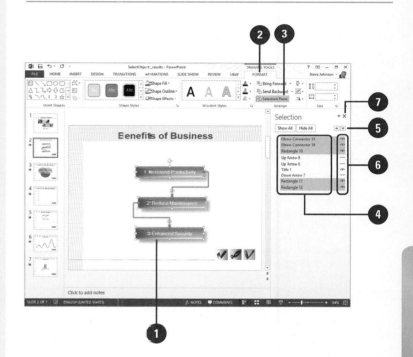

Inserting Pictures and Multimedia

5

Introduction

Although well-illustrated slides can't make up for a lack of content, you can capture your audiences' attention if your slides are vibrant and visually interesting. You can easily enhance a slide by adding a picture—one of your own or one of the hundreds that come with Microsoft PowerPoint. If you have the appropriate hardware, such as a sound card and speakers, you can also include audio files and video clips in your presentation.

Microsoft Office comes with a vast array of online Clip Art, and there are endless amounts available through other software packages or on the web. When going online to look at clips, you can categorize them so that it's easier to find the best choice for your presentation. You can use the Microsoft Office.com web site to search for and download clip art images or use Bing image search on the web.

With all of your digital photos or scanned pictures, you can organize them in an album. Certain elements, such as adding text or oval frames, make cataloging your pictures an easier process. If you need to modify your pictures, you can resize them, compress them for storage, change their brightness or contrast, recolor them, or change their shape by cropping them.

WordArt is another feature that adds detail to your slide presentation. Available in other Office programs, WordArt can bring together your slides—you can change its color, shape, shadow, or size. Because WordArt comes with so many style choices, time spent customizing your slides is minimal.

Another element that will give your presentation a real professional look and feel is the addition of video or audio clips. Imagine watching a slide show presentation with music playing at key points or starting a slide show with a video clip that loosens up the audience.

What You'll Do

Locate and Insert Online Pictures

Insert a Picture from an Online Service

Insert a Picture from a SkyDrive or SharePoint

Insert a Picture from a File

Insert a Pictures from a Slide Layout

Examine Picture File Formats

Create a Photo Album

Insert a Picture Screen Shot

Apply a Style, Shape and Border to a Picture

Apply Picture Effects

Modify Picture Size

Compress and Correct a Picture

Crop, Rotate and Recolor a Picture

Remove a Picture Background

Create and Format WordArt Text

Apply and Modify WordArt Text Effects

Insert, Edit, and Format Videos and Audio

Set Video and Audio Play Options

Play Videos and Audio

Record Audio

Compress or Optimize Media

Locating and Inserting Online Pictures

If you need a picture to insert into a presentation and don't have one, you can search for and insert clip art from Office.com (**New!**) or a picture from the web using Bing Image Search (**New!**). Office.com is a clip gallery that Microsoft maintains on its web site. Clip art includes photos and illustrations, such as vector images, which are mathematically defined to make them easy to resize and manipulate. To add an online picture to a presentation, you click the Online Pictures button on the Insert tab, and then locate, select, and insert the picture you want.

Locate and Insert Online Clip Art from Office.com

1. Click the **Insert** tab.

2. Click the **Online Pictures** button.

3. In the Search Office.com box, enter search criteria to locate the online picture you want.

   ◆ To cancel the search, click the **Close** button in the Search box.

4. Click the **Search** button or press Enter.

5. Select the picture(s) you want.

   ◆ To preview a larger picture, point to a picture, and then click the **View Larger** button.

6. Click **Insert**.

7. Select the picture, and then move and resize it, as desired.

Did You Know?

You can insert bitmaps. A bitmap is an image made up of dots. Bitmaps do not lend themselves as easily to resizing because the dots can't expand and contract when you enlarge or shrink your image. You can create a bitmap in a graphics program, such as Adobe Photoshop, Microsoft Paint, or Paint Shop Pro, or by taking a digital photo.

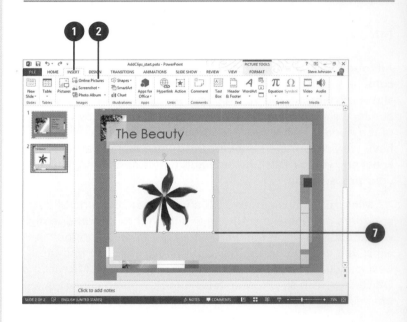

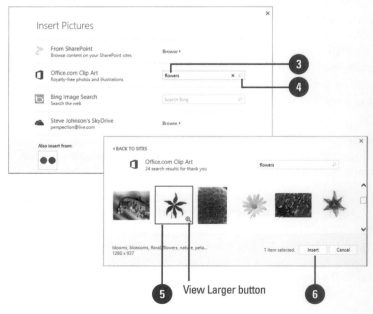

View Larger button

Locate and Insert Online Pictures from Bing Image Search

① Click the **Insert** tab.

② Click the **Online Pictures** button.

③ In the Search Bing box, enter search criteria to locate the online picture you want.

   ◆ To cancel the search, click the **Close** button in the Search box.

④ Click the **Search** button or press Enter.

⑤ If prompted, click **Show all web results**. If a message bar appears, read it, then click the **Close** button to dismiss it.

⑥ Select the picture(s) you want.

   ◆ To preview a larger picture, point to a picture, and then click the **View Larger** button.

⑦ Click **Insert**.

⑧ Select the picture, and then move and resize it, as desired.

Did You Know?

You can select multiple pictures from within a search. To select multiple pictures in consecutive order, press Shift, click first image, and then click the last image. To select multiple pictures in non-consecutive order, press Ctrl, and then click images.

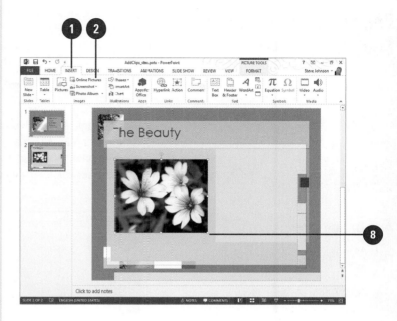

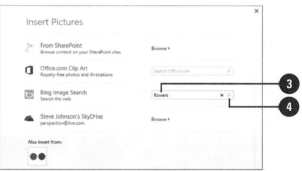

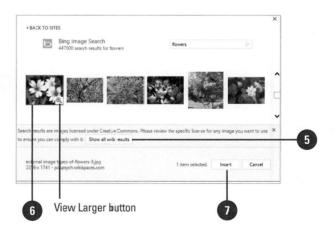

View Larger button

Inserting Pictures from an Online Service

If you have an account for an online service (**New!**) for images and video, such as Flickr or YouTube, you can insert pictures into a presentation directly from the service. Before you can use an online service, you need to add them (establishing a connection to your Microsoft account) to PowerPoint, which requires an established account with a user name and password. In addition to the image and video online services, you can also establish connections to access pictures stored on other online services, such as a SkyDrive (**New!**) or Office 365 SharePoint (**New!**). To add an online picture from an online service to a presentation, you click the Online Pictures button on the Insert tab, click the service icon, and then locate, select, and insert the picture you want.

Add Online Services

1. Click the **File** tab, and then click **Account** (**New!**).

2. Click **Add a service** (**New!**), point to a service type (options vary):

   ◆ **Images & Videos**, and then click **Flickr** or **YouTube**.

   ◆ **Storage**, and then click **Office 365 SharePoint** or **SkyDrive**.

3. Follow the on-screen instructions to sign-in and connect to the service.

   After the service is connected to your Microsoft account, it appears in the list of connected services.

4. To manage or remove a connected service, click the **Manage** or **Remove** link; options vary depending on the service.

   When you manage a connected service, your web browser opens, displaying options for the account.

5. Click the **Back** button to exit the File tab.

Insert Pictures from an Image Online Service

1. Click the **Insert** tab.

2. Click the **Online Pictures** button.

3. If the online service isn't connected, click the online service icon, such as Flickr, click **Connect**, and then enter your user name and password to establish a connection to the online service.

   The online service appears in the Insert Pictures window.

4. To manage the account, click the **Manage** link, make any option changes, click **Save**, and then close your web browser.

5. Click the **See more** link for more pictures.

   ◆ To quickly insert a recent picture, click one from the Recently Used list in the Insert Pictures window.

6. Select the picture(s) you want.

   ◆ To preview a larger picture, point to a picture, and then click the **View Larger** button.

7. Click **Insert**.

8. Select the picture, and then move and resize it, as desired.

3 Flickr

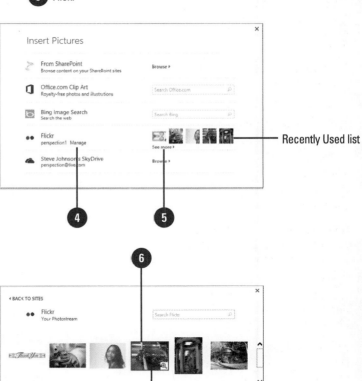

Recently Used list

4 **5**

6

View Larger button **7**

Inserting a Picture from a SkyDrive or SharePoint

If you have pictures stored on a SkyDrive (**New!**) or Office 365 SharePoint (**New!**), you can access them from Online Pictures on the Insert tab. Before you can use an online service, you need to add them (establishing a connection to your Microsoft account) to PowerPoint, which requires an established account with a user name and password. After you establish a connection, you can browse for pictures directly on the SkyDrive or Office 365 SharePoint sites.

Insert a Picture from SkyDrive or SharePoint

1. Click the **Insert** tab.

2. Click the **Online Pictures** button.

3. Click **Browse** for SharePoint or SkyDrive.

   The main folder for your SkyDrive or SharePoint site appears.

4. Navigate to the folder that contains the picture files you want to insert.

5. Click the file you want to insert.

6. Click **Insert**.

See Also

See "Inserting Pictures from an Online Service" on page 162 for information on adding an online service to connect to a SkyDrive or Office 365 SharePoint site.

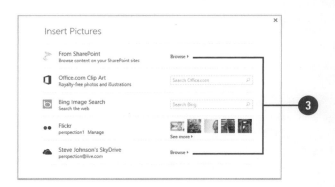

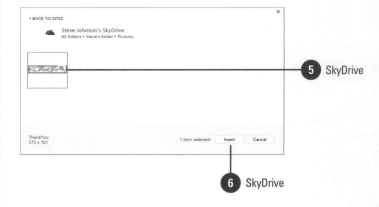

5 SkyDrive

6 SkyDrive

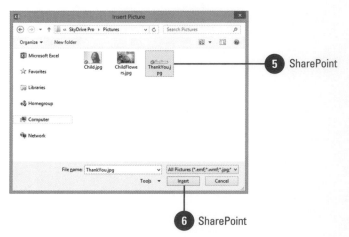

5 SharePoint

6 SharePoint

Inserting a Picture from a File

PowerPoint makes it possible for you to insert pictures, graphics, scanned photographs, art, photos, or artwork from a collection of stock images or other program into a slide. When you use the Picture button on the Insert tab, you specify the source of the picture. When you insert pictures from files on your hard disk drive, scanner, digital camera, or web camera, PowerPoint allows you to select multiple pictures, view thumbnails of them, and insert them all at once, which speeds up the process.

Insert a Picture from a File

1. Click the **Insert** tab.

2. Click the **Pictures** button.

3. Navigate to the folder that contains the picture files you want to insert.

4. Click the file you want to insert.

5. Click **Insert**.

   ◆ To link a picture file, click the **Insert** button arrow, and then click **Link to File**.

   ◆ To insert and link a picture file, click the **Insert** button arrow, and then click **Insert and Link**.

   TROUBLE? *If you see a red "x" instead of a picture in your presentation, then you don't have a graphics filter installed on your computer for that image.*

Did You Know?

You can change a picture. If you no longer want to use a picture, you can change it instead of deleting it and inserting another one. Select the picture, click the Change Picture button on the Format tab, select a picture, and then click Insert.

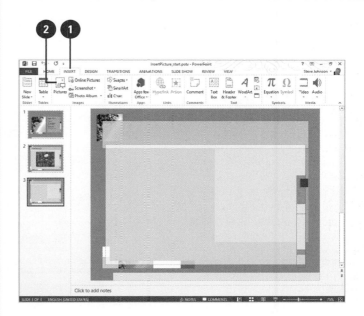

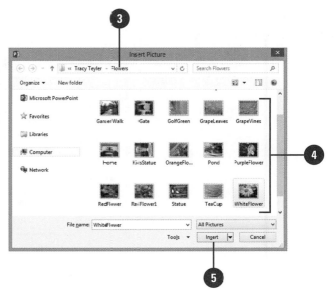

Inserting a Picture from a Slide Layout

When you create a slide, you can specify a layout with placeholder objects to fill in later. One of the placeholders is for content, such as a table, chart, SmartArt, picture, online picture, or video. The content placeholder contains an icon for each type of content. To insert a picture from a file or online service, click the Pictures or Online Pictures icon in the placeholder, where you can select the picture you want.

Insert a Picture from a Slide Layout

1. Click the **Home** tab.

2. Select the slide you want to apply a slide layout.

3. Click the **Layout** button, and then click a slide layout that includes the Pictures or Online Pictures content placeholder.

   ◆ **Create a New Slide.** To create a new slide, click the **New Slide** button arrow, and then click a slide layout that includes the Pictures or Online Pictures content placeholder.

4. In the content placeholder, click the **Pictures** or **Online Pictures** icon.

5. Navigate to the pictures you want to insert.

6. Click the file you want to insert.

7. Click **Insert**.

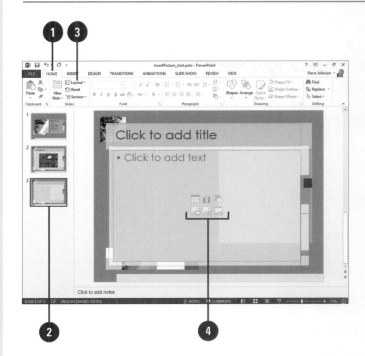

Examining Picture File Formats

The following table lists the default graphic formats available in PowerPoint. If the graphic format you need is not in the list, you can use Office Setup's maintenance feature to install additional graphic formats using the Add or Remove Features option. See "Maintaining and Repairing Office" on page 422 for more information on using the feature.

Supported Graphic File Formats		
Insert Picture file type	Extension	Used to insert
Enhanced Windows Metafile	.emf	A 32-bit graphic (Windows 95 and later)
Windows Metafile	.wmf	A 16-bit graphic (Windows 3.x and later)
JPEG (Joint Photographic Experts Group)	.jpeg, .jpg .jfif, .jpe	A graphic for use on web pages; supports 16 millions colors; best for photographs
PNG (Portable Network Graphics)	.png	A graphic for use on web pages; the future replacement for GIF, but not yet
Windows Bitmap	.bmp, .dib, .rle	A graphic; colors are represented in a format independent of the output
GIF (Graphics Interchange Format)	.gif	A graphic for use on web pages; support 256 colors; best for scanned images and animation
Compressed Enhanced Windows Metafile	.emz	A compressed version of the Enhanced Windows Metafile
Compressed Windows Metafile	.wmz	A compressed version of the Windows Metafile
Compressed Macintosh PICT	.pcz	A compressed version of the Macintosh PICT
TIFF (Tag Image File Format)	.tiff, .tif	A graphic for use in print; best for bitmaps; good at any resolution
Encapsulated PostScript	.eps	A graphic for use on printers; the format uses the postscript language
Macintosh PICT	.pct, .pict	A default graphic on the Macintosh
WordPerfect Graphics	..wpg	A default graphic for the WordPerfect program

Creating a Photo Album

If you have a large collection of pictures, you can use PowerPoint to create a photo album. A PowerPoint photo album is a presentation that you can use to display your photographs and pictures. PowerPoint makes it easy for you to insert multiple pictures from your hard disk into your photo album. You can also customize the photo album by applying themes and using special layout options, such as oval frames and captions under each picture. When you setup captions in a photo album, PowerPoint automatically uses picture file name as caption placeholder text, which you can change later. You can also change the appearance of a picture in the photo album by adjusting rotation, contrast, and brightness.

Create a New Photo Album

1. Click the **Insert** tab.

2. Click the **Photo Album** button arrow, and then click **New Photo Album**.

3. Click **File/Disk**.

4. Navigate to the folder that contains the picture files you want to insert.

5. Select the pictures you wish to include in the new photo album; hold down the Ctrl key to select multiple pictures.

6. Click **Insert**.

7. Select or clear the pictures you want to show or hide.

8. Click the **Picture Layout** list arrow, and then click a picture layout.

9. Click the **Frame Shape** list arrow, and then click a frame shape.

10. If you want to change the picture order or remove one, click a picture, and then use the **Up**, **Down**, or **Remove** buttons.

11. Click **Create**.

12. Click the **File** tab, click **Save As**, click **Computer**, click **Browse**, type a file name, and then click **Save**.

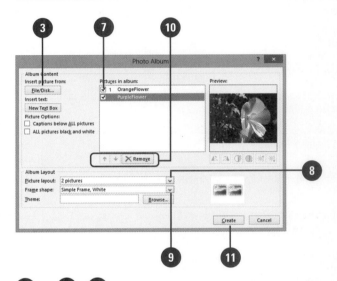

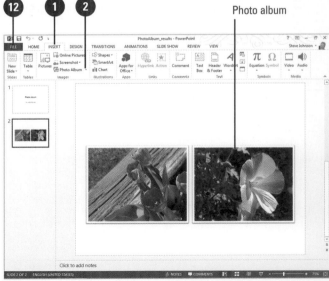

Photo album

Edit a Photo Album

1. Open the photo album presentation.

2. Click the **Insert** tab.

3. Click the **Photo Album** button arrow, and then click **Edit Photo Album**.

4. To add captions, select the **Captions below ALL pictures** check box.

    TROUBLE? *If the check box is not available, you need to select another picture layout.*

5. To add a text box for spacing purposes, select the picture you want to use, and then click **New Text Box**.

6. To change the appearance of a picture, do one of the following:

    ◆ **Rotate.** Click these buttons to rotate the picture.

    ◆ **Contrast.** Click these buttons to increase or decrease contrast.

    ◆ **Brightness.** Click these buttons to increase or decrease brightness.

7. To apply a theme, click **Browse**, locate and select a theme file, and then click **Select**.

8. Click **Update**.

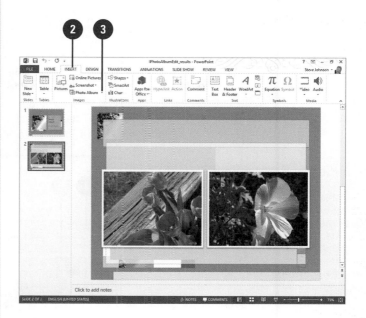

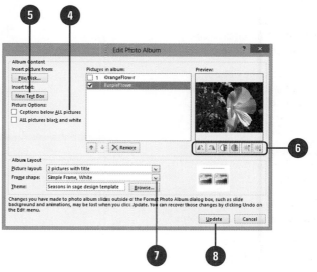

Did You Know?

You can share your photo album with others. You can print it, publish it to the web, or send it as an attachment in an e-mail.

Inserting a Picture Screen Shot

If you're working on a training manual, presentation, or document that requires a picture of your computer screen, then the Screenshot button on the Insert tab just made your life a lot easier. You use the Screen Clipping tool to drag a selection around the screen area that you want to capture, and then select the picture from the Screenshot gallery. The Screenshot gallery holds multiple screen shots, so you can capture several screens before you insert them into your presentation. After you insert the screen shot into a presentation, you can use the tools on the Picture Tools tab to edit and improve it.

Insert a Picture Screen Shot

1. Click the **Insert** tab.

2. Click the **Screenshot** button.

3. Click **Screen Clipping**.

4. Display the screen you want to capture, and then drag the large plus cursor to select the screen area to capture.

5. Click the **Screenshot** button, and then click the thumbnail of the screen shot you want to insert.

6. Use the tools on the **Format** tab under Picture Tools to edit and improve the screen shot.

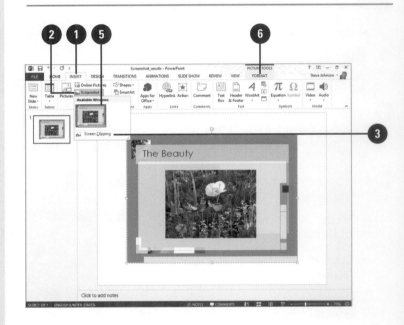

Did You Know?

You can copy the window or screen contents. To make a copy of the active window, press Alt+Print Scrn. To copy the entire screen as it appears on your monitor, press Print Scrn.

See Also

See "Cropping and Rotating a Picture" on page 182 for more information on cropping out part of a screen shot picture you don't want.

Adding an Artistic Style to a Picture

With the Artistic Quick Style gallery, you can transform a picture into a piece of artwork. The Artistic Quick Style gallery makes it easy to change the look of a picture to a sketch, drawing, or painting. The Picture Quick Style gallery provides a variety of different formatting options—such as Pencil Sketch, Line Drawing, Watercolor Sponge, Mosaic Bubble, Glass, Pastels Smooth, Plastic Wrap, Photocopy, and Paint Strokes—to create a professional look. To quickly see if you like an Artistic Quick Style, point to a thumbnail in the gallery to display a live preview of it in the selected shape. If you like it, you can apply it.

Add an Artistic Style to a Picture

1 Click the picture you want to change.

2 Click the **Format** tab under Picture Tools.

3 Click the **Artistic Effects** button.

The current style appears highlighted in the gallery.

4 Point to a style.

A live preview of the style appears in the picture.

5 Click the style you want from the gallery to apply it to the selected picture.

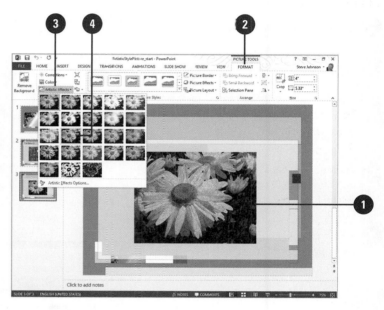

Adding a Quick Style to a Picture

Instead of changing individual attributes of a picture—such as shape, border, and effects—you can quickly add them all at once with the Picture Quick Style gallery. The Picture Quick Style gallery provides a variety of different formatting combinations. To quickly see if you like a Picture Quick Style, point to a thumbnail in the gallery to display a live preview of it in the selected shape. If you like it, you can apply it.

Add a Quick Style to a Picture

1 Click the picture you want to change.

2 Click the **Format** tab under Picture Tools.

3 Click the scroll up or down arrow, or click the **More** list arrow in the Picture Styles group to see additional styles.

The current style appears highlighted in the gallery.

4 Point to a style.

A live preview of the style appears in the current shape.

5 Click the style you want from the gallery to apply it to the selected picture.

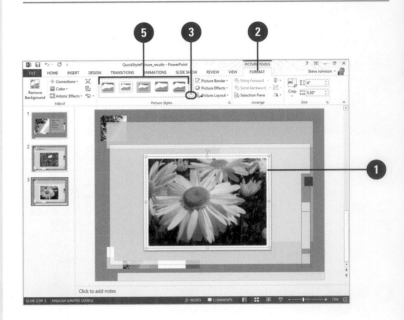

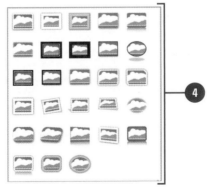

Did You Know?

You can save a shape as a picture in the PNG format. Right-click the shape, click Save As Picture, type a name, and then click Save.

Applying a Shape to a Picture

After you insert a picture into your presentation, you can select it and apply one of Office's shapes to it. The picture appears in the shape just like it has been cropped. The Crop to Shape gallery makes it easy to choose the shape you want to use. Live preview is not available with the Crop to Shape gallery. You can try different shapes to find the one you want. If you don't find the one you want, you can use the Reset Picture button to return the picture back to its original state.

Apply a Shape to a Picture

1. Click the picture you want to change.

2. Click the **Format** tab under Picture Tools.

3. Click the **Crop** button arrow, and then point to **Crop to Shape**.

4. Select the shape you want to apply to the selected picture.

Did You Know?

You can quickly return a picture back to its original form. Select the picture, click the Format tab, and then click the Reset Picture button.

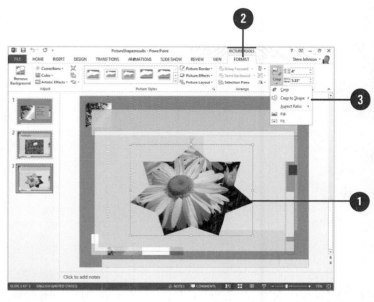

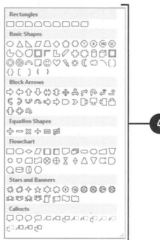

Applying a Border to a Picture

After you insert a picture, you can add and modify the picture border by changing individual outline formatting using the Picture Border button on the Format tab under Picture Tools. The Picture Border button works just like the Shape Outline button, and provides similar options to add a border, select a border color, and change border width and style. You can try different border combinations to find the one you want. If you want to use a color from another element on the screen, you can use the eyedropper (**New!**) to select it. If you don't find one that works for you, you can use the No Outline command on the Picture Border gallery to remove it.

Apply a Border to a Picture

① Click the picture you want to change.

② Click the **Format** tab under Picture Tools.

③ Click the **Picture Border** button.

④ Click a color, or point to **Weight**, or **Dashes**, and then select a style, or click **More Lines** to select multiple options.

◆ **Select a Color from the Screen.** Click **Eyedropper** (**New!**), point to a color on the screen, and then click to apply it to the selection. To cancel the eyedropper, press Esc.

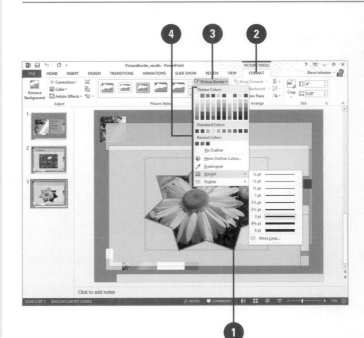

Did You Know?

You can remove a border. Select the picture, click the Format tab, click the Picture Border button, and then click No Outline.

You can apply a border to any object. The Shape Outline button works just like the Picture Border button and provides similar options to add a border, select a border color, and change border width and style.

Applying Picture Effects

You can change the look of a picture by applying effects, such as shadows, reflections, glow, soft edges, and 3-D rotations. You can also apply effects to a shape by using the Picture Effects gallery for quick results, or by using the Format Shape pane (**New!**) for custom results. From the Picture Effects gallery you can apply a built-in combination of 3-D effects or individual effects to a picture. To quickly see if you like a picture effect, point to a thumbnail in the Picture Effects gallery to display a live preview of it. If you like it, you can apply it. If you no longer want to apply a picture effect to an object, you can remove it. Simply, select the picture, point to the effect type on the Picture Effects gallery, and then select the No effect type option.

Add an Effect to a Picture

1. Click the picture you want to change.

2. Click the **Format** tab under Picture Tools.

3. Click the **Picture Effects** button, and then point to one of the following:

   ◆ **Preset** to select No 3-D, one of the preset types, or 3-D Options.

   ◆ **Shadow** to select No Shadow, one of the shadow types, or Shadows Options.

   ◆ **Reflection** to select No Reflection, one of the Reflection Variations, or Reflection Options.

   ◆ **Glow** to select No Glow, one of the Glow Variations, More Glow Colors, or Glow Options.

   ◆ **Soft Edges** to select No Soft Edges or a point size to determine the soft edge amount, or Soft Edges Options.

   ◆ **3-D Rotation** to select No Rotation, one of the rotation types, or 3-D Options.

   When you point to an effect, a live preview of the style appears in the current shape.

4. Click the effect you want from the gallery to apply it to the selected shape.

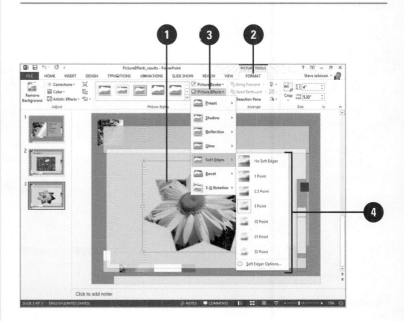

Modifying Picture Size

Once you have inserted a picture, clip art and other objects into your presentation, you can adapt them to meet your needs. Perhaps the clip is too small to be effective, or you don't quite like the colors it uses. Like any object, you can resize or move the picture. You can use the sizing handles to quickly resize a picture or use height and width option in the Size group on the Format tab to resize a picture more precisely. If you want to set multiple options at the same time, you can use the Size and Position dialog box. You can make sure your pictures keep the same relative proportions as the original and provide the best scaling size for a slide show on a specific monitor size.

Resize a Picture

1. Click the object you want to resize.

2. Drag one of the sizing handles to increase or decrease the object's size.

    ◆ Drag a middle handle to resize the object up, down, left, or right.

    ◆ Drag a corner handle to resize the object proportionally.

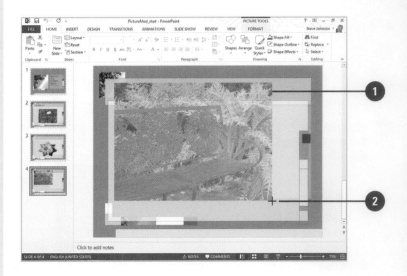

Resize a Picture Precisely

1. Click the object you want to resize.

2. Click the **Format** tab under Picture Tools.

3. Click the up and down arrows or enter a number (in inches) in the Height and Width boxes on the Ribbon and press Enter.

    If the **Lock aspect ratio** check box is selected in the Format Picture pane (under Size), height or width automatically changes when you change one of them. Click the **Size Dialog Box Launcher** to change the option.

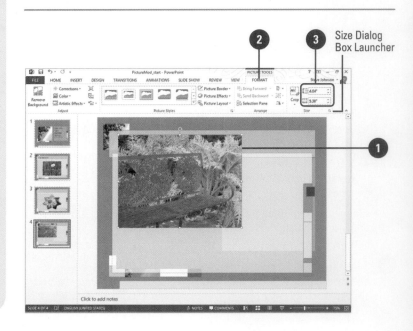

Scale a Picture Precisely

① Click the object you want to resize.

② Click the **Format** tab under Picture Tools.

③ Click the **Size Dialog Box Launcher**.

The Format Picture pane opens, displaying format options (**New!**).

④ Do any of the following:

- ◆ **Keep the picture proportional.** Select the **Lock aspect ratio** check box.

- ◆ **Keep the picture the same relative size.** Select the **Relative to original picture size** check box.

⑤ To scale a picture for the best slide show look on a specific slide monitor, select the **Best scale for slide show** check box, and then select a resolution size.

⑥ Click the up and down arrows or enter a number in the Height and Width boxes in one of the following:

- ◆ **Size.** Enter a size in inches.

- ◆ **Scale.** Enter a percentage size.

If the Lock aspect ratio check box is selected, height or width automatically changes when you change one of them.

⑦ If you want to remove your changes, click **Reset**.

⑧ Click the **Close** button in the pane.

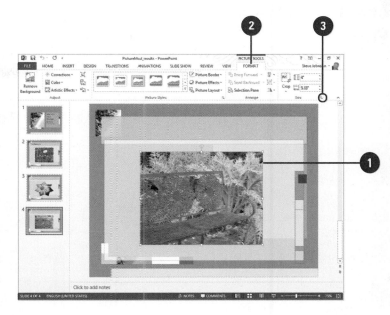

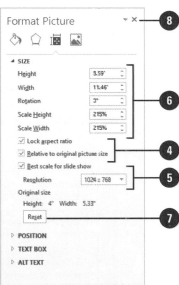

Compressing a Picture

PowerPoint allows you to compress pictures in order to minimize the file size of the image. In doing so, however, you may lose some visual quality, depending on the compression setting. You can pick the resolution that you want for the pictures in a presentation based on where or how they'll be viewed (for example, on the web or printed). You can also set other options, such as Delete cropped areas of picture, to get the best balance between picture quality and file size or automatically compress pictures when you save your presentation.

Compress a Picture

1. Click to select the pictures you want to compress.

2. Click the **Format** tab under Picture Tools.

3. Click the **Compress Pictures** button.

4. Select the **Apply only to this picture** check box to apply compression setting to only the selected picture. Otherwise, clear the check box to compress all pictures in your presentation.

5. Select or clear the **Delete cropped areas of pictures** check box to reduce file.

6. Click the **Print**, **Screen**, **E-mail**, or **Document** option to specify a target output.

7. Click **OK**.

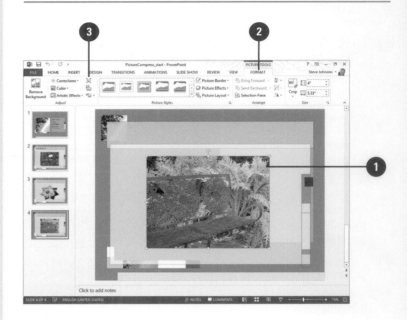

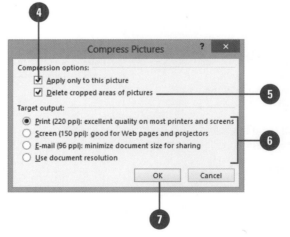

Correcting a Picture

Once you have inserted a picture, you can control the image's colors, brightness, and contrast using Picture tools. The brightness and contrast controls let you make simple adjustments to the tonal range of a picture. The brightness and contrast controls change a picture by an overall lightening or darkening of the image pixels. In addition, you can sharpen and soften pictures by a specified percentage. If you want to set unique or multiple options, you can use the Format Picture pane (**New!**). You can experiment with the settings to get the look you want. If you don't like the look, you can use the Reset Picture button to return the picture back to its original starting point.

Change Brightness and Contrast or Sharpen and Soften

1. Click the picture you want to change.

2. Click the **Format** tab under Picture Tools.

3. Click the **Corrections** button, and then do one of the following:

   - **Brightness and Contrast.** Click a brightness and contrast option.

     A positive brightness lightens the object colors by adding more white, while a negative brightness darkens the object colors by adding more black. A positive contrast increases intensity, resulting in less gray, while a negative contrast to decrease intensity, resulting in more gray.

   - **Sharpen and Soften.** Click a sharpen and soften option.

4. To set custom correction percentages, click the **Corrections** button, click **Picture Corrections Options**, specify the options you want in the Format Picture pane (**New!**), and then click the **Close** button in the pane.

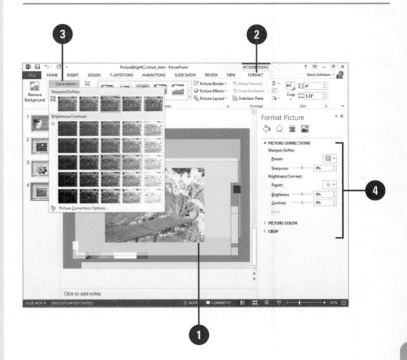

Recoloring a Picture

You can recolor clip art and other objects to match the color scheme of your presentation. For example, if you use a flower clip art as your business logo, you can change shades of pink in the spring to shades of orange in the autumn. The Color Picture Quick Style gallery provides a variety of different recolor formatting combinations. To quickly see if you like a Color Picture Quick Style, point to a thumbnail in the gallery to display a live preview of it in the selected shape. If you like it, you can apply it. You can also use a transparent background in your picture to avoid conflict between its background color and your presentation's background. With a transparent background, the picture takes on the same background as your presentation.

Recolor a Picture

1 Click the picture whose color you want to change.

2 Click the **Format** tab under Picture Tools.

3 Click the **Color** button.

4 Click one of the Color options.

◆ **Recolor.** Click an option to apply a color type:

No Recolor. Click this option to remove a previous recolor.

Grayscale. Converts colors into whites, blacks and shades of gray between black and white.

Sepia. Converts colors into very light gold and yellow colors like a picture from the old west.

Washout. Converts colors into whites and very light colors.

Black and White. Converts colors into only white and black.

◆ **Color Saturation** or **Color Tone.** Click an option to apply a color saturation or tone based on the recolor selection.

◆ **More Variations.** Point to this option to select a specific color.

◆ **Picture Color Options.** Click this option to set custom recolor options by percentage.

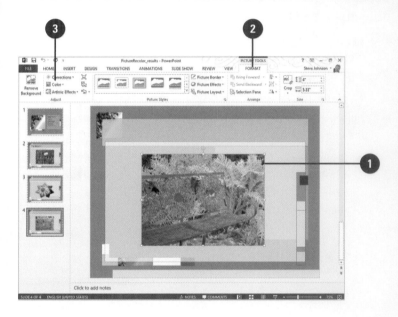

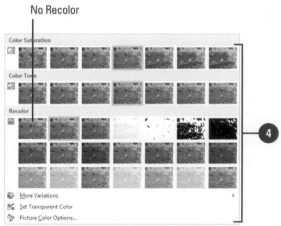

No Recolor

Set a Transparent Background

1. Click the picture you want to change.

2. Click the **Format** tab under Picture Tools.

3. Click the **Color** button, and then click **Set Transparent Color**.

4. Move the pointer over the object until the pointer changes shape.

5. Click the color you want to set as transparent.

6. Move the pointer over the picture where you want to apply the transparent color, and then click to apply it.

7. When you're done, click outside the image.

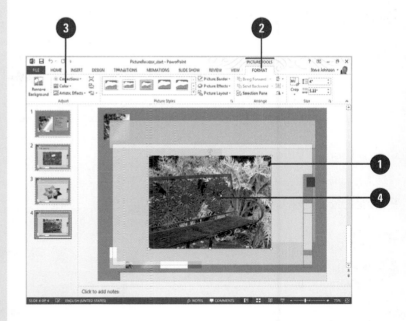

Did You Know?

Why is the Set Transparent Color command dimmed? Setting a color as transparent works only with bitmaps. If you are working with an object that is not a bitmap, you will not be able to use this feature.

You can't modify some pictures in PowerPoint. If the picture is a bitmap (.BMP, .JPG, .GIF, or .PNG), you need to edit its colors in an image editing program, such as Adobe Photoshop, Microsoft Paint, or Paint Shop Pro.

You can reset a picture back to its original state. Click the picture you want to reset, click the Format tab under Picture Tools, and then click the Reset Picture button.

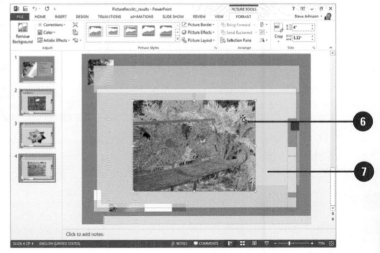

Cropping and Rotating a Picture

You can crop clip art to isolate just one portion of the picture. Because clip art uses vector image technology, you can crop even the smallest part of it and then enlarge it, and the clip art will still be recognizable. You can also crop bitmapped pictures, but if you enlarge the area you cropped, you lose picture detail. Use the Crop button to crop an image by hand. In addition, you can crop a picture while maintaining a selected resize aspect ratio or crop a picture based on a fill or fit. You can also rotate a picture by increments or freehand.

Crop a Picture Quickly

1 Click the picture you want to crop.

2 Click the **Format** tab under Picture Tools.

3 Click the **Crop** button.

4 Drag the sizing handles until the borders surround the area you want to crop.

5 Click outside the image when you are finished.

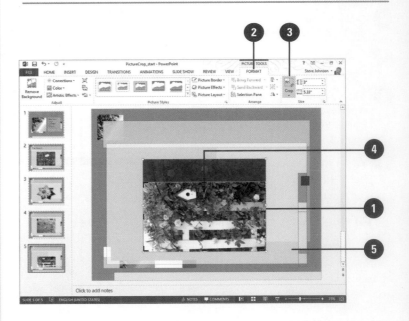

Crop a Picture with an Aspect Ratio

1 Click the picture you want to crop.

2 Click the **Format** tab under Picture Tools.

3 Click the **Crop** button arrow, point to **Aspect Ratio**, and then select an aspect ratio.

4 Drag the sizing handles until the borders surround the area you want to crop.

5 Click outside the image when you are finished.

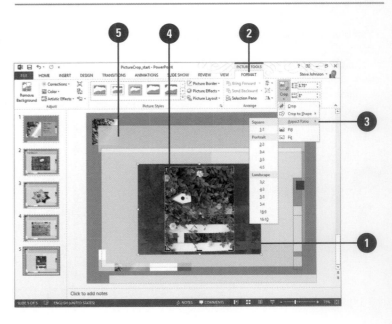

Crop a Picture with a Fill or Fit

1. Click the picture you want to crop.

2. Click the **Format** tab under Picture Tools.

3. Click the **Crop** button arrow, and then select an option:

   ◆ **Fill.** Resizes the picture so the entire picture area is filled while maintaining the aspect ratio. Any area outside of the picture area is cropped.

   ◆ **Fit.** Resizes the picture so the entire picture displays inside the picture area while maintaining the aspect ratio.

4. Drag the sizing handles until the borders surround the area you want to crop.

5. Click outside the image when you are finished.

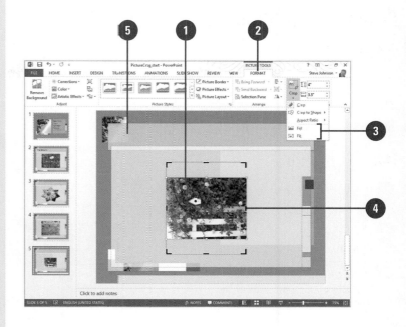

Rotate a Picture

1. Click the object you want to rotate.

2. Position the pointer (which changes to the Free Rotate pointer) over the circle arrow rotate lever at the top of the object, and then drag to rotate it.

3. Click outside the object to set the rotation.

Did You Know?

You can rotate or flip a picture. Select the picture, click the Format tab, click the Rotate button, and then click Rotate Right 90, Rotate Left 90, Flip Vertical, Flip Horizontal, or click More Rotation Options.

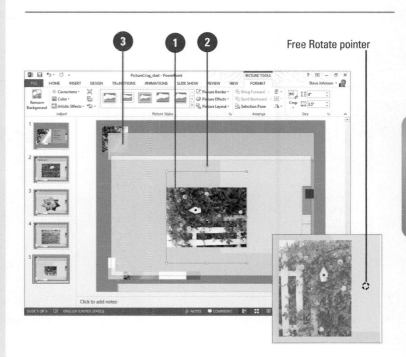

Free Rotate pointer

Removing a Picture Background

Sometimes you want to use an element from a picture instead of the entire picture. With the Remove Background command, you can specify the element you want in a picture, and then remove the background. You can use automatic background removal or you can manually draw lines to specify which parts of the picture background you want to keep and which to remove.

Remove a Picture Background

1. Click the picture you want to change.

2. Click the **Format** tab under Picture Tools.

3. Click the **Remove Background** button.

4. Drag the handles on the marquee lines to specify the part of the picture you want to keep. The area outside the marquee gets removed.

5. Click the **Keep Changes** button to close and keep the removal or click the **Discard All Changes** button to close and cancel the automatic removal.

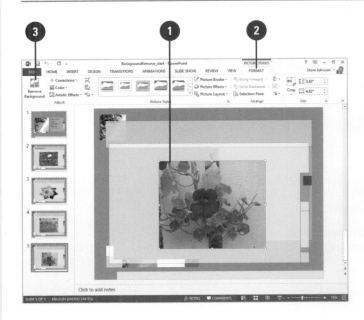

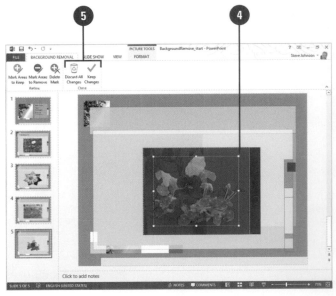

Remove a Picture Background Manually

1. Click the picture you want to change.

2. Click the **Format** tab under Picture Tools.

3. Click the **Remove Background** button.

4. Drag the handles on the marquee lines to specify the part of the picture you want to keep. The area outside the marquee gets removed.

5. To manually specify which areas to keep and which areas to remove, do the following:

   ◆ **Mark Areas to Keep.** Click the button, and then draw lines to specify which parts of the picture you do not want automatically removed.

   ◆ **Mark Areas to Remove.** Click the button, and then draw lines to specify which parts of the picture you do want removed in addition to those automatically marked.

   ◆ **Delete Mark.** Click the button, and then click marked lines to remove them.

6. Click the **Keep Changes** button to close and keep the removal or click the **Discard All Changes** button to close and cancel the automatic removal.

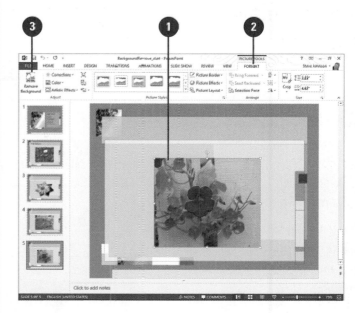

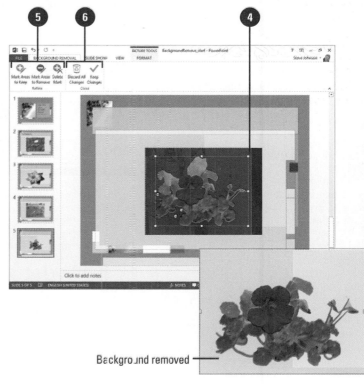

Background removed

Creating WordArt Text

The WordArt feature lets you create stylized text to draw attention to your most important words. Most users apply WordArt to short phrases or even just a word, such as *GROWING A GARDEN*. You should apply WordArt to a slide sparingly. Its visual appeal and unique look require uncluttered space. When you use WordArt, you can choose from a variety of text styles that come with the WordArt Quick Style gallery, or you can create your own using tools in the WordArt Styles group. To quickly see if you like a WordArt Quick Style, point to a thumbnail in the gallery to display a live preview of it in the selected text. If you like it, you can apply it. You can also use the free angle handle (pink diamond) inside the selected text box to adjust your WordArt text angle.

Insert WordArt Text

1. Click the **Insert** tab.

2. Click the **WordArt** button, and then click one of the WordArt styles.

   A WordArt text box appears on the slide with selected placeholder text.

3. Type the text you want WordArt to use.

4. If applicable, use the Font and Paragraph options on the Home tab to modify the text you entered.

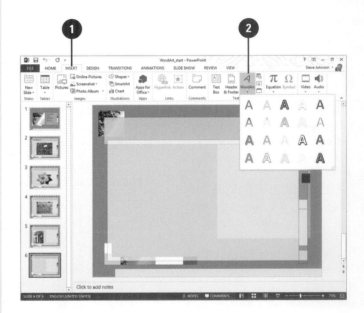

Did You Know?

You can convert text to WordArt. Select the text, click the Home tab, and then click the WordArt text style you want from the Ribbon.

You can remove WordArt text. Select the WordArt text you want to remove, click the Format tab, click the Quick Styles button, and then click Clear WordArt.

Edit WordArt Text

1. Click the WordArt object you want to edit.

2. Click to place the insertion point where you want to edit, and then edit the text.

3. Click outside the object to deselect it.

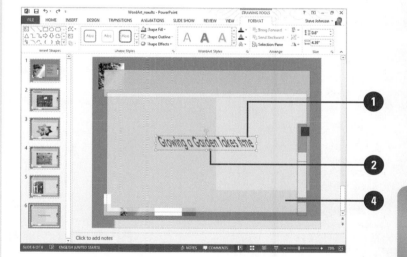

Adjust WordArt Text Angle

1. Click the WordArt object you want to change.

2. Drag the free angle handle (pink diamond) to adjust text angle in the direction you want.

3. When you're done, release the mouse button.

4. Click outside the object to deselect it.

Formatting WordArt Text

In addition to applying one of the preformatted WordArt styles, you can also create your own style by shaping your text into a variety of shapes, curves, styles, and color patterns. The WordArt Styles group gives you tools for changing the fill and outline of your WordArt text. To quickly see if you like a WordArt Style, point to a thumbnail in the gallery to display a live preview of it in the selected text. If you like it, you can apply it.

Apply a Different WordArt Style to Existing WordArt Text

1 Click the WordArt object whose style you want to change.

2 Click the **Format** tab under Drawing Tools.

3 Click the scroll up or down arrow, or click the **More** list arrow in the WordArt Styles group to see additional styles.

   The current style appears highlighted in the gallery.

4 Point to a style.

   A live preview of the style appears in the current shape text.

5 Click the style you want from the gallery to apply it to the selected shape.

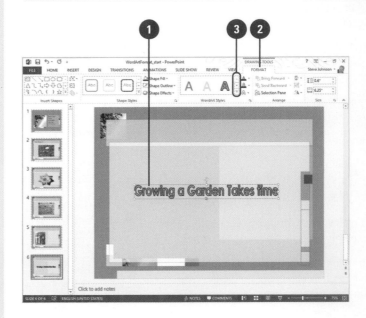

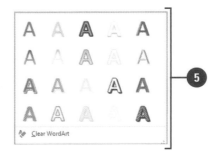

Did You Know?

You can add more formatting to WordArt text. Select the WordArt object, click the Home tab, and then use the formatting button in the Font and Paragraph groups.

You can change the WordArt fill color to match the background. Click the WordArt object, right-click the object, click Format Shape, click the Background option, and then click the Close button in the pane.

Apply a Fill to WordArt Text

1. Click the WordArt object you want to change.

2. Click the **Format** tab under Drawing Tools.

3. Click the **Text Fill** button, and then click or point to one of the following:

   ◆ **Color** to select a theme or standard color.

   ◆ **Eyedropper** to select a color from the screen with an eyedropper (**New!**).

   ◆ **Picture** to select a picture file.

   ◆ **Gradient** to select No Gradient, one of the shadow types, or More Gradients.

   ◆ **Texture** to select one of the of the texture types, or More Textures.

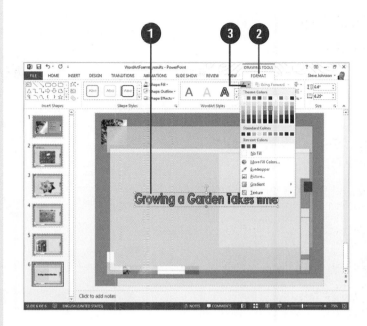

Apply an Outline to WordArt Text

1. Click the WordArt object you want to change.

2. Click the **Format** tab under Drawing Tools.

3. Click the **Text Outline** button.

4. Click a color, or point to **Weight** or **Dashes**, and then select a style.

   ◆ **Eyedropper** to select an outline color from the screen with an eyedropper (**New!**).

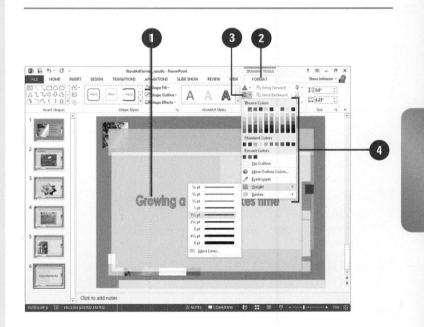

Applying WordArt Text Effects

You can change the look of WordArt text by applying effects, such as shadows, reflections, glow, soft edges, 3-D rotations, and transformations. You can apply effects to a shape by using the Text Effects gallery for quick results. From the Text Effects gallery you can apply a built-in combination of 3-D effects or individual effects to WordArt text. To quickly see if you like the effect, point to a thumbnail in the Text Effects gallery to display a live preview of it. If you like it, you can apply it. If you no longer want to apply the effect, you can remove it. Simply, select the WordArt text, point to the effect type on the Text Effects gallery, and then select the No effect type option.

Apply an Effect to WordArt Text

1. Click the WordArt object you want to change.

2. Click the **Format** tab under Drawing Tools.

3. Click the **Text Effects** button, and then point to one of the following:

   ◆ **Shadow** to select No Shadow, one of the shadow types, or Shadows Options.

   ◆ **Reflection** to select No Reflection, one of the Reflection Variations, or Reflection Options.

   ◆ **Glow** to select No Glow, one of the Glow Variations, More Glow Colors, or Glow Options.

   ◆ **Bevel** to select No Bevel, one of the bevel variations, or 3-D Options.

   ◆ **3-D Rotation** to select No Rotation, one of the rotation types, or 3-D Rotation Options.

   ◆ **Transform** to select No Transform, or one of the transform types (Follow Path or Warp).

   When you point to an effect, a live preview of the style appears in the current shape.

4. Click the effect you want from the gallery to apply it to the selected shape.

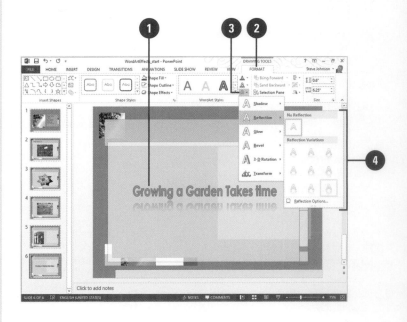

Modifying WordArt Text Position

You can apply a number of text effects to your WordArt objects that determine alignment and direction. The effects of some of the adjustments you make are more pronounced for certain WordArt styles than others. Some of these effects make the text unreadable for certain styles, so apply these effects carefully. You can apply effects to a shape by using the Format Shape pane (**New!**) for custom results. You can also use the free rotate handle (circle arrow) at the top of the selected text box to rotate your WordArt text.

Change WordArt Text Direction

1. Right-click the WordArt object you want to change, and then click **Format Shape**.

2. Click **Text Options** in the Format Shape pane (**New!**).

3. Click **Text Box** (**New!**).

4. Click the **Vertical alignment** or **Horizontal alignment** list arrow, and then select an option: **Top**, **Middle**, **Bottom**, **Top Center**, **Middle Center**, or **Bottom Center**.

5. Click the **Text Direction** list arrow, and then select an option: **Horizontal**, **Rotate all text 90°**, **Rotate all text 270°**, or **Stacked**.

6. Click the **Close** button in the pane.

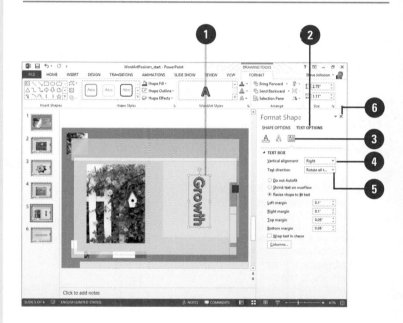

Rotate WordArt Text

1. Click the WordArt object you want to change.

2. Position the pointer (which changes to the Free Rotate pointer) over the circle arrow rotate lever at the top of the object, and then drag to rotate it.

3. When you're done, release the mouse button.

4. Click outside the object to deselect it.

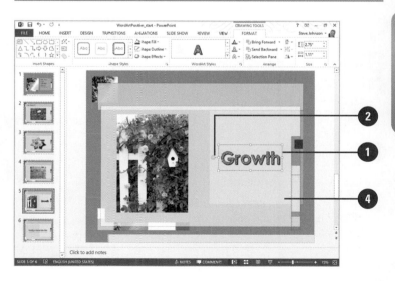

Inserting Videos and Audio

You can insert videos or audio into a presentation. You can insert a video from a file, SkyDrive (**New!**), Bing Video Search (**New!**), or a social media web site, such as YouTube, using an embed code. Videos can be either animated pictures—also known as animated GIFs—or they can be digital videos. When you insert a video, it becomes part of the presentation, and not a linked file. When you insert an audio from a file or Office.com, a small icon appears representing the sound. PowerPoint supports the following audio file formats—ADTS, AIFF, AU, MP3, MP4, WAV, WMA, QuickTime Audio, and Advanced Audio Coding (AAC) (**New!**)—and video file formats—ASF, AVI, MP4 (**New!**), MPEG-2 TS, MPG or MPEG, WMV, MOV with H.264 (**New!**) or QT (QuickTime movie or video), SWF (Flash). You can play a video or audio using the playback bar or the Playback tab under Video or Audio Tools. You can also play audio in the background (**New!**).

Insert a Video or Audio from a File

1. Click the **Insert** tab.

2. Click the **Video** or **Audio** button arrow, and then click **Video on My PC** or **Audio on My PC**.

3. Locate and select a video or audio file.

4. Click **Insert**.

   ◆ To link a video to a presentation, click the **Insert** button arrow, and then click **Link to File**.

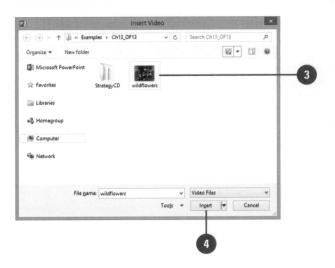

Play a Video or Audio

1. Select the video or audio icon.

2. To play audio in the background, click the **Play in Background** button (**New!**) on the Playback tab under Audio Tools.

3. Click the **Play/Pause** button on the playback bar or on the Playback tab under Video or Audio Tools.

4. To change the volume, click the **Mute/Unmute** button or point to it, and then adjust the volume slider.

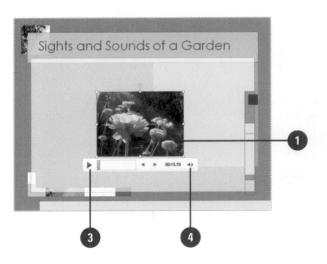

Insert an Online Video or Audio

1. Click the **Insert** tab.

2. Click the **Video** or **Audio** button arrow, and then click **Online Video** or **Online Audio**.

3. Search Office.com Clip Art (audio) or Bing Video Search, or browse your SkyDrive (video) (**New!**), select the file, and then click **Insert**.

4. Select the media clip, and then click the **Playback** tab under Video or Audio Tools.

5. Click the **Start** list arrow, and then select an option:

   ◆ **Automatically.** Plays the media clip automatically when you go to the slide.

   ◆ **On Clicked.** Play the media clip only when you click it.

   ◆ **Play Across Slides.** Play the media clip across slides.

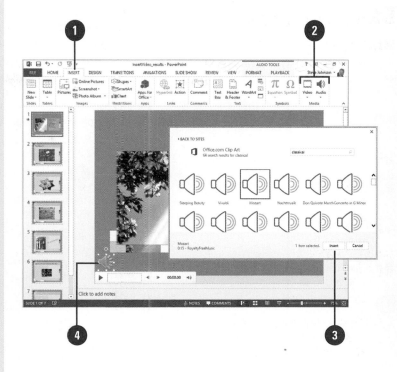

Insert a Video from a Web Site

1. Click the **Insert** tab.

2. Click the **Video** or **Audio** button arrow, and then click **Online Video** or **Online Audio**.

3. To copy an embed code, open your browser, go to the web page with the embed code you want to use, select the embed code, and then press Ctrl+C to copy it. Close your browser.

4. In PowerPoint, press Ctrl+V to paste the embed code in the Paste embed code here text box (**New!**), or use the YouTube search (**New!**) to find and select a YouTube video.

5. Click **Insert**.

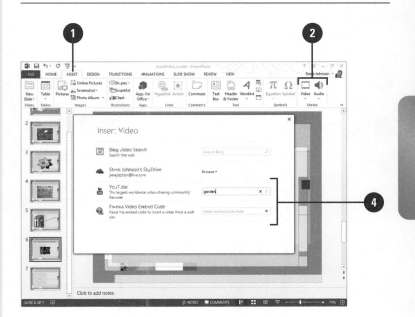

Editing Videos and Audio

After you insert a video or audio, you can trim the start or end to remove the parts you don't want and make it shorter. In the Trim Video or Trim Audio dialog box, you can drag the marker for the start point (green) or end point (red) or specify exact times to adjust the start and end time you want for the video or audio. You cannot trim sections within a video or audio. In addition to trimming, you can also add a fade effect to a video or audio and add text to a video. Adding text to a video is useful for creating titles, captions, and credits.

Trim a Video or Audio

1. Click the video or audio object you want to change.

2. Click the **Playback** tab under Video or Audio Tools.

3. Click the **Trim Video** or **Trim Audio** button.

4. Point to the start point (green marker), and then drag it to a new starting point, or specify an exact Start Time.

   ◆ You can click a marker, and then click the **Previous Frame** and **Next Frame** buttons to locate an exact time.

   ◆ You can click the **Play/Pause** button to advance the video or audio.

5. Point to the end point (red marker), and then drag it to a new end point, or specify an exact End Time.

6. Click **OK**.

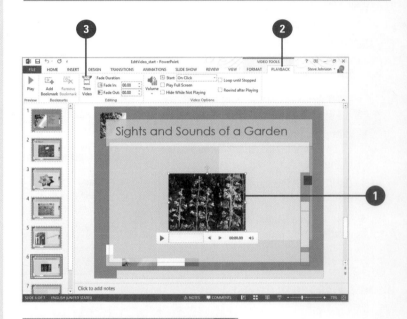

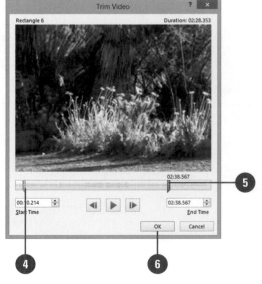

Add a Fade Effect

1. Click the video or audio object you want to change.

2. Click the **Playback** tab under Video or Audio Tools.

3. Specify the number of seconds you want to play a fade effect in the Fade In or Fade Out box.

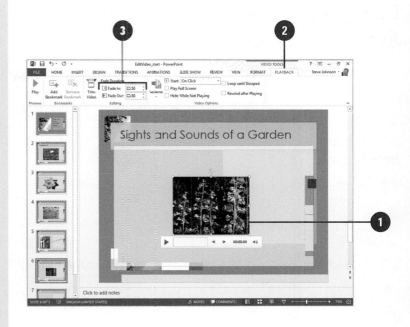

Add Text to a Video

1. Click the video object you want to change.

2. Click the **Insert** tab.

3. Click the **Text Box** button.

4. Point to where you want the text box, drag to draw a text box, and then enter text.

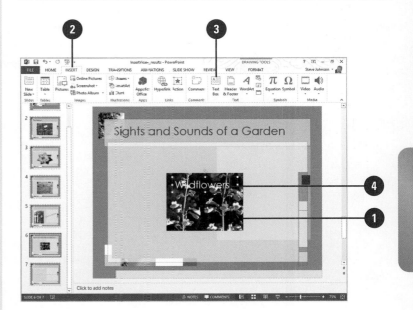

Adding Bookmarks to Videos and Audio

After you insert a video or audio, you can add bookmarks to indicate time points in a video or audio clip. Bookmarks are useful as a way to trigger animations or jump to a specific location in a video. When you add a bookmark, a small bookmark dot appears on the timeline. The bookmark dot provides a visual marker on the timeline, which you can use to select it. The bookmarks are named Bookmark 1, Bookmark 2, etc. for reference in animations.

Add or Remove Video or Audio Bookmarks

1. Click the video or audio object you want to change.

2. Click the **Playback** tab under Video or Audio Tools.

3. Play and pause the video or audio where you want to insert a bookmark.

4. Click the **Add Bookmark** button.

   A dot appears on the timeline. The bookmarks are named Bookmark 1, Bookmark 2, etc.

5. To remove a bookmark, click the bookmark (dot), and then click the **Remove Bookmark** button.

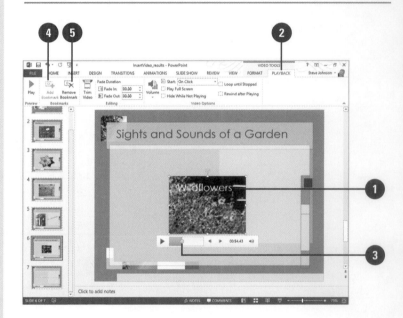

Formatting Videos

In addition to editing videos, you can also use the Format tab under Video Tools to apply formatting—such as image correction, video styles, effects, and borders—to the video, which are similar to Picture Tools. The poster frame is a preview image used when a video is not being played. You can create a poster frame from the current frame or an image from a file. Just like any other object in PowerPoint, you can change it's stacking order, alignment, position, and size—under Video Tools. If you don't like the changes you have made to a video, you can use the Reset Design button to restore it.

Format a Video

1. Click the video object you want to format; options are limited for a Flash object.

2. Click the **Format** tab under Video or Audio Tools.

3. Select from the available buttons:

   ◆ **Corrections.** Select a brightness and contrast option.

   ◆ **Color.** Select a recolor variation.

   ◆ **Poster Frame.** Creates a preview image for the video. Display a frame, and then select Current Frame, or Image from File to use a existing image.

   ◆ **Reset Design.** Resets the video back to the original. Click the Reset Design button arrow, and then click Reset Design or Reset Design & Size.

   ◆ **Video Styles**, **Video Shape**, **Video Border**, or **Video Effects.** Click to apply a pre-defined style, change the video to a shape, add a border, or apply an effect, such as shadow, glow, reflection, or 3-D rotation.

   ◆ **Arrange** or **Size.** Use the Arrange options (Bring Forward, Send Backward, Align, Group, or Rotate) or Size options (Crop button or Video Height and Width). You can also drag a resize handle to resize a video.

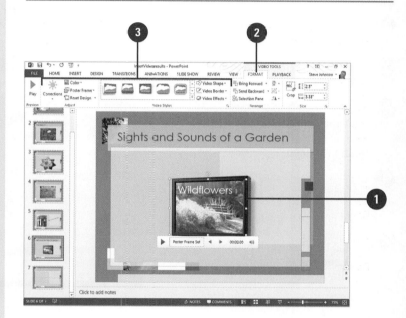

Setting Video and Audio Play Options

After you insert video, audio, or audio objects, you can set play options to determine how they will play back. You can change settings so they play continuously or just one time. Videos and audio can play in either Normal view or Slide Show view. You can also view and play movies using the full screen or play audio in the background (**New!**). To play sound and movies, you need to have Microsoft DirectShow or Microsoft Windows Media Player installed on your system, which you can download from the Microsoft web site.

Change Video Play Options

1 Click the video object you want to change options.

2 Click the **Playback** tab under Video Tools.

3 To adjust slide show volume, click the **Volume** button, and then click an option: **Low**, **Medium**, **High**, or **Mute** (no audio).

4 Change the available video settings.

- ◆ To change the way a video plays, click the **Start** list arrow, and then select an option: **Automatically**, **On Clicked**, or **Play across slides**.

- ◆ To hide video, select the **Hide While Not Playing** check box.

- ◆ To play continuously, select the **Loop Until Stopped** check box.

- ◆ To resize the video to fit the screen, select the **Play Full Screen** check box.

- ◆ To automatically rewind the video, select the **Rewind After Playing** check box.

5 To add a fade in or out to a video or audio, specify the number of seconds you want to play a fade effect in the **Fade In** or **Fade Out** box.

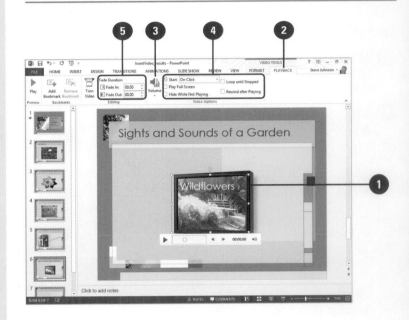

Change Audio Play Options

1. Click the audio object you want to change options.

2. Click the **Playback** tab under Audio Tools.

3. To adjust slide show volume, click the **Volume** button, and then click an option: **Low**, **Medium**, **High**, or **Mute** (no audio).

4. Change the available video or audio settings.

   ◆ To change the way a video plays, click the **Start** list arrow, and then select an option: **Automatically**, **On Clicked**, or **Play across slides**.

   ◆ To hide an audio, select the **Hide While Not Playing** check box.

   ◆ To play continuously, select the **Loop Until Stopped** check box.

   ◆ To automatically rewind the audio, select the **Rewind After Playing** check box.

   ◆ To play audio in the background (**New!**), click the **Play in Background** or **No Style** button.

5. To add a fade in or out to an audio, specify the number of seconds you want to play a fade effect in the **Fade In** or **Fade Out** box.

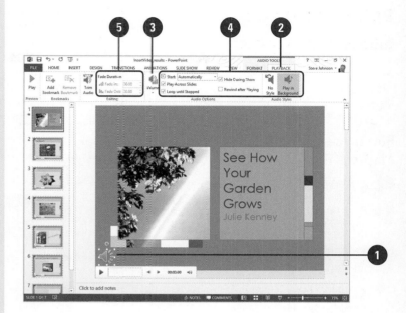

Playing Videos and Audio

After you insert video or audio objects, you can play them several different ways. You can play it back using the playback bar or the Playback tab under Video or Audio Tools. Videos and audio can play in either Normal view or Slide Show view during a slide show. You can modify them so they play continuously or just one time. Before you can play audio, or audio from video, you need a sound card and speakers installed on your computer.

Play a Video or Audio Using the Playback Bar

① Select the video or audio icon.

② Click the **Play/Pause** button on the playback bar.

TIMESAVER *Press Alt+P to play/pause the video or audio.*

◆ To move 0.25 seconds, click the **Move Forward** or **Move Backwards** button on the playback bar.

③ To change the volume, click the **Mute/Unmute** button or point to it, and then adjust the volume slider.

Did You Know?

Having problems playing a video. If your video doesn't play, check the list of compatible video file formats (see the Insert Video dialog box). If a video plays white, the path exceeds 128 characters. If a video plays black, your hardware accelerator is incompatible.

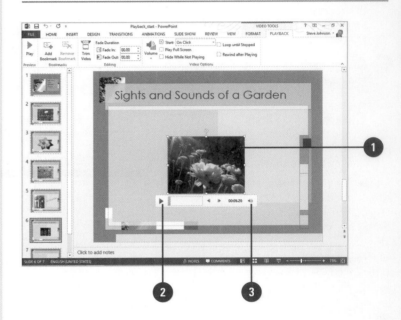

Other Ways to Play a Video or Audio

◆ To play a video or audio in Normal view, select the video object or audio icon, click the **Playback** tab, and then click the **Play/Pause** button.

◆ To play a video, audio, or animated picture in Slide Show view, click the **Slide Show** button, and then display the slide with the media you want to play.

Depending on your play options, you may need to click the video object or audio icon to play it.

Did You Know?

You cannot insert a digital video from a video DVD. PowerPoint is unable to add a video from a video DVD. However, some third-party add-ins, such as PFCMedia, let you play a video DVD in a presentation.

You can delay the start of a video. Click the video, click the Animation tab, and then click the Custom Animation button. In the pane, click the arrow next to the video, and then click Effects Options. Click the Effect tab, click From Time (under Start Playing), and then enter the total number of seconds for the delay.

Play/Pause button

Playback tab

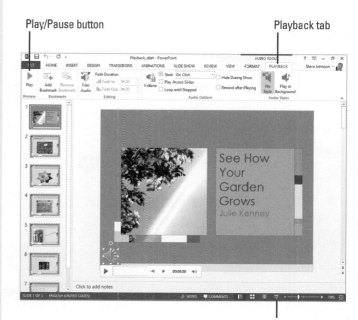

Slide show button

Recording Audio

You can add voice narration or audio in a slide show when you are either creating a slide show for individuals who can't attend a presentation or archiving a meeting for presenters to review later and hear comments made during the presentation. If you want to add voice narration or audio to a slide, you can record an audio clip directly into PowerPoint. Before you can record audio, you need a microphone, sound card, and speakers installed on your computer.

Record Audio on a Slide

1 Click the **Insert** tab.

2 Click the **Audio** button arrow, and then click **Record Audio**.

3 Type a name for the audio.

4 Click the **Record** button (red dot).

5 Click the **Stop** button when you are finished.

6 Click **OK**.

An audio icon appears on the slide.

Did You Know?

You can delete an audio. Click the audio icon, and then press Delete.

You can turn off audio narration. Click the Slide Show tab, click the Set Up Slide Show button, select the Show Without Narration check box, and then click OK.

See Also

See "Recording a Narration" on page 332 for more information and additional ways to record sound.

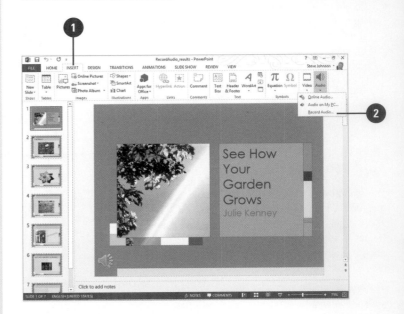

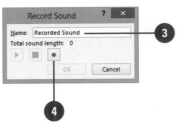

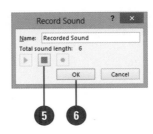

Compressing Media

When you create a presentation with audio and video, the file size of the presentation can become quite large, which creates problems when you want to send it in an e-mail or view it over the Internet. With the Compress Media button—which only shows when you have audio or video media in the presentation—on the Info screen, you can compress the media in a presentation to reduce the overall size of the file. You can select from three quality options: Presentation, Internet, and Low.

Compress Media in a Presentation

1. Open the presentation with the media you want to compress.

2. Click the **File** tab, and then click **Info**.

3. Click the **Compress Media** button.

4. Click any of the following quality options:

   ◆ **Presentation Quality.** Compresses the presentation to save space while maintaining audio and video quality.

   ◆ **Internet Quality.** Compresses the presentation for optimal use when streaming over the Internet.

   ◆ **Low Quality.** Compresses the presentation with the highest compression to create the smallest file size.

5. Review the compression results.

6. Click **Close**.

7. To undo the previous compress, click the **Compress Media** button, and then click **Undo**.

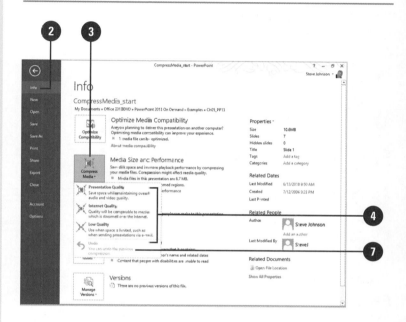

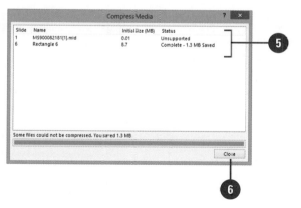

Optimizing Media

When you create a presentation with audio and video, you can avoid playback issues on other computers or devices by optimizing the media for compatibility. If you have problems with older media, convert it to modern media formats, such as H.264 and Advanced Audio Coding (AAC). With the Optimize Compatibility button (**New!**)—which only shows when you have audio or video media in the presentation that could present compatibility issues—on the Info screen, you can optimize the media in a presentation for use on different devices.

Optimize Media in a Presentation for Compatibility

1 Open the presentation with the media you want to optimize.

2 Click the **File** tab, and then click **Info**.

3 Click the **Optimize Compatibility** button (**New!**).

4 Review the summary of resolutions of potential playback issues.

5 If you have linked videos, click the **View Links** option to break the link for each one, so the media become embedded.

6 If you have videos inserted using an earlier version of PowerPoint, such as version 2007, you'll need to upgrade your media format to ensure proper playback.

◆ **Upgrade Media.** Click the **File** tab, click **Info**, and then click **Convert**.

7 Click **Close**.

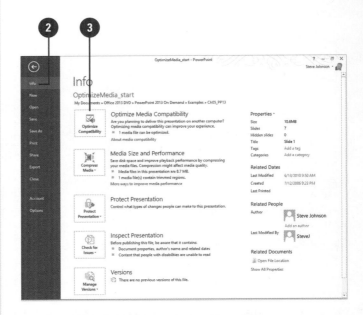

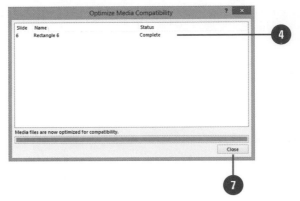

Inserting Charts and Related Material

Introduction

An effective presentation draws on information from many sources. Microsoft PowerPoint helps you seamlessly integrate information into your presentations using shared data from Office programs.

In PowerPoint and other Microsoft Office programs, you can insert SmartArt graphics to create diagrams that convey processes or relationships. PowerPoint offers a wide-variety of built-in SmartArt graphic types from which to choose, including graphical lists, process, cycle, hierarchy, relationship, matrix, pyramid, picture, and Office.com. Using built-in SmartArt graphics makes it easy to create and modify charts without having to create them from scratch. If you already have text on a slide, you can quickly convert your text to a SmartArt graphic.

Instead of adding a table of dry numbers, insert a chart. Charts add visual interest and useful information represented by lines, bars, pie slices, or other markers. Office uses Microsoft Excel to embed and display the information in a chart.

In PowerPoint, you can insert an object created in another program into a presentation using technology known as **object linking and embedding (OLE)**. OLE is a critical feature for many PowerPoint users because it lets you share objects among compatible programs when you create presentations. When you want to make any changes or enhancements to the objects, you can edit the inserted object without having to leave PowerPoint. OLE makes it easy to add graph and organization charts to present information visually. If you have information in other programs, such as Microsoft Word or Microsoft Excel, you can insert it in to your presentation with the help of OLE.

What You'll Do

Create SmartArt Graphics

Use the Text Pane with SmartArt Graphics

Modify, Resize and Format a SmartArt Graphic

Format a Shape in a SmartArt Graphic

Create and Modify an Organization Chart

Insert a Chart and Import Data

Select, Enter and Edit Chart Data

Modify the Data Worksheet

Select a Chart Type, Layout and Style

Select, Change, and Format Chart Elements

Change chart Titles, Labels, Lines, and Bars

Save a Chart Template

Insert, Modify and Format a Table

Add a Quick Style and Effects to a Table

Share Information Among Documents

Embed and Link an Object

Insert a Microsoft Excel Chart or Word Document

Creating SmartArt Graphics

SmartArt graphics allow you to create diagrams that convey processes or relationships. PowerPoint provides a wide variety of built-in SmartArt graphic types, including graphical lists, process, cycle, hierarchy, relationship, matrix, pyramid, picture, and Office.com. Using built-in SmartArt graphics makes it easy to create and modify charts without having to create them from scratch. If you already have text on a slide, you can quickly convert your text to a SmartArt graphic. To quickly see if you like a SmartArt graphic layout, point to a thumbnail in the gallery to display a live preview of it in the selected shape. If you like it, you can apply it.

Create a SmartArt Graphic

1. Click the **Insert** tab.

2. Click the **SmartArt** button.

   TIMESAVER *In a content placeholder, you can click the SmartArt icon to start.*

3. In the left pane, click a category, such as All, List, Process, Cycle, Hierarchy, Relationship, Matrix, Pyramid, Picture, or Office.com.

4. In the right pane, click a SmartArt graphic style type.

5. Click **OK**.

   The SmartArt graphic appears with a Text pane to insert text.

6. Label the shapes by doing one of the following:

   ◆ Type text in the [Text] box.

      You can use the arrow keys to move around the Text pane.

   ◆ Click a shape, and then type text directly into the shape.

7. When you're done, click outside of the SmartArt graphic.

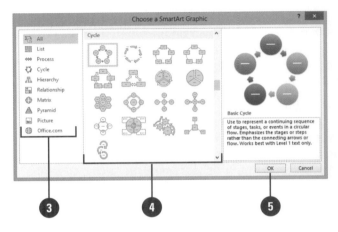

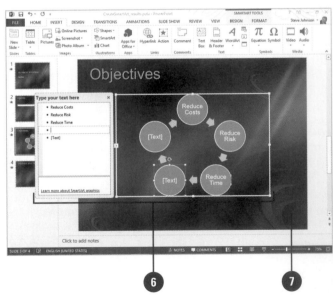

Convert Text to a SmartArt Graphic

1. Select the text box with the text you want to convert to a SmartArt graphic.

2. Click the **Home** tab.

3. Click the **Convert to SmartArt Graphic** button.

    The gallery displays layouts designed for bulleted lists.

4. To view the entire list of layout, click **More SmartArt Graphics**.

5. Point to a layout.

    A live preview of the style appears in the current shape.

6. Click the layout for the SmartArt graphic you want from the gallery to apply it to the selected shape.

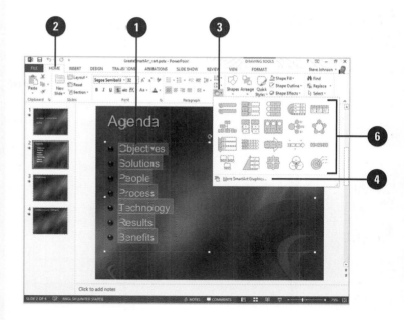

Did You Know?

You cannot drag text into the Text pane. Although you can't drag text into the Text pane, you can copy and paste text.

You can create a blank SmartArt graphic. In the Text pane, press Ctrl+A to select all the placeholder text, and then press Delete.

Shorter amounts of text work best for SmartArt graphics. Most of the layouts for SmartArt graphics work the best with smaller amounts of text. However, if you have larger amounts, layouts in the List category work better than others.

Placeholder text doesn't print or show during a slide show. Placeholder text in the SmartArt graphic doesn't print or show during a slide show.

SmartArt Graphic Purposes

Type	Purpose
List	Show non-sequential information
Process	Show steps in a process or timeline
Cycle	Show a continual process
Hierarchy	Show a decision tree or create an organization chart
Relationship	Illustrate connections
Matrix	Show how parts relate to a whole
Pyramid	Show proportional relationships up and down
Picture	Convert a picture to a SmartArt graphic
Office.com	Show SmartArt graphics from Office.com

Using the Text Pane with SmartArt Graphics

After you create a layout for a SmartArt graphic, a Text pane appears next to your selected SmartArt graphic. The bottom of the Text pane displays a description of the SmartArt graphic. The Text pane and SmartArt graphic contain placeholder text. You can change the placeholder text in the Text pane or directly in the SmartArt graphic. The Text pane works like an outline or a bulleted list and the text corresponds directly with the shape text in the SmartArt graphic. As you add and edit content, the SmartArt graphic automatically updates, adding or removing shapes as needed while maintaining the design. If you see a red "x" in the Text pane, it means that the SmartArt graphic contains a fixed number of shapes, such as Counterbalance Arrows (only two).

Show or Hide the Text Pane

1. Click the SmartArt graphic you want to modify.

2. Click the **Design** tab under SmartArt Tools.

3. Do any of the following:

   ◆ **Show**. Click the **Text Pane** button, or click the control with two arrows along the left side of the SmartArt graphic selection to show the Text pane.

   ◆ **Hide**. Click the **Text Pane** button, click the **Close** button on the Text pane, deselect the SmartArt graphic.

   The Text Pane button toggles to show or hide the Text pane.

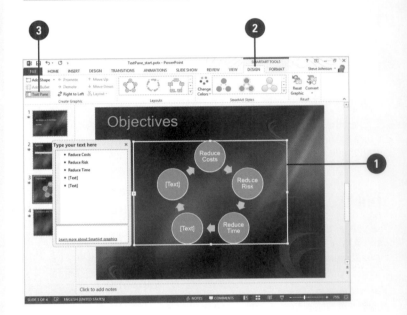

Did You Know?

You can resize the Text pane. To resize the Text pane, point to any edge (pointer changes to double-headed arrow), and then drag to resize it.

You can move the Text pane. To move the Text pane, drag the top of the pane. The Text pane location resets when you exit PowerPoint.

Work with Text in the Text Pane

① Click the SmartArt graphic you want to modify.

② Click the **Design** tab under SmartArt Tools.

③ If necessary, click the **Text Pane** button to show the Text pane.

④ Do any of the following tasks:

◆ **New line**. At the end of a line, press Enter.

◆ **Indent line right**. Press Tab, or click the **Promote** button.

◆ **Indent line left**. Press Shift+Tab, or click the **Demote** button.

◆ **Delete line**. Select the line text, and then press Delete.

Did You Know?

You can format text in the Text pane. When you apply formatting to text in the Text pane, it doesn't display in the Text pane, but it does display in the SmartArt graphic.

You can remove a shape from a SmartArt graphic. Select the SmartArt graphic, click the shape you want to remove, and then press Delete.

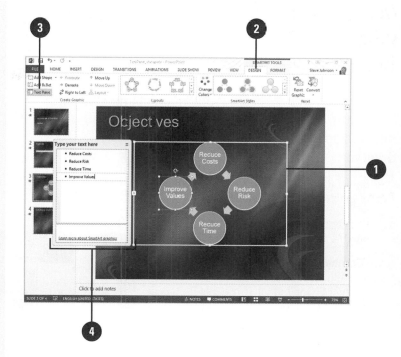

Modifying a SmartArt Graphic

After you create a SmartArt graphic, you can add, remove, change, or rearrange shapes to create a custom look. For shapes within a SmartArt graphic, you can change the shape from the Shape gallery or use familiar commands, such as Bring to Front, Send to Back, Align, Group, and Rotate, to create your own custom SmartArt graphic. If you no longer want a shape you've added, simply select it, and then press Delete to remove it.

Add a Shape to a SmartArt Graphic

1. Select the shape in the SmartArt graphic you want to modify.

2. Click the **Design** tab under SmartArt Tools.

3. Click the **Add Shape** button to insert a shape at the end, or click the **Add Shape** button arrow, and then select the position where you want to insert a shape.

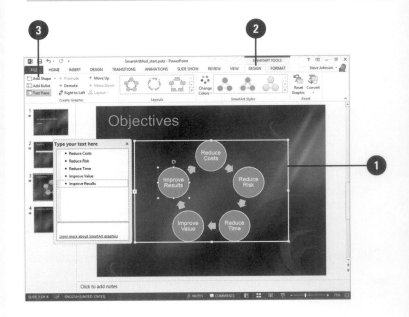

Change Shapes in a SmartArt Graphic

1. Select the shapes in the SmartArt graphic you want to modify.

2. Click the **Format** tab under SmartArt Tools.

3. Click the **Change Shape** button, and then click a shape.

Did You Know?

You can reset a SmartArt graphic back to its original state. Select the SmartArt graphic, click the Design tab under SmartArt Tools, and then click the Reset Graphic button.

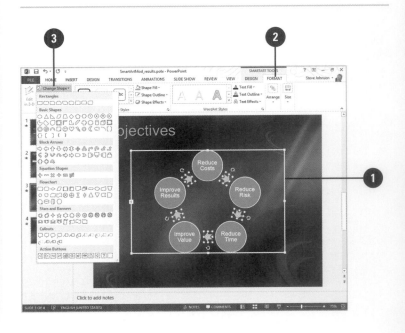

Resizing a SmartArt Graphic

You can change the size of individual shapes within a SmartArt graphic or of an entire SmartArt graphic. If the size of an individual shape within a SmartArt graphic changes, the other shapes in the graphic may also change based on the type of layout. When you resize a shape with text or increase or decrease text size, the text automatically resize to fit the shape depending on the space available in the SmartArt graphic. When you resize an entire SmartArt graphic, shapes within it scale proportionally or adjust to create the best look.

Resize a SmartArt Graphic

1. Select the shapes in the SmartArt graphic or the entire SmartArt graphic you want to modify.

2. Click the **Format** tab under SmartArt Tools.

3. Use one of the following methods:

   ◆ Drag a middle handle to resize the object up, down, left, or right.

   ◆ Drag a corner handle to resize the object proportionally.

   ◆ Click the **Size** button, and then specify the size you want.

   ◆ Click the **Larger** or **Smaller** button to increase or decrease the object in standard increments.

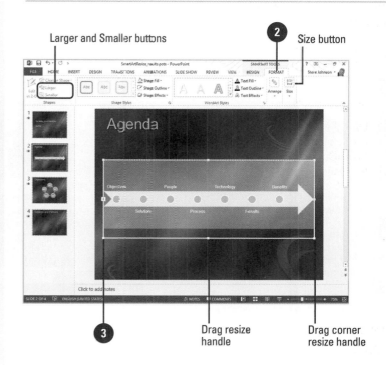

Larger and Smaller buttons

Size button

Drag resize handle

Drag corner resize handle

Did You Know?

You can arrange shapes in a SmartArt graphic. Select the shape in the SmartArt graphic, click the Format tab under SmartArt Tools, click the Arrange button, and then use the arrange button options: Bring To Front, Send To Back, Align, Group, or Rotate.

You can edit a SmartArt graphic shape in 2-D. Select the SmartArt graphic with the 3-D style, click the Format tab under SmartArt Tools, and then click the Edit In 2-D button.

Formatting a SmartArt Graphic

If your current SmartArt graphics don't quite convey the message or look you want, you can use live preview to quickly preview layouts in the Quick Styles and Layout Styles groups and select the one you want. If you only want to change the color, you can choose different color schemes using theme colors by using the Change Color button. If the flow of a SmartArt graphic is not the direction you want, you can change the orientation.

Apply a Quick Style to a SmartArt Graphic

1. Click the SmartArt graphic you want to modify.

2. Click the **Design** tab under SmartArt Tools.

3. Click the scroll up or down arrow, or click the **More** list arrow in the Quick Styles group to see additional styles.

   The gallery displays the current layout with different theme colors.

4. Point to a style.

   A live preview of the style appears in the current shape.

5. Click the layout for the SmartArt graphic you want from the gallery.

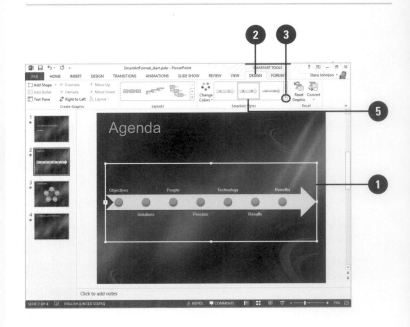

Change a SmartArt Graphic Orientation

1. Click the SmartArt graphic you want to modify.

2. Click the **Design** tab under SmartArt Tools.

3. Click the **Right to Left** button.

   The button toggles, so you can click it again to switch back.

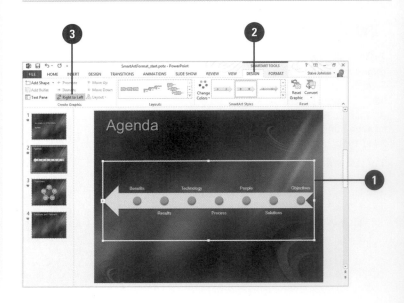

Change a SmartArt Graphic Layout

1. Click the SmartArt graphic you want to modify.

2. Click the **Design** tab under SmartArt Tools.

3. Click the scroll up or down arrow, or click the **More** list arrow in the Layout Styles group to see additional styles.

   The gallery displays layouts designed for bulleted lists.

4. To view the entire list of diagram layouts, click **More Layouts**.

5. Point to a layout.

   A live preview of the style appears in the current shape.

6. Click the layout for the SmartArt graphic you want from the gallery.

7. If you opened the entire list of layouts, click **OK**.

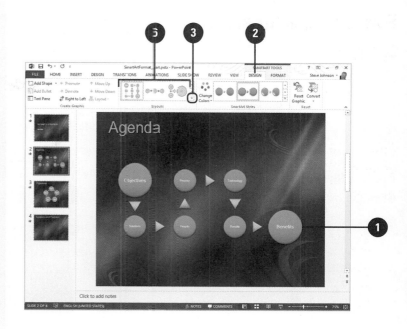

Change a SmartArt Graphic Colors

1. Click the SmartArt graphic you want to modify.

2. Click the **Design** tab under SmartArt Tools.

3. Click the **Change Colors** button.

   The gallery displays the current layout with different theme colors.

4. Point to a style.

   A live preview of the style appears in the current shape.

5. Click the layout for the SmartArt graphic you want from the gallery.

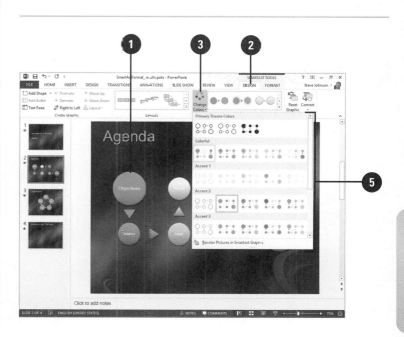

Formatting a Shape in a SmartArt Graphic

In the same way you can apply shape fills, outlines, and effects to a shape, you can also apply them to shapes in a SmartArt graphic. You can modify all or part of the SmartArt graphic by using the Shape Fill, Shape Outline, and Shape Effects buttons. Shape Fill can be set to be a solid, gradient, texture or picture, or set the Shape Outline to be a solid or gradient. In addition, you can change the look of a SmartArt graphic by applying effects, such as glow and soft edges. If a shape in a SmartArt graphic contains text, you can use WordArt style galleries to modify shape text.

Apply a Shape Fill to a SmartArt Graphic

1. Select the shapes in the SmartArt graphic you want to modify.

   TIMESAVER *You can hold Ctrl while you click to select multiple shapes, or press Ctrl+A to select all the shapes.*

2. Click the **Format** tab under SmartArt Tools.

3. Click the **Shape Fill** button.

4. Click a color, **No Fill**, or **Picture** to select an image, or point to **Gradient**, or **Texture**, and then select a style.

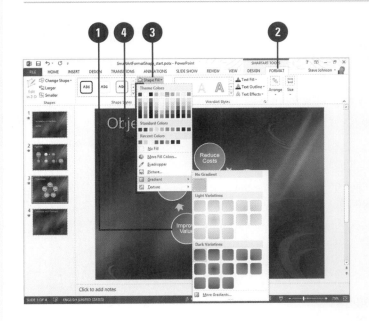

Apply a Shape Outline to a SmartArt Graphic

1. Select the shapes in the SmartArt graphic you want to modify.

2. Click the **Format** tab under SmartArt Tools.

3. Click the **Shape Outline** button.

4. Click a color or **No Outline**, or point to **Weight** or **Dashes**, and then select a style.

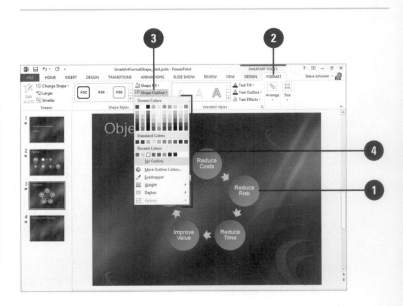

Apply a Shape Effect to a SmartArt Graphic

1. Select the shapes in the SmartArt graphic you want to modify.

2. Click the **Format** tab under SmartArt Tools.

3. Click the **Shape Effects** button, and then point to one of the following:

   - **Preset** to select No 3-D, one of the preset types, or 3-D Options.

   - **Shadow** to select No Shadow, one of the shadow types, or Shadow Options.

   - **Reflection** to select No Reflection, one of the Reflection Variations, or Reflection Options.

   - **Glow** to select No Glow, one of the Glow Variations, More Glow Colors, or Glow Options.

   - **Soft Edges** to select No Soft Edges, a point size to determine the soft edge amount, or Soft Edge Options.

   - **Bevel** to select No Bevel, one of the bevel types, or 3-D Options.

   - **3-D Rotation** to select No Rotation, one of the rotation types, or 3-D Rotation Options.

   When you point to an effect, a live preview of the style appears in the current shape.

4. Click the effect you want from the gallery to apply it to the selected shape.

5. If you selected an option command, the Format pane (**New!**) opens, displaying additional options. When you're done, click the **Close** button in the pane.

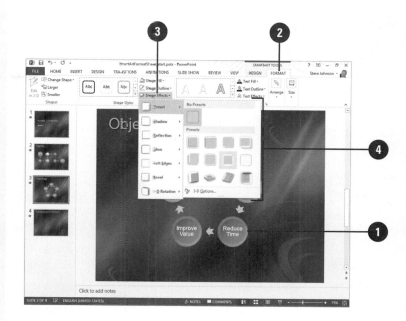

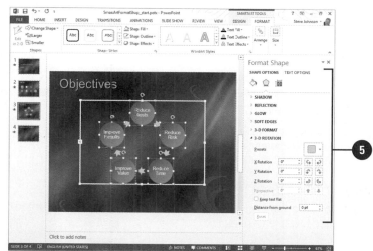

Adding Pictures to a SmartArt Graphic

With SmartArt graphic layouts, you can insert pictures in the SmartArt shapes. In addition to the pictures, you can also add descriptive text using the Text pane or shape itself. The process is very simple. Insert a SmartArt picture layout, insert pictures, and then add descriptive text. If you already have pictures in your presentation, you can convert them to a SmartArt graphic.

Add a SmartArt Graphic to a Picture

1. Use either of the following to add pictures to a SmartArt graphic:

    ◆ **Create New.** Click the **Insert** tab, click the **SmartArt** button, click **Picture**, click a layout, and then click **OK**.

    ◆ **Convert Picture.** Select a picture, click the **Format** tab under Picture Tools, click the **Picture Layout** button, and then select a layout.

2. To add a shape, click the **Design** tab under SmartArt Tools, click the **Add Shape** button arrow, and then select the type of shape you want to add.

3. To add a picture, double-click a graphic placeholder, select a picture file, and then click **Insert**.

4. Label the shapes by doing one of the following:

    ◆ Type text in the [Text] box.

    ◆ Click a shape, and then type text directly into the shape.

Selected picture

Convert picture

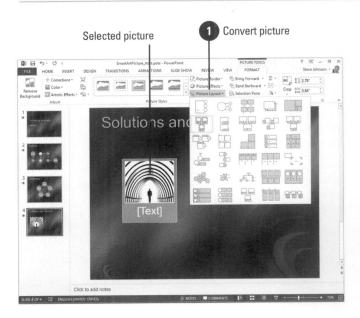

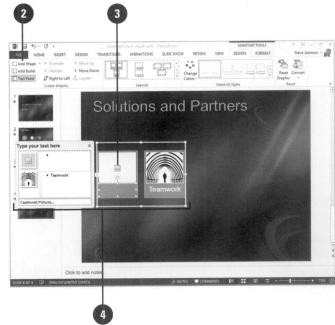

Converting a SmartArt Graphic to Shapes

A SmartArt graphic is an easy and powerful way to visually convey text and graphics. However, it's only supported in PowerPoint 2007-2013. If you wanted to share a PowerPoint 2013 presentation with someone who still uses PowerPoint 2003 or earlier, you would need to convert your SmartArt graphics to shapes, and then save your presentation in the PowerPoint 97-2003 (.ppt) file format. You can quickly convert a SmartArt graphic to a group of individual shapes or text by using the Convert button on the Design tab under SmartArt Tools.

Convert a SmartArt Graphic to Shapes

1. Select the SmartArt graphic you want to modify.

2. Click the **Design** tab under SmartArt Tools.

3. Click the **Convert** button, and then click **Convert to Shapes** or **Convert to Text**.

   The Convert to Shapes command creates a group of individual shapes, while the Convert to Text command creates a text box.

4. To ungroup the converted SmartArt graphic to shapes, click the **Format** tab under Drawing Tools, click the **Group** button, and then click **Ungroup**.

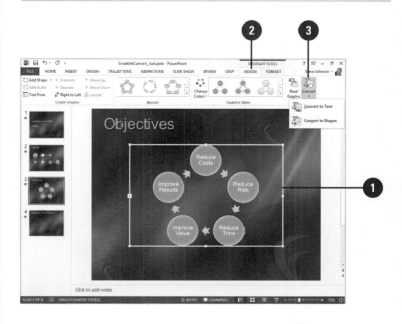

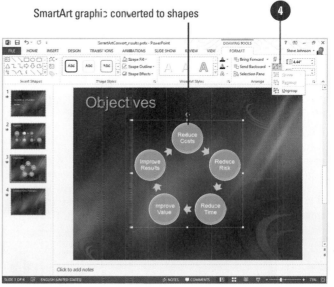

SmartArt graphic converted to shapes

Creating an Organization Chart

An organization chart shows the reporting relationships between individuals in an organization. For example, you can show the relationship between a manager and employees within a company. You can create an organization chart using a SmartArt graphic or using Microsoft Organization Chart. If you're creating a new organization chart, a SmartArt graphic is your best choice. If you need to match an existing organization chart from a previous version of PowerPoint, Microsoft Organization Chart is your best choice. A SmartArt graphic organization chart makes it easy to add shapes using the graphic portion or the Text pane.

Create an Organization Chart Using a SmartArt Graphic

1. Click the **Insert** tab.

2. Click the **SmartArt** button.

3. In the left pane, click **Hierarchy**.

4. In the right pane, click a SmartArt organization chart type.

5. Click **OK**.

   The SmartArt graphic appears with a Text pane to insert text.

6. Label the shapes by doing one of the following:

   ◆ Type text in the [Text] box.

     You can use the arrow keys to move around the Text pane.

   ◆ Click a shape, and then type text directly into the shape.

7. To add shapes from the Text pane, place the insertion point at the beginning of the text where you want to add a shape, type the text you want, press Enter, and then to indent the new shape, press Tab or to de-indent, press Shift+Tab.

8. When you're done, click outside of the SmartArt graphic.

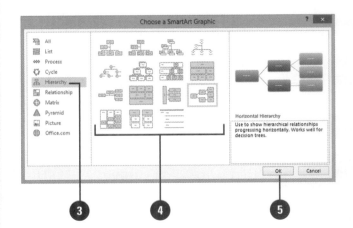

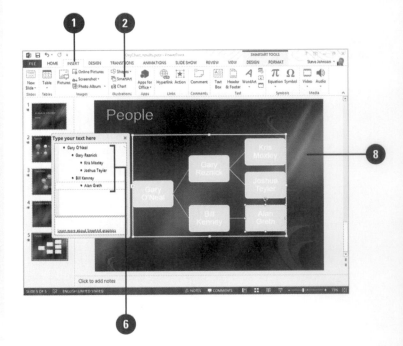

Add a Shape to an Organization Chart

1. Select the shapes in the SmartArt graphic you want to modify.

2. Click the **Design** tab under SmartArt Tools.

3. Click the shape with the layout you want to change.

4. Click the **Add Shape** button arrow, and then select the option you want:

   - **Add Shape After** or **Add Shape Before.** Inserts a shape at the same level.

   - **Add Shape Above** or **Add Shape Below.** Inserts a shape one level above or below.

   - **Add Assistant.** Inserts a shape above, but it's displayed at the same level at the end in the Text pane.

5. When you're done, click outside of the SmartArt graphic.

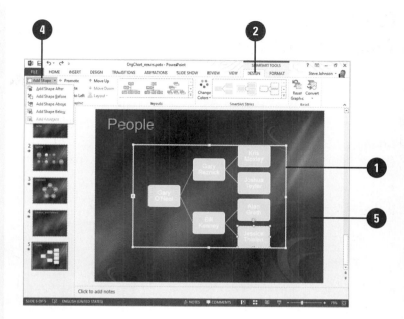

Modifying an Organization Chart

Like any SmartArt graphic, you can add special effects—such as soft edges, glows, or 3-D effects, and animation—to an organization chart. If your organization chart doesn't quite look the way you want, live preview can help you preview layouts in the Quick Styles and Layout Styles groups and select the one you want. If you only want to change the color, you can choose different color schemes using theme colors by using the Change Color button.

Change the Layout or Apply a Quick Style to an Organization Chart

1. Click the SmartArt graphic you want to modify.

2. Click the **Design** tab under SmartArt Tools.

3. Click the scroll up or down arrow, or click the **More** list arrow in the Layouts group or Quick Styles group to see additional styles.

   The gallery displays different layouts or the current layout with different theme colors.

4. Point to a style.

   A live preview of the style appears in the current shape.

5. Click the layout or style for the SmartArt graphic you want from the gallery.

   ◆ **Change Colors.** Click the **Change Colors** button, and then select a color scheme.

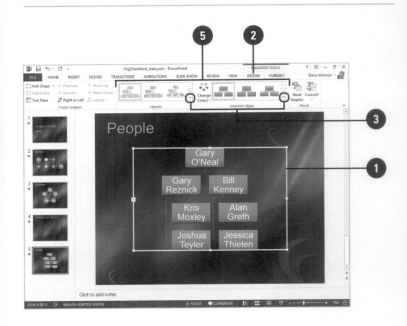

Did You Know?

You can change organization chart lines to dotted lines. Right-click the line you want to modify, click Format Shape, click Line Style, click Dash type, click a style, and then click Close.

Modify an Organization Chart Layout Using a SmartArt Graphic

1. Select the shapes in the SmartArt graphic you want to modify.

2. Click the **Design** tab under SmartArt Tools.

3. Click the shape with the layout you want to change.

4. Click the **Organization Chart Layout** button, and then select the option you want:

   ◆ **Standard.** Traditional top down chart.

   ◆ **Both.** Relational left and right chart.

   ◆ **Left Hanging** or **Right Hanging.** Left or right hanging down chart.

5. When you're done, click outside of the SmartArt graphic.

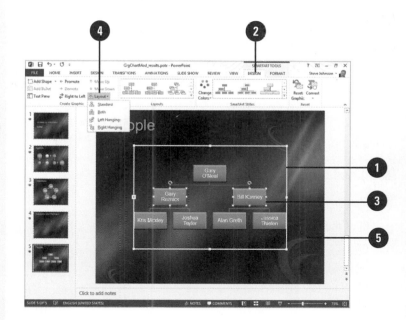

Did You Know?

You can change the colors of an organization chart. Click the SmartArt graphic you want to modify, click the Design tab under SmartArt Tools, click the Change Colors button, and then click the color theme you want.

Inserting a Chart

Instead of adding a table of dry numbers, insert a chart. Charts add visual interest and useful information represented by lines, bars, pie slices, or other markers. PowerPoint uses Microsoft Excel 2013 to embed (**New!**) and display the information in a chart: the **worksheet**, a spreadsheet-like grid of rows and columns that contains your data; and the **chart**, the graphical representation of the data. A worksheet contains cells to hold your data. A **cell** is the intersection of a row and column. A group of data values from a row or column of data makes up a **data series**. Each data series has a unique color or pattern on the chart.

Insert and Create a Chart

1. Click the **Insert** tab.

2. Click the **Chart** button.

   > **TIMESAVER** *In a content placeholder, you can click the Chart icon to start.*

3. Click a category in the left pane.

   - **Recent.** Click to display and use recently used templates for easy access (**New!**).

   - **Templates.** Click to display and use custom chart templates.

4. Click the chart type you want.

5. Click **OK**.

   A Microsoft Excel worksheet opens on top of your PowerPoint presentation (**New!**), displaying a sample chart.

   The chart data appears with a blue fill, while the data series appear with a red and purple fill for easy identification (**New!**).

6. To create a chart, change the sample data in the Excel worksheet. You can enter, paste, or import data.

7. To close the worksheet and view the chart, click the **Close** button on the Excel worksheet and return to PowerPoint.

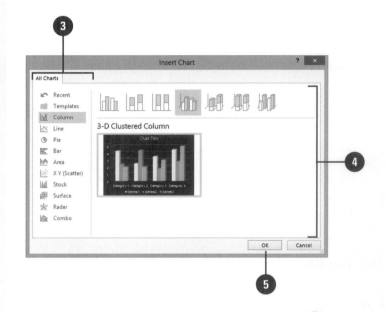

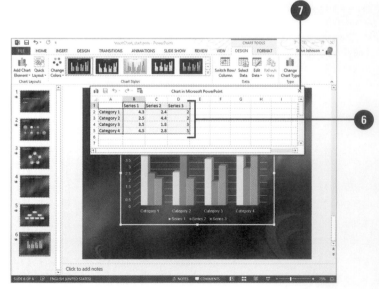

Open and View Chart Data

1. Click the chart you want to modify.

   A chart consists of the following elements.

   ◆ **Data markers**. A graphical representation of a data point in a single cell in the datasheet. Typical data markers include bars, dots, or pie slices. Related data markers constitute a data series.

   ◆ **Legend**. A pattern or color that identifies each data series.

   ◆ **X-axis**. A reference line for the horizontal data values.

   ◆ **Y-axis**. A reference line for the vertical data values.

   ◆ **Tick marks**. Marks that identify data increments.

2. Click the **Design** tab under Chart Tools.

3. Click the **Edit Data** button, and then click **Edit Data (New!)** or **Edit Data in Excel 2013**.

   A Microsoft Excel worksheet opens and tiles next to your PowerPoint presentation.

4. To close the worksheet and view the chart, click the **Close** button on the Excel worksheet and return to PowerPoint.

Did You Know?

You can create a chart from a slide layout. To create a chart on a new slide, click the New Slide button on the Home tab, choose a slide layout with the content or chart option from the gallery, and then click the chart icon in the placeholder to add the chart.

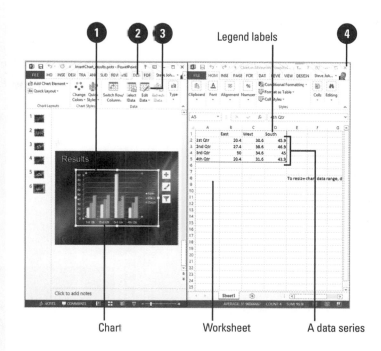

Chart   Worksheet   A data series

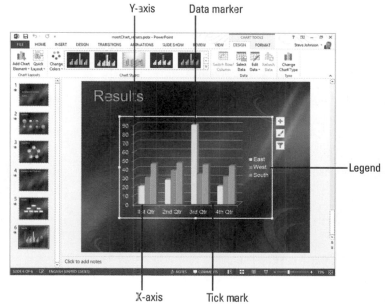

Selecting Chart Data

Use Microsoft Excel worksheet to edit your data. Select the data first in the worksheet. If you click a cell to select it, anything you type replaces the contents of the cell. If you double-click the cell, however, anything you type is inserted at the location of the cursor. You can select one cell at a time, or you can manipulate blocks of adjacent data called **ranges**. For example, the sample data below is a range.

Select Data in the Worksheet

1 Click the chart you want to modify, click the **Edit Data** button on the Design tab under Chart Tools, and then click **Edit Data** (**New!**) or **Edit Data in Excel 2103**.

2 Use one of the following to select a cell, row, column, or datasheet.

◆ To select a cell, click it.

◆ To select an entire row or column, click the row heading or column heading button.

◆ To select a range of cells, drag the pointer over the cells you want to select, or click the upper-left cell of the range, press and hold Shift, and then click the lower-right cell. When you select a range of cells, the active cell is white, and all other selected cells are outlined in black.

3 To close the worksheet and view the chart, click the **Close** button on the Excel worksheet and return to PowerPoint.

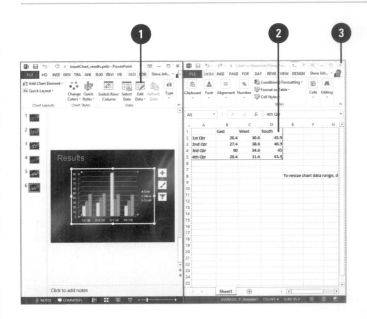

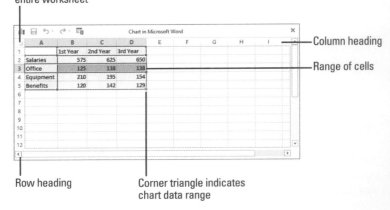

Click to select the entire worksheet

Column heading

Range of cells

Row heading

Corner triangle indicates chart data range

Entering Chart Data

You can enter chart data in the worksheet either by typing it or by inserting it from a different source. The worksheet is designed to make data entry easy, so direct typing is best when you're entering brief, simple data. For more complex or longer data, and when you're concerned about accuracy, insert and link your data to the chart. When you first insert a chart, the worksheet contains sample labels and numbers. If you're entering data by typing, click a cell to make it the active cell, and then select the sample information and replace it with your own.

Enter Data in the Worksheet

1. Click the chart you want to modify, click the **Edit Data** button on the Design tab under Chart Tools, and then click **Edit Data (New!)** or **Edit Data in Excel 2103**.

2. To delete the sample data, click the upper-left heading button to select all the cells, and then press Delete.

3. Click the cell to make it active.

4. Type the data you want to enter in the cell.

5. Press Enter to move down one row or press Tab to move right to the next cell.

6. To resize the table, select the data for the chart, click the **Design** tab in Excel, click the **Resize Table** button, and then click **OK**.

7. To close the worksheet and view the chart, click the **Close** button on the Excel worksheet and return to PowerPoint.

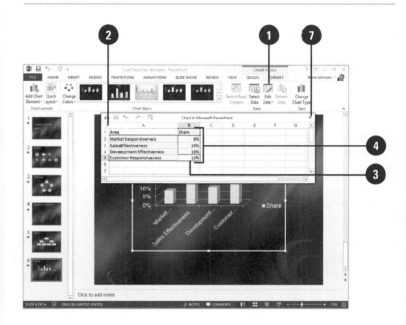

Did You Know?

You can turn automatic completion of cell entries on or off. Excel completes text entries that you start to type. Click the File tab, click Options, click Advanced in the left pane, select or clear Enable AutoComplete For Cell Values check box, and then click OK.

Editing Chart Data

You can edit chart data in an Excel worksheet one cell at a time, or you can manipulate a range of data. If you're not sure what data to change to get the results you want, use the Edit Data Source dialog box to help you. In previous versions, you were limited to 32,000 data points in a data series for 2-D charts. Now you can have as much as your memory to store. You can work with data ranges by series, either Legend or Horizontal. The Legend series is the data range displayed on the axis with the legend, while the Horizontal series is the data range displayed on the other axis. Use the Collapse Dialog button to temporarily minimize the dialog to select the data range you want. After you select your data, click the Expand Dialog button to return back to the dialog box.

Edit Data in the Worksheet

1. Click the chart you want to modify, click the **Edit Data** button on the Design tab under Chart Tools, and then click **Edit Data** (**New!**) or **Edit Data in Excel 2103**.

2. To delete the sample data, click the upper-left heading button to select all the cells, and then press Delete.

3. In the worksheet, use any of the following methods to edit cell contents:

   ◆ To replace the cell contents, click the cell, type the data you want to enter in the cell. It replaces the previous entry.

   ◆ To edit the cell content, double-click the selected cell where you want to edit.

   Press Delete or Backspace to delete one character at a time, and then type the new data.

4. Press Enter to move the insertion point down one row or press Tab to move the insertion point right to the next cell.

5. To close the worksheet and view the chart, click the **Close** button on the Excel worksheet and return to PowerPoint.

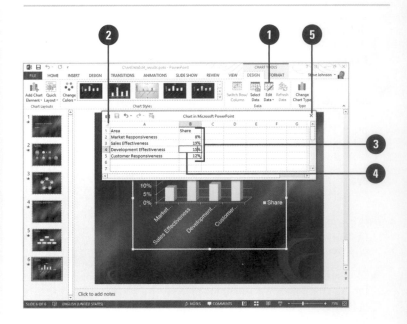

Edit the Data Source

1. Click the chart you want to modify, click the **Select Data** button on the Design tab under Chart Tools.

2. In the Select Data Source dialog box, use any of the following:

   IMPORTANT *Click the* ***Collapse Dialog*** *button to minimize the dialog, so you can select a range in the worksheet. Click the* ***Expand Dialog*** *button to maximize it again.*

   - ◆ **Chart data range.** Displays the data range in the worksheet of the plotted chart.

   - ◆ **Switch Row/Column.** Click to switch plotting the data series in the chart from rows or columns.

   - ◆ **Add.** Click to add a new Legend data series to the chart.

   - ◆ **Edit.** Click to make changes to a Legend or Horizontal series.

   - ◆ **Remove.** Click to remove the selected Legend data series.

   - ◆ **Move Up and Move Down.** Click to move a Legend data series up or down in the list.

   - ◆ **Hidden and Empty Cells.** Click to plot hidden worksheet data in the chart and determine what to do with empty cells.

3. Click **OK**.

4. To close the worksheet and view the chart, click the **Close** button on the Excel worksheet and return to PowerPoint.

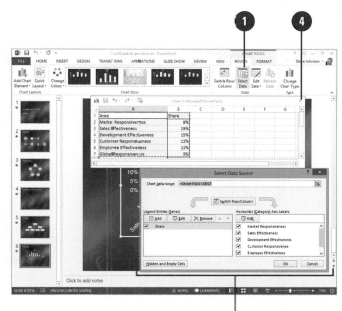

Use buttons to edit chart data

Chart data range

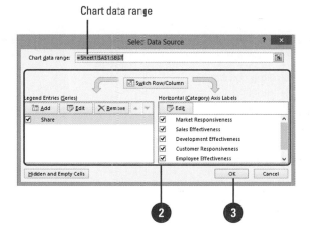

Importing Data

PowerPoint makes it easy to insert data from other sources, such as a plain text file, Microsoft Access database, or a Microsoft Excel worksheet. You have control over how much of the data in a file you want to insert, and, in the case of an imported text file, you can indicate how Excel should arrange your data once it is imported.

Import Data into the Worksheet

1. Click the chart you want to modify, click the **Edit Data** button on the Design tab under Chart Tools, and then click **Edit Data in Excel 2103**.

2. In Excel, click the cell where you want the data to begin. You cannot select cells already used in a PowerPoint chart. If you want, delete them first.

3. Click the **Data** tab.

4. Click the **Get External Data** button arrow, and then click the button with the type of data you want to import.

5. Double-click the file that contains the data you want to import.

6. If you are importing a text file, follow the Text Import Wizard steps, and then click **Finish**.

7. If you are importing Excel data, select the sheet that contains the data you want to import in the Import Data dialog box.

   ◆ Select the option how you want to view this data in your workbook: **Table**, **PivotTable Report**, **PivotChart and PivotTable Report**, or **Only Create Connection**.

   ◆ Select where you want to put the data. Click the **New worksheet** option or click the **Existing worksheet** option, and then specify a cell or range of data.

8. Click **OK**.

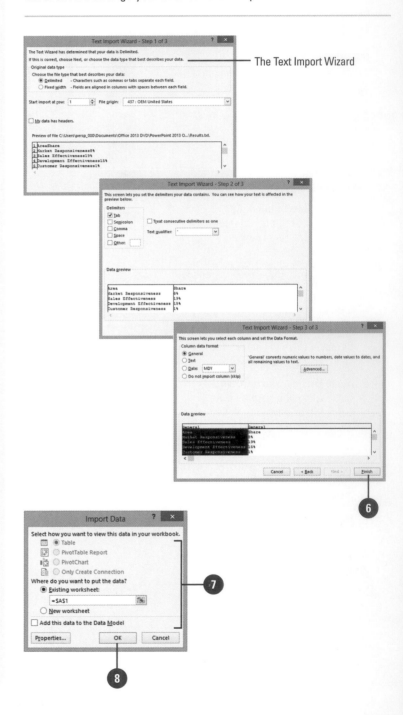

The Text Import Wizard

Paste Data into the Worksheet

1. In the source program, open the file that contains the data you want to paste.

2. Select the data you want to paste.

3. Click the **Home** tab.

4. Click the **Copy** button.

5. Switch to PowerPoint, and then click the Microsoft Excel chart.

6. Click the **Edit Data** button on the Design tab under Chart Tools.

7. If necessary, switch to the datasheet and clear its contents.

8. Paste the data into the datasheet using one of the following methods.

   ◆ To paste the data without linking it, click the **Home** tab, and then click the **Paste** button.

   ◆ To link the data, click the **Home** tab, click the **Paste** button arrow, click **Paste Link**, and then click **OK**.

9. To resize the table, select the data for the chart, click the **Design** tab in Excel, click the **Resize Table** button, and then click **OK**.

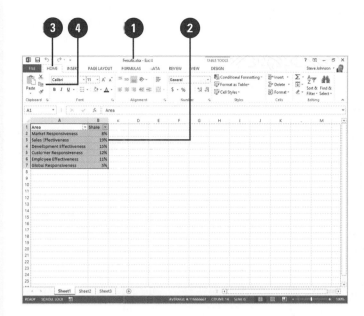

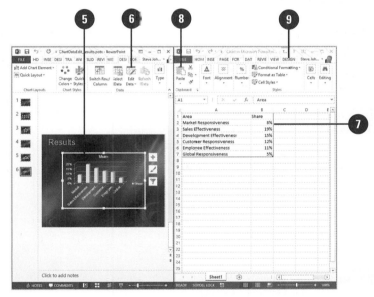

Did You Know?

You can switch the data series around. In PowerPoint, click the chart, click the Design tab under Chart Tools, and then click the Switch Row/Column button.

Office pastes charts from PowerPoint as a picture. If you paste a chart from PowerPoint into a program other than PowerPoint, Word, or Excel, the chart is pasted as a picture. A workaround is to copy the chart from Excel.

Modifying the Data Worksheet

After you enter or edit data in the worksheet, you might need to change the column widths to fit the data. If you see #### in a cell, it means there is not enough room in the column to display the data. You need to increase the column width to display the data. If you need to change one column, you can use the mouse to quickly change the column width. To uniformly change several columns to the same column width, you can use the Column Width command on the Format menu. You may need to reformat the datasheet itself—its size and how it displays the data—to make it easier to read. For example, you can format numbers in currency, accounting, percentage, and scientific formats. You can also change the fonts used in the graph.

Change the Width of a Column

◆ To increase or decrease the width of a column, show the data in the worksheet, position the pointer on the vertical line to the right of the column heading, and then drag the pointer until the column is the correct width.

◆ To adjust a datasheet column to display the widest data entered (also known as Best Fit), show the data in the worksheet, position the pointer on the line to the right of the column heading, and then double-click to adjust the column width.

If a series of number signs (#) appears in a cell, it means the cell is not wide enough to display the entire cell contents. Widen the column to view the data.

Double-click the line to the right of the column heading to resize the column to the widest entry.

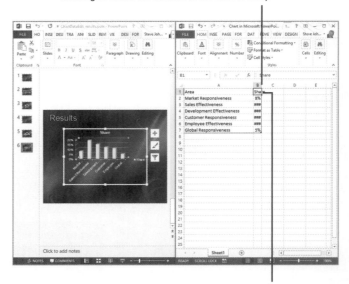

Drag the pointer until the column is the correct width.

Did You Know?

You can specify a precise column width. Click a cell in the column you want to format, click the Home tab, click the Cells button, click the Format button, and then click Width to enter a column width, click Standard Width to change the standard column width, or click AutoFit Selection to change the column to the smallest size possible to fit the data.

Insert Cells, Rows, and Columns

1. In the worksheet, select the cells you want to modify.

2. Click the **Home** tab.

3. Click where you want to insert cells:

   ◆ To insert a column, click the column heading to the right of where you want the new column.

   ◆ To insert a row, click the row heading below where you want the new row.

   ◆ To insert a single cell, click an adjacent cell.

4. Click the **Insert Cells** button arrow, and then click the insert option you want.

Format the Worksheet

1. In the worksheet, select the cells you want to modify.

2. Click the **Home** tab.

3. Use the options on the Ribbon to make the formatting changes you want.

   ◆ To apply a theme, click the **Cell Styles** button, and then click the style you want.

   ◆ To format individual attributes, use the options in the Font and Alignment groups to make the formatting changes you want.

   ◆ To format numbers, use the options in the Number groups to make the formatting changes you want.

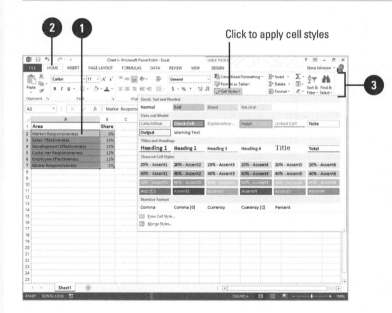

Click to apply cell styles

Selecting a Chart Type, Layout and Style

Your chart is what your audience sees, so make sure to take advantage of PowerPoint's pre-built chart layouts and styles to make the chart appealing and visually informative. Start by choosing the chart type that is suited for presenting your data. There are a wide variety of chart types, available in 2-D and 3-D formats, from which to choose. For each chart type, you can select a predefined chart layout and style to apply the formatting you want. If you want to format your chart beyond the provided formats, you can customize a chart. Save your customized settings so that you can apply that chart formatting to any chart you create. To change a chart design, you can use layout, style, and color options on the Design tab under Chart Tools or use the Chart Styles button (**New!**) (one of three) in the upper-right corner of the selected chart.

Change a Chart Type

1. Select the chart you want to change.

2. Click the **Design** tab under Chart Tools.

3. Click the **Change Chart Type** button.

4. Click the chart type you want.

5. Click **OK**.

Did You Know?

You can reset chart formatting. Click the chart you want to reset, click the Format tab under Chart Tools, and then click Reset To Match Style.

You can delete a chart. Click the chart object, and then press Delete.

You can create macros with chart elements. When you create a macro with charts, it now can include formatting changes to charts and other objects.

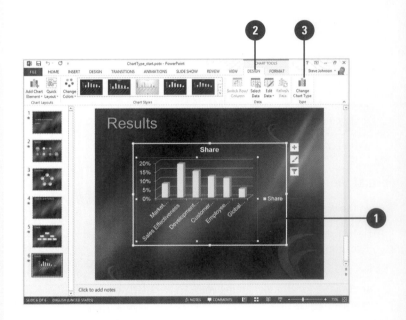

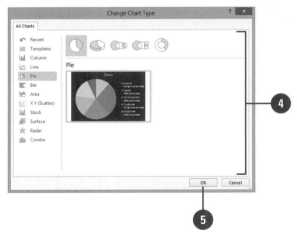

Apply a Chart Layout and Style

① Select the chart you want to change.

② Click the **Design** tab under Chart Tools.

③ To change the chart layout, click the **Quick Layout** button (**New!**), and then click the layout you want.

④ To quickly change the chart style and colors, click the **Chart Styles** button (**New!**) near the chart, click **STYLE** or **COLOR**, and then click a style or color. You can also use options on the Design tab:

◆ **Style.** Click the scroll up or down arrow, or click the **More** list arrow in the Chart Styles group, and then click the chart style you want.

◆ **Color.** Click the **Change Colors** button, and then click a color.

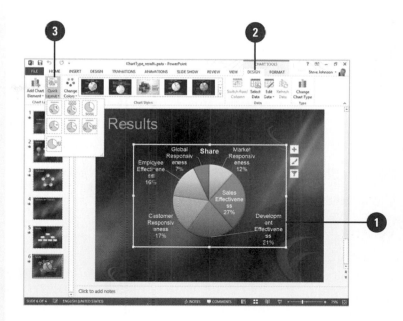

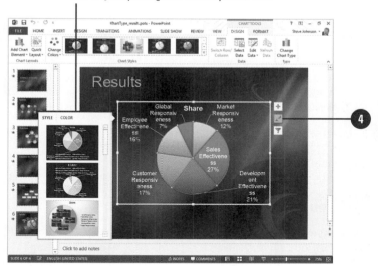

Use to quickly change the chart style and color

Selecting and Changing Chart Elements

Chart objects are the individual elements that make up a chart, such as an axis, the legend, or a data series. The **plot area** is the bordered area where the data are plotted. The **chart area** is the area between the plot area and the chart object selection box. Before you can format a chart object, you need to select it first. You can select a chart object directly on the chart or use the Chart Elements list arrow on the Ribbon. Once you select a chart object, you can use options on the Format tab to modify them. In the same way you can apply shape fills, outlines, and effects to a shape, you can also apply them to shapes in a chart.

Select a Chart Object

1. Select the chart you want to change.

2. Click the **Format** tab under Chart Tools.

3. Click the **Chart Elements** list arrow.

4. Click the chart object you want to select.

   When a chart object is selected, selection handles appear.

   TIMESAVER *To select a chart object, click a chart element directly in the chart; if it's hard to view, increase the zoom size to make elements easier to select.*

5. Use the Home, Design, Layout, or Format tabs to change the selected chart element.

Did You Know?

You can quickly access chart formatting options. Double-click a chart element to open a formatting pane.

You can arrange and size a chart just like other objects. On the Format tab under Chart tools, use Arrange options (Bring Forward, Send Backward, or Align) and Size options (Shape Height and Width).

Selected chart element

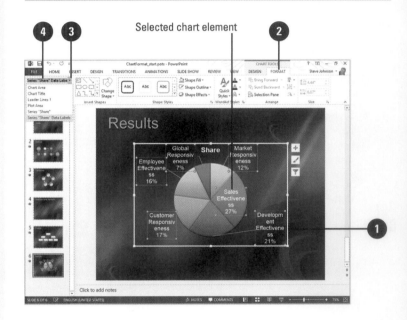

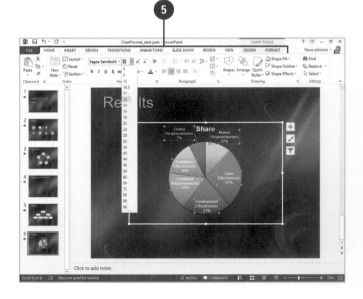

Change a Chart Object Option

1. Select the chart or a chart element you want to change.

   When a chart object is selected, selection handles appear.

2. Click the **Format** tab under Chart Tools.

3. Click the **Format Selection** button.

   TIMESAVER *Double-click a chart element to open a Format pane.*

4. Select the options you want. The available options change depending on the chart object.

5. Click the **Close** button in the pane.

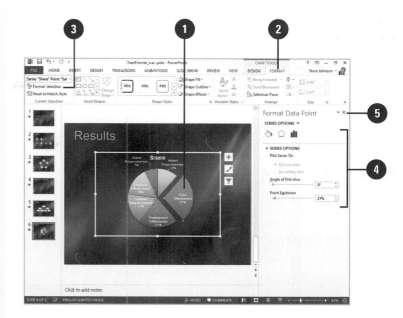

Apply Shape Styles to a Chart Object

1. Select the chart element you want to modify.

2. Click the **Format** tab under Chart Tools.

3. Click the **Shape Fill**, **Shape Outline**, or **Shape Effects** button, and then click or point to an option.

   ◆ **Fill.** Click a color, No Fill, or Picture to select an image, or point to Gradient, or Texture, and then select a style.

   ◆ **Outline.** Click a color or No Outline, or point to Weight, or Dashes, and then select a style.

   ◆ **Effects.** Point to an effect category (Preset, Shadow, Reflection, Glow, Soft Edges, Bevel, or 3-D Rotations), and then select an option.

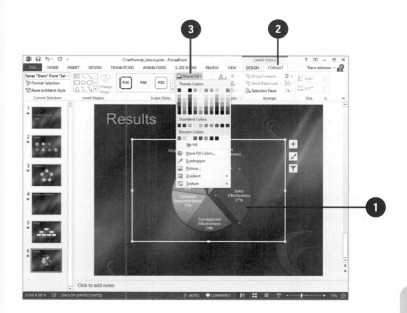

Formatting Chart Elements

Before you can format a chart element, you need to select it first. You can select a chart element directly on the chart or use the Chart Elements list arrow on the Ribbon. After you select a chart element, you can use the Format Selection button to open the Format pane (**New!**), where you can change formatting options, including number, fill, border color and styles, shadow, 3-D format, and alignment. Formatting options vary depending on the selected chart element. In the same way you can apply shape fills, outlines, and effects to a shape, you can also apply them to elements and shapes in a chart.

Format a Chart Object

1. Select the chart element you want to modify.

2. Click the **Format** tab under Chart Tools.

3. Click the **Format Selection** button.

   ◆ You can also double-click a chart element.

4. In the Format pane (**New!**), click a button (Fill & Line, Effects, or Options), expand a category, and then select the options you want.

   Some common formatting option categories include the following:

   ◆ **Number** to change number formats.

   ◆ **Fill** to remove or change the fill color, either solid, gradient, picture, or texture.

   ◆ **Border** to remove or change the border color and styles, either solid or gradient line.

   ◆ **Shadow** to change shadow options, including color, transparency, size, blur, angle, and distance.

   ◆ **3-D Format** to change 3-D format options, including bevel, depth, contour, and surface.

   ◆ **Alignment** to change text alignment, direction, and angle.

   ◆ **Series Options** to change gap depth and width, and shape.

5. Click the **Close** button in the pane.

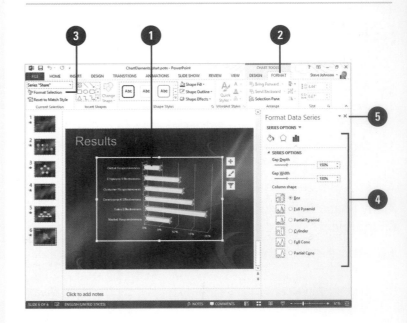

Working with Chart Elements

The layout of a chart typically comes with a chart title, X and Y axes, axis titles, and a legend. However, you can also include other elements, such as data labels, a data table, gridlines. A **legend** is a set of labels that helps the reader connect the colors and patterns in a chart with the data they represent. Legend text is derived from the data series plotted within a chart. If the legend chart location doesn't work with the chart type, you can reposition it. **Data labels** show data values in the chart to make it easier for the reader to see, while a **Data table** shows the data values in a table next to the chart. To change elements, you can use the Add Chart Element button on the Design tab under Chart Tools or use the Chart Elements button (**New!**) (one of three) in the upper-right corner of the selected chart. If you want a customized look, you can double-click an element to set options using the Format pane (**New!**).

Change the Chart Elements

1. Select the chart you want to modify.

2. Click the **Design** tab under Chart Tools.

3. To quickly show or hide chart elements, click the **Chart Elements** button near the chart, and then select or clear the element check box (**New!**), or click an arrow, and then a command.

4. Click the **Add Chart Element** button (**New!**), and then point to one of the following options:

   ◆ **Axes** to display the horizontal and vertical axes.

   ◆ **Axis Titles** to display the horizontal and vertical axis titles.

   ◆ **Chart Tile** to display or position the main chart title. Double-click the text box to modify text.

   ◆ **Data Labels** to show or hide data labels.

   ◆ **Data Table** to show or hide a data table along with the chart.

   ◆ **Gridlines** to display different types of gridlines.

   ◆ **Legend** to display or position the chart legend.

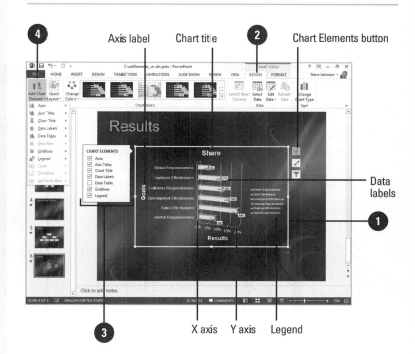

Changing Chart Titles

The layout of a chart typically comes with a chart title, axis titles, and a legend. However, you can also include other elements, such as data labels, and a data table. You can show, hide, or change the positions of these elements to achieve the look you want. The chart title typically appears at the top of the chart. However, you can change the title position to appear as an overlap text object on top of the chart. When you position the chart title as an overlay, the chart is resized to the maximum allowable size. In the same way, you can also reposition horizontal and vertical axis titles to achieve the best fit. If you want a more custom look, you can set individual options using the Format pane (**New!**).

Change Chart Title

1. Select the chart you want to modify.

2. Click the **Design** tab under Chart Tools.

3. Click the **Add Chart Elements** button, point to **Chart Titles**, and then click one of the following:

   ◆ **None** to hide the chart title.

   ◆ **Centered Overlay Title** to insert a title on the chart without resizing it.

   ◆ **Above Chart** to position the chart title at the top of the chart and resize it.

   ◆ **More Title Options** to set custom chart title options.

4. Double-click the text box to place the insertion point, and then modify the text.

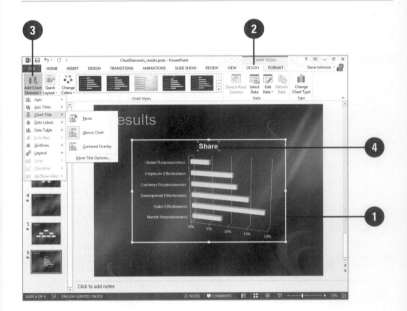

Did You Know?

You can insert a picture into a chart. Select the chart, click the Format tab under Chart Tools, click the Shape Fill button, click Picture, find and select a picture, and then click Insert.

You can insert a text box or shape into a chart. Select the chart, click the Format tab under Chart Tools, click the Text Box button or a shape button, draw an element. For text, type text.

Changing Chart Labels

A legend is a set of text labels that helps the reader connect the colors and patterns in a chart with the data they represent. Legend text is derived from the data series plotted within a chart. You can rename an item within a legend by changing the text in the data series. If the legend chart location doesn't work with the chart type, you can reposition the legend at the right, left, top or bottom of the chart or overlay the legend on top of the chart on the right or left side. Data labels show data values in the chart to make it easier for the reader to see, while a Data table shows the data values in an associated table next to the chart. You can have data labels appears as callouts (**New!**) or just about any shape (**New!**), and even add leader lines (**New!**) to them. You can use the Format tab under Chart Tools to change and format data labels. If you want a customized look, you can set individual options using the Format pane (**New!**). In addition, you can change the label display for axes and show or hide major or minor gridlines.

Change the Chart Legend, Data Labels, and Axis Titles

1. Select the chart you want to modify.

2. Click the **Design** tab under Chart Tools.

3. Click the **Add Chart Elements** button, point to one of the following, and then click an available option.

   - **Axes.** Click to show, hide, or position axis labels or tick marks.

   - **Axis Titles.** Click to add or remove an axis title on the chart.

   - **Chart Title.** Click to add, remove, or position a chart title.

   - **Data Labels.** Click to show or hide data labels on the chart for each data series (**New!**).

   - **Data Table.** Click to show or hide a table next to the chart with the chart data.

   - **Gridlines.** Click to show or hide major or minor gridlines.

   - **Legend.** Click to select a legend position on the chart.

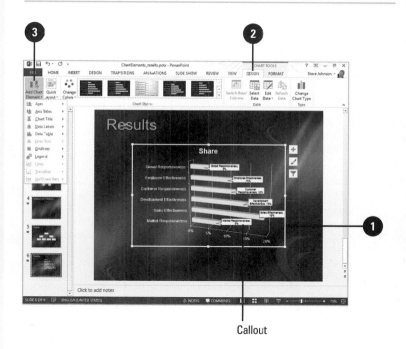

Callout

Changing Line and Bar Charts

If you're using a line or bar chart, you can add trendlines, series lines, drop lines, high-low lines, up/down bars, or error bars with different options to make the chart easier to read. **Trendlines** are graphical representations of trends in data that you can use to analyze problems of prediction. For example, you can add a trendline to forecast a trend toward rising revenue. **Series lines** connect data series in 2-D stacked bar and column charts. **Drop lines** extend a data point to a category in a line or area chart, which makes it easy to see where data markers begin and end. **High-low lines** display the highest to the lowest value in each category in 2-D charts. Stock charts are examples of high-low lines and up/down bars. **Error bars** show potential error amounts graphically relative to each data marker in a data series. Error bars are usually used in statistical or scientific data. To format these charts, you can use the Add Chart Element button (**New!**) on the Design tab under Chart Tools.

Format Line and Bar Charts

1. Select the line or bar chart you want to modify.

2. Click the **Design** tab under Chart Tools.

3. Click the **Add Chart Element** button (**New!**), and then point to one of the following options:

   ◆ **Trendline** to remove or add different types of trendlines: Linear, Exponential, Linear Forecast, and Two Period Moving Average.

   ◆ **Lines** to hide Drop Lines, High-Low Lines or Series Lines, or show series lines on a 2-D stacked Bar/Column Pie or Pie or Bar of Pie chart.

   ◆ **Up/Down Bars** to hide Up/Down Bars, or show Up/Down Bars on a line chart.

   ◆ **Error Bars** to hide error bars or show error bars with using Standard Error, Percentage, or Standard Deviation.

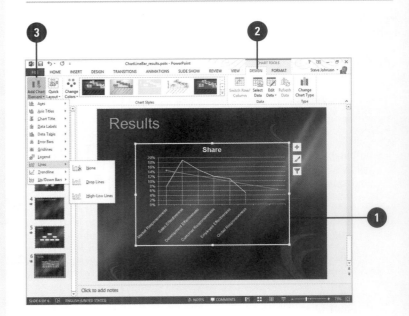

Filtering Chart Data

Instead of using the Select Data Source dialog box to make changes to the data series in a chart, you can quickly filter chart data and category names with the Chart Filters button. With the Chart Filters button (**New!**) (one of three) in the upper-right corner of the selected chart, you can specify what data points and label names you want to appear on the chart. The Chart Filters menu allows you to quickly preview filter changes to data series and categories, apply filter changes, change the data series range, and open the Select Data Source dialog box to make additional data changes.

Filter the Chart Data and Category Names

1 Select the chart you want to modify.

2 Click the **Design** tab under Chart Tools.

3 Click the **Chart Filter** button (**New!**).

4 Click the **Values** tab.

5 To preview a chart filter, point to a data series or category on the menu.

6 To filter on or off chart data series or categories, select or clear the element check box.

7 To edit or change the chart data, click the **Select Data** link to open the Select Data Source dialog box to further customize the data.

8 To show or hide data series or category label names, click the **Names** tab, and then select an option on the menu.

9 To apply the change, click the **Apply** button (**New!**) on the menu.

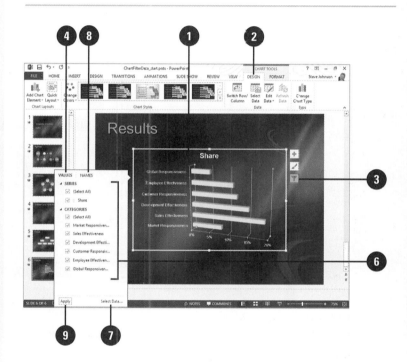

Saving a Chart Template

A chart template file (.crtx) saves all the customization you made to a chart for use in other presentations. You can save any chart in a presentation as a chart template file and use it to form the basis of your next presentation chart, which is useful for standard company financial reporting. Although you can store your template anywhere you want, you may find it handy to store it in the Templates/Charts folder that Microsoft Office uses to store its templates. If you store your design templates in the Templates/Charts folder, those templates appear as options when you insert or change a chart type using My Templates. When you create a new chart or want to change the chart type of an existing chart, you can apply a chart template instead of re-creating it.

Create a Custom Chart Template

1 Click the chart you want to save as a template.

2 Right-click the chart, and then click **Save As Template**.

◆ The Save As Template button on the Design tab under Chart Tools is no longer available in PowerPoint 2013 (**New!**).

3 Make sure the Charts folder appears in the Save in box.

Microsoft Office templates are typically stored in the following location:

Windows 8 or 7. C:/Users/*your name*/AppData/Roaming/Microsoft/Templates/Charts

4 Type a name for the chart template.

5 Click **Save**.

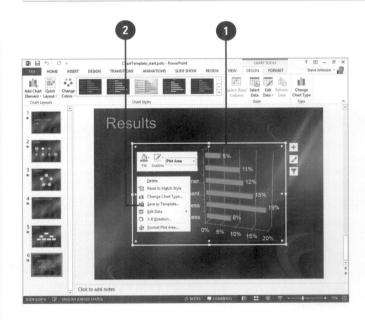

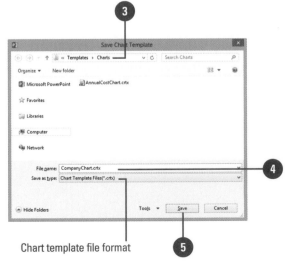

Chart template file format

Apply a Chart Template

1. Use one of the following methods:

   ◆ **New Chart.** Click the **Insert** tab, and then click **Insert Chart**.

   ◆ **Change Chart.** Select the chart you want to change, click the **Design** tab under Chart Tools, and then click the **Change Chart Type** button.

2. In the left pane, click **Templates**.

3. Click the custom chart type you want.

4. Click **OK**.

Did You Know?

You can manage chart templates in the Charts folder. In the Chart Type dialog box, you can click the Manage Templates button to open the Charts folder and move, copy, or delete chart templates (.crtx). When you're done, click the Close button to return back to the Chart Type dialog box, and then click Cancel.

You can set a chart as the default. In the Chart Type dialog box, click Templates in the left pane, right-click the chart you want, and then click Set As Default Chart, and then click Cancel.

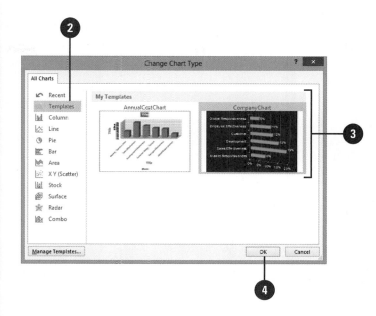

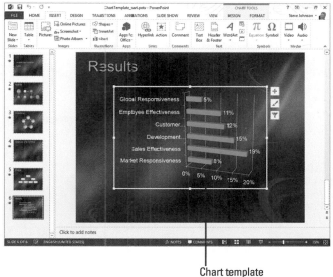

Chart template

Inserting a Table

A **table** neatly organizes information into rows and columns, now up to a maximum of 75x75. The intersection of a column and row is called a **cell**. Enter text into cells just as you would anywhere else in PowerPoint, except that pressing the Tab key moves you from one cell to the next. PowerPoint tables behave much like tables in Word. You can insert tables by specifying a size, or drawing rows and columns to create a custom table. If you like to use Microsoft Excel worksheets, you can also insert and create an Excel table in your presentation.

Insert a Table Quickly

1. In Normal view, display the slide to which you want to add a table.

2. Click the **Insert** tab.

3. Click the **Table** button, and then drag to select the number of rows and columns you want, or click **Insert Table**, enter the number of columns and rows you want, and then click **OK**.

4. Release the mouse button to insert a blank grid in the presentation.

5. When you're done, click outside of the table.

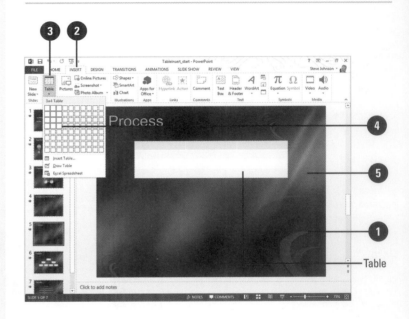

Draw a Table

1. In Normal view, display the slide to which you want to add a table.

2. Click the **Insert** tab.

3. Click the **Table** button, and then click **Draw Table**.

4. Drag the table size you want.

5. Drag horizontal lines to create rows and vertical lines to create columns.

6. When you're done, click outside of the table.

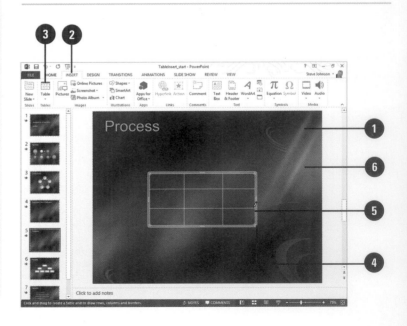

Insert an Excel Table

1. In Normal view, display the slide to which you want to add a table.

2. Click the **Insert** tab.

3. Click the **Table** button, and then click **Insert Excel Spreadsheet**.

   An Excel worksheet appears on your slide.

4. If necessary, drag the lower-right corner sizing handle to enlarge the size of the worksheet.

5. Use the commands on the Ribbon in Excel to modify the worksheet.

6. When you're done, click outside of the table.

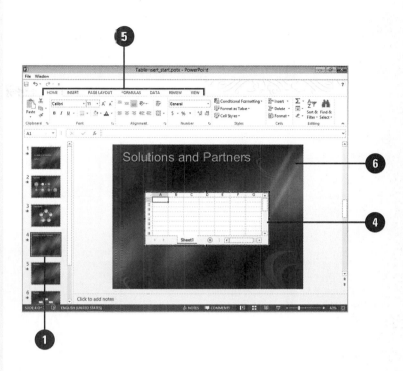

Enter Text and Move Around a Table

The insertion point shows where text you type will appear in a table. Choose one of the following after you type text in a cell.

- Press Enter to start a new paragraph within that cell.

- Press Tab to move the insertion point to the next cell to the right (or to the first cell in the next row).

- Use the arrow keys or click anywhere in the table to move the insertion point to a new location.

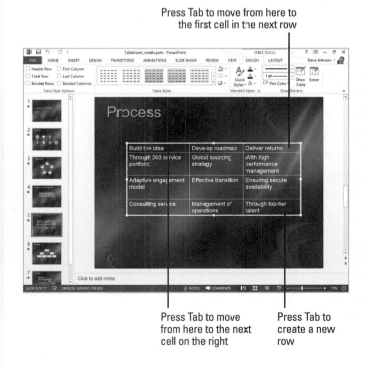

Press Tab to move from here to the first cell in the next row

Press Tab to move from here to the next cell on the right

Press Tab to create a new row

Modifying a Table

After you create a table or begin to enter text in one, you might want to add more rows or columns to accommodate the text you are entering in the table. PowerPoint makes it easy for you to format your table. You can change the alignment of the text in the cells (by default, text is aligned on the left of a cell). You can also modify the appearance and size of the cells and the table.

Insert and Delete Columns and Rows

1. Click in a table cell next to where you want the new column or row to appear.

2. Click the **Layout** tab under Table Tools.

3. To insert columns and rows, click the **Insert Above**, **Insert Below**, **Insert Left**, or **Insert Right** buttons.

4. To delete columns and rows, click the **Delete** button, and then click **Delete Columns** or **Delete Rows**.

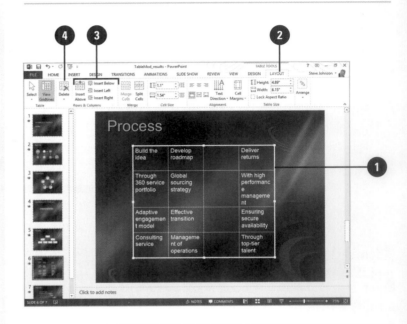

Change Cells Margins and Table Sizes

1. Select the text you want to align in the cells, rows, or columns.

2. Click the **Layout** tab under Table Tools.

3. To resize the table manually, drag a corner or middle resize handle.

   To set a specific size for the table, click the **Table Size** button, and then specify a height and width. To keep the size proportional, select the **Lock Aspect Ratio** check box.

4. To change margins, click the **Cell Margins** button, and then click a cell size margin option: Normal, None, Narrow, Wide, or Custom Margins.

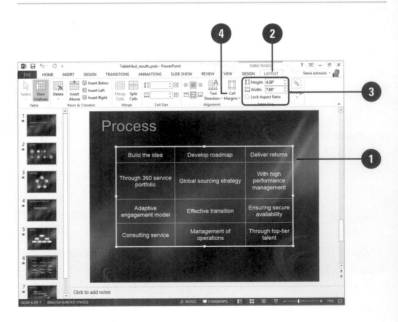

Adjust Row Height and Column Width

1. Move the pointer over the boundary of the row or column you want to adjust until the pointer changes into a resizing pointer.

2. Drag the boundary to adjust the row or column to the size you want.

Did You Know?

You can merge or split cells. Select the cells you want to merge or the cell you want to split, and then click the Merge Cells or Split Cells button in the Merge group on the Layout tab.

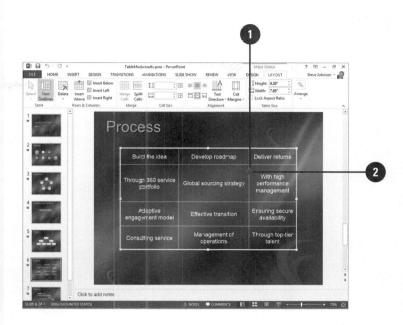

Align Text Within Cells, Rows, and Columns

1. Select the text you want to align in the cells, rows, or columns.

2. Click the **Layout** tab under Table Tools.

3. To align text in a cell, row or column, click one of the alignment buttons in the Alignment group: **Align Left**, **Center**, **Align Right**, **Align Top**, **Center Vertically**, or **Align Bottom**.

4. To evenly distribute the height and width of the selected row and columns, select the row or column, and then click **Distribute Rows** or **Distribute Columns**.

5. To change the direction of text in a cell, select a cell, row or column, click the **Text Direction** button, and then select an option.

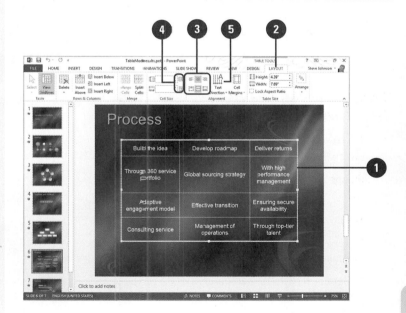

Formatting a Table

When you create a table, you typically include a header row or first column to create horizontal or vertical headings for your table information. You can use Quick Style options, such as a header or total row, first or last column, or banded rows and columns, to show or hide a special row and column formatting. The Total Row option displays a row at the end of the table for column totals. The Banded Row or Banded Column option formats even rows or columns differently from odd rows or columns to make a table easier to view. You can also insert a picture (from a file or online (**New!**)) into a table to create a more polished look.

Format Table Columns

1. Click the table you want to change.

2. Click the **Design** tab under Table Tools.

3. Select any of the following row and column check box options:

   ◆ **First Column** to format the first column of the table as special.

   ◆ **Last Column** to format the last column of the table as special.

   ◆ **Banded Column** to format even columns differently than odd columns.

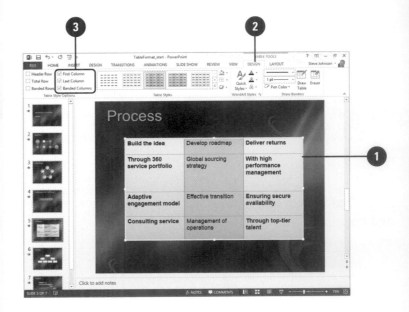

Format Table Rows

1. Click the table you want to change.

2. Click the **Design** tab under Table Tools.

3. Select any of the following row and column check box options:

   ◆ **Header Row** to format the top row of the table as special.

   ◆ **Total Row** to format the bottom row of the table for column totals.

   ◆ **Banded Rows** to format even rows differently than odd rows.

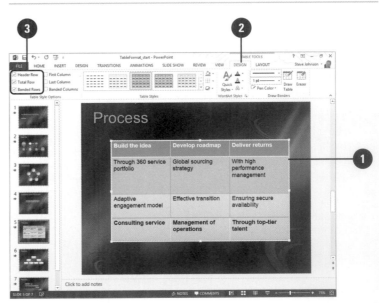

Add Pictures to a Table

1. Select the cells where you want to insert a picture, and then right-click one of the selected cells.

2. Click **Format Shape**.

3. In the Format pane (**New!**), click **Fill & Line** button under Shape Options, and then expand the **Fill** category.

4. Click the **Picture or texture fill** option.

5. Click **File** or **Online** (**New!**).

6. Locate and select the file you want to insert, and then click **Insert**.

7. Select or clear the **Tile picture as texture** check box.

8. Click the **Close** button in the pane.

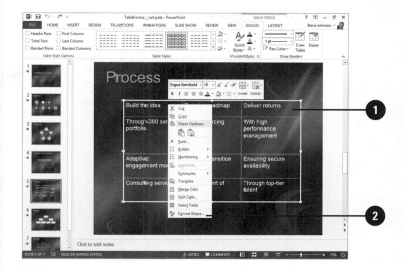

Did You Know?

You can add or remove lines from a table. Select the table you want to change, and then click the Design tab under Table Tools. In the Draw Borders group, select a pen style, weight, and color. Click the Draw Table button, and then drag the pencil pointer from one boundary to another to add cells. Click the Eraser button, and then click on a border to erase a cell. Press Esc when you're done.

You can show or hide gridlines in a table. Select the table you want to change, click the Layout tab under Table Tools, and then click View Gridlines to toggle it on and off.

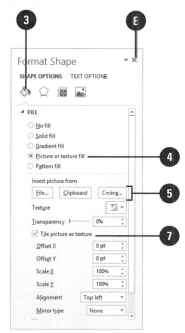

Adding a Quick Style to a Table

Instead of changing individual attributes of a table, such as shape, border, and effects, you can quickly add them all at once with the Table Quick Style gallery. The Table Quick Style gallery provides a variety of different formatting combinations. To quickly see if you like a Table Quick Style, point to a thumbnail in the gallery to display a live preview of it in the selected shape. If you like it, you can apply it. In addition to applying one of the preformatted tables from the Table Quick Style gallery, you can also create your own style by shaping your text into a variety of shapes, curves, styles, and color patterns.

Add a Quick Style to a Table

1. Click the table you want to change, or select the cells you want to modify.

2. Click the **Design** tab under Table Tools.

3. Click the scroll up or down arrow, or click the **More** list arrow in the Table Styles group to see additional styles.

   The current style appears highlighted in the gallery.

   TIMESAVER *Click the gallery title bar arrow to narrow down the list of styles: All, Document Matching, Light, Medium, or Dark.*

4. Point to a style.

   A live preview of the style appears in the current shape.

5. Click the style you want from the gallery to apply it to the selected table.

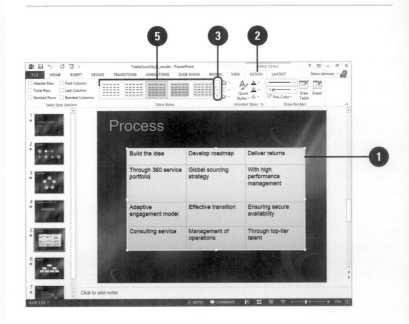

Did You Know?

You can clear table formatting. Select the table you want to change, click the Design tab under Table Tools, click the More list arrow in the Table Styles group, and then click Clear Table.

Apply a Fill to a Table

1. Click the table you want to change, or select the cells you want to modify.

2. Click the **Design** tab under Table Tools.

3. Click the **Shading** button, and then click or point to one of the following:

   ◆ **Color** to select a theme or standard color.

   ◆ **Picture** to select a picture file.

   ◆ **Gradient** to select No Gradient, one of the shadow types, or More Gradients.

   ◆ **Texture** to select one of the texture types, or More Textures.

   ◆ **Table Background** to select a theme or standard color.

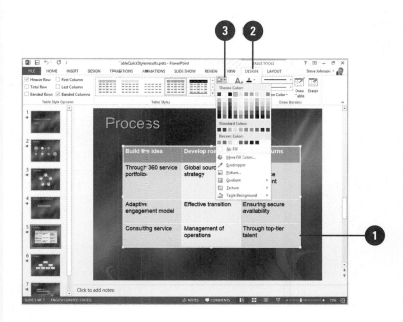

Apply an Outline to a Table

1. Click the table you want to change, or select the cells you want to modify.

2. Click the **Design** tab under Table Tools.

3. Click the **Border** button.

4. Click a border option, such as No Border, All Borders, Outside Borders, Inside Horizontal Border, Inside Vertical Border, Diagonal Down Border, or Diagonal Up Border.

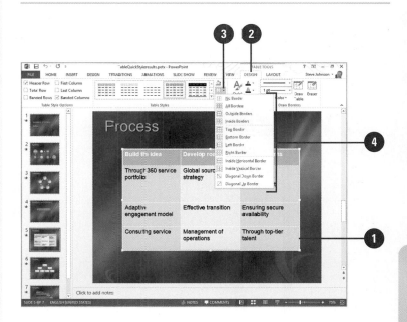

Applying Effects to a Table

You can change the look of a table by applying effects, such as shadows, reflections, glow, soft edges, 3-D rotations, and transformations. Apply effects to a table by using the Table Effects gallery for quick results. From the Table Effects gallery you can apply a built-in combination of 3-D effects or individual effects to a table. To quickly see if you like the effect, point to a thumbnail in the Table Effects gallery to display a live preview of it. If you like it, you can apply it. If you no longer want to apply the effect, you can remove it. Simply, select the table, point to the effect type on the Table Effects gallery, and then select the No effect type option.

Apply an Effect to a Text

1. Click the table you want to change.

2. Click the **Design** tab under Table Tools.

3. Click the **Tables Effects** button, and then point to one of the following:

   ◆ **Cell Bevel** to select No Bevel or one of the bevel variations.

   ◆ **Shadow** to select No Shadow, one of the shadow types (Outer or Inner), or Shadows Options.

   ◆ **Reflection** to select No Reflection, one of the Reflection Variations, or Reflection Options.

   When you point to an effect, a live preview of the style appears in the current shape.

4. Click the effect you want from the gallery to apply it to the selected shape.

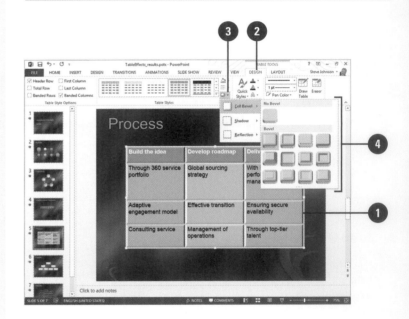

Sharing Information Among Documents

Object linking and embedding (OLE) is a familiar innovation in personal computing. OLE lets you insert an object created in one program into a document created in another program. Terms that you'll find useful in understanding how you can share objects among documents include:

Embedding and Linking

Term	Definition
Source program	The program that created the original object
Source file object	The file that contains the original
Destination program	The program that created the document into which you are inserting the object
Destination file	The file into which you are inserting the object

For example, if you place an Excel chart in your PowerPoint presentation, Excel is the source program and PowerPoint is the destination program. The chart is the source file; the presentation is the destination file. There are three ways to share information in Windows programs: pasting, embedding, and linking.

Pasting

You can cut or copy an object from one document and then paste it into another using the Cut, Copy, and Paste commands on the source and destination program ribbons.

Embedding

When you **embed** an object, you place a copy of the object in the destination file, and when you activate the object, the tools from which it was created (the **source program**) become available in your presentation. For example, if you insert and then click an Excel chart in your PowerPoint presentation, the Excel ribbon replaces the PowerPoint ribbon, so you can edit the chart if necessary. With embedding, any changes you make to the chart in the presentation do not affect the original file.

Linking

When you link an object, you insert a representation of the object itself into the **destination file**. The tools of the source program are available, and when you use them to edit the object you've inserted, you are actually editing the source file. Moreover, any changes you make to the source file are reflected in the destination file. You can edit the linked object from either file, although changes are stored in the source file. For example, you might link an Excel chart to a Word document and a PowerPoint slide so you can update the chart from any of the files. If you break the link between a linked object and its source file, the object becomes embedded.

Embedding and Linking an Object

You can embed or link objects in several ways. If you are creating a new object you want to embed or link, use the Insert Object button. If you want to embed an existing file, you can also use Insert Object and specify whether you want to also link the object. If your object is already open in its source program, you can copy the object, and in some cases, paste it onto a slide, automatically embedding it. Finally, you can use the Paste Special command to **paste link** a copied object—pasting and linking it at the same time.

Insert a New Object

1. Click the **Insert** tab, and then click the **Insert Object** button.

2. Click the **Create new** option.

3. Click the type of object you want to insert.

4. Click **OK**.

5. Use the source program tools to edit the object.

6. When you're done, click outside the object.

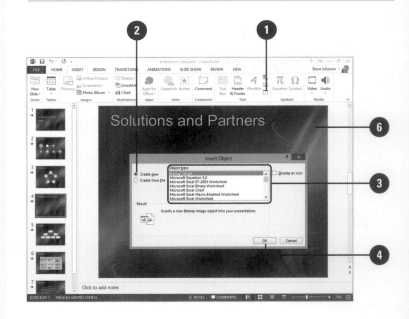

Insert a File

1. Click the **Insert** tab, and then click the **Insert Object** button.

2. Click the **Create from file** option.

3. Click **Browse**.

4. Click the **Look in** list arrow, and then select the file you want to insert, and then click **OK**.

5. To embed the object, clear the **Link** check box, if necessary. To link it, select the **Link** check box.

6. Click **OK**.

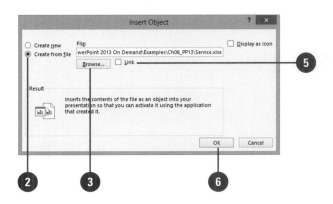

Paste Link an Object

1. In the source program, select the object you want to paste link.

2. Click the **Home** tab.

3. Click the **Cut** or **Copy** button.

4. Switch to your presentation.

5. Click the **Home** tab.

6. Click the **Paste** button arrow, and then click **Paste Special**.

7. Click the **Paste link** option.

8. Click the object type you want.

9. Click **OK**.

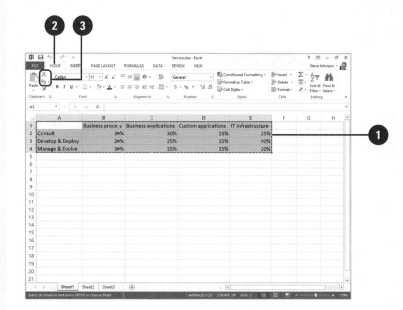

Did You Know?

You can paste text in different formats. The Paste Special command allows you to paste text on the Clipboard to other parts of a presentation or other documents in different formats: HTML Format, Formatted Text (RTF), or Unformatted Text.

You can insert objects as icons. In the Insert Object dialog box, select the Display As Icon check box. If you insert an object as an icon, you can double-click the icon to view the object. This is especially handy for kiosk presentations.

You can work with embedded objects. If you click an embedded object, you simply select it. You can then resize it in PowerPoint. If you double-click an embedded object, you activate it and the source toolbars and menus appear.

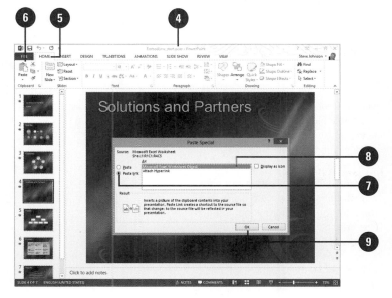

Modifying Links

When you modify a linked object, it is usually updated in the destination document. However, if it doesn't automatically update, you can update the link manually. All Office 2013 programs give you some control over the links you have established. You can convert a linked object to another object type. The convert to object types vary depending on the source type.

Edit a Linked Object

1. Open the presentation that contains the links you want to update.

2. Double-click the object.

   The source program opens.

3. Make changes you want.

4. Click the **File** tab (or **File** menu, depending on the program), and then click **Exit** (or *Exit program name*).

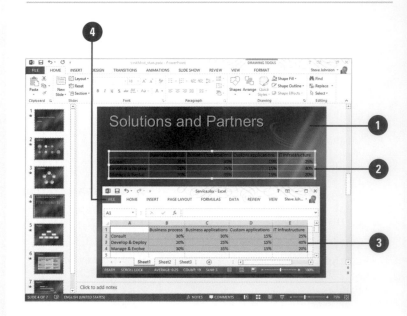

Did You Know?

You can change the source of a linked object. Double-click the linked object to open it, close the original file, open a new one, place the data you want in the file, and then save and exit the source program.

You can update the source of a linked object. Open the source file directly from the source program (not through PowerPoint), make the changes you want, and then save and exit the program. Open PowerPoint with the linked object. Double-click the object, and then exit the program to update the object in PowerPoint.

Convert a Linked Object

1. Right-click the linked object whose file type you want to convert.

2. Point to **Linked *x* Object**, where *x* is Worksheet, Equation, or some file type, depending on the object type.

3. Click **Convert**.

4. Click the new object type you want.

5. Click **OK**.

Did You Know?

You can reconnect a broken link. After you break the connection to a linked object, you must reinsert the object into your presentation to reconnect.

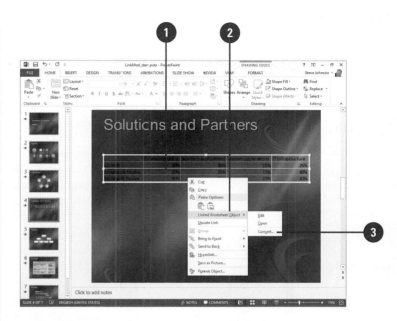

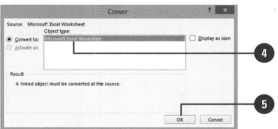

For Your Information

Reducing the Size of Embedded Objects

If you no longer need to edit an embedded object, you can reduce the size of the object in PowerPoint by removing the OLE related data and compressing the picture. OLE objects include a Windows® Metafile (WMF) picture of the image. PowerPoint normally compresses images very efficiently, but it can't compress images in WMFs, so copying and pasting or dragging images into your files can make your files quite large. To remove the OLE data, right-click the embedded object, point to Grouping on the shortcut menu, and then click Ungroup. Next, right-click the image again, point to Grouping on the shortcut menu, and then click Regroup. Ungrouping throws away the OLE data and leaves just the picture in a form that PowerPoint can now compress. Remember, once you ungroup the embedded object, you cannot restore the OLE data without creating a new embedded object.

Inserting a Microsoft Excel Chart

If you need to create chart for backwards compatibility with Power-Point 97-2003, you can embed an Excel object for Excel 97-2003. You can insert a Microsoft Excel chart from any version into PowerPoint by inserting the chart as an embedded object in a slide. An embedded object is an object that maintains a direct connection to its original program, known as the source program. After you insert an embedded object, you can easily edit it by double-clicking it, which opens the program in which it was originally created. Embedding objects increases the file size of a presentation because the embedded object is stored in the presentation. To reduce the file size of the presentation, you can link an object instead of embedding it. A linked object appears in the slide, but it actually contains a "link" back to the original file, known as the source document. When you link an object, the original object is stored in its source document, where it was created. You must have Microsoft Excel installed on your computer to insert an Excel chart or worksheet.

Insert a New Excel Chart

1. Click the **Insert** tab, and then click the **Insert Object** button.

2. Click the **Create new** option.

3. Click **Microsoft Excel Chart**.

4. Click **OK**.

5. Use the commands on the Ribbon to modify the chart.

6. When you're done, click outside the object.

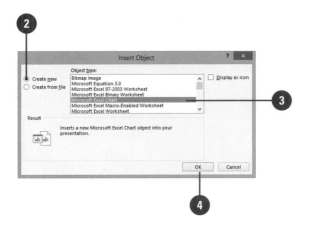

Did You Know?

You can drag a chart from Excel to PowerPoint. Open both Excel and PowerPoint, select the chart in Excel, and then drag it into PowerPoint. If the PowerPoint presentation is not visible, drag the chart to the presentation button on the taskbar to display PowerPoint.

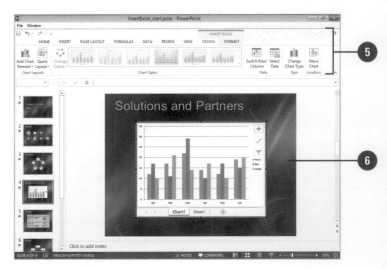

Import a Microsoft Excel Worksheet or Chart

1. Click the **Insert** tab, and then click the **Insert Object** button.

2. Click the **Create from file** option, click the **Browse** button, locate and select the chart you want, and then click **OK**.

3. To link the chart, click the **Link** check box.

4. Click **OK**.

5. Use the commands on the Ribbon to modify the worksheet or chart.

6. When you're done, click outside the worksheet.

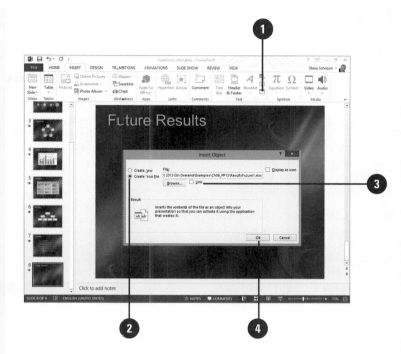

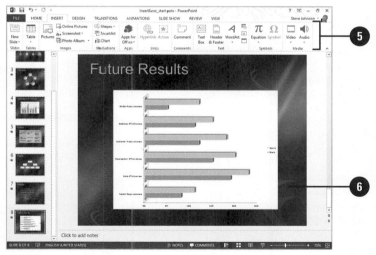

Inserting a Microsoft Word Document

If you need to create a chart for backwards compatibility with PowerPoint 97-2003, you can embed a Word document object for Word 97-2003. You can insert a Microsoft Word table from any version into PowerPoint by inserting the document as an embedded object in a slide. When you insert a new or existing Word document, a Microsoft Word document appears on the PowerPoint slide. Double-click your embedded object to open Word and edit the document. A Ribbon will also open which assists you in creating and formatting the document. You must have Microsoft Word installed on your computer to insert a Word document.

Insert a Word Document

1. Click the **Insert** tab, and then click the **Insert Object** button.

2. Click the **Create new** option, and then click **Microsoft Word 97-2003 Document** or **Microsoft Word Document**, or click the **Create from file** option, click the **Browse** button, and then locate and select the file you want.

3. Click **OK**.

4. Double-click the Word object, if necessary.

   A Microsoft Word document opens in the PowerPoint slide.

5. Use the commands on the Ribbon in Word to modify the document.

6. When you're done, click outside of the object.

> ## See Also
>
> *See "Sharing Information Among Documents" on page 253 for more information about an embedded object.*

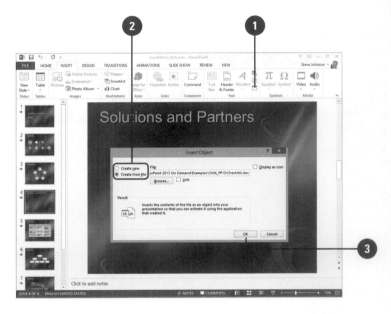

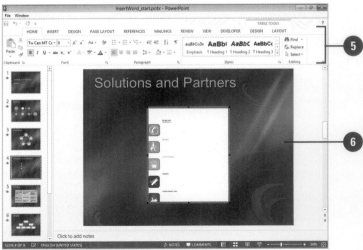

Creating a Web Presentation

Introduction

With Microsoft PowerPoint, you can incorporate action buttons and hyperlinks within your presentation to add an element of connectivity to your work. If you add action buttons to your slides, you can click a button in a slide show to jump instantly to another slide, presentation, or program file. If you add hyperlinks to objects, you can jump to Internet and intranet locations. You can also customize your hyperlink by adding sound to it.

PowerPoint provides you with the tools you need to save your slides for use on the web in a variety of web graphic file formats, such as GIF, JPEG, or PNG. In addition to slides, you can also save a presentation as a picture presentation. Each slide is saved as a picture in the presentation. This is useful for distributing your presentation as a single file to others, yet still protecting your content.

You can no longer save a presentation as a web page in PowerPoint. However, if you have web presentation saved in a previous version of PowerPoint, you can open the HTML (Hypertext Markup Language) file in PowerPoint 2013. After you open a web presentation, you can preview it as it would appear on the web.

If you want more information about PowerPoint and related resources, check out Office.com. Microsoft Office.com offers tips, software updates, tools, and general information to help you work with your PowerPoint presentation as well as other Office documents.

What You'll Do

Add Action Buttons

Add Hyperlinks to Objects

Create Hyperlinks to External Elements

Insert Hyperlinks

Use and Remove Hyperlinks

Save Slides as Web Graphics

Save a Presentation as Web Graphics

Explore XML

Save an XML Presentation

Open a Web Page

Preview a Web Page

Get Documents from the Web

Access Office Information on the Web

Adding Action Buttons

When you create a self-running presentation to show at a kiosk, you might want a user to be able to move easily to specific slides or to a different presentation altogether. To give an audience this capability, insert **action buttons**, such as Back, Forward, Home, Help, or Return, which a user can click to jump to a different slide or presentation. Clicking an action button activates a **hyperlink**, a connection between two locations in the same presentation or in different documents.

Insert an Action Button

1. Click the **Home** or **Insert** tab.

2. Click the **Shapes** button, and then choose the action button (at the bottom) you want, such as Back, Forward, Home, Information, Return, Movie, Document, Sound, or Help.

3. Drag the pointer to insert the action button, and then release the mouse button when the action button is the size you want.

4. Fill in the hyperlink settings you want as needed.

5. Click **OK**.

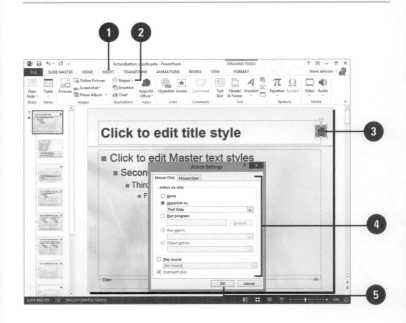

Test an Action Button

1. Click the **Slide Show View** button.

2. Display the slide containing the action button.

3. Click the action button.

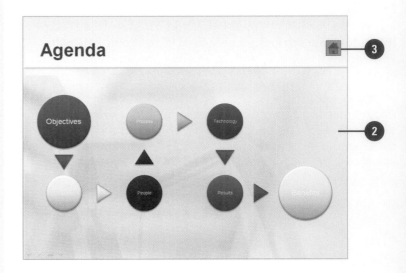

Create an Action Button to Go to a Specific Slide

1. Click the **Home** or **Insert** tab.

2. Click the **Shapes** button, and then click the **Custom** action button (at the bottom far right).

3. Drag the pointer to insert the action button on the slide.

4. Click the **Hyperlink To** option, click the list arrow, and then click **Slide** from the list of hyperlink destinations.

5. Select the slide you want the action button to jump to.

6. Click **OK**.

7. Click **OK**.

8. Select the action button object, and then type the name of the slide the action button points to.

9. Click outside the action button to deselect it.

10. Run the slide show and test the action button.

Did You Know?

You can insert the Return action button to help navigate the slide show. If you want to return to the slide you were previously viewing, regardless of its location in the presentation, insert the Return action button.

You can create a square action button. Press and hold Shift as you drag to create a square action button.

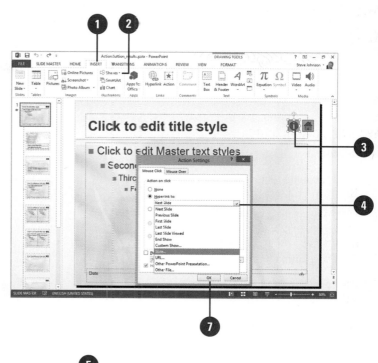

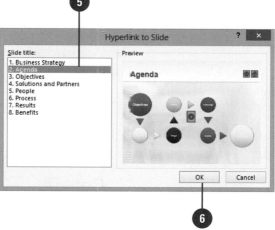

Adding Hyperlinks to Objects

You can turn one of the objects on your slide into an action button so that when you click or move over it, you activate a hyperlink and jump to the new location. You can point hyperlinks to almost any destination, including slides in a presentation and web pages on the web. Use the Action Settings dialog box to add sound to a hyperlink. You can add a default sound such as Chime, Click, or Drum Roll, or select a custom sound from a file.

Add a Hyperlink to a Slide Object

1. Click the object (not within a SmartArt graphic) you want to modify.

2. Click the **Insert** tab.

3. Click the **Action** button.

4. Click the **Mouse Click** or **Mouse Over** tab.

5. Click the **Hyperlink to** option.

6. Click the **Hyperlink to** list arrow.

7. Click a destination for the hyperlink.

8. Click **OK**.

9. Run the slide show and test the hyperlink by pointing to or clicking the object in the slide show.

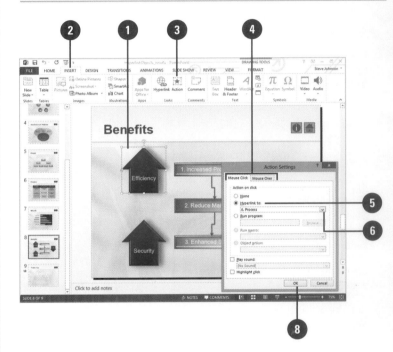

Did You Know?

You can edit a hyperlink quickly. Right-click the object with the hyperlink, and then click Edit Hyperlink.

You can highlight a click or mouse over. When you click or move over a hyperlink, you can highlight the object. In the Action Settings dialog box, select the Highlight Click or Highlight When Mouse Over check box.

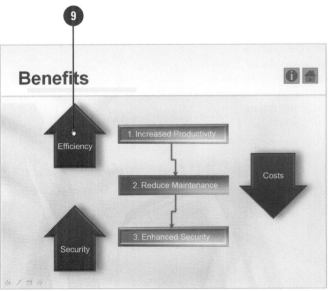

Add a Sound to a Hyperlink

1. Click the object (not within a SmartArt graphic) you want to modify.

2. Click the **Insert** tab.

3. Click the **Action** button.

4. Click the **Mouse Click** or **Mouse Over** tab.

5. Select the **Play sound** check box.

6. Click the **Play Sound** list arrow, and then click the sound you want to play when the object is clicked during the show.

   ◆ **Custom Sound.** Or scroll to the bottom of the Play Sound list, and then click Other Sound, locate and select the sound you want to use, and then click OK.

7. Click **OK**.

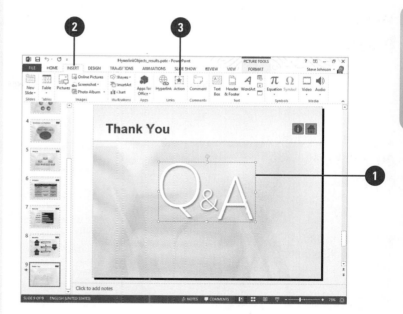

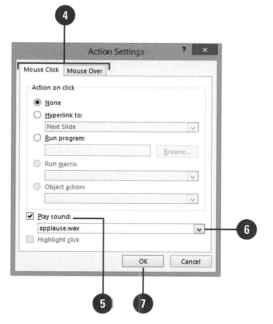

Did You Know?

You can create an action button for a sound. Click the Slide Show menu, point to Action Buttons, click the Sound action button, drag to create the sound action button, click the Play Sound list arrow, select the sound you want, and then click OK.

Creating Hyperlinks to External Elements

You can create hyperlinks in your presentation that access other sources, such as another presentation, a file, a web site, or even a program. This feature is especially useful for kiosk presentations, where you want to make information available to your audience, even if you can't be there to provide it. Depending on your audience, you can set a hyperlink to be activated by clicking the hyperlink with the mouse or by moving the mouse over the hyperlink.

Create a Hyperlink to Another Presentation

1. Click the object (not within a SmartArt graphic) you want to modify.

2. Click the **Insert** tab, and then click the **Action** button.

3. Click the **Hyperlink To** option.

4. Click the list arrow, and then click **Other PowerPoint Presentation** from the list of hyperlinks.

5. Locate and select the presentation you want, and then click **OK**.

6. Select the slide you want to link to.

7. Click **OK**, and then click **OK** again.

Create a Hyperlink to an External File

1. Click the object (not within a SmartArt graphic) you want to modify.

2. Click the **Insert** tab, and then click the **Action** button.

3. Click the **Hyperlink To** option.

4. Click the list arrow, and then click **Other File** in the list of hyperlinks.

5. Locate and select the file on your computer, and then click **OK**.

6. Click **OK**, and then click **OK** again.

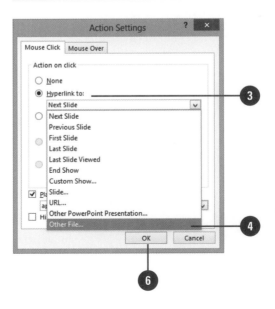

Create a Hyperlink to a Web Page

1 Click the object (not within a SmartArt graphic) you want to modify.

2 Click the **Insert** tab, and then click the **Action** button.

3 Click the **Hyperlink to** option.

4 Click the **Hyperlinks to** list arrow, and then click **URL**.

5 Enter the URL of the web page.

6 Click **OK**.

7 Click **OK** again.

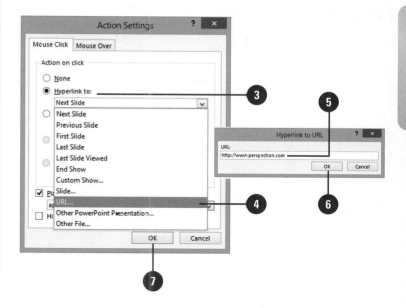

Create a Hyperlink to a Program

1 Click the object (not within a SmartArt graphic) you want to modify.

2 Click the **Insert** tab, and then click the **Action** button.

3 Click the **Run Program** option.

4 Click **Browse**, and then locate and select the program you want.

5 Click **OK**.

6 Click **OK** again.

Did You Know?

You can use Mouse Over instead of Mouse Click. Set a hyperlink to be activated by clicking the hyperlink with the mouse or by moving the mouse over the hyperlink. To set a hyperlink to be activated by moving the mouse over it, click the Mouse Over tab in the Action Settings dialog box.

Inserting Hyperlinks

When you reference information included earlier in a presentation, you had to duplicate material or add a footnote. Now you can create a **hyperlink**—a graphic object or colored, underlined text that you click to move (or **jump**) to a new location (or **destination**). The destination can be in the same presentation, another file on your computer or network, or a web page on your intranet or the Internet. PowerPoint inserts an absolute link—a hyperlink that jumps to a fixed location—to an Internet destination. PowerPoint inserts a relative link—a hyperlink that changes when the hyperlink and destination paths change—between documents. You must move the hyperlink and destination together to keep the link intact.

Insert a Hyperlink Within a Presentation

1. Click where you want to insert the hyperlink, or select the text or object you want to use as the hyperlink.

2. Click the **Insert** tab.

3. Click the **Insert Hyperlink** button.

4. Click **Place In This Document**.

5. Click a destination in the presentation.

   The destination can be a PowerPoint slide, slide title, or custom show.

6. Type the text you want to appear as the hyperlink, if available.

7. Click **ScreenTip**.

8. Type the text you want to appear when someone points to the hyperlink.

9. Click **OK**.

10. Click **OK**.

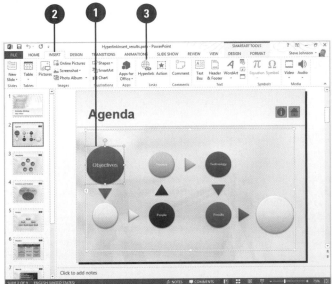

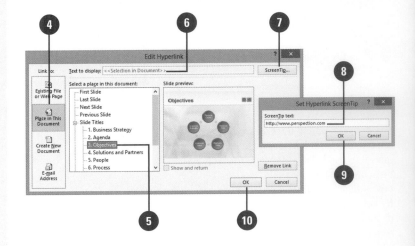

Insert a Hyperlink Between Documents

1 Click where you want to insert the hyperlink, or select the text or object you want to use as the hyperlink.

2 Click the **Insert** tab.

3 Click the **Insert Hyperlink** button.

4 Click **Existing File Or Web Page**.

5 Enter the name and path of the destination file or web page.

◆ Or click the **Bookmark** button; select the bookmark, and then click **OK**.

6 Type the text you want to appear as the hyperlink, if available.

7 Click **ScreenTip**.

8 Type the text you want to appear when someone points to the hyperlink.

9 Click **OK**.

10 Click **OK**.

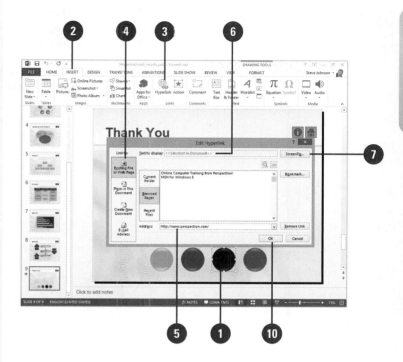

Did You Know?

You can create a hyperlink to send e-mail messages. Click where you want to insert the hyperlink, click the Insert tab, click the Insert Hyperlink button on the Insert tab, click E-Mail Address, enter the recipients e-mail address, enter a subject, enter the hyperlink display text, and then click OK.

For Your Information

Understanding Web Addresses and URLs

Every web page has a **uniform resource locator** (URL), a web address in a form your browser program can decipher. Like postal addresses and e-mail addresses, each URL contains specific parts that identify where a web page is located. For example, the URL for Perspection's web page is http://www.perspection.com where "http://" shows the address is on the web and "www.per-spection.com" shows the computer that stores the web page. As you browse various pages, the URL includes their folders and file names.

Using and Removing Hyperlinks

Hyperlinks connect you to information in other documents. Rather than duplicating the important information stored in other documents, you can create hyperlinks to the relevant material. When you click a hyperlink for the first time (during a session), the color of the hyperlink changes, indicating that you have accessed the hyperlink. If a link becomes outdated or unnecessary, you can easily revise or remove it. PowerPoint repairs broken links. Whenever you save a presentation with hyperlinks, PowerPoint checks the links and repairs any that aren't working. For example, if a file was moved, PowerPoint updates the location.

Use a Hyperlink

① In Slide Show view, position the mouse pointer (which changes to a hand pointer) over any hyperlink.

② Click the hyperlink.

Depending on the type of hyperlink, the screen

◆ Jumps to a new location within the same presentation.

◆ Jumps to a location on an intranet or Internet web site.

◆ Opens a new file and the program in which it was created.

◆ Opens Outlook and displays a new e-mail message.

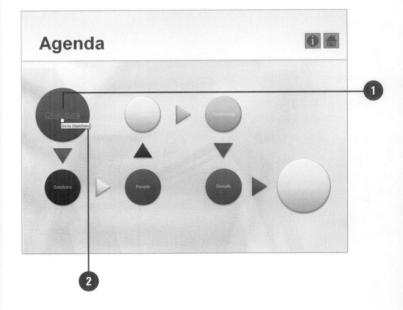

Edit a Hyperlink

1. Right-click the hyperlink you want to edit, and then click **Edit Hyperlink**.

2. If you want, change the display text, if available.

3. If you want, click **ScreenTip**, edit the custom text, and then click **OK**.

4. If necessary, change the destination.

5. Click **OK**.

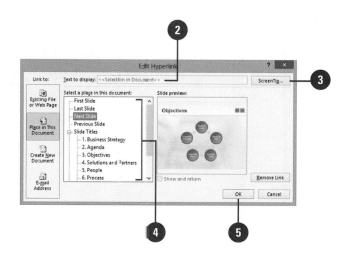

Remove a Hyperlink

1. Right-click the hyperlink you want to remove.

2. Click **Remove Hyperlink**.

   TIMESAVER *Drag the I-beam pointer across the hyperlink to select it, and then press Ctrl+Shift+F9 to delete a hyperlink.*

3. If necessary, delete the text or object.

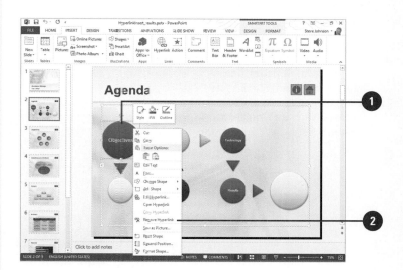

Did You Know?

You can format a hyperlink. You can change the look of a hyperlink just as you do other text—select it and apply attributes. Select the hyperlink, click the Home tab, and then use WordArt styles, and formatting buttons, such as Bold, Italic, Underline, Font, and Font Size. You can also use Shape styles on the Format tab under Drawing Tools.

Saving Slides as Web Graphics

As you develop a web site, you can incorporate slides from any of your PowerPoint presentations. You can save any slide in a presentation in the GIF, JPEG, or PNG web graphic format. **Graphics Interchange Format (GIF)** is a form of compression for line drawings or other artwork. Office converts to GIF such images as logos, graphs, line drawings, and specific colored objects. **Joint Photographic Experts Group (JPEG)** is a high-quality form of compression for continuous tone images, such as photographs. Office converts to JPEG such images as photographs or other images that have many shades of colors. **Portable Network Graphics Format** is a new bit-mapped graphics format similar to GIF.

Save a PowerPoint Slide as a Web Graphic

1. Open the presentation with the slide you want to save as a web graphic, and then display the slide.

2. Click the **File** tab, click **Save As**, click **Computer**, and then click **Browse** or select a recent folder.

4. Click the **Save as type** list arrow, and then click **GIF Graphics Interchange Format**, **JPEG File Interchange Format**, or **PNG Portable Network Graphics Format**.

5. Click the **Save in** list arrow, and then select a location for the file.

6. Type a name for the file.

7. Click **Save**.

8. Click **All Slides** or **Just This One**.

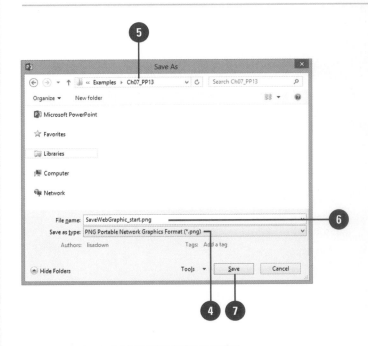

See Also

See "Saving a Presentation with Different Formats" on page 28 and "Saving Slides in Different Formats" on page 307 for information on saving files with different file formats.

Saving a Presentation as Web Graphics

Instead of saving individual slides in a presentation as graphics, you can save each slide in a presentation as a graphic. With the PowerPoint Picture Presentation file with the .pptx file format, you can convert each slide in a presentation to a picture. In other words, everything on a slide, including shapes, text, and images, is converted to a picture. This is useful for distributing your presentations to others with PowerPoint, yet still protecting your content.

Convert Presentation Slides to Web Graphics

1. Open the PowerPoint presentation you want to save.

2. Click the **File** tab, click **Save As**, click **Computer**, and then click **Browse** or select a recent folder.

3. Click the **Save as type** list arrow, and then click **PowerPoint Picture Presentation (*.pptx)**.

   ◆ You can also click the **File** tab, click **Export**, click **Change File Type**, click **PowerPoint Picture Presentation (*.pptx)**, and then click **Save As**.

4. Click the **Save in** list arrow, and then select a location for the file.

5. Type a name for the file.

6. Click **Save**.

7. Click **Cancel** or **Save As**.

   If you select Save As, specify a file name, location, and PowerPoint presentation file type, and then click Save.

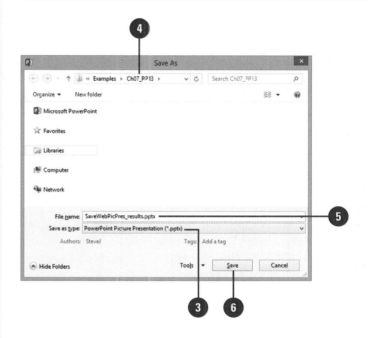

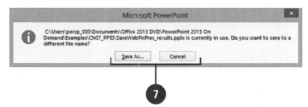

See Also

See "Saving a Presentation with Different Formats" on page 26 and "Saving Slides in Different Formats" on page 303 for information on saving files with different file formats.

Exploring XML

Introduction

XML (Extensible Markup Language) is a platform-independent universal language that enables you to create documents in which data is stored independently of the format so you can use the data more seamlessly in other forms. XML is a markup language just like HTML. You mark up a document to define the structure, meaning, and visual appearance of the information in the document.

When you mark up a document, using XML or HTML, you use codes called **tags** that define the appearance or structure of the document. In HTML, the tags define the appearance and location of your data, while in XML, the tags define the structure and meaning of your data. For a HTML document, the tags determine where titles, text, and information goes in a document. For a XML document, the tags defines the kind of data, which makes it possible to reuse or exchange data. The

You cannot use HMTL in place of XML. However, you can wrap your XML data in HTML tags and display it in a web page. HTML is limited to a predefined set of tags, while XML allows you to create tags that describe your data and its structure. This makes XML an extensible markup language.

In order to share XML data among programs and operating systems, it needs to be **well-formed**, which means it conforms to a standard set of XML rules. In addition to well-formed data, XML also uses schemas and transforms. A **schema** is an XML file (.xsd extension instead of the typical .xml) with a set of rules that defines the elements and content used in an XML document. XML schemas are created by developers who understand XML. The schema is used to validate the data in an XML document and help prevent corrupted data. After you validate an XML data file with a schema, you can apply a **transform** that allows you to reuse the data in different forms, such as a document or worksheet, or exchange the data with a data system, such as a database. The XML data file, schema, and transform make up the components of a XML system.

Microsoft Office XML

XML is supported in Microsoft Office 2013 through PowerPoint, Word, and Excel. Each of these Office programs uses XML as the default file format. XML allows you to work with the Office interface and create XML documents, without ever knowing the XML language. In Word and Excel, you can use the Developer tab to work with XML structure, schema, and documents. In Access and Excel, you can import and export XML data. Office programs can work with schemas, transforms, and data from other suppliers as long as the XML is well-formed.

XML Benefits

The XML format significantly reduces file sizes, provides enhanced file recovery, and allows for increased compatibility, confidentially, sharing, reuse, and transportability. The XML format uses ZIP and other compression methods to reduce the file size by as much as 75%. Since XML separates the data from the structure and meaning, it's easier for Office programs to recover data or remove sensitive information. In fact, you can even open a damaged file in Microsoft Notepad to recover some of the information. The XML format is also royalty free, which makes it more available.

Saving an XML Presentation

When you save a presentation, PowerPoint 2013 saves it by default in a XML file format (.pptx). PowerPoint allows you to create and save documents as XML (Extensible Markup Language), without ever knowing the XML language. The XML format significantly reduces file sizes, provides enhanced file recovery, and allows for increased compatibility, sharing, reuse, and transportability.

Save an XML Presentation

1. Open the PowerPoint presentation you want to save.

2. Click the **File** tab, click **Save As**, click **Computer**, and then click **Browse** or select a recent folder.

3. Click the **Save as type** list arrow, and then click **PowerPoint XML Presentation (*.xml)**.

4. Click the **Save in** list arrow, and then click the drive or folder where you want to save the file.

5. Type a presentation file name.

6. Click **Save**.

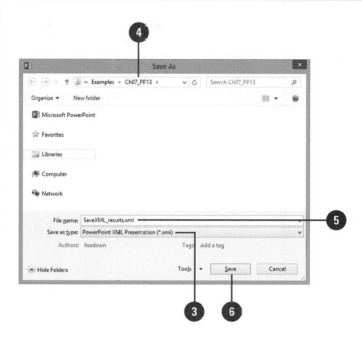

For Your Information

Understanding Extensions: PPTX vs. PPTM

PowerPoint 2013 files with the default "x" at the end of the extension (.pptx) cannot contain Visual Basic for Application (VBA) macros or ActiveX controls, which decreases the security risks associated with files that contain embedded code. PowerPoint 2013 files with an "m" at the end of the extension (.pptm) contain VBA macros and ActiveX controls. The embedded code is even stored in a separate section within the .pptm file to make it easier to isolate if necessary. The two different extensions make it easier for antivirus software to identify potential threats and block documents with unwanted macros or controls.

Opening a Web Page

You can no longer save a presentation as a web page in PowerPoint 2010-2013. However, if you have web presentation saved in a previous version of PowerPoint or created in another program, you can open the HTML (Hypertext Markup Language) file in PowerPoint 2013. This allows you to quickly view the web page without having to switch to another program. You can open web pages in the following file formats: HTM, HTML, MHT, and MHTML   (single file format).

Open a Presentation as a Web Page in PowerPoint

1. Click the **File** tab, click **Open**, click **Computer**, and then click **Browse** or select a recent folder.

2. Click the **Files of type** list arrow, and then click **All Web Pages**.

3. Click the **Look in** list arrow, and then select the folder where the file is located.

4. Click the web presentation file.

5. Click **Open**.

   ◆ To open the web page in your browser, click the **Open** button arrow, and then click **Open in Browser**.

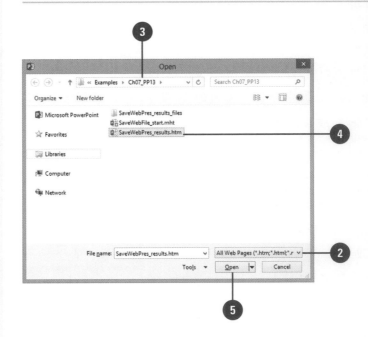

Did You Know?

You can change the appearance of web pages and Help Viewer window. In the Internet Options dialog box for Windows, click Accessibility on the General tab, select the Ignore Colors Specified On Web pages check box, and then click OK. In the Internet Properties dialog box, click Colors to select text and background colors or Fonts to change text style.

Getting Documents from the Web

File Transfer Protocol (FTP) is an inexpensive and efficient way to transfer files between your computer and others on the Internet. You can download or receive, from another computer, any kind of file, including text, graphics, sound, and video files. To download a file, you need an ID and password to identify who you are. Anonymous FTP sites are open to anyone; they usually use *anonymous* as an ID and your *e-mail address* as a password. You can also save the FTP site address to revisit the site later.

Add FTP Locations

1. Click the **File** tab, click **Open**, click **Computer**, and then click **Browse**.

2. Click **Computer** in the left pane.

3. Right-click a blank area, and then click **Add a network location**.

4. Follow the Add Network Location wizard to create a link to an FTP site or other network, and then click **Finish** to complete it.

   ◆ To complete the process, you need the complete address for a FTP site, and a user name and password.

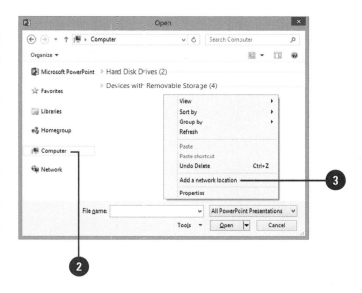

Access a FTP Site

1. Click the **File** tab, click **Open**, click **Computer**, and then click **Browse**.

2. Click **Computer** in the left pane.

3. Double-click the FTP site to which you want to log in.

4. Enter a password (your E-mail address or personal password), and then select a log on option.

5. Click **Log On**.

6. Select a folder location, and then select a file.

7. Click **Open**.

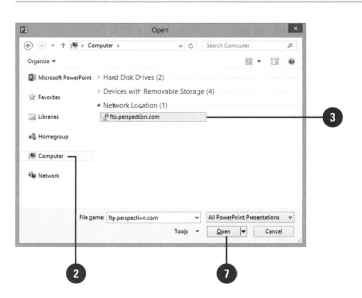

Finalizing a Presentation and Its Supplements

Introduction

As you finish developing your presentation in PowerPoint, you can add some last-minute enhancements that will help with your delivery of the slide show. By creating a summary slide in the beginning of your presentation, your audience will know the scope of your presentation. Before finalizing your presentation, you should make sure that you embed truetype fonts into your presentation. This will ensure that your slide show appears correctly, regardless of the fonts installed on the various computers that you might be using.

Handouts are printed materials that you supply to your audience. Typically, handouts include an outline for the audience to follow as you speak, a copy of the slides in your presentation (printed one or more slides to a page), or a set of pages with blank lines next to reduced images of the slides for note taking. PowerPoint gives you many options for printing handouts, including editing and formatting them with the Handout Master. Most speakers feel more comfortable giving a presentation with a script in front of them, and you can easily create one in Notes Page view. With **speaker notes**, you can control the success of your presentation delivery.

As you take your presentation to various clients, it may be necessary to translate your slide show into another language. You might also want to export your notes to Microsoft Word to further customize them. You can save your slides in different formats—you might want to save them as part of a web page, or maybe a different version of PowerPoint for other clients. PowerPoint allows you to save a presentation as an XPS or PDF file, which are secure fixed-layout formats you can send to others. You can also preview your presentation before printing or print as black and white or color to review your presentation in different print formats.

What You'll Do

Change Slide Setup Options

Prepare Handouts and Speaker Notes

Customize Notes Pages

Change Proofing Options and Set Languages for Proofing

Check Spelling and Use Custom Dictionaries

Insert Research Material

Find the Right Words

Translate Text to Another Language and Use Multiple Languages

Export Notes and Slides to Word

Document Presentation Properties

Check Compatibility and Accessibility

Save Slides in Different Formats

Save Outline Text as a Document

Create a PDF and an XPS Document

Select Printing Options

Preview a Presentation

Print a Presentation and Outline

Changing Slide Setup Options

Before you print a presentation, you can use the Page Setup dialog box to set the proportions of your presentation slides—standard (4:3) and wide screen (16:9) (**New!**)—and their orientation on the page. You can also control slide numbering in the Number Slides From box. For a new presentation, PowerPoint opens with default slide page settings: on-screen slide show, landscape orientation, and slides starting at number one. Notes, handouts, and outlines are printed in portrait orientation.

Control Slide Size

1 Click the **Design** tab.

2 Click the **Slide Size** button (**New!**), and then click **Standard (4:3)**, **Widescreen (16:9)**, or **Custom Slide Size**.

3 For a custom slide size, click the **Slides sized for** list arrow.

4 Click the size you want.

◆ **On-Screen Show** for slides that fit computer monitor with ratios of 4:3 (standard), 16:9 (wide screen HDTV's), or 16:10 (wide screen laptops).

◆ **Letter Paper** for slides that fit on 8.5-by-11-inch paper.

◆ **Ledger Paper** for slides that fit on 11-by-17-inch paper.

◆ **A3 Paper**, **A4 Paper**, **B4 (ISO) Paper**, or **B5 (ISO) Paper** for slides that fit on international paper.

◆ **35mm Slides** for 11.25-by-7.5-inch slides.

◆ **Overhead** for 10-by-7.5-inch slides that fit transparencies.

◆ **Banner** for 8-by-1-inch slides that are typically used as advertisements on a web page.

◆ **Widescreen** for slides on a widescreen (16:9) (**New!**).

◆ **Custom** to enter the measurements you want in the width and height boxes.

5 Click **OK**.

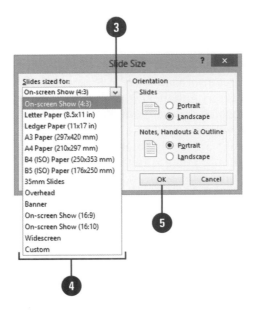

Customize Slide Proportions

1. Click the **Design** tab.

2. Click the **Slide Size** button (**New!**), and then click **Custom Slide Size**.

3. Enter a specific width in inches.

4. Enter a specific height in inches.

5. Click **OK**.

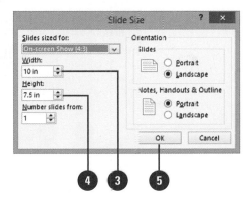

Change Slide Orientation

1. Click the **Design** tab.

2. Click the **Slide Size** button (**New!**), and then click **Custom Slide Size**.

3. To orient your slides, click the **Portrait** or **Landscape** option.

4. To orient your notes, handouts, and outline, click the **Portrait** or **Landscape** option in the Notes, Handouts & Outline area.

5. Click **OK**.

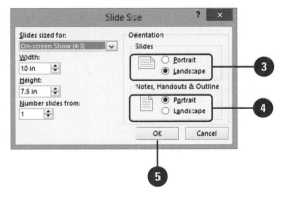

For Your Information

Using Portrait and Landscape Together

In PowerPoint, you can have only one slide orientation in a presentation. However, if you want to use portrait and landscape slide orientation in the same presentation, you can do it by creating a link between two presentations. For best results, place both presentations in the same folder on your system. First, you create a link from the first presentation to the second presentation, and then create a link from the second presentation back. *See "Creating a Hyperlink to External Elements" on page 266 for instructions on creating a link to another presentation or file.*

Preparing Handouts

Prepare your handouts in the Print screen, where you can specify what to print. You can customize your handouts by formatting them in the handout master first, using the formatting and drawing tools. You can also add a header and footer to include the date, slide number, and page number, for example. In the Print screen, you can choose to print one, two, three, four, six, or nine slides per page.

Format the Handout Master

1. Click the **View** tab.

2. Click the **Handout Master** button.

3. Click the **Slides Per Page** button, and then select an option with how many slides you want per page.

4. Select or clear the **Header**, **Date**, **Footer**, or **Page Number** check boxes to show or hide handout master placeholders.

5. To add a background style, click the **Background Styles** button, and then click a style or **Format Background** to customize one.

6. Use the formatting tools on the Home tab or drawing tools on the Format tab to format the handout master placeholders.

7. Click the **Close Master View** button.

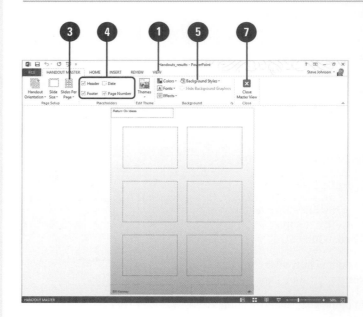

Did You Know?

What are the dotted rectangles in the handout master? The dotted rectangles are placeholders for slides and for header and footer information.

You can add headers and footers to create consistent handouts. Headers and footers you add to the handout master are also added to notes pages and the printed outline.

Add Headers and Footers to Handouts

1. Click the **Insert** tab.

2. Click the **Header & Footer** button.

3. Click the **Notes and Handouts** tab.

4. Select the check boxes with the options you want and then enter the information you want to appear on your handouts.

   ◆ **Date and time.**

   ◆ **Page number.**

   ◆ **Header.**

   ◆ **Footer.**

5. Click **Apply To All**.

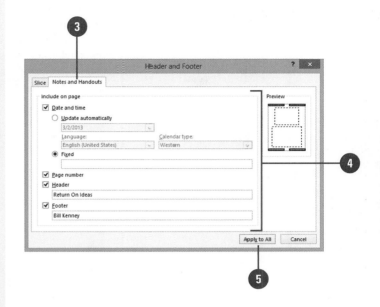

Print Handouts

1. Click the **File** tab, and then click **Print**.

2. Click the **Print What** list arrow, and then select one of the nine options:

   ◆ **1, 2, or 3 Slides.**

   ◆ **4, 6, or 9 Slides Horizontal.**

   ◆ **4, 6, or 9 Slides Vertical.**

3. Click **Print**.

Did You Know?

You can add a frame around printed slides. Click the File tab, click Print, click the Print What list arrow, select Frame Slides, and then click Print.

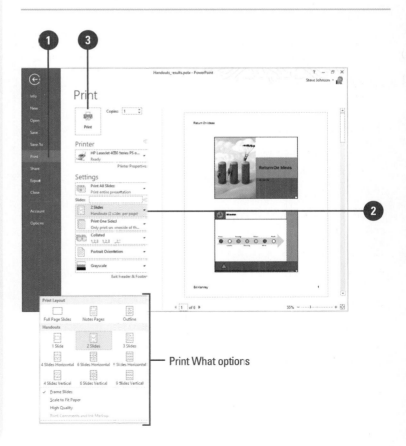

Print What options

Preparing Speaker Notes

You can add speaker notes to a slide in Normal view using the Notes pane. Also, every slide has a corresponding **notes page** that displays a reduced image of the slide and a text placeholder where you can enter speaker's notes. Once you have created speaker's notes, you can reference them as you give your presentation, either from a printed copy or from your system. You can enhance your notes by including objects on the notes master.

Enter Notes in Normal View

1. Click on the slide for which you want to enter notes.

2. To show or hide the Notes pane, click the **Notes** button on the Status bar.

3. Click to place the insertion point in the Notes pane, and then type your notes.

Did You Know?

You can view more of the Notes pane. To see more of the Notes pane in Normal view, point to the top border of the Notes pane until the pointer changes to a double-headed arrow, and then drag the border until the pane is the size you want.

You export notes and slides to Microsoft Word. Click the Send To Microsoft Word button on the Quick Access Toolbar (add it if necessary), click the page layout option you want for handouts, click the Paste Link option if you want to create a link, and then click OK.

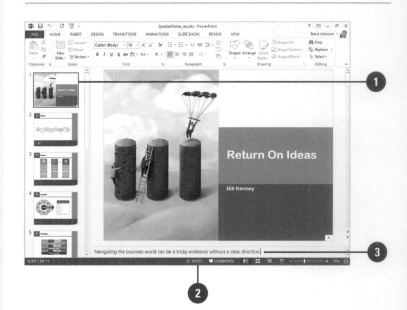

Enter Notes in Notes Page View

1. Switch to the slide for which you want to enter notes.

2. Click the **View** tab.

3. Click the **Notes Page** button.

4. If necessary, click the **Zoom** list arrow, and then increase the zoom percentage to better see the text you type.

5. Click the text placeholder.

6. Type your notes.

Did You Know?

Why don't the objects on the Notes master appear in the Notes pane in Normal view? The objects that you add to the Notes master will appear when you print the notes pages. They do not appear in the Notes pane of Normal view or when you save your presentation as a web page.

See Also

See "Customizing Notes Pages" on page 286 for more information on customizing and formatting the Notes master.

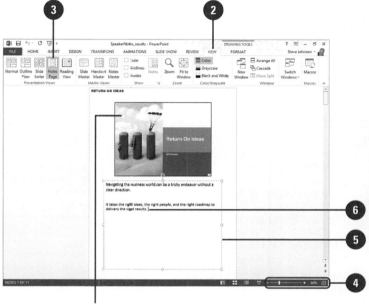

Reduced image of slide

Customizing Notes Pages

You can add dates, numbering, and header and footer text to your notes pages just as you do to your slides. If you have removed objects from the master and decide you want to restore them, you can reapply any of the master placeholders (the slide image, the date, header, and so on) without affecting objects and text outside the placeholders. Moreover, if you delete the slide placeholder or text placeholder from a notes page, you can easily reinsert it.

Add a Header and Footer to Notes Pages

1. Click the **Insert** tab.

2. Click the **Header & Footer** button.

3. Click the **Notes and Handouts** tab.

4. Select the check boxes with the options you want and then enter the header and footer information you want.

   ◆ **Date and time.**

   ◆ **Page number.**

   ◆ **Header.**

   ◆ **Footer.**

5. Click **Apply To All**.

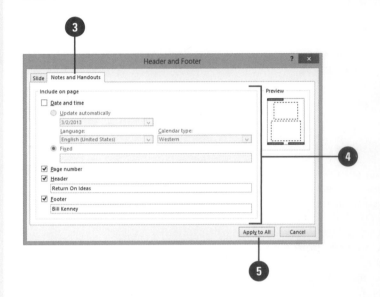

Reinsert Notes Placeholders on the Notes Master

1. Click the **View** tab.

2. Click the **Notes Master** button.

3. Select the **Header**, **Slide Image**, **Footer**, **Date**, **Body**, or **Page Number** check boxes in the Placeholder group corresponding to the placeholders you want to reinsert.

4. Click the **Close Master View** button.

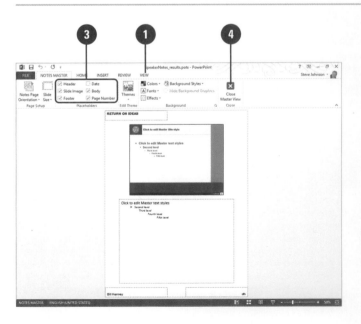

Format the Notes Master

1 Click the **View** tab.

2 Click the **Notes Master** button.

3 Select or clear the **Header**, **Slide Image**, **Footer**, **Date**, **Body** or **Page Number** check boxes to show or hide notes master placeholders.

4 To add a background, use any of the following:

◆ **Background Styles.** Click the **Background Styles** button, and then click a style or **Format Background** to customize one.

◆ **Theme Styles.** Click the **Color**, **Fonts**, or **Effects** button, and then select an option.

5 If you want, add objects to the notes master that you want to appear on every page, such as a picture or a text object.

◆ **Hide Background Graphics.** Select to hide an inserted picture as a background.

6 Use the formatting tools on the **Home** tab or drawing tools on the **Format** tab to format the handout master text placeholders.

7 To add a header and footer, click the **Insert** tab, and then click the **Header & Footer** button.

8 Click the **Close Master View** button.

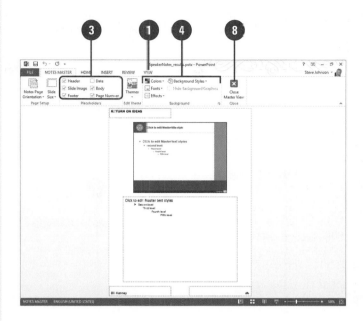

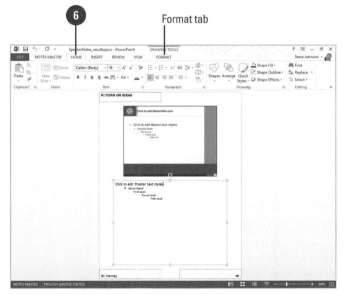

Format tab

Did You Know?

You can change the notes page orientation. Click the View tab, click the Notes Master button, click the Notes Page Orientation button, and then click Portrait or Landscape.

Changing Proofing Options

You can customize the way PowerPoint and Microsoft Office spell check a presentation by selecting proofing settings in PowerPoint Options. Some spelling options apply to PowerPoint, such as Check spelling as you type or Check grammar with spelling (**New!**), while other options apply to all Microsoft Office programs, such as Ignore Internet and File Addresses, and Flag Repeated Words. If you have ever mistakenly used their instead of *there*, you can use contextual grammar to fix it. While you work in a presentation, you can can set options to have the spelling check search for mistakes in the background.

Change PowerPoint Proofing Options

1. Click the **File** tab, and then click **Options**.

2. In the left pane, click **Proofing**.

3. Select or clear the PowerPoint spelling options you want.

   ◆ **Check spelling as you type.** Select to automatically correct spelling errors and AutoCorrect as you type.

   ◆ **Hide spelling and grammar errors.** Clear to displays errors with a red wavy line. If you select this, you must also select Check spelling as you type (above).

   ◆ **Check grammar with spelling.** Select to correct grammar usage errors like the use of *their* vs *there* along with spelling errors (**New!**).

4. To recheck spelling and grammar (if enabled), click **Recheck Document** (**New!**).

5. Click **OK**.

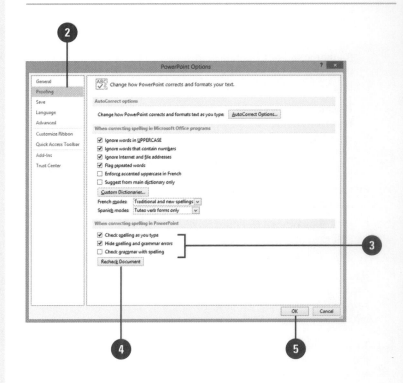

Change Office Proofing Options

1. Click the **File** tab, and then click **Options**.

2. In the left pane, click **Proofing**.

3. Select or clear the spelling options you want.

   ◆ **Ignore words in UPPERCASE**.

   ◆ **Ignore words that contain numbers**.

   ◆ **Ignore Internet and file addresses**.

   ◆ **Flag repeated words**.

   ◆ **Enforce accented uppercase in French**.

   ◆ **Suggest from main dictionary only**. Select to exclude your custom dictionary.

      ◆ To work with custom dictionaries, click **Custom Dictionaries**.

   ◆ **French or Spanish modes**. Select an option for working with French or Spanish.

4. Click **OK**.

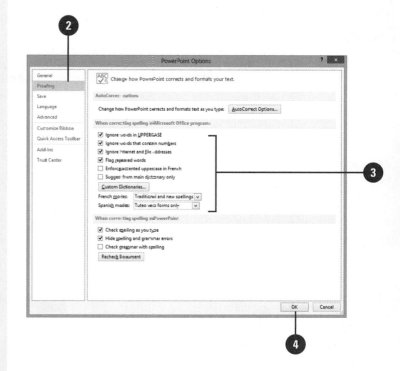

See Also

See "Using Custom Dictionaries" on page 294 for information on working with custom dictionaries.

Setting Languages for Proofing

If your text is written in more than one language, you can designate the language of selected text so spell check uses the right dictionary. For international Microsoft Office users, you can change the language that appears on their screens by enabling different languages. Users around the world can enter, display, and edit text in all supported languages. When you're working with more than one language at a time in a presentation, you can enable a language option to make it easier to switch between languages when typing and editing text. You can also select the Automatically switch keyboard to match language of surround text option in the Advanced pane of the PowerPoint Options dialog box to work more efficiently with multiple languages.

Set a Language for Proofing

1. Select the text you want to mark.

2. Click the **Review** tab.

3. Click the **Language** button, and then click **Set Proofing Language**.

4. Click the language you want to assign to the selected text.

5. To skip this text during spell checking, select the **Do not check spelling** check box.

6. To set a language as the default, select the language, click **Default**, and then click **Yes**.

7. Click **OK**.

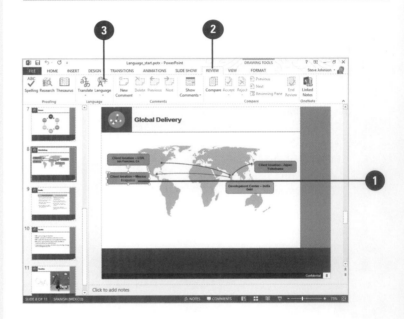

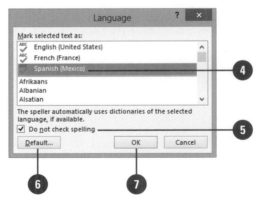

Did You Know?

There is a Multilingual AutoCorrect.
Office supports an AutoCorrect list for each language. For example, the English AutoCorrect list capitalizes all cases of the single letter "i;" in Swedish however, "i" is a preposition and is not capitalized.

Set an Option to Automatically Switch Keyboard Language

1 Click the **File** tab, and then click **Options**.

2 In the left pane, click **Advanced**.

3 Select the **Automatically switch keyboard to match language of surrounding text** check box.

◆ If the option is not available, you need to enable a keyboard layout for a language in the Language pane of the PowerPoint Options dialog box.

4 Click **OK**.

See Also

See "Using Multiple Languages" on page 300 for information on enabling a keyboard layout to use with Microsoft Office programs.

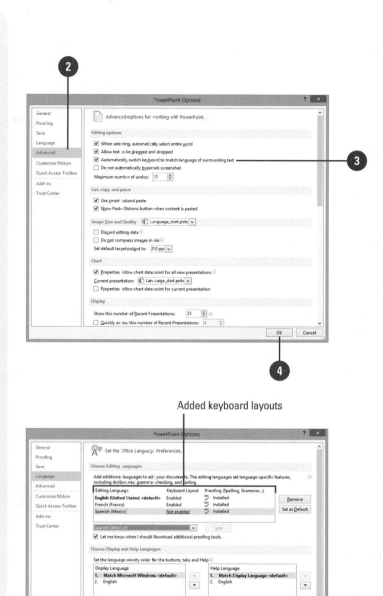

Added keyboard layouts

Checking Spelling

As you type, a red wavy line appears under words not listed in PowerPoint's dictionary (such as misspellings, names, technical terms, or acronyms) or duplicate words (such as *the the*). You can correct these errors as they arise or after you finish the entire presentation. PowerPoint's spelling checker checks the spelling of the entire presentation, including all slides, outlines, notes pages, and handout pages. You can use the Spelling button on the Review tab to check the entire presentation using the Spelling pane (**New!**), or when you encounter a wavy red line under a word, you can right-click the word and choose the correct spelling or add it to your custom dictionary from the list on the shortcut menu. If you have a dictionary Office app installed, you can view or hear dictionary information. If you work with different languages, you can conveniently change the language for spelling in the Spelling pane (**New!**).

Correct Spelling as You Type

1. Right-click a word with a red wavy underline.

2. Choose an option:

   ◆ Click the correct spelling.

   ◆ Click **Ignore All** to skip any other instances of the word

   ◆ Click **Add to Dictionary** to include it in your custom dictionary.

See Also

See "Changing Proofing Options" on page 288 for information on setting options to correct spelling as you type.

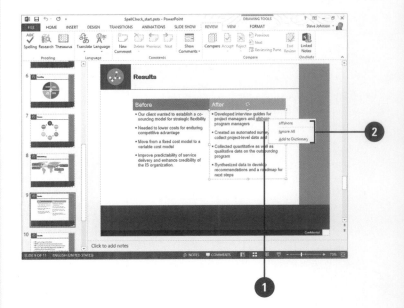

Check Spelling All at Once

1 Click the **Review** tab.

2 Click the **Spelling** button.

3 To change the language, click the **Language** list arrow, and then select a language (**New!**)

4 In the Spelling pane (**New!**), choose an option:

◆ Click **Ignore** to skip the word, or click **Ignore All** to skip every instance of the word.

◆ Click a suggestion, and then click **Change** or **Change All**.

◆ Click **Add** to add a word to your dictionary, so it doesn't show up as a misspelled word in the future.

◆ View the dictionary information (**New!**) from an installed dictionary Office app. Click the Audio icon to hear information.

◆ If no suggestion is appropriate, click in the presentation and edit the text yourself. Click **Resume** to continue.

5 When the spelling check is complete, click **OK**, or click the **Close** button in the pane to end the spelling check.

Did You Know?

You can make spell check ignore text or an entire style. Select the word or phrase that you want to mark. Click the Review tab, click the Language button, click Set Proofing Language, select the Do Not Check Spelling check box, and then click OK.

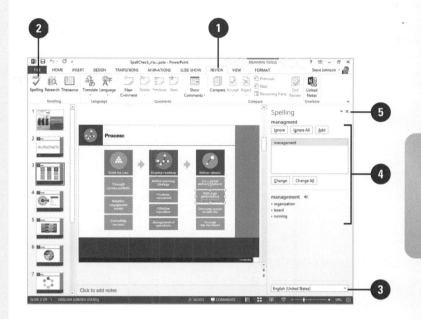

Using Custom Dictionaries

Before you can use a custom dictionary, you need to enable it first. You can enable and manage custom dictionaries by using the Custom Dictionaries dialog box. In the dialog box, you can change the language associated with a custom dictionary, create a new custom dictionary, or add or remove existing custom dictionary. If you need to manage dictionary content, you can also change the default custom dictionary to which the spelling checker adds words, as well as add, delete, or edit words. All the modifications you make to your custom dictionaries are shared with all your Microsoft Office programs, so you only need to make changes once. If you mistakenly type an obscene or embarrassing word, such as *ass* instead of *ask*, spell check will not catch it because both words are spelled correctly. You can avoid this problem by using an exclusion dictionary. When you use a language for the first time, Office automatically creates an exclusion dictionary. This dictionary forces the spelling checker to flag words you don't want to use.

Use a Custom Dictionary

1. Click the **File** tab, and then click **Options**.

2. In the left pane, click **Proofing**.

3. Click **Custom Dictionaries**.

4. Select the check box next to **CUSTOM.DIC (Default)**.

5. Click the **Dictionary language** list arrow, and then select a language for a dictionary.

6. Click the options you want:

   ◆ Click **Edit Word List** to add, delete, or edit words.

   ◆ Click **Change Default** to select a new default dictionary.

   ◆ Click **New** to create a new dictionary.

   ◆ Click **Add** to insert an existing dictionary.

   ◆ Click **Remove** to delete a dictionary.

7. Click **OK** to close the Custom Dictionaries dialog box.

8. Click **OK**.

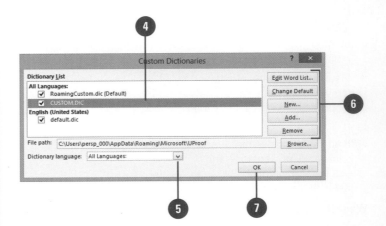

Find and Modify the Exclusion Dictionary

① In Windows Explorer, go to the folder location where the custom dictionaries are stored.

◆ **Windows 8 or 7.** C:\Users*user name*\AppData\Roaming\ Microsoft\UProof

TROUBLE? *If you can't find the folder, change folder settings to show hidden files and folders.*

② Locate the exclusion dictionary for the language you want to change.

◆ The file name you want is ExcludeDictionary *Language CodeLanguage LCID*.lex.

For example, ExcludeDictionary EN0409.lex, where EN is for English.

Check Help for an updated list of LCID (Local Identification Number) numbers for each language.

③ Open the file using Microsoft Notepad or WordPad.

④ Add each word you want the spelling check to flag as misspelled. Type the words in all lowercase and then press Enter after each word.

⑤ Save and close the file.

UProof folder with Office dictionaries

Inserting Research Material

With the Research pane, you can access data sources and insert research material right into your text without leaving your PowerPoint presentation. The Research pane can help you to access electronic dictionaries, thesauruses, research sites on the web, such as Bing, Factiva iWorks, and HighBeam Research, and proprietary company information. You can select one reference source or search in all reference books. The Research pane allows you to quickly and easily find information and incorporate it into your work. Once you find it, you can copy and paste it into your presentation. If you have a hard time finding research information on a specific topic, you can use the Research Options command to enable and update additional reference books and research web sites from which to search.

Research a topic

1. Click the **Review** tab.

2. Click the **Research** button.

3. Type the topic you would like to research.

4. Click the list arrow, and then select a reference source, or click **All Reference Books**.

5. To customize which resources are used for research, click **Research options**, select the reference books and research sites you want, and then click **OK**.

6. Click the **Start Searching** button (green arrow).

7. Select the information in the Research pane that you want to copy.

   To search for more information, click one of the words in the list or click a link to an online site.

8. Select the information you want, and then copy it. In the Research pane, you can point to the item you want, click the list arrow, and then click **Copy**.

9. Paste the information into your presentation.

10. When you're done, click the **Close** button in the pane.

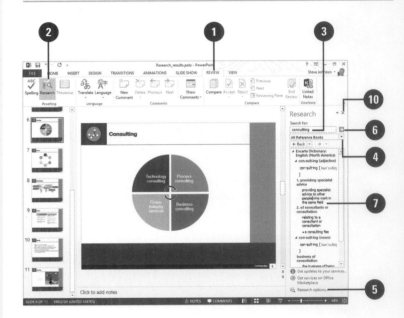

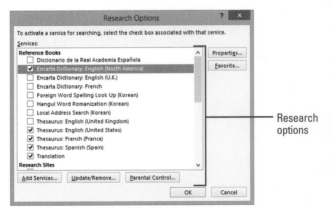

Research options

Finding the Right Words

Repeating the same word in a presentation can reduce a message's effectiveness. Instead, replace some words with synonyms or find antonyms. This feature can save you time and improve the quality and readability of your presentation. You can also select a Thesaurus for another language. Foreign language thesauruses can be accessed at the bottom of the Thesaurus pane (**New!**). If you have an App for Office dictionary installed from the Office Store, a definition appears in the pane (**New!**). If you want to replace the selected word with a synonym or other available alternative, you can use a shortcut menu to insert it.

Use the Thesaurus

1. Select the text you want to translate.

2. Click the **Review** tab.

3. Click the **Thesaurus** button.

   TIMESAVER *Press Shift+F7 to open the Thesaurus pane.*

4. Click the **Language** list arrow, and then select a language.

5. Point to the word in the pane.

6. Click the list arrow, and then click one of the following:

   ◆ **Insert** to replace the word you looked up with the new word.

   ◆ **Copy** to copy the new word and then paste it within the presentation.

7. To change the text, type a word or click a word in the pane.

8. When you're done, click the **Close** button in the pane.

Did You Know?

You can view a definition of the selected word. If you have an App for Office dictionary installed from the Office Store, a definition appears in the Thesaurus pane (**New!**).

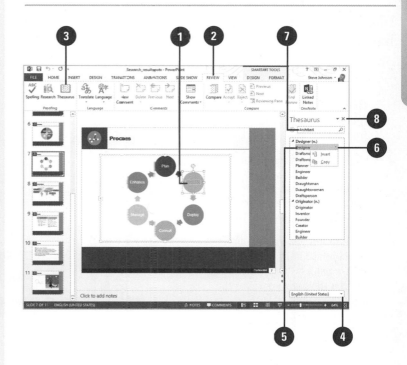

Translating Text to Another Language

If you need to quickly translate a word into another language, you can enable the Mini Translator that translates words when you point to them. The Mini Translator also includes a toolbar, which provides options to copy the translation to the Clipboard or play the word audibly. Before you get started, you need to choose the translation language you want to use. If you don't get the results you want, you can also use the Research pane to translate text. With the Research pane, you can translate single words or short phrases into different languages by using bilingual dictionaries and incorporate it into your work.

Translate Text Using the Mini Translator

1. Click the **Review** tab.

2. Click the **Translate** button, click **Choose Translation Language**, specify a language for the Mini Translator, and then click **OK**.

3. Click the **Translate** button, and then click the Mini Translator language you set for translation to highlight the icon next to the command.

4. Point to the word you want to display the Mini Translator with the translated word. You can also use the toolbar to perform the following options:

   ◆ **Expand.** Opens the Research pane with more options.

   ◆ **Copy.** Copies the translation to the Clipboard.

   ◆ **Play** and **Stop.** Plays or stops the word audibly.

   ◆ **Help.** Opens Help.

5. To turn off the Mini Translator, click the **Translate** button, and then click the Mini Translator language to clear the highlighted icon next to the command.

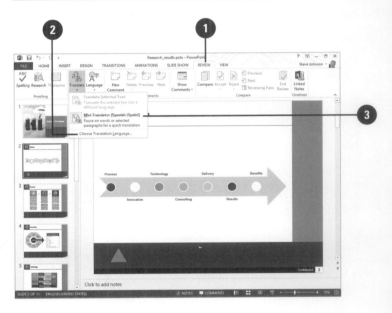

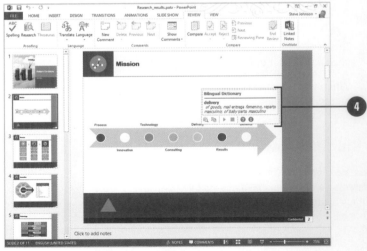

Translate Text Using the Research Pane

① Select the text you want to translate.

② Click the **Review** tab.

③ Click the **Translate** button, and then click **Translate Selected Text**.

If this is the first you have used translation services, click **OK** to install the bilingual dictionaries and enable the service.

④ If necessary, click the list arrow, and then click **Translation**.

⑤ Click the **From** list arrow, and then select the language of the selected text.

⑥ Click the **To** list arrow, and then select the language you want to translate into.

⑦ To customize which resources are used for translation, click **Translation options**, select the look-up options you want, and then click **OK**.

⑧ Right-click the translated text in the Research pane that you want to copy, and then click **Copy**.

⑨ Paste the information into your presentation.

⑩ When you're done, click the **Close** button in the pane.

See Also

See "Using Multiple Languages" on page 300 for information on adding languages to use with Microsoft Office programs.

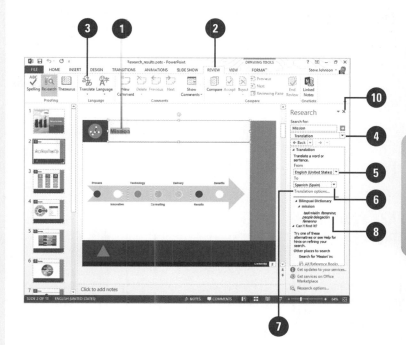

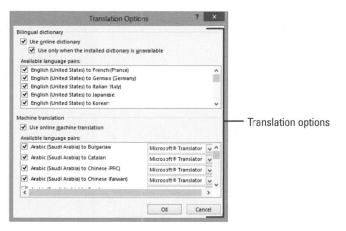

Translation options

Using Multiple Languages

International Microsoft Office users can change the language that appears on their screens by changing the default language settings. Users around the world can enter, display, and edit text in all supported languages—including European languages, Japanese, Chinese, Korean, Hebrew, and Arabic—to name a few. You'll probably be able to use Office programs in your native language. If the text in your presentation is written in more than one language, you can automatically detect languages or designate the language of selected text so the spelling checker uses the right dictionary. You can set preferences for editing, display, ScreenTip, and Help languages. If you don't have the keyboard layout or related software installed, you can click links to add or enable them.

Add a Language to Office Programs

1. Click the **File** tab, click **Options**, and then click **Language**.

   ◆ You can also click **Microsoft Office 2013 Language Preferences** on the All Apps screen (Win 8) or on the Start menu under Microsoft Office and Microsoft Office Tools (Win 7).

2. Click the **Language** list arrow, and then select the language you want to enable.

3. Click **Add**.

4. To enable the correct keyboard layout for the installed language, click the **Not enabled** link to open the Text Services and Input Language dialog box, where you can select a keyboard layout, and then click **OK**.

5. Set the language priority order for the buttons, tabs, and Help for the Display and Help languages.

6. Set your ScreenTip language to Match Display Language or a specific language.

7. Click **OK**, and then click **Yes** (if necessary) to quit and restart PowerPoint.

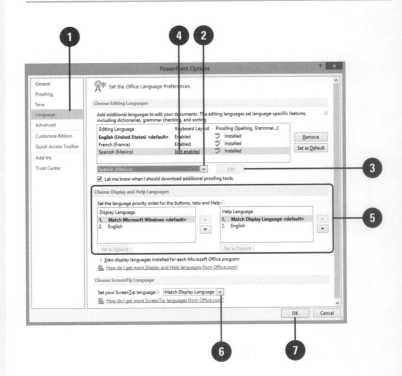

Exporting Notes and Slides to Word

You can send both your notes and slides to Word so that you can use a full array of word processing tools. This is especially handy when you are developing more detailed materials, such as training presentations and manuals. By default, PowerPoint pastes your presentation into a Word document. If you change the presentation after sending it to Word, the changes you make to the presentation are not reflected in the Word document. If you click the Paste Link option in the Send to Microsoft Word dialog box, however, you create a link between the Word document and the presentation, and changes you make in one are reflected in the other.

Create Handouts in Word

1. Click the **File** tab, and then click **Export**.

2. Click **Create Handouts**, and then click the **Create Handouts** button.

3. Click the page layout option you want for handouts.

4. To create a link to the presentation, click the **Paste Link** option.

5. Click **OK**.

   Word starts, creates a new document, and inserts your presentation slides with the page layout you selected.

6. Print the document in Word, editing and saving it as necessary.

7. When you're done, click the **Close** button to quit Word.

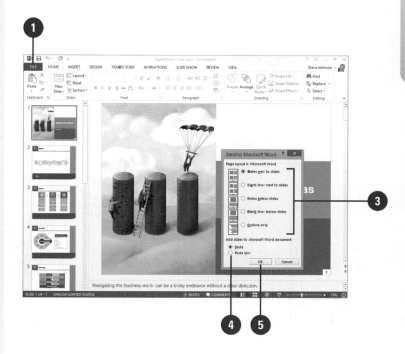

Documenting Presentation Properties

PowerPoint automatically documents presentation properties while you work—such as file size, save dates, and various statistics—and allows you to document other properties, such as title, author, subject, keywords, category, and status. You can view or edit standard document properties or create advanced custom properties by using the Document Properties Panel, which is actually an XML-based Microsoft InfoPath form hosted in PowerPoint. You can use document properties—also known as metadata—to help you manage and track files; search tools can use the metadata to find a presentation based on your search criteria. If you associate a document property to an item in the presentation, the document property updates when you change the item.

View and Edit Standard Presentation Properties

1. Click the **File** tab, and then click **Info**.

2. Click the **Properties** button, and then click **Show Document Panel**.

3. Enter the standard properties, such as author, title, subject, keywords, category, status, and comments, in the Document Properties Panel.

4. Click the **Close** button on the Document Properties Panel.

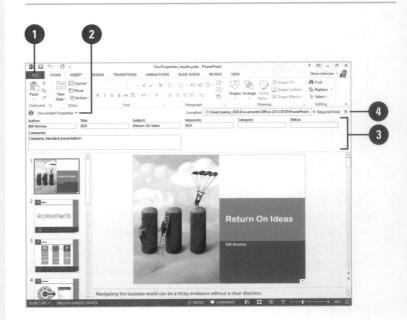

Did You Know?

Your Document Properties Panel might look different. If you save your presentation to a SharePoint library or a document management server, your Document Properties Panel might have additional properties.

You can view document properties when you open or save a file. In the Open or Save As dialog box, select the presentation you want, click the arrow next to the Views, and then click Details to view file size and last changed date, or click Properties to view all information.

Display Advanced Properties

1 Click the **File** tab, and then click **Info**.

2 Click the **Properties** button, and then click **Advanced Properties**.

3 Click the tabs to view and add information:

◆ **General**. To find out file location or size.

◆ **Summary**. To add title and author information for the presentation.

◆ **Statistics**. To display the number of slides, paragraphs, words and other details about the presentation.

◆ **Contents**. To display slide titles and information about fonts and design templates used in the presentation.

4 Click **OK**.

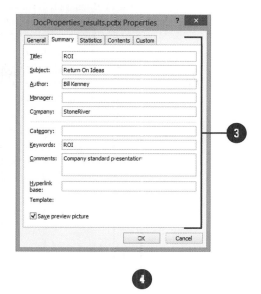

Customize Properties

1 Click the **File** tab, and then click **Info**.

2 Click the **Properties** button, and then click **Advanced Properties**.

3 Click the **Custom** tab.

4 Type the name for the custom property or select a name from the list.

5 Select the data type for the property you want to add.

6 Type a value for the property.

7 Click **Add**.

8 Click **OK**.

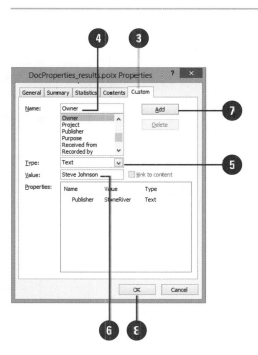

Checking Accessibility

The Accessibility Checker identifies potential difficulties that people with disabilities might have reading or interactive with an Office document. The Accessibility Checker generates a list of errors and warning and possible fixes in the Accessibility Checker panel. Use the information to determine what caused each issue and for suggestions on how to fix it. In addition to the Accessibility Checker, you can also add alternative text (also known as alt text) to objects and other items to provide information for people with visual impairments who may be unable to easily or fully see it. Alternative text also helps people with screen readers understand the content in a presentation. You can create alternative text for shapes, pictures, charts, tables, SmartArt graphics, or other objects. When you point to an object with alternative text in a screen reader or DAISY (digital Accessible Information System) or in most browsers, the alternative text appears.

Check Accessibility

1. Click the **File** tab, and then click **Info**.

2. Click the **Check For Issues** button, and then click **Check Accessibility**.

   PowerPoint checks compatibility for content that people with disabilities might find difficult to read.

3. View the compatibility summary information of errors and warnings in the Accessibility Checker panel.

4. Select an issue under Inspection Results to find out how to fix it under Additional Information.

5. When you're done, click the **Close** button in the panel.

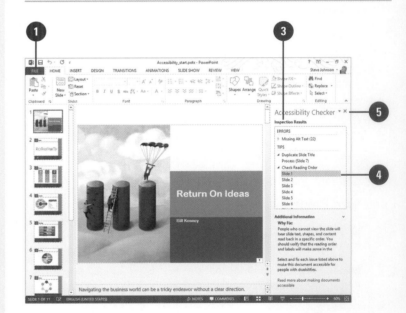

Add Alternative Text

1. Select the text or object you want to add alternative text.

2. If you want to find the objects that don't have alternative text, check accessibility (previous page), click the plus sign (+) next to Missing Alt Text, and then select an object from the list to display it.

3. Right-click the object or item, point to and/or click a command (varies depending on the object or item), such as **Format Shape**, **Alternative Text** or **Alt Text**.

   The Format pane (**New!**) opens, displaying options.

4. Click the **Size & Properties** button (**New!**) under Shape Options.

5. Expand **Alt Text**, if necessary, in the pane.

6. Type a title and description.

7. When you're done, click the **Close** button in the panel.

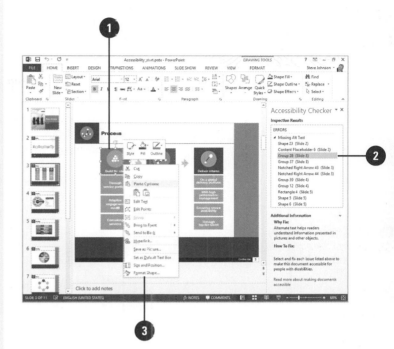

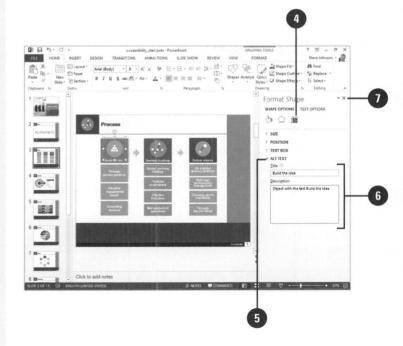

Checking Compatibility

The Compatibility Checker identifies the potential loss of functionality when you save a PowerPoint 2013 presentation in the PowerPoint 97-2003 Presentation file format. The Compatibility Checker generates a report that provides a summary of the potential losses and the number of occurrences in the presentation. Use the report information to determine what caused each message and for suggestions on how to change it. If the loss is due to a new feature in PowerPoint 2013—such as custom layouts or Artistic and Quick Styles applied to shapes, pictures, and WordArt—you might be able to simply remove the effect or feature. In other cases, you might not be able to do anything about it. To maintain a visual appearance, SmartArt graphics and other objects with new effects are converted to bitmaps to preserve their overall look and cannot be edited.

Check Compatibility

1. Click the **File** tab, and then click **Info**.

2. Click the **Check For Issues** button, and then click **Check Compatibility**.

   PowerPoint checks compatibility of the presentation for non supported features in earlier versions of the PowerPoint program.

3. View the compatibility summary information, so you can make changes, as necessary.

4. To have the compatibility checker review the presentation when the PowerPoint saves the file in 97-2003 file format, select the **Check compatibility when saving in PowerPoint 97-2003 formats** check box.

5. Click **OK**.

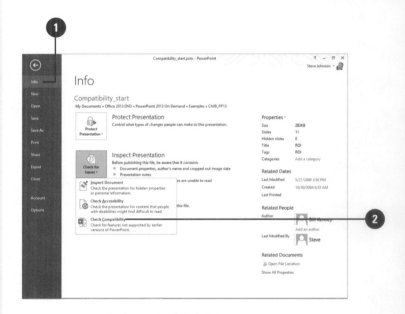

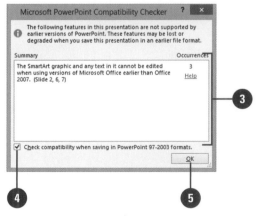

Saving Slides in Different Formats

You can save PowerPoint presentations in a number of formats so that many different programs can access them. For example, you might want to save a presentation slide as a web graphic image in the .jpg or .gif format to use in a web page that you can view in a web browser. Or you can save a presentation slide as a graphic image that you can open in a graphics editor. When you're saving presentation slides, PowerPoint asks if you want to save the current slide only or all the slides in your presentation, which can be a big timesaver.

Save a Slide as a Graphic Image

1. In Normal view, display the slide you want to save.

2. Click the **File** tab, and then click **Export**.

3. Click **Change File Type**.

4. Select the graphics format you want to use, either **PNG** or **JPEG**, or **Save as Another File Type**.

5. Click the **Save As** button.

6. Click the **Save as type** list arrow, and then select a graphics format, if necessary.

7. Click the **Save in** list arrow, and then click the drive or folder where you want to save the file.

8. Type a file name.

9. Click **Save**.

10. Click **Every Slide** to save all slides as separate graphic image files, or click **Current Slide Only** to save just the current slide. If necessary, click **OK**.

See Also

See "Examining Picture File Formats" on page 167 for information on the different graphic file formats.

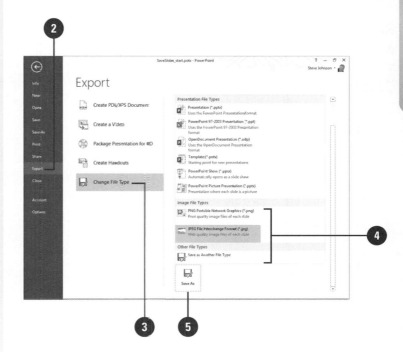

Saving Outline Text as a Document

When you need the text portion of a presentation for use in another program, you can save the presentation text in a format called Rich Text Format (RTF). Saving an outline in RTF allows you to save any formatting that you made to the presentation text in a common file format that you can open in other programs. As long as Microsoft Word is installed on your computer, you can export a presentation outline directly from PowerPoint into a report in Word with the Send to Microsoft Word feature. PowerPoint launches Word and sends or copies the outline in the presentation to a blank Word document.

Save a Presentation as an Outline

1 Click the **File** tab, click **Save As**, click **Computer**, and then click **Browse**.

2 Click the **Save as type** list arrow, and then click **Outline/RTF**.

3 Click the **Save in** list arrow, and then click the drive or folder where you want to save the file.

4 Type the file name.

5 Click **Save**.

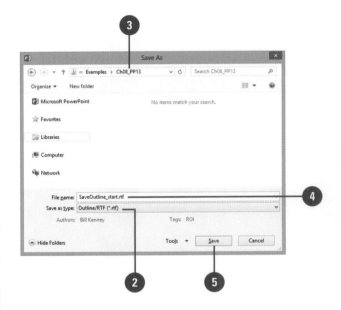

Send an Outline to Word

1 Click the **File** tab, and then click **Export**.

2 Click **Create Handouts**, and then click the **Create Handouts** button.

3 Click the **Outline Only** option.

4 Click **OK**.

Microsoft Word starts, creating a new document, and inserts the presentation slide outline information.

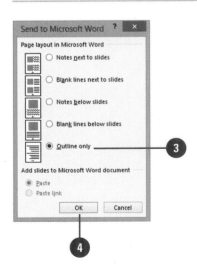

Creating a PDF Document

Portable Document Format (PDF) is a fixed-layout format developed by Adobe Systems that retains the form you intended on a computer monitor or printer. A PDF is useful when you want to create a document primarily intended to be read and printed, not modified. PowerPoint allows you to save a document as a PDF file, which you can send to others for review in an e-mail. To view a PDF file, you need to have Acrobat Reader—free downloadable software from Adobe Systems—installed on your computer.

Save a Document as a PDF Document

1. Click the **File** tab, click **Export**, and then click **Create PDF/XPS Document**.

2. Click the **Create PDF/XPS** button.

3. Click the **Save as type** list arrow, and then click **PDF**.

4. Click the **Save in** list arrow, and then click the folder where you want to save the file.

5. Type a PDF file name.

6. To open the file in Adobe Reader after saving, select the **Open file after publishing** check box.

7. Click the **Standard** or **Minimum size** option to specify how you want to optimize the file.

8. Click **Options**.

9. Select the publishing options you want, such as what to publish, range to publish, whether to include non-printing information, or PDF options.

10. Click **OK**.

11. Click **Publish**.

12. If necessary, install Adobe Acrobat Reader and related software as directed.

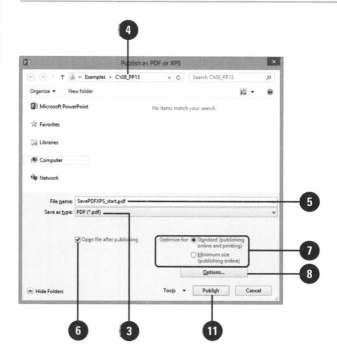

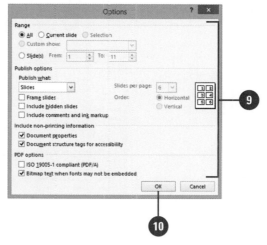

Creating an XPS Document

XML Paper Specification (XPS) is a secure fixed-layout format developed by Microsoft that retains the form you intended on a monitor or printer. An XPS is useful when you want to create a document primarily intended to be read and printed, not modified. PowerPoint allows you to save a document as an XPS file, which you can send to others for review in an e-mail. XPS includes support for digital signatures and is compatible with Windows Rights Management for additional protection. The XPS format also preserves live links with documents, making files fully functional. To view an XPS file, you need to have a viewer—free downloadable software from Microsoft Office.com—installed on your computer.

Save a Document as an XPS Document

1. Click the **File** tab, click **Export**, and then click **Create PDF/XPS Document**.

2. Click the **Create PDF/XPS** button.

3. Click the **Save as type** list arrow, and then click **XPS Document.**

4. Click the **Save in** list arrow, and then click the folder where you want to save the file.

5. Type an XPS file name.

6. To open the file in viewer after saving, select the **Open file after publishing** check box.

7. Click the **Standard** or **Minimum size** option to specify how you want to optimize the file.

8. Click **Options**.

9. Select the publishing options you want, such as what to publish, range to publish, whether to include non-printing information, or XPS options.

10. Click **OK**.

11. Click **Publish**.

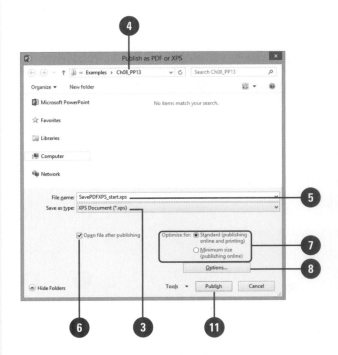

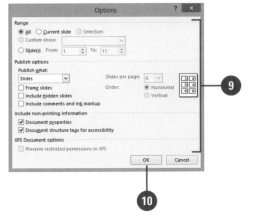

Selecting Printing Options

You can customize the way PowerPoint prints presentations and supplements by selecting printing settings in PowerPoint Options. These PowerPoint preferences determine the internal process of printing a presentation. You can set options that allow you to print a presentation while you continue to work and provide you with the best quality print out. If you use the same print options most of the time, you can set print preferences in PowerPoint Options to save you some time.

Change Printing Options

1. Click the **File** tab, and then click **Options**.

2. In the left pane, click **Advanced**.

3. Select or clear the printing options you do or don't want.

   - **Print in background.** Select to print as you continue to work.

   - **Print TrueType fonts as graphics.** Select to print fonts as vector graphic for better print quality.

   - **Print inserted objects at printer resolution.** Select to print charts and tables with the best print quality.

   - **High Quality.** Select to print with the highest color and resolution settings available.

   - **Align transparent graphics at printer resolution.** Select to print transparent graphics at the printer set resolution.

4. Click the **When printing this document** list arrow, and then click the presentation in which you want to set print options.

5. Click the option you want for the specified presentation:

   - **Use the most recent used print settings.**

   - **Use the following print settings.** Print what, Color/grayscale, Print hidden slides, Scale to fit paper, or Frame slides.

6. Click **OK**.

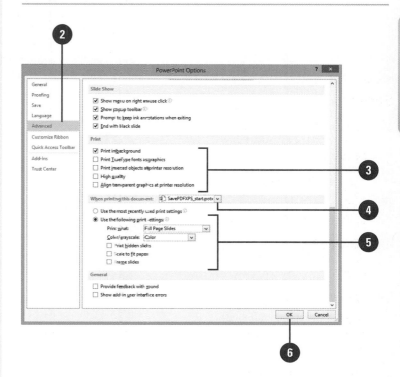

Previewing a Presentation

Before printing, you should verify that the page looks the way you want. You save time, money, and paper by avoiding duplicate printing. Print Preview shows you the exact placement of your data on each printed page. You can view all or part of your presentation as it will appear when you print it. You have the option of switching between various views, such as notes, slides, outlines, and handouts. Print Preview shows you the pages based on the properties of the selected printer. For example, if the selected printer is setup to print color, Print Preview displays in color. If you are using a black and white printer, you can preview your color slides in pure black and white or grayscale in print preview to verify that they will be legible when you print them. The Print screen on the File tab makes it easy to zoom in and out to view a presentation more comfortably, switch between pages, preview page breaks, set print options, and print all from the same place.

Preview a Presentation

1. Click the **File** tab, and then click **Print**.

2. Click the **Zoom to Page** button to toggle the zoom in and out to the page.

3. To adjust the zoom, drag the **Zoom** slider or click the **Zoom In** or **Zoom Out** buttons.

4. To switch pages, click the **Next Page** or **Previous Page** button, or enter a specific page in the Current Page box.

5. If you want to print, click the **Print** button.

See Also

See "Printing a Presentation" on page 310 for information on printing a presentation.

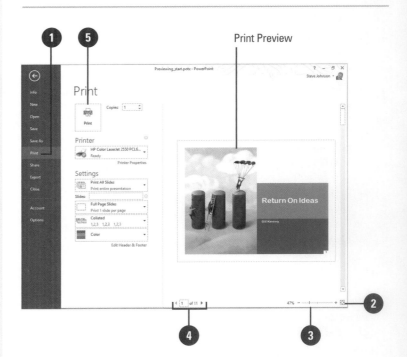

Print Preview

Change Preview Options

① Click the **File** tab, and then click **Print**.

② Click the **Print What** list arrow, and then choose any of the following:

- ◆ **Print Layout or Handouts.** Click an icon to select what to print (slides, notes pages, outline, or handouts).

- ◆ **Frame Slides.** Click to add a frame to slides.

- ◆ **Scale to Fit Paper.** Click to scale slide to fit paper.

- ◆ **High Quality.** Click to print with high quality settings.

- ◆ **Print Comments and Ink Markup.** Click to print review comments and mark ups.

③ To change the preview color, click the **Color/Grayscale** list arrow, and then click **Color**, **Grayscale**, or **Pure Black and White**.

④ If you want to print, click the **Print** button.

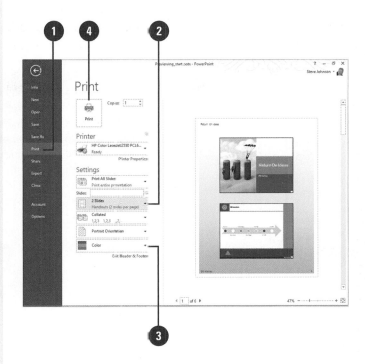

Preview Slides in Pure Black and White or Grayscale

① Click the **View** tab.

- ◆ Or, if in Print Preview, click the **Color/Grayscale** list arrow.

② Click the **Black and White** or **Grayscale** button.

③ On the Black and White or Grayscale tab, click the button with the specific color method you want to use.

④ When you're done, click the **Back To Color View** button.

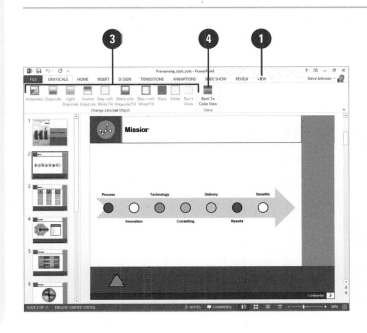

Printing a Presentation

You can print all the elements of your presentation—the slides, outline, notes, and handouts—in either color or black and white. PowerPoint makes it easy to print your presentation; it detects the type of printer that you choose—either color or black and white—and then prints the appropriate version of the presentation. When you're ready to print your presentation, you can choose several printing options on the Print screen on the File tab, such as choosing a printer, selecting the number of slides, notes, or handouts you want printed and the number of copies, and specifying whether to print in color or grayscale. You can also use the Header and Footer dialog box to control the appearance of headers and footers on the pages. You can quickly print a copy of your presentation without using the Print screen by clicking the Quick Print button on the Quick Access Toolbar.

Print All or Part of a Presentation

1. Click the **File** tab, and then click **Print**.

   TIMESAVER *To print without the Print screen, press Ctrl +P, or click the Quick Print button on the Quick Access Toolbar.*

2. Click the **Printer** list arrow, and then click the printer you want to use.

3. To change printer properties, click the **Printer Properties** link, select the options you want, and then click **OK**.

4. Select whether you want to print the entire presentation or only the slides you specify.

5. Select the other print options you want to use, such as what to print, collated, orientation, or color/ grayscale.

6. To change the header and footer, click the **Edit Header & Footer** link, select the options you want, and then click **Apply to All**.

7. Click **Print**.

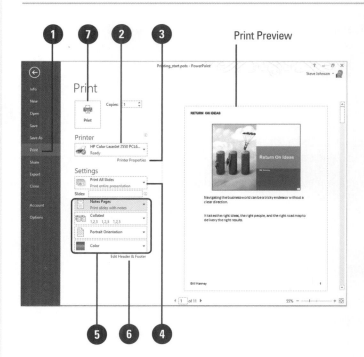

Print a Custom Show

1. Click the **File** tab, and then click **Print**.

2. Click the **Print Range** list arrow, and then click the custom show you want to print.

3. Change settings in the Print screen as necessary.

4. Click **Print**.

Print a Single Slide or a Range of Slides

1. To print selected slides, select the slide you want to print in the Slides pane or Slide Sorter view.

2. Click the **File** tab, and then click **Print**.

3. If necessary, click the **Print Range** list arrow, and then click **Print Current Slide**, **Print Selection**, or **Custom Range**.

4. For a custom range, specify the range of slides you want to print.

5. Click **Print**.

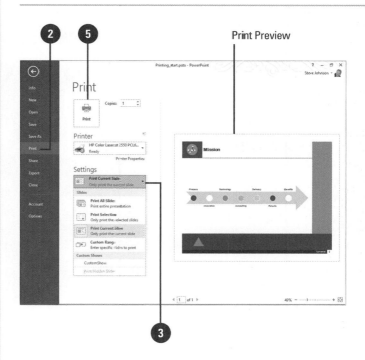

Printing an Outline

When you print an outline, PowerPoint prints the presentation outline as shown in Outline view. What you see in the Outline pane is what you get on the printout. PowerPoint prints an outline with formatting according to the current view setting. Set your formatting to display only slide titles or all of the text levels, and choose to display the outline with or without formatting. From the Print screen you can choose to preview your outline before printing.

Print an Outline

1. Click the **View** tab, and then click the **Outline View** button.

2. In the Outline pane, format your outline the way you want it to be printed.

   ◆ Display only slide titles or all text levels.

   ◆ Display with or without formatting. Right-click the outline, and then click **Show Text Formatting**.

3. Click the **File** tab, and then click **Print**.

4. Click the **Print What** list arrow, and then click **Outline**.

5. Change settings in the Print screen as necessary.

6. Click **Print**.

Did You Know?

You can scale slides to fit your paper when you print. Click the File tab, click Print, click the Print What list arrow, select the Scale To Fit Paper, and then click Print.

See Also

See "Inserting and Developing an Outline" on page 52 for information on saving a presentation as an outline.

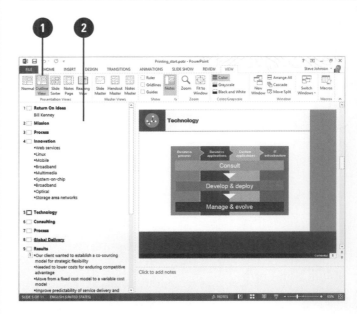

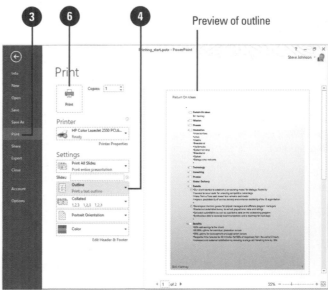

Preview of outline

Preparing a Slide Show

Introduction

Microsoft PowerPoint provides many tools to help you coordinate your slide show as a complete multimedia production. After all your effort to create your presentation, the final details could be the lasting memory of your slide show.

Before you can deliver a slide show, you need to select the type of show you want. Will your show be presented by a speaker, or be self running? Will your show include narration or animation? These are some of the details you will need to set up for your slide show. Some presentations include slides that are appropriate for one audience but not for another. PowerPoint lets you create custom slide shows that include only a selection of slides, in whatever order you want, intended for a given audience.

After setting up your slide show requirements, you can add other special features to customize your show. Elements such as creating transitions between slides, adding special visual, sound, and animation effects. Using animations— effects that animate your slide elements, such as text flying in from the right or fading text after it's been shown, can increase the interest in your slide show.

PowerPoint includes tools that let you time your presentation to make sure that it is neither too long nor too short. You can set the timing of your slides as you rehearse your slide show. To make sure each slide has enough time on the screen. You might want to add a narration to your slide show or a music clip to play during a planned coffee break in your presentation. You can also create a self-running presentation to package for off-site clients or to run at a trade show.

What You'll Do

Create Slide Transitions

Add and Remove Animation

Use Specialized Animation

Coordinate Multiple Animations

Animate a SmartArt Graphic

Trigger Animations

Use the Animation Painter

Add Slide Timings

Record a Narration

Set Up a Slide Show

Create a Custom Slide Show

Hide Slides

Create a Self-Running Presentation

Work with Fonts

Creating Slide Transitions

If you want to give your presentation more visual interest, you can add transitions between slides. For example, you can create a fading out effect so that one slide fades out as it is replaced by a new slide, or you can have one slide appear to push another slide out of the way. If you like a more excite or dynamic effect, you can use transitions with 3-D motion effects, such as 3D rotation or orbit. You can also add sound effects to your transitions, though you need a sound card and speakers to play them. To quickly see if you like a transition, point to one in the Transition Quick Style gallery to display a live preview of it. When you add a transition effect to a slide, the effect takes place between the previous slide and the selected slide.

Apply a Transition to an Individual or All Slides

1. Click the slide(s) to which you want to add a transition effect.

2. Click the **Transitions** tab.

3. Click the scroll up or down arrow, or click the **More** list arrow in the Transition To This Slide group.

4. Point to a transition to view a live preview, and then click the transition effect you want.

   ◆ To remove a slide transition, click **None**.

5. Click the **Effect Options** button, and then an option for the selected effect, such as direction or color.

6. To apply the current transition to all slides in the presentation, click the **Apply To All** button.

Did You Know?

You can quickly view a slide's transition quickly in Slide Sorter view. In Slide Sorter view, click a slide's transition icon to view the transition effect.

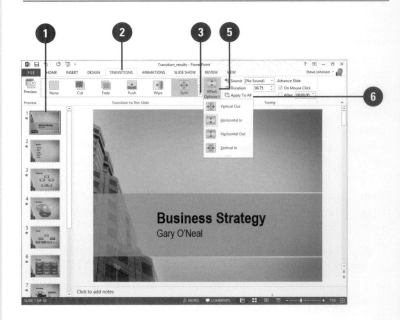

Set Transition Timing

1. In Normal or Slide Sorter view, click or display the slide whose transition effect you want to edit.

2. Click the **Transitions** tab.

3. Specify a duration for the selected transition.

4. To have the slide advance in a slide show after a certain time, select the **After** check box, and then specify a duration.

5. To apply the settings to all slides, click the **Apply To All** button.

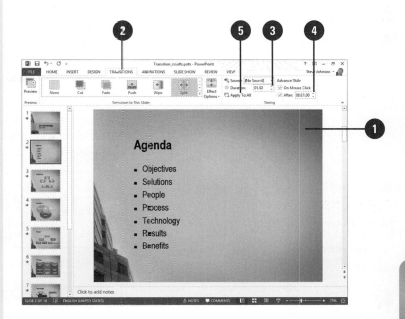

Add Sound to a Transition

1. In Normal or Slide Sorter view, click or display the slide to which you want to add a transition sound.

2. Click the **Transitions** tab.

3. Click the **Transition Sound** list arrow, and then click a sound you want, or choose an option:

   ◆ Click **[No Sound]** or **[Stop Previous Sound]** to specify the command.

   ◆ Click **Other Sound** to select a sound file.

   ◆ Click **Loop Until Next Sound** to toggle the sound loop option.

4. To apply the settings to all slides, click the **Apply To All** button.

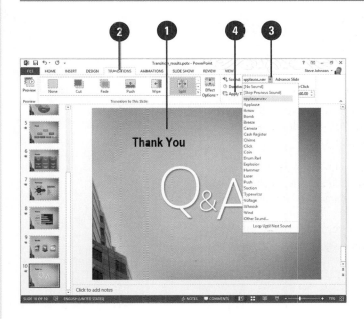

Adding and Removing Animation

You can use animation to introduce objects onto a slide one at a time or with special animation effects. For example, a bulleted list can appear one bulleted item at a time, or a picture or chart can fade in gradually. There are four types of animations: Entrance, Exit, Emphasis and Motion Path (animations along a line). You can apply one or more animations to the same object. To quickly see if you like an animation, point to a name in the Animation list to display a live preview of it. If you like it, you can apply it. You can also design your own customized animations, including those with your own effects and sound elements. If you no longer want to use an animation, you can remove it.

Apply and Preview a Animation Effect to Text or an Object

1. Select the text or object you want to animate.

2. Click the **Animations** tab.

3. Click the **Animation** list arrow, and then point to an animation.

    A live preview of the style appears in the current shape.

4. Click the animation you want.

5. To add multiple animations, click the **Add Animation** button, and then click the animation you want.

6. To preview an animation, click the **Preview** button.

    ◆ To stop an animation, click the **Preview** button again.

    ◆ To automatically preview an animation after adding or changing one, click the **Preview** button arrow, and then click **AutoPreview** to select it.

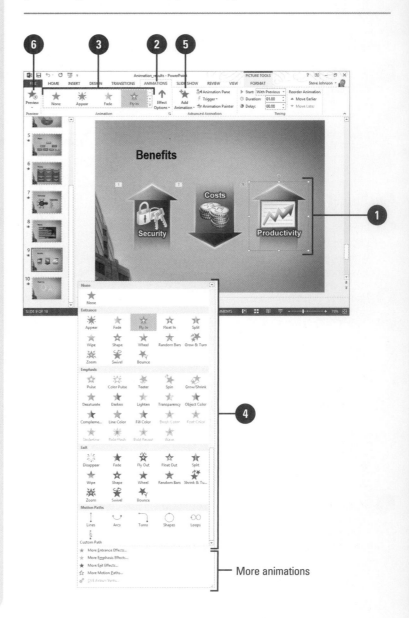

More animations

Remove an Animation

1. In Normal view, select the object you want to animate.

2. Click the **Animations** tab.

3. Click the **Animations** list arrow, and then click **None**.

Did You Know?

You can view a slide's animation quickly in Slide Sorter view. In Slide Sorter view, click a slide's animation icon to view the animation.

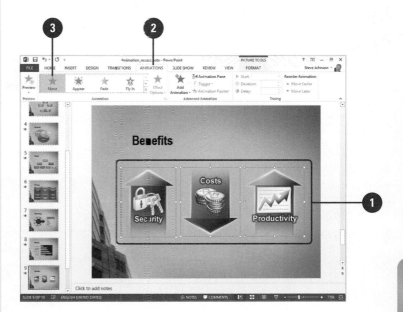

Add Sound to an Animation

1. In Normal view, select the object you want to animate.

2. Click the **Animations** tab.

3. Click the **Animations Pane** button.

4. In the Animation Order list, click the list arrow of the animation to which you want to add a sound, and then click **Effect Options**.

5. Click the **Sound** list arrow, and then click the sound effect you want.

   ◆ To add your own sound, click **Other Sound** from the list, select the sound you want, and then click **OK**.

6. Click **OK**.

7. Click the **Play From** button to hear the animation effect.

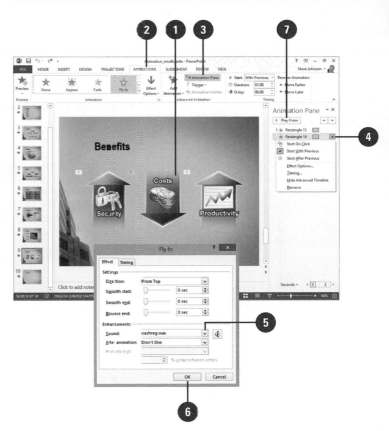

Using Specialized Animations

Using specialized animations, you can quickly apply animations specific to certain objects using the Animations tab. For example, for a text object, you can introduce the text on your slide all at once or by word or letter. Similarly, you can introduce bulleted lists one bullet item at a time and apply different effects to older items, such as graying the items out as they are replaced by new ones. You can animate charts by introducing chart series or chart categories one at a time. When you create a motion path animation, the original object stays put, and PowerPoint displays a ghost image as it moves along the path to the end (**New!**).

Animate Text or Bulleted Lists

1. In Normal view, select the text object you want to animate.

2. Click the **Animations** tab.

3. Click the **Animation** list arrow, and then click an animation (Entrance, Emphasis, Exit, or Motion Paths).

    ◆ For some motion paths, click points to create a path (**New!**).

4. Click the **Effect Options** button, and then specify any of the following:

    ◆ **Direction.** Select a direction for the animation: **Down**, **Left**, **Right**, or **Up**.

    ◆ **Sequence.** Select a grouping for the animation: **As One Object**, **All At Once**, or **By Paragraph**.

    ◆ **Origin.** Select **Locked** or **Unlocked**.

    ◆ **Path.** Select **Edit Points** to change the animation path, or **Reverse Path Direction**.

5. To dim text after the animation, click the **Animation Dialog Box Launcher**, click the **After Animation** list arrow, click the dim text color or option you want, and then click **OK**.

6. To see the animation effect, click the **Preview** button.

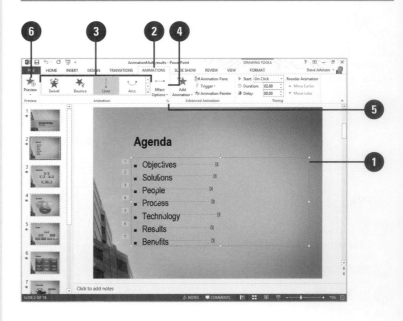

Other animation options

Dim text after the animation

Animate Shape Elements

1. In Normal view, select the shape you want to animate.

2. Click the **Animations** tab.

3. Click the **Animation** list arrow, and then click an animation (Entrance, Emphasis, Exit, or Motion Paths).

   - For some motion paths, click points to create a path.

4. Click the **Effect Options** button, and then select a direction.

5. To see the animation effect, click the **Preview** button.

Did You Know?

You can view a slide's animation quickly in Slide Sorter view. In Slide Sorter view, click a slide's animation icon to view the animation.

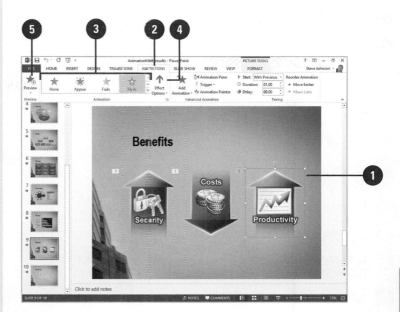

Animate Chart Elements

1. In Normal view, select the chart you want to animate.

2. Click the **Animations** tab.

3. Click the **Animation** list arrow, and then click an animation (Entrance, Emphasis, Exit, or Motion Paths).

   - For some motion paths, click points to create a path.

4. Click the **Effect Options** button, and then select a grouping sequence (**As One Object**, **By Series**, **By Category**, **By Element in Series**, or **By Element in Category**).

5. To see the animation effect, click the **Preview** button.

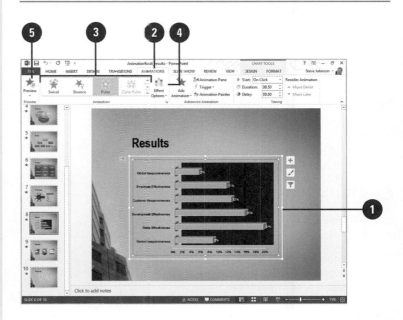

Coordinating Multiple Animations

The Animation pane helps you keep track of your animations by listing all animated objects in a single location. Use these lists if your slides contain more than one animation, because they help you determine how the animations will work together. You can control the animation of each object, the order each object appears, the time between animation effects, when an animation takes place—on click or video bookmark trigger—and remove unwanted animations.

Work with Multiple Animations

1. In Normal view, select the slide objects you want to change.

2. Click the **Animations** tab.

3. Click the **Animation Pane** button.

4. Click an animated object in the Animation pane to select it.

5. To select animation options, click the list arrow, and then select an option. To remove an animation, click **Remove**.

6. To play the animations and display a timing line, click the **Play** button.

   ◆ To zoom the pane in or out, click the **Seconds** button, and then click **Zoom In** or **Zoom Out**.

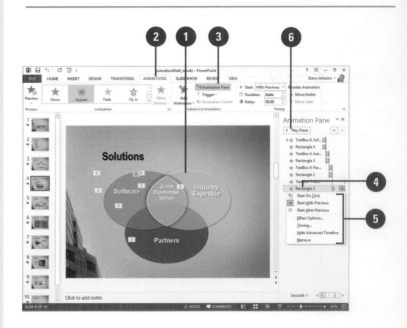

Modify the Animation Order

1. In Normal view, select the slide object you want to re-order.

   Animation sequence numbers appear next to animated objects indicating the animation order.

2. Click the **Animations** tab.

3. Click the **Move Earlier** or **Move Later** button.

   ◆ In the Animation pane, you can select an animation, and then click the **Re-Order Up** or **Down** arrow button.

4. To see the animation effect, click the **Preview** button.

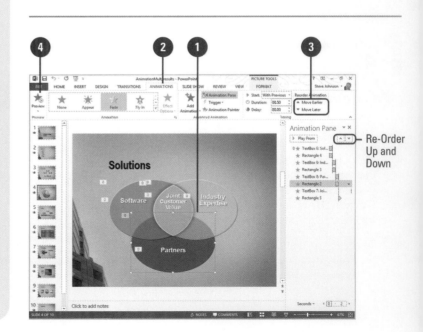

Re-Order Up and Down

Set Time Between Animations

1. In Normal view, select the slide object you want to animate.

2. Click the **Animations** tab.

3. Click the **Start** list arrow, and then click **After Previous**, **With Previous**, or **On Click**.

4. Use the **Duration** arrows to select the number of seconds to play this animation.

5. Use the **Delay** arrows to select the number of seconds to wait before playing this animation.

6. To see the animation effect, click the **Preview** button.

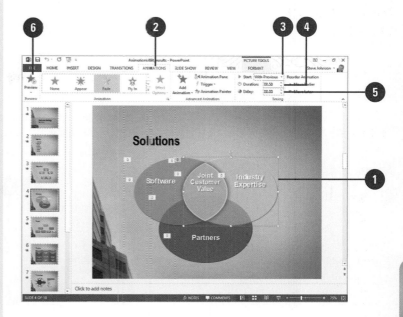

Modify an Animation

1. In Normal view, select the object with the animation you want to change.

2. Click the **Animations** tab.

3. Click the **Animations Pane** button.

4. In the Animation Order list, click the list arrow of the animation to which you want to add a sound, and then click **Effect Options**.

5. Adjust the options for the selected animations.

6. Click **OK**.

7. Click the **Play** button to hear the animation effect.

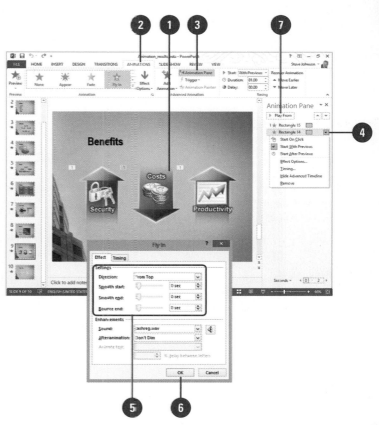

Animating a SmartArt Graphic

SmartArt graphics allow you to create diagrams that convey processes or relationships. You can add animation to a SmartArt graphic to show information in phases on a slide one at a time or with special animation effects. The easiest way to apply animation effects to a slide show is to use animation commands on the Animations tab. To quickly see if you like an animation, point to a name in the Animation list to display a live preview of it. If you like it, you can apply it. You can also design your own customized animations, including those with your own special effects and sound elements.

Animate a SmartArt Graphic

1 Select the SmartArt graphic you want to animate.

2 Click the **Animations** tab.

3 Click the **Animation** list arrow, and then point to an animation.

A live preview of the style appears in the current shape.

4 Click the animation you want.

◆ **None.** Removes the animation effect.

5 Click the **Effect Options** button, and then an option for the selected effect (options vary depending on the SmartArt graphic):

◆ **As One Object.** Animates the SmartArt object as a whole.

◆ **All at Once.** Animates all shapes at the same time.

◆ **One by One.** Animates each shape individually one at a time.

6 To see the animation effect, click the **Preview** button.

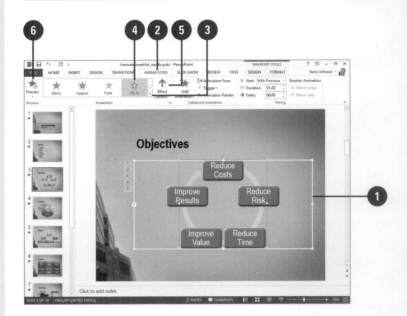

Apply a Customized Animation to a SmartArt Graphic

1 Select the SmartArt graphic or individual shape you want to animate.

2 Click the **Animations** tab.

3 Click the **Add Animations** button, and then click the animation you want, or one of the More commands to display additional effects.

4 Click the **Effect Options** button, and then click a direction.

5 To see the animation effect, click the **Preview** button.

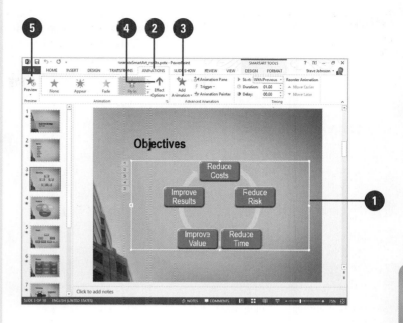

Reverse the Order of a SmartArt Graphic Animation

1 Select the SmartArt graphic you want to reverse.

2 Click the **Animations** tab.

3 Click the **Animation Pane** button.

4 In the Animation Order list, click the list arrow of the animation to which you want to reverse, and then click **Effect Options**.

5 Click the **SmartArt Animation** tab.

6 Select the **Reverse order** check box.

7 Click **OK**, and then click the **Play** button to see the animation effect.

Triggering Animations

You can control when an animation takes place by using an animation timing, clicking an object, or specifying a bookmark in a video. The Trigger button on the Animations tab allows you to select an On Click of or On Bookmark item. Before you can use a bookmark to trigger an animation, you need to add a bookmark to a video in your presentation using the Playback tab under Video Tools when you select a video.

Trigger an Animation

1. In Normal view, select the slide object that has the animation you want to trigger.

2. Click the **Animations** tab.

3. Click the **Trigger** button, and then point to:

   ◆ **On Click of.** Select the object you want to trigger the animation.

   ◆ **On Bookmark.** Select the video bookmark you want to trigger the animation.

4. To see the animation effect, click the **Slide Show** button, and then click the object to trigger it.

5. To remove a trigger, click the **Trigger** button, point to **On Click of** or **On Bookmark**, and then select the trigger to deselect it.

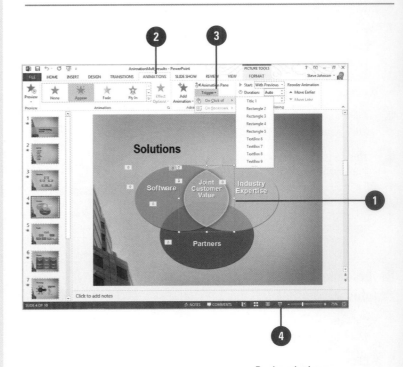

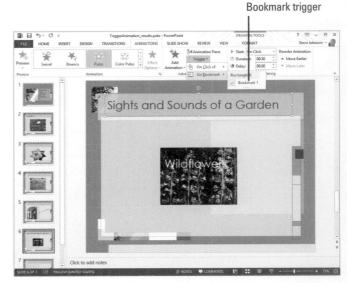

Bookmark trigger

Using the Animation Painter

After you create an animation, you might want to apply those same animation changes to another object in your presentation. You can use the Animation Painter to quickly copy it to another object, just like the Format Painter. The Animation Painter lets you "pick up" the animation of one selection and apply, or "paint," it to another. To apply an animation style to more than one item, double-click the Animation Painter button on the Animations tab instead of a single-click. The double-click keeps the Animation Painter active until you want to press Esc to disable it, so you can apply animations to any text or object you want in your presentation.

Apply an Animation to Another Object

1. Select the text or object with the animation you want to use.

2. Click the **Animations** tab.

3. Click the **Animation Painter** button.

4. Click the object you want to apply the animation.

   ◆ To apply the animation to multiple objects, double-click the **Animation Painter** button; press Esc to exit.

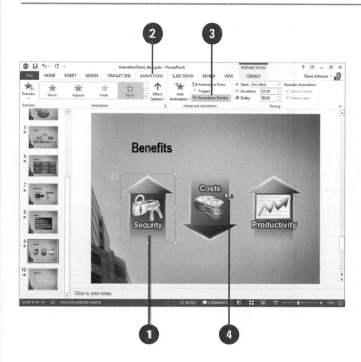

Adding Slide Timings

Use slide timing features to make sure that your presentation is not too long or too fast. You can specify the amount of time given to each slide or use Rehearse Timings. By rehearsing timings, you can vary the amount of time each slide appears on the screen. If you want the timings to take effect, make sure the show is set to use timings in the Set Up Show dialog box. In Slide Show View, a mouse click always advances a slide, even if the set timing has not elapsed, and holding down the mouse button prevents a timed transition until you release it.

Set or Edit Timings Between Slides

1. Click the slide(s) to which you want to set or change slide timings.

2. Click the **Transitions** tab.

3. Select the **After** check box.

4. Enter the time (in seconds) before the presentation automatically advances to the next slide after displaying the entire slide.

5. To apply the settings to all slides, click the **Apply To All** button.

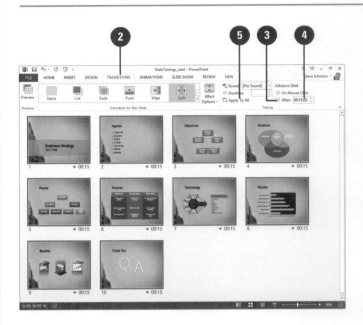

Did You Know?

You can use the mouse to control slide timings. In Slide Show View, a mouse click always advances a slide, even if the set timing has not elapsed, and holding down the mouse button prevents a timed transition from occurring until you release the mouse button.

Create Timings Through Rehearsal

1 Click the **Slide Show** tab.

2 Click the **Rehearse Timings** button.

3 As the slide show runs, rehearse your presentation by clicking or pressing Enter to go to the next transition or slide.

4 When you're done, click **Yes** to accept the timings.

5 To test timings, start the slide show and note when the slides advance too quickly or too slowly.

6 Review and edit individual timings in Slide Sorter view.

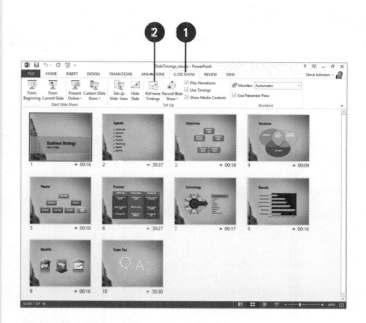

Recording a Narration

If you are creating a self-running presentation, you might want to add a narration to emphasize the points you make. PowerPoint lets you record your own narration as you rehearse your slide show. You can record a narration before you run a slide show, or you can record it during the presentation and include audience comments. As you record the narration, you can pause or stop the narration at any time. When you play back a narration, the recording is synchronized with the presentation, including all slide transitions and animations. You can also delete a voice narration, as with any other PowerPoint object. You will need to set up a microphone and a sound card before recording a slide show.

Record a Narration and Slide Show

1. Click the **Slide Show** tab.

2. Click the **Record Slide Show** button arrow, and then click **Start Recording from Beginning** or **Start Recording from Current Slide**.

3. Select the **Narrations and laser pointer** check box, and then select or clear the **Slide and animation timings** check box.

4. Click **Start Recording**.

5. Speak clearly into the microphone and record your narration for each slide.

   ◆ To pause the narration, click the Pause button on the Recording toolbar or right-click anywhere on the screen, and then click **Pause Recording**. To resume, click **Resume Recording**.

   ◆ To end the narration, right-click anywhere on the screen, and then click **End Show**.

   The recorded slide show timings are automatically saved and the slide show appears in Slide Show view.

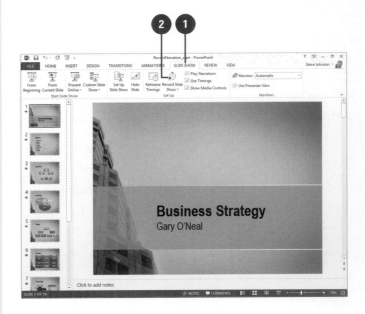

Clear Timings or Narration

1. Click the **Slide Show** tab.

2. Click the **Record Slide Show** button arrow, and then point to **Clear**.

3. Click any of the following options:

   ◆ **Clear Timing on Current Slide.**

   ◆ **Clear Timing on All Slides.**

   ◆ **Clear Narration on Current Slide.**

   ◆ **Clear Narration on All Slides.**

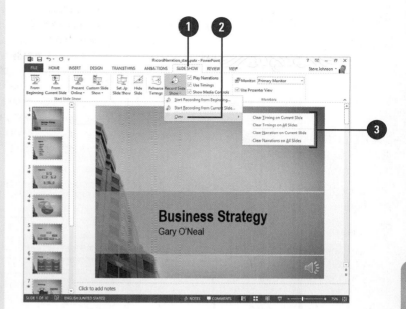

Did You Know?

You can show a presentation without narration. To show a presentation with narration on a computer without sound hardware installed, click the Slide Show tab, click the Set Up Show button, select the Show Without Narration check box to avoid problems running the presentation, and then click OK.

See Also

See "Recording Audio" on page 202 for more information and additional ways to record sound.

Setting Up a Slide Show

PowerPoint offers several types of slide shows appropriate for a variety of presentation situations, from a traditional big-screen slide show to a show that runs automatically on a computer screen at a conference kiosk. When you don't want to show all of the slides in a PowerPoint presentation to a particular audience, you can specify only a range of slides to show, or you can hide individual slides. You can also save a presentation to open directly into Slide Show view or run continuously.

Set Up a Show

1 Click the **Slide Show** tab.

2 Click the **Set Up Slide Show** button.

3 Choose the show type you want.

- Click the **Presented by a speaker** option to run a full screen slide show.

- Click the **Browsed by an individual** option to run a slide show in a window and allow access to commands.

- Click the **Browsed at a kiosk** option to create a self-running, unattended slide show for a booth or kiosk.

4 Select or clear the following show options check boxes:

- **Loop continuously until 'Esc'.** Select to replay the slide show again until you stop it.

- **Show without narration.** Select to not play narration.

- **Show without animation.** Select to not play animation.

- **Disable hardware graphics acceleration.** Select to if you have a display problem (**New!**).

5 Select the **Manually** or **Using timings, if present** option.

6 If you have multiple monitors, click the **Slide show monitor** list arrow, and then select an option (**New!**).

7 Click the **Resolution** list arrow, and then click **Use Current Resolution**, or select a resolution (**New!**).

8 Click **OK**.

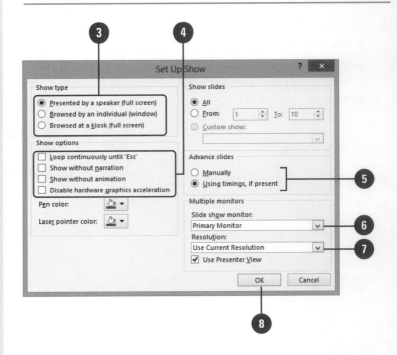

For Your Information

How Do You Choose a Screen Resolution?

The quality of a display system depends on its screen resolution, how many pixels it can display, and how many bits are used to represent each pixel. The screen resolution signifies the number of dots (pixels) on the entire screen. A higher screen resolution, such as 1024 by 768, makes items appear smaller, while a lower screen resolution, such as 640 by 480, makes items appear larger, which can help make a slide show easier to view.

Show a Custom Show or Range of Slides

1. Click the **Slide Show** tab.

2. Click the **Set Up Show** button.

3. To show a range of slides, click the **From** option, and then enter the first and last slide numbers of the range you want to show.

4. To show a custom show, click the **Custom Show** option, and then select a custom show.

5. Click **OK**.

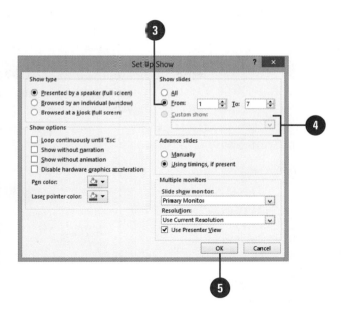

Set Pen and Laser Pointer Color

1. Click the **Slide Show** tab.

2. Click the **Set Up Show** button.

3. Click the **Pen color** or **Laster pointer color** list arrow, and then select a color.

4. Click **OK**.

Did You Know?

You can turn your mouse into a laser pointer. In Slide Show view, hold down Ctrl, click the left mouse button, and the begin pointing. You can also click the Pen button on the Slide Show toolbar, and then click Laser Pointer.

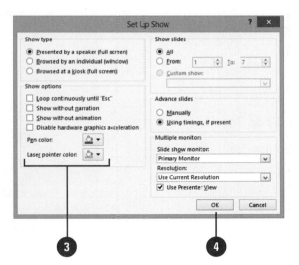

Creating a Custom Slide Show

If you plan to present a slide show to more than one audience, you don't have to create a separate slide show for each audience. Instead, you can create a custom slide show that allows you to specify which slides from the presentation you will use and the order in which they will appear. You can also edit a custom show which you've already created. Add, remove, and rearrange slides in a custom show to fit your various needs.

Create a Custom Slide Show

1. Click the **Slide Show** tab.

2. Click the **Custom Slide Show** button, and then click **Custom Shows**.

3. Click **New**.

4. Type a name for the show.

5. Click the slide check boxes, and then click **Add**. To remove a slide, select it in the Slides In Custom Show list, and then click **Remove**.

6. Click **OK**.

7. Click **Close**.

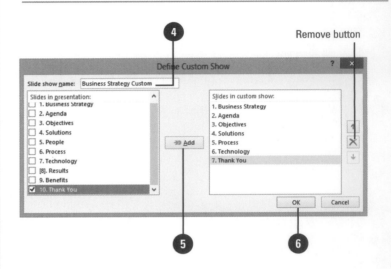

Show a Custom Slide Show

1. Click the **Slide Show** tab.

2. Click the **Custom Slide Show** button, and then click **Custom Shows**.

3. Click the custom slide show you want to run.

4. Click **Show**.

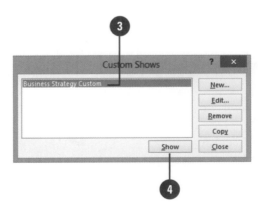

Did You Know?

You can print a custom show. Click the File tab, click Print, click the Print Range list arrow, select a custom show, and then click Print.

Edit a Custom Slide Show

1. Click the **Slide Show** tab.

2. Click the **Custom Slide Show** button, and then click **Custom Shows**.

3. Click the show you want to edit.

4. Click **Edit**.

5. To add a slide, click the slide in the Slides In Presentation list and then click the **Add** button. The slide appears at the end of the Slides In Custom Show list.

6. To remove a slide from the show, click the slide in the Slides In Custom Show list, and then click the **Remove** button.

7. To move a slide up or down in the show, click the slide in the Slides In Custom Show list, and then click the **Up Arrow** or **Down Arrow** button.

8. Click **OK**.

9. Click **Close**.

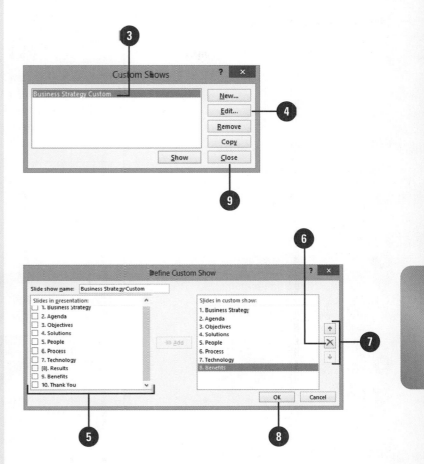

Did You Know?

You can delete a custom slide show. Click the Slide Show tab, click the Custom Slide Show button, click Custom Shows, click the show you want to delete, click Remove, and then click Close.

You can use the Set Up Show command to display a custom slide show. Click the Slide Show tab, click the Set Up Show button, click the Custom Show option, click the Custom Show list arrow, select the custom slide show, and then click OK.

Hiding Slides

Instead of creating a custom show for a slide show, you can also hide slides in your presentation. This is useful if you have a few slides that you don't want to show. You can quickly hide one or more selected slides by using the Hide Slide button. When you hide a slide, a circle with a line through it appears over the slide number in the Slide pane or Slide Sorter view. If you have hidden slides in a presentation, you can still print them by using the Print Slides option in the Print Range on the Print Screen. If you want to show a hidden slide, you can select it and then use the Hide Slide button again.

Hide Slides

1. In Slide Sorter view or Normal view, select or display the slide you want to hide.

2. Click the **Slide Show** tab.

3. Click the **Hide Slide** button.

   The slide number in the Slide pane or Slide Sorter view appears with a circle and a line through it.

4. To show a hidden slide, click it, and then click the **Hide Slide** button again.

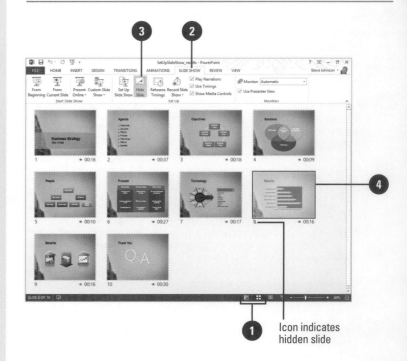

Icon indicates hidden slide

Creating a Self-Running Presentation

Self-running slide shows are a great way to communicate information without needing someone to run the show. You might want to set up a presentation to run unattended in a kiosk at a trade show or place it on your company's Intranet to run at the user's convenience. The slides will advance automatically, or a user can advance the slides or activate hyperlinks. You can use the Set Up Show dialog box to select the Browsed at a Kiosk (Full Screen) and other related options to create a self-running slide show.

Set Up a Self-Running Slide Show

1. Click the **Slide Show** tab.

2. Click the **Set Up Slide Show** button.

3. Select the **Manually** or **Using timings, if present** option, where you can advance the slides manually or automatically.

4. Click the **Browsed at a kiosk (full screen)** option.

   The Loop continuously until 'Esc' option is selected and grayed out; the options in Step 3 are also grayed out.

5. Select additional show options check boxes as appropriate.

6. Click **OK**.

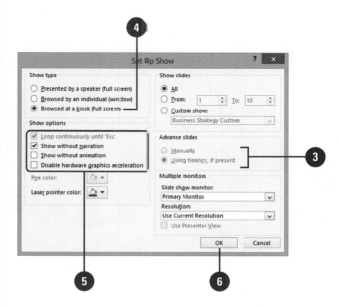

Did You Know?

Certain tools are active in a self-navigating show. A self-navigating show turns off all navigation tools except action buttons and other action settings available to the user.

You can run a slide show continuously. Open the presentation you want to run, click the Slide Show tab, click the Set Up Show button, select the Loop Continuously Until 'Esc' check box, and then click OK.

Working with Fonts

PowerPoint offers an assortment of tools for working with the fonts in your presentation. If you are using nonstandard fonts, you can embed the fonts you use so they "travel" with your presentation. Then, if the computer you use to show your presentation does not have all your fonts installed, the presentation quality will not suffer.

Embed TrueType Fonts in a Presentation

1. Click the **File** tab, and then click **Options**.

   TIMESAVER *If you're in the Save As dialog box, click the Tools button arrow, and then click Save Options.*

2. In the left pane, click **Save**.

3. Click the list arrow next to Preserve fidelity when sharing this presentation, and then select the presentation you want to embed fonts.

4. Select the **Embed fonts in the file** check box.

5. Click the option you want.

   ◆ **Embed only the characters used in the presentation (best for reducing file size).**

   ◆ **Embed all characters (best for editing by other people).**

6. Click **OK**.

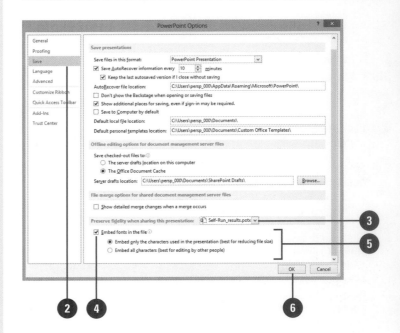

Did You Know?

Embedding fonts increase the presentation size. When you embed all characters in a presentation, you embed all the characters in the font set, and then increases file size.

Frequently Asked Questions

What's the Difference Between the Fonts?

There are two basic types of fonts: scalable and bitmapped. A **scalable font** (also known as **outline font**) is based on a mathematical equation that creates character outlines to form letters and numbers of any size. The two major scalable fonts are Adobe's Type 1 PostScript and Apple/Microsoft's TrueType or OpenType. Scalable fonts are generated in any point size on the fly and require only four variations for each typeface. A **bitmapped font** consists of a set of dot patterns for each letter and number in a typeface for a specified type size. Bitmapped fonts are created or prepackaged ahead of time and require four variations for each point size used in each typeface. Although a bitmapped font designed for a particular font size will always look the best, scalable fonts eliminate storing hundreds of different sizes of fonts on disk.

Presenting a Slide Show

Introduction

When you're done preparing your slide show, it's time to consider how to show it to your audience. Microsoft PowerPoint gives you several ways to give and share your presentations. When you are presenting the show in person, you can use PowerPoint's slide navigation tools to move around your presentation. You can move forward and backward or move to a specific slide by using various navigation keys on the keyboard and on-screen Slide Show tools.

As you're presenting your slide show, you can highlight key ideas by using the mouse as a pointer or pen/highlighter. By annotating your slide show, you can give extra emphasis on a topic or goal for your audience. Annotations can be saved as enhancements to your presentation for later. If you are presenting a slide show using a second monitor or projection screen, PowerPoint includes the tools you need to properly navigate the display equipment.

If you are taking your presentation to another site, you might not need the entire PowerPoint package. Rather than installing PowerPoint on the sites' computer, you can pack your presentation into one compressed file, storing it on a CD. Once you reach your destination, you can expand the compressed file onto your client's computer and play it, regardless of whether that computer has PowerPoint installed.

What You'll Do

Start a Slide Show

Navigate a Slide Show

Navigate a Slide Show with Touch

Annotate a Slide Show

Deliver a Show on Multiple Monitors

Display a Show in Presenter View

Save a Presentation as a Slide Show

Save a Presentation as a Video

Package a Presentation on CD

Broadcast a Presentation Online

Give a Presentation at an Online Lync Meeting

Communicate Online with Lync

Show a Presentation with the PowerPoint Viewer

Customize the PowerPoint Viewer

Show Multiple Presentations

Starting a Slide Show

Once you have set up your slide show, you can start the show at any time. As you run your slide show, you can use the Slide Show toolbar, or Pop-up toolbar, to access certain PowerPoint commands without leaving Slide Show view. One of the commands is a Zoom button (**New!**), which allows you to see an enlarge view of an area. Another is the See all slides button (**New!**), which allows you to go to slides out of order.

Start a Slide Show

1. Click the **Slide Show** tab.

   TIMESAVER *Click the Slide Show View button on the Status bar to start a slide show quickly from the current slide.*

2. Click the **From Beginning** or **From Current Slide** button.

3. Move the mouse pointer to display the Slide Show toolbar.

4. Click a button on the Slide Show toolbar.

   ◆ **Next or previous slide.** Click to go between slides.

   ◆ **Pen and laser pointer tools.** Click to change pen options.

   ◆ **See all slides.** Click to display the Slide Navigator (**New!**).

   ◆ **Zoom in.** Click, move the zoom view, and then click (**New!**). Right-click to zoom out.

   ◆ **More Options.** Click to display an options menu.

   TIMESAVER *Press Esc to stop a slide show.*

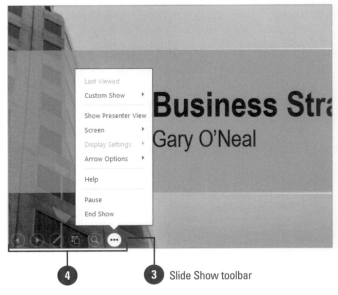

3 Slide Show toolbar

Set Slide Show Options

1 Click the **File** tab, and then click **Options**.

2 In the left pane, click **Advanced**.

3 Select the slide show and pop-up toolbar check box options you want.

◆ **Show menu on right mouse click.** Select to show a shortcut menu when you right-click a slide during a slide show.

◆ **Show popup toolbar.** Select to show the popup toolbar at the bottom of a full screen presentation.

◆ **Prompt to keep ink annotations when exiting.** Select to be prompted to save your changes when you write on slides during a slide show.

◆ **End with black slide.** Select to insert a black slide at the end of the presentation.

4 Click **OK**.

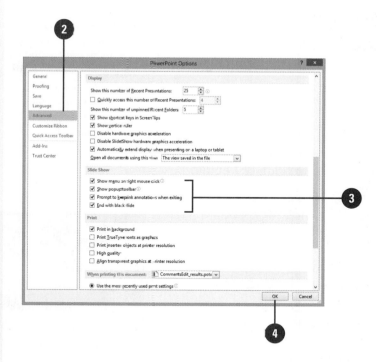

Navigating a Slide Show

In Slide Show view, you advance to the next slide by clicking the mouse button, pressing the Spacebar, or pressing Enter. In addition to those basic navigational techniques, PowerPoint provides keyboard shortcuts that can take you to the beginning, the end, or any particular slide in your presentation. You can also use Slide Navigator (**New!**) to access slides or sections or navigation commands on the shortcut menu to access slides in custom slide shows. After a period of inactivity during a normal full-screen slide show, PowerPoint hides the pointer and Slide Show toolbar.

Go to a Specific Slide or Section

1. In Slide Show view, move the mouse to display the Slide Show toolbar, and then click the **See all slides** button.

    TIMESAVER *Pinch two fingers to display the Navigation pane.*

    Slide Navigator appears (**New!**) with slides and sections in Slide Show view.

2. Click the slide title or section to which you want to go.

3. To go back to the slide show without selecting a slide or section, click the **Back** button (**New!**).

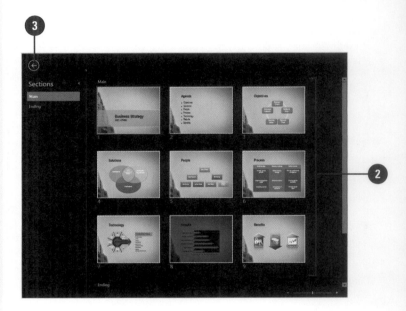

Did You Know?

You can switch to another program in Slide Show view. In Slide Show view, right-click a blank area on the slide, click Screen, and then click Show Taskbar (**New!**). Use the taskbar to switch between programs.

Use Slide Show View Navigation Shortcuts

◆ Refer to the adjacent table for information on Slide Show view navigation keyboard shortcuts.

Did You Know?

You can turn your mouse into a laser pointer. In Slide Show view, hold down Ctrl, click the left mouse button, and the begin pointing. You can also click the Pen button on the Slide Show toolbar, and then click Laser Pointer. To change the laser pointer color, click the Slide Show tab, click the Set Up Show button, click the Laser Pointer Color list arrow, select a color, and then click OK.

Slide Show View Shortcuts

Action	Result
Mouse click	Moves to the next slide
Right-mouse click	Moves to the previous slide (only if the Shortcut Menu On Right-Click option is disabled)
Press Enter	Moves to the next slide
Press Home	Moves to the first slide in the show
Press End	Moves to the last slide in the show
Press Page Up	Moves to the previous slide
Press Page Down	Moves to the next slide
Enter a slide number and press Enter	Moves to the slide number you specified when you press Enter
Press B	Displays a black screen; press again to return
Press W	Displays a white screen; press again to return
Press Esc	Exits Slide Show view

Go to a Custom Slide Show or Section

1. In Slide Show view, click the **More Options** button on the Slide Show toolbar or right-click a slide.

2. Click (on More Options) or point to **Custom Show**.

3. Click the custom slide show that you want to go to.

See Also

See "Creating a Custom Slide Show" on page 336 for information on creating a custom slide show.

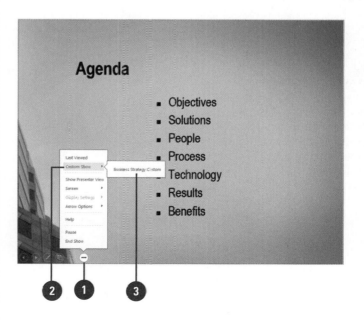

Navigating a Slide Show with Touch

If you're working with PowerPoint on a touch screen device, all you need is your finger to make gestures (**New!**). A gesture is the movement of one or more fingers on a touch screen or pad. For example, touching the screen is called tapping or dragging your finger with a flicking motion at the end of the movement is called swiping. You can swipe, tap, scroll, zoom, and pan within any PowerPoint view to navigate between and work with slides. You can select an object or range of text to edit it, swipe right or left to switch slides, or pinch/stretch to zoom in or out. To make PowerPoint easier to use with touch screens, the program provides Touch/Mouse Mode (**New!**), which adds or removes more space between commands on the Ribbon.

Use Touch Gestures in Slide Show View

1 In Slide Show view, use any of the following gestures:

- ◆ **Next or Previous Slide.** Swipe (touch and flick) right or left.

- ◆ **Zoom.** Stretch two fingers to zoom in. Touch and slide to scroll around in the zoom. Tap the screen or pinch two fingers to zoom out.

- ◆ **Navigation Pane.** Pinch two fingers to display the Navigation pane. Touch and slide up or down to scroll. Tap a slide to display it.

- ◆ **Slide Show Toolbar.** Tap the screen to display the Slide Show toolbar. Tap buttons and menu items to execute commands. Tap or drag to use annotation, eraser, and pointer options.

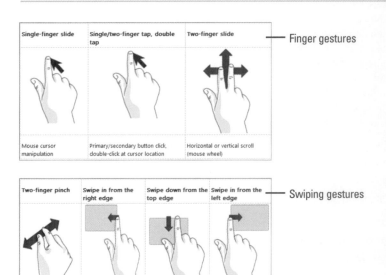

Finger gestures

Swiping gestures

Use Touch/Mouse Mode

1. Click the **Quick Access Toolbar** list arrow, and then click **Touch/Mouse Mode**.

   This adds the button to the Quick Access Toolbar.

2. Click **Touch/Mouse Mode** button on the Quick Access Toolbar.

3. Click **Mouse** or **Touch**.

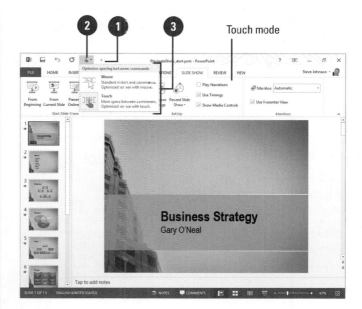

Touch mode

Did You Know?

You can use touch commands. In Office, you can use the following touch commands:

Click - Tap in the file.

Double-click - Double-tap in the file.

Drag - Tap and slide.

Zoom - Pinch or stretch two fingers.

Pan - Pinch or stretch two fingers and drag.

Scroll - Touch and slide up or down.

Swipe - Touch and flick right or left.

Select - Tap an object. For multiple objects, select one (tap and hold), and then tap others. For text, tap and drag.

You can make text and objects bigger. In Windows, open the Control Panel, tap Appearance & Personalization, tap Display, and tap Medium - 125% or Larger - 150%, and then tap Apply.

Annotating a Slide Show

When you are presenting your slide show, you can turn your mouse pointer into a pen tool to highlight and circle your key points or a laser pointer tool (**New!**) to point to areas on the screen. If you decide to use a pen tool, you might want to set its color to match the colors in your presentation. When you are finished, you can turn the pen back to the normal mouse pointer. Mark ups you make on a slide with the pen tool during a slide show can be saved with the presentation, and then turned on or off when you re-open the presentation for editing.

Change Pointer Options

1. In Slide Show view, move the mouse to display the Slide Show toolbar.

2. Click the **More Options** button, click **Arrow Options**, and then click a pointer option.

   ◆ **Automatic** hides the pointer until you move the mouse.

   ◆ **Visible** makes the pointer visible.

   ◆ **Hidden** makes the pointer invisible throughout the presentation.

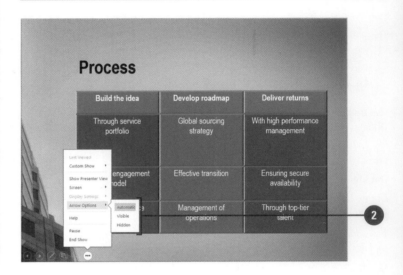

Use a Pen in a Slide Show

1. In Slide Show view, move the mouse to display the Slide Show toolbar.

2. Click the **Pen** button, and then click an option.

   ◆ A writing tool (**Highlighter** or **Pen**) or a pointing tool (**Laser Pointer** (**New!**)).

   ◆ **Ink Color.** Select an ink color.

3. Drag the mouse pointer to draw on your slide presentation with the pen or highlighter.

4. To remove ink, click the **Pen** button, and then click **Eraser** for individual ink, or click **Erase All Ink on Slide** for all ink.

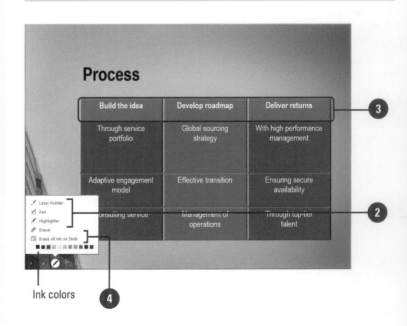

Ink colors

Save Annotations and Turn Them On and Off

1. In Slide Show view, right-click a slide.

2. Point to **Pointer Options**.

3. Click a pen or highlighter, and then make an annotation on a slide.

4. Right-click the slide, and then click **End Show**.

5. Click **Keep** when asked if you want to keep your ink annotations for editing.

6. In Normal view, click the **Review** tab.

7. Click the **Show Markup** button arrow, and then click **Show Markup** to select (show) or deselect (hide) it.

8. Click the **File** tab, click **Close**, and then click **Save** to save the changes.

   When you re-open this presentation, you can view the Mark ups in Normal or Slide Sorter view, and then turn them off or on.

Did You Know?

You can quickly turn the pen back to the mouse pointer. To turn the pen back to the normal mouse pointer, right-click a slide in Slide Show view, point to Pointer Options, and then click Arrow.

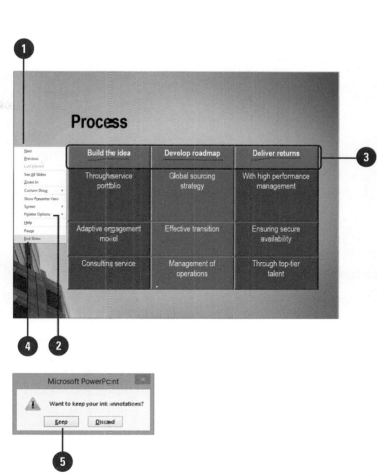

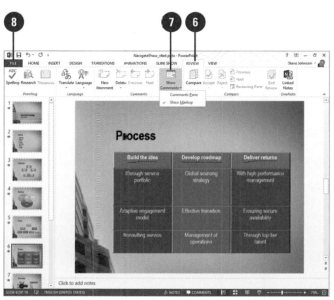

Delivering a Show on Multiple Monitors

If your computer is connected to two monitors, you can view a slide show on one monitor while you control it from another. This is useful when you want to control a slide show and run other programs that you don't want the audience to see. You can specify which monitor you want to use (**New!**) and the resolution (**New!**). PowerPoint can even sense your computer setup and choose the right monitor for you. When you display your slide show on multiple monitors, you can present it using PowerPoint's Presenter Tools in the Presenter view, which allows presenters to have their own view that is not visible to the audience. In addition to including details about what bullet or slide is coming next, this view also enables you to see your speaker notes and lets you jump directly to any slide. You can only use Presenter view and run the presentation from one monitor.

Turn on Multiple Monitor Support in PowerPoint

1. Click the **Slide Show** tab.

2. Click the **Set Up Slide Show** button.

3. Select the **Show Presenter View** check box.

4. Click the **Slide show monitor** list arrow (**New!**), and then select the option or monitor where you want to display the slide show.

   ◆ **Automatic.** PowerPoint automatically senses your computer setup and chooses the right monitor.

   ◆ **Primary Monitor.** Selects the primary monitor selected in your Windows setup.

5. Click the **Resolution** list arrow (**New!**), and then select **Use Current Resolution** or a specific screen size.

6. Click **OK**.

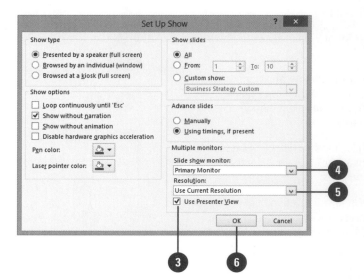

Turn on Multiple Monitor Support in Windows

1. In the desktop, right-click or tap-hold a blank area of the desktop, and then click or tap **Screen resolution**.

2. If the secondary monitor doesn't appear, click or tap **Detect**.

3. Click or tap the **Multiple displays** list arrow, and then select an option:

   ◆ **Duplicate these displays.**

   ◆ **Extend these displays.**

   ◆ **Show desktop only on 1.**

   ◆ **Show desktop only on 2.**

4. Select a monitor icon or drag an icon to represent how you want to move items from one monitor to another.

5. Select any of the following monitor options:

   ◆ **Display.** Changes the display driver.

   ◆ **Resolution.** Changes the screen resolution; drag the slider.

   ◆ **Orientation.** Changes the screen to landscape or portrait.

6. To change the primary display, select a non primary monitor, and then select the **Make this my main display** check box.

7. Click or tap **OK**.

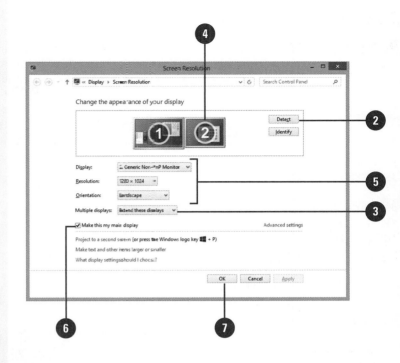

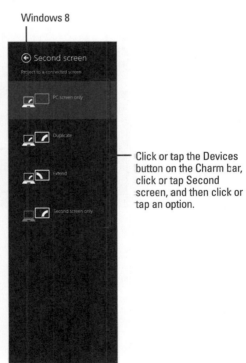

Windows 8

Click or tap the Devices button on the Charm bar, click or tap Second screen, and then click or tap an option.

Displaying a Show in Presenter View

With Presenter view (**New!**), you can deliver a slide show on one monitor while you control it from another. You can use Presenter view with one monitor (**New!**) to practice or two monitors to deliver it. When you want to use two monitors, be sure to turn on multiple monitor support in Windows Display Settings and select a Presenter view monitor setting (**New!**) in PowerPoint. In Presenter view, you can view the presentation time, current slide, speaker notes, and next slide, and use slide show view options. You can also use options to show the taskbar to run other programs, change display settings, and end the slide show.

Use Presenter View

1. Click the **Slide Show** tab.

2. Click the **Monitor** list arrow (**New!**), and then click **Automatic** (auto select) or **Primary Monitor**.

3. Select the **Use Presenter View** check box.

4. Click the **From Beginning** or **From Current Slide** button or click the **Slide Show** button on the Status bar.

5. For a single monitor, click the **More Options** button, and then click **Show Presenter View** (**New!**).

6. Use any of the following options in Presenter view (**New!**):

   ◆ **Show Taskbar.** Click to show or hide the taskbar, where you can switch to other programs.

   ◆ **Display Settings.** Click to switch between Presenter View and Slide Show view or create a duplicate slide show.

7. Use the navigation and tools in Presenter View to display the presentation.

   ◆ For other options, click the **More Options** button, and then select the option you want.

8. Press Esc or click **End Slide Show** to exit Presenter view.

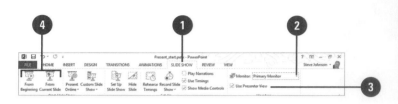

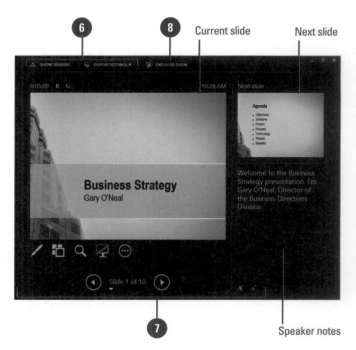

Current slide

Next slide

Speaker notes

Work with Presenter View

1. Click the **Slide Show** tab.

2. Click the **Monitor** list arrow (**New!**), and then click **Automatic** (auto select) or **Primary Monitor**.

3. Select the **Use Presenter View** check box.

4. Click the **From Beginning** or **From Current Slide** button or click the **Slide Show** button on the Status bar.

5. For a single monitor, click the **More Options** button, and then click **Show Presenter View** (**New!**).

6. Use any of the following options in Presenter view (**New!**):

   ◆ **Previous slide or next slide.** Click to navigate to slides.

   ◆ **Pen and laser pointer tools.** Click to select pen type, ink color, erase and arrow options.

   ◆ **See all slides.** Click to select a slide out of sequence.

   ◆ **Pen and laser pointer tools.** Click to select pen type, ink color, erase and arrow options.

   ◆ **Black or unblack slide.** Click to black or unblack the screen.

   ◆ **Speaker notes.** Click the **Larger Text** or **Smaller Text** buttons to change the notes text size.

7. For timer options, click the **Pause** or **Restart** buttons for the timer.

8. Press Esc or click **End Slide Show** to exit Presenter view.

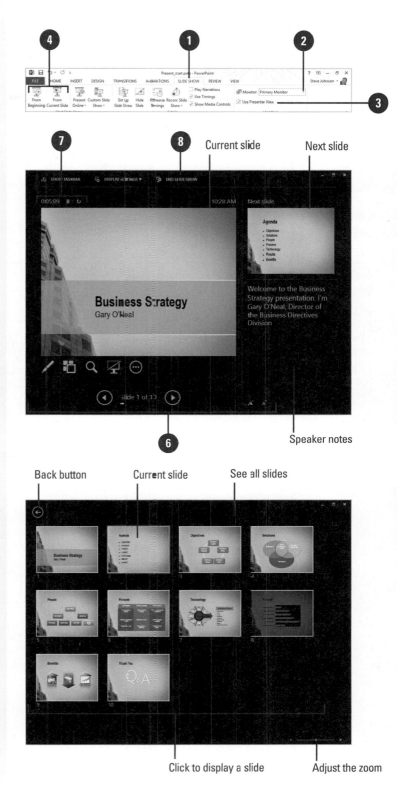

Current slide

Next slide

Speaker notes

Back button

Current slide

See all slides

Click to display a slide

Adjust the zoom

Saving a Presentation as a Slide Show

When you're giving a professional slide show presentation, you might not want your audience to see you start it from PowerPoint. Instead, you can save a presentation as a PowerPoint Show to open directly into Slide Show view. You can use the Save As dialog box to save a presentation as a PowerPoint Show (.ppsx) or PowerPoint Macro-Enabled (.ppsm). After you save a presentation as a PowerPoint Show file, you can create a shortcut to it on your desktop and then simply double-click the PowerPoint Show file to start it directly in Slide Show view. You need the Microsoft PowerPoint Viewer—available free online at *www.microsoft.com*—or PowerPoint software installed on your system to display the slide show.

Save a Presentation as a PowerPoint Show

1. Click the **File** tab, click **Save As**, click **Computer**, and then click **Browse**.

   ◆ You can also click the **File** tab, click **Export**, click **Change File Type**, and then click **PowerPoint Show**.

2. Specify a name and location for the slide show file.

3. Click the **Save as type** list arrow, and then click **PowerPoint Show** or **PowerPoint Macro-Enabled Show**.

4. Click **Save**.

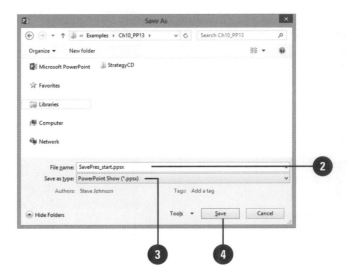

Saving a Presentation as a Video

Sometimes sharing a presentation as a video is the best approach. In PowerPoint, you can save a complete presentation, including slide timings and narration as a Windows Media Video (.wmv). After you save a presentation as a video file, you can share it with others on a web site, DVD, or network. It's a single file that you can run on most systems. If you need the video in a different video format, you need to use a third-party conversation software to convert the Windows Media Video file into another video format, such as MP4 or QuickTime.

Save a Presentation as a Video

1. Click the **File** tab, and then click **Export**.

2. Click **Create a Video**.

3. Click the **Resolution** list arrow, and then select any of the following:

   ◆ **Computer & HD Displays.** Creates for large screen (960 x 720).

   ◆ **Internet & DVD.** Creates for medium screen (640 x 480).

   ◆ **Portable Devices.** Creates for small screen (320 x 240).

4. Click the **Timing** list arrow, and then click **Don't Use Recorded Timings and Narrations** or **Use Recorded Timings and Narrations**, and then specify a time.

5. Click the **Create Video** button.

6. Specify a name and location for the video.

7. Click **Save**.

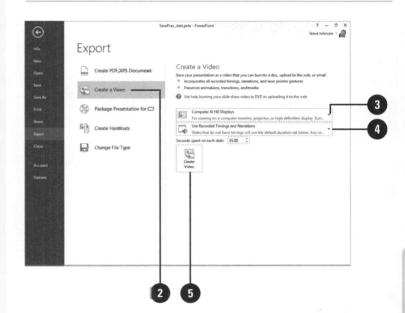

Packaging a Presentation on CD

The Package for CD feature allows you to copy one or more presentations and all of the supporting files, including linked files, on CD. You can choose packaging options to automatically or manually run your presentations. The PowerPoint Viewer is a program included on the packaged CD used to run presentations on computers that don't have PowerPoint installed. If you are packaging your presentation for use on your laptop, a DVD, or a network, you can use Package for CD to package your presentation to a folder or a network. PowerPoint doesn't support direct burning to DVDs, so you need to use DVD burning software to import the presentation files and create a DVD. Before you package your presentation, you can inspect it for hidden data and personal information.

Package a Presentation on CD or to a Folder

1. Click the **File** tab, click **Export**, and then click **Package Presentation for CD**.

2. Click the **Package for CD** button.

3. Type a name for the CD.

4. To add additional files to the CD, click **Add**, select the files you want, and then click **Open**.

   ◆ To reorder presentations, click **Move Up** or **Move Down**.

5. Click **Options**.

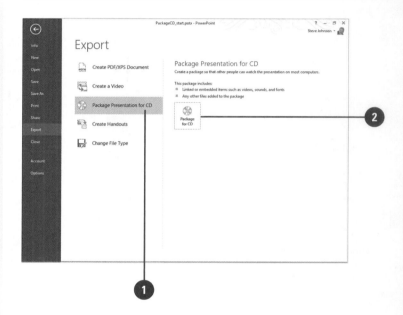

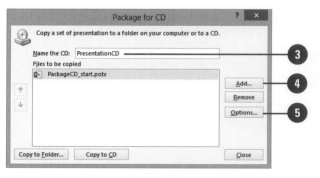

6 To link any external files, select the **Linked files** check box.

7 To ensure fonts are available on the play back computer, select the **Embedded TrueType fonts** check box.

8 If you want, type a password to open or modify the presentation.

9 To remove data, select the **Inspect presentations for inappropriate or private information** check box.

10 Click **OK**.

11 Click **Copy to CD**, and then follow the CD writer instructions, or click **Copy to Folder**, specify a folder location, and then click **OK**.

If a message alert appears, click the buttons you want to complete the process.

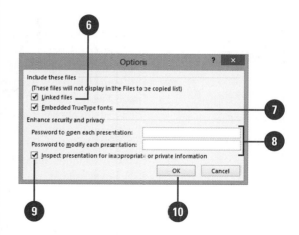

Copy to Folder options

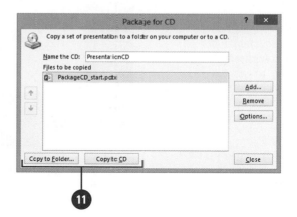

Broadcasting a Presentation Online

If you want to share an Office document (**New!**) with others at different locations, the Office Presentation Service allows you to deliver the document as a presentation over the Internet. The Office Presentation Service is a free service provided by Microsoft for use with your Microsoft account. Before you start the online broadcast, you send a URL link to your remote audience via an e-mail or copied link that they can use to access and watch your show in their browser. If you have notes in OneNote (**New!**), you can show them too. In the browser delivery of your show, some features are changed, including transitions shown as fades, no audio or video, no ink annotations, can't follow a hyperlink, and screensavers and e-mail popup can disrupt the view.

Join in to a Presentation Broadcast Online

1. Open the email, instant message, or document with the join in link for the presentation.

2. Click the link.

   ◆ You can also open your web browser, and then paste in the copied link.

   Your default web browser opens, displaying the document in the PowerPoint Web App.

3. To follow along with the presenter, click **Follow Presenter**. Available when you're not in sync with presenter.

4. To view shared meeting notes from OneNote in a new tab, click **Shared Meeting Notes**.

5. To download the broadcast document, if made available by the presenter, click the **File** tab, click **Save As**, click **Download**, specify a name and location, and then click **Save As**.

6. To create a PDF of the broadcast document, click the **File** tab, click **Print**, and then click **Print to PDF**; click a link to view it or click Close.

7. To disconnect from the broadcast, click the **Close** button on your web browser.

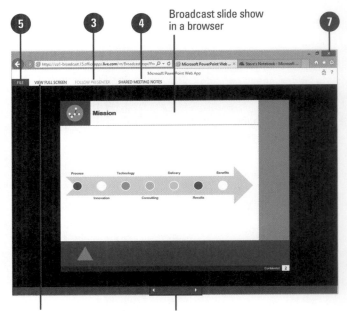

Broadcast slide show in a browser

Click to show in Full Screen (in a separate window)

Slide navigation

Broadcast a Presentation Online

1. Click the **File** tab, click **Share**, and then click **Present Online**.

2. Click the **Present Online** list arrow, and then select **Office Presentation Service**.

3. To allow users to download the presentation, select the **Enable remote viewers to download the presentation** check box.

4. Click the **Present Online** button.

   ◆ You can also click the **Present Online** button on the Slide Show tab, and then click **Office Presentation Service**.

5. Click the **Copy Link**, **Send in Email** or **Send in IM** link to share the link for others to access the broadcast.

6. Click **Start Presentation**.

7. As the presenter, navigate the presentation in Slide Show View.

   ◆ **Presenter View.** Right-click the screen, and then click **Show Presenter View**.

8. If you end the slide show, you can use any of the following buttons on the Present Online tab:

   ◆ **From Beginning or From Current Slide.** Use to start the slide show.

   ◆ **Monitor.** Use to select a display monitor for the slide show.

   ◆ **Use Presenter View.** Select to show in Presenter View.

   ◆ **Share Meeting Notes.** Use to share notes from OneNote.

   ◆ **Send Invitations.** Use to invite more people to the meeting.

9. To end the broadcast, click the **End Online Presentation** button on the Present Online tab, and then click **End Online Presentation**.

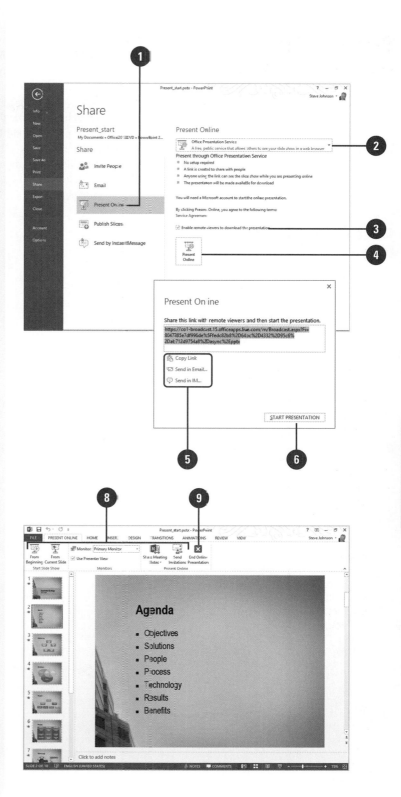

Giving a Presentation at an Online Lync Meeting

With Lync, you can present a document to an online meeting. With the Present Online command (**New!**), you can start a Lync meeting with the currently opened document. Microsoft Lync is an instant messaging program that allows you to hold online meetings with an audio and video experience. Lync uses a SharePoint or Office 365 site as the meeting or conversation host. During the meeting, you can use navigation buttons to move from slide to slide or use slide thumbnails (like Slide Sorter view), display speaker's notes, and share OneNote. You can switch to it in order to invited attendees to participate in the meeting and send instant messages. If not everyone is able to attend, you can also record the meeting (More Options) to play it back later.

Give a Presentation at an Online Lync Meeting

1. Click the **File** tab, click **Share**, and then click **Present Online**.

2. Click the **Present Online** list arrow, and then select **Microsoft Lync**.

3. Click the **Present Online** button.

   ◆ You can also click the **Present Online** button on the Slide Show tab, and then click **Microsoft Lync**.

4. Click **Start a new Lync Meeting**, and then click **OK**. If prompted, sign-in to the meeting with your SharePoint credentials.

5. Specify an audio and video option.

6. Click **OK**.

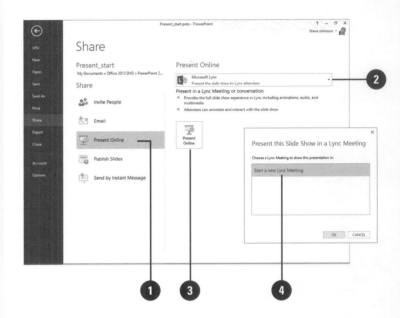

(7) In the Conversation window, wait for the presentation to open.

(8) Use the arrow buttons to deliver the slides. Click **Thumbnails** to display slides, or click **Notes** to display speaker notes.

(9) Use the action buttons to do any of the following:

- ◆ **Dial Pad.** Use to make a phone call.
- ◆ **Video.** Use to start or stop a video conversation.
- ◆ **Presentable Content.** Use to present content, including presentations, whiteboard drawing, notes (from OneNote) and attachments.
- ◆ **People.** Use to invite more participants.

(10) When you're done, click **Stop Presenting**.

(11) To end the meeting, click the **More Options** button, click **End Meeting**, and then click **OK**.

Did You Know?

You can record an online meeting in Lync. In the Conversation window in Lync, click the More Options button, and then click Start Recording. When you're done, click the Stop button to edit it.

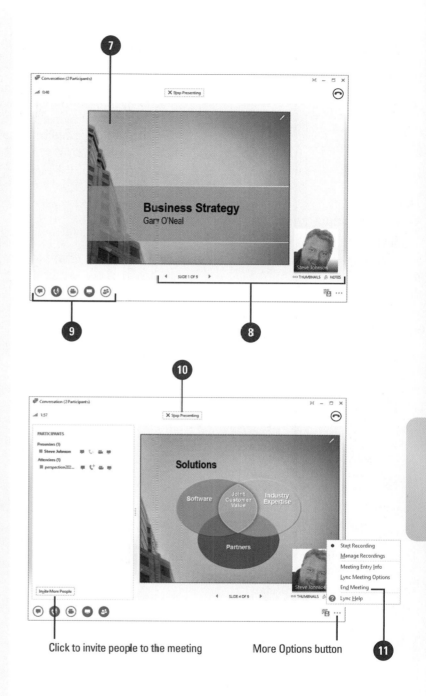

Click to invite people to the meeting   More Options button

Communicating Online with Lync

Microsoft Lync (**New!**) is an instant messaging program that allows you to send and receive instant messages, hold video chats, and share files. Lync uses a SharePoint or Office 365 site as the host location for the online communication. Before you can use Lync, you need to sign-in to the online site. During the conversation, you can send instant messages, make a call, start/stop video, present content, such as your desktop, a program, a PowerPoint presentation, a whiteboard, polls, or notes from OneNote, or invite and work with participants. If not everyone is able to attend, you can also record the session to play it back later. You can manage the recording with the Lync Recording Manager tool (**New!**).

Communicate with Lync

1. Start **Lync 2013**.
   - ◆ **Windows 8.** Click the tile on the Start screen.
   - ◆ **Windows 7.** Click **Start** on the taskbar, point to **All Programs**, and then point to **Microsoft Office**.

2. If prompted, enter a user name and password to sign-in.

3. Double-click a contact.

4. Type text to have a conversation; press Enter to send; press Shift+Enter to start a new line.

5. Use the action buttons to do any of the following:
   - ◆ **Dial Pad.** Use to make a phone call.
   - ◆ **Video.** Use to start or stop a video conversation.
   - ◆ **Presentable Content.** Use to present content, including presentations, whiteboard drawing, notes (from OneNote) and attachments.
   - ◆ **People.** Use to invite more participants.

6. To start a recording, click the **More Options** button, and then click **Start Recording**. Click the **Stop** button to end it.

7. When you're done, click the **Close** button.

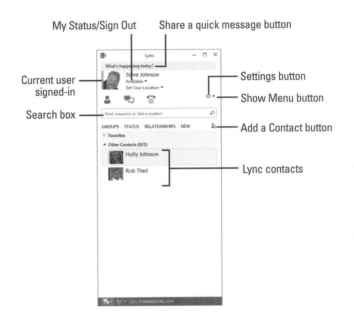

My Status/Sign Out — Share a quick message button

Current user signed-in — Settings button — Show Menu button

Search box — Add a Contact button — Lync contacts

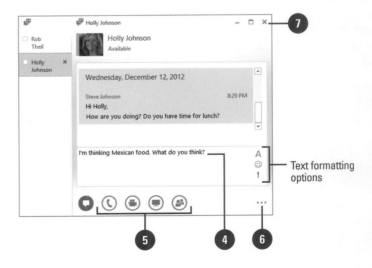

Text formatting options

Add Contacts in Lync

1. In Lync, click the **Add a Contact** button.

2. Click **Add a Contact in My Organization**, or point to **Add a Contact Not in My Organization**, and then select a contact type.

3. Enter the contact e-mail address.

4. Specify which group to place the contact, and a privacy option.

5. Click **OK**.

   The contact is added to the contacts list and synced to the SharePoint site.

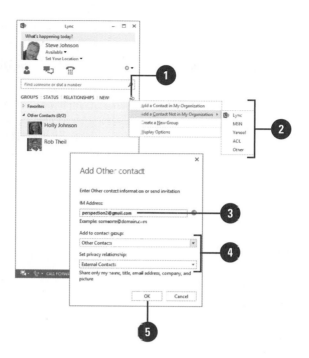

Manage Lync Recordings

1. Start **Lync Recording Manager**.

   ◆ **Windows 8.** Click the tile on the All Apps screen.

   ◆ **Windows 7.** Click **Start** on the taskbar, point to **All Programs**, point to **Microsoft Office**, and then point to **Office 2013 Tools**.

2. Select the recording you want to manage.

3. To play a recording, click **Play**, and then select a player.

4. To rename the title, click **Rename**, and then type a new title.

5. To publish the recording as an MP4, click **Publish**, specify a name and location, and then click **OK**.

6. To delete a recording, click **Delete**, and then click **Yes** to confirm.

7. To exit, click the **Close** button.

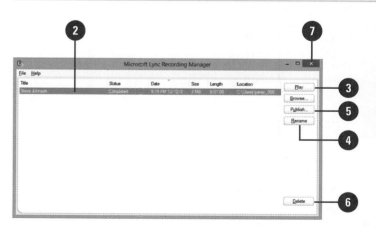

Publishing options

Player options

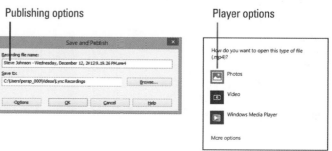

Showing a Presentation with the PowerPoint Viewer

The PowerPoint Viewer is a program used to run presentations on computers that don't have Microsoft PowerPoint installed. This Viewer is used as part of the Package for CD feature, but you can also use the Viewer independently. You can download the PowerPoint Viewer from the Microsoft Office.com web site in the downloads section if you need it on the road. You can start the PowerPoint Viewer from the Start screen (Win 8) or Start menu (Win 7) under All Programs or use the Search box if unavailable. You open your presentation from the PowerPoint Viewer just like you open them from the Open dialog box. If a presentation contains password protection, the PowerPoint Viewer prompts you for a password.

Show a Presentation with the PowerPoint Viewer

1. Start **Microsoft PowerPoint Viewer**.
   - ◆ **Windows 8.** Click the tile on the All Apps screen.
   - ◆ **Windows 7.** Click **Start** on the taskbar, and then point to **All Programs**.

   TROUBLE? *If the viewer is not available, search for the pptview.exe file, which you can double-click to start.*

2. If necessary on first run, click **Accept** for the license agreement.

3. If you want to open a specific file type, click the **Files of type** list arrow, and then click a file type.

4. If the file is located in another folder, click the **Look in** list arrow, and then navigate to the file.

5. Select the presentation you want to show.

6. Click **Open**.

7. Navigate the slide show.

8. To stop the show, press Esc at any time or click **Cancel** at the end to close the PowerPoint Viewer.

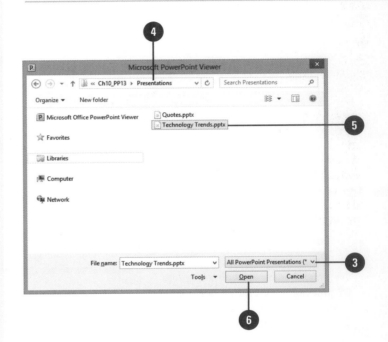

Customizing the PowerPoint Viewer

You can use the Run command within Microsoft Windows to customize the way the PowerPoint Viewer starts and functions. In the Run dialog box, you can enter a command to start the PowerPoint Viewer without the startup splash screen, at a specific slide, and using a playlist (showing consecutive presentations). You can also show the Open dialog box at the end of the show and print a presentation. The command you enter uses switches and parameters to perform the functions you want. A switch determines the function you want to perform. In the command-line, the switch appears after the program name (PPTVIEW.EXE) with a a space, followed by a slash (/) and the name of the switch. The switch is followed in some cases by a space and a parameter, which gives direction. A parameter is typically a file name. For example, "c:*path to folder*\PPTVIEW.EXE /N3 "pres.pptx"", where "c:*path to folder*\PPTVIEW.EXE" is the command, /N3 is the switch, and "pres.pptx" is the parameter. The path to folder is the location where the PPTVIEW.EXE file is stored. It's typically located in "c:\programs files\microsoft office\office14\PPTVIEW.EXE"

Use the Run Command to Start the PowerPoint Viewer

1. Click the **Run** tile on the All Apps screen (Win 8) or click **Start** on the taskbar (Win 7), point to **All Programs**, point to **Accessories**, and then click **Run**.

2. Refer to the adjacent table for commands to enter.

   You can use only one switch at a time. Quotation marks are required if there are spaces in the path or file name; they are optional when there are no spaces.

3. Click **OK**.

Command-line Switches

Switch	Action
/D	Show the Open dialog box when presentation ends. Example: "c:*path to folder*\PPTVIEW.EXE" /D
/L	Read a playlist of PowerPoint presentations contained within a text file. Example: "c:*path to folder*\PPTVIEW.EXE" /L "playlist.txt"
/N#	Open the presentation at a specified slide number. Example: "c:*path to folder*\PPTVIEW.EXE" /N3 "pres.pptx"
/S	Start the Office PowerPoint Viewer 2007 without showing the splash screen. Example: "c:*path to folder*\PPTVIEW.EXE" /S
/P	Send the presentation to a printer and print the file. Example: "c:*path to folder*\PPTVIEW.EXE" /P "pres.pptx"

Did You Know?

You can create a shortcut to reuse a command-line switch. Right-click the Windows desktop, point to New, and then click Shortcut. In the wizard, type the full path to the Viewer or click Browse to find it, add a switch and parameter to the path command-line, click Next, type a shortcut name, and then click Finish.

Showing Multiple Presentations

If you want to deliver more than one slide show at a time, you can create and use a playlist. A **playlist** is a simple text file than contains a list of presentation file names in the order that you want to deliver them. File names in a playlist file need to include the full path to the presentation unless they are located in the same location as the PowerPoint Viewer. It is not possible to add command-line switches to the presentation file name in the playlist.

Create and Show a Playlist

1. Open a text editor, such as Notepad or WordPad.

2. Type the presentations files you want to use on separate lines.

   If the presentation files are not in the same location as the Viewer, be sure to include full paths.

3. Save the text file with the name you want, such as playlist.txt, and then exit the program.

   To avoid problems, place the text file, and presentation files in the same folder as the PowerPoint Viewer.

4. Click the **Run** tile on the All Apps screen (Win 8) or click **Start** on the taskbar (Win 7), point to **All Programs**, point to **Accessories**, and then click **Run**.

5. Type "c:*path to folder*\ PPTVIEW.EXE" /L "playlist.txt"

   Quotation marks are required if there are spaces in the path or file name; they are optional when there are no spaces.

6. Click **OK**.

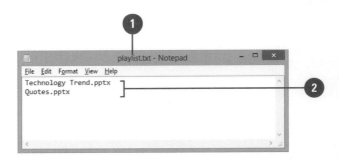

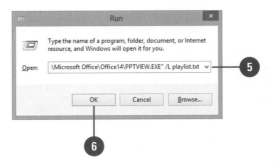

See Also

See "Customizing the PowerPoint Viewer" on page 365 for information on using the Run command, command-line switches, and parameters.

Reviewing and Securing a Presentation

11

Introduction

When you've developed content in your presentation and want feedback, you can electronically send a PowerPoint presentation to reviewers so that they can read, revise, and comment on the presentation without having to print it. Instead of reading handwritten text or sticky notes on your printout, you can get clear and concise feedback right in your presentation.

Adding a password to protect your presentation is not only a good idea for security purposes, it's an added feature to make sure that changes to your presentation aren't accidentally made by unauthorized people. Not only can you guard who sees your presentation, you can set rights on who can add changes and comments to your presentation.

The **Trust Center** is a place where you set security options and find the latest technology information as it relates to document privacy, safety, and security from Microsoft. The Trust Center allows you to set security and privacy settings—Trusted Publishers, Trusted Locations, Trusted Document, Add-ins, ActiveX Settings, Macro Settings, Message Bar, File Block Settings, and Privacy Options—and provides links to Microsoft privacy statements, a customer improvement program, and trustworthy computing practices. If you receive a security warning when you open a presentation, you can set options in the Trust Center to enable macro or active content. If you trust the content provider, you can add the trusted publishers or location to alleviate the warning in the future.

After you finish making changes to your presentation, you can quickly send it to another person for review using e-mail an Internet Fax service, or instant message.

What You'll Do

Add and Edit Comments in a Presentation

Inspect Documents

Compare and Merge Presentations

Create and Link OneNotes

Work with OneNote

Add Password Protection to a Presentation

Add a Digital Signature

Mark a Presentation as Read-Only

Review a Presentation Using E-Mail

Send a Presentation by Internet Fax

Send a Presentation by Instant Message

Avoid Harmful Attacks

Use the Trust Center

Select Trusted Publishers and Locations

Set Document Related Security Options

Set App Catalog Security Options

Set Add-In, ActiveX and Macro Security Options

Change Message Bar Security Options

Set Privacy Options

Work with Office Safe Modes

Adding Comments to a Presentation

When you review a presentation, you can insert comments to the author or other reviewers. **Comments** are like electronic adhesive notes tagged with your name. They typically appear in comment bubbles in PowerPoint. You can use comments to get feedback from others or to remind yourself of revisions you plan to make. A comment bubble (**New!**) and Comments pane (**New!**) are visible only when you show comments using the Show Comments button (**New!**). You can attach one or more comments to a letter or word on a slide, or to an entire slide. When you insert a comment, PowerPoint creates a comment bubble icon and opens the Comments pane, where you enter your comments. When you're reviewing a presentation, you can use the Show Comments button on the Review tab to show and hide markups or the Comments pane. In the Comments pane (**New!**), you can create new comments, move between comments, delete comments, or reply to comments.

Insert a Comment

1. Click the slide where you want to insert a comment or select an object.

2. Click the **Review** tab.

3. Click the **New Comment** button.

4. Type your comment in the Comments pane. Press Shift+Enter to insert a paragraph break in the comment.

5. Press Enter or click outside the comment.

    A comment bubble icon (**New!**) appears on the slide.

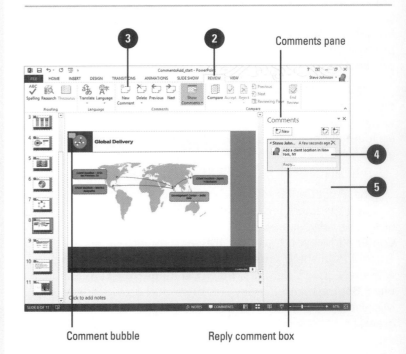

Comments pane

Comment bubble

Reply comment box

Did You Know?

You can move a comment bubble. Drag a comment bubble icon (**New!**) to a new location on the same slide.

My reviewer initials and name are incorrect. You can change them in PowerPoint Options. Click the File tab, click Options, click General, enter your User name and Initials in the boxes provided, and then click OK.

Read a Comment

1 Click the **Review** tab.

2 Click the **Show Comments** button arrow, and then click **Comments Pane** to show all comments.

◆ You can also click the **Show Comments** button to show (button highlighted) or hide (button not highlighted) comments and markups.

TIMESAVER *Click a bubble icon (**New!**) or the Comments button on the Status bar to open the Comments pane.*

3 Read the comment in the pane.

4 Click the **Previous** or **Next** button to read another comment.

5 When you reach the end of the presentation, click **Continue** to start at the beginning again or **Cancel**.

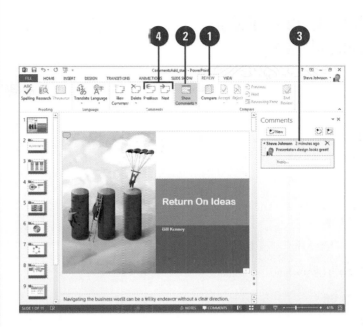

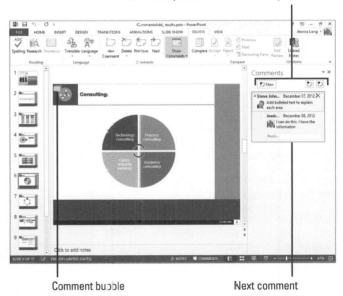

Comment options in the Comments pane

Comment bubble   Next comment

Did You Know?

You can show or hide markup or Comments pane. Click the Show Comments button arrow, and then click Show Markup (**New!**) or Comments Pane (**New!**).

You can show annotations. During a slide show you can add annotations, which you can save. When you show markups, annotations are included. You can select, move, and delete them.

You cannot merge PowerPoint 2013 comments back into a PowerPoint 2003 presentation. If you use PowerPoint 2003 or earlier to send your presentation for review, reviewers who use PowerPoint 2013 can view and add commands, but you cannot merge their comments into your presentation.

Editing Comments in a Presentation

PowerPoint uses a different color comment for each reviewer, which is based on the User name and Initials settings in PowerPoint Options. When you add or edit a comment, the color of the review comment changes to the reviewer's color, and changes the comment name and date. You can use the Previous and Next button to quickly review each comment. When you're done, you can delete one comment at a time, all the comments on a slide, or all the comments in the presentation. In the Comments pane (**New!**), you can move between comments, reply to comments, or delete comments.

Change Reviewers

1. Click the **File** tab, and then click **Options**.

2. In the left pane, click **General**.

3. Enter a User name and Initials.

4. Click **OK**.

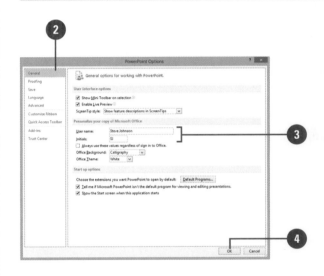

Edit a Comment

1. Click the **Review** tab.

2. Click the **Show Comments** button to open the Comments pane.

   TIMESAVER *Click a comment bubble to open the comment in the Comments pane.*

3. Click in the comment you want to edit to place the insertion point.

4. Make your editing changes.

5. Click outside the comment.

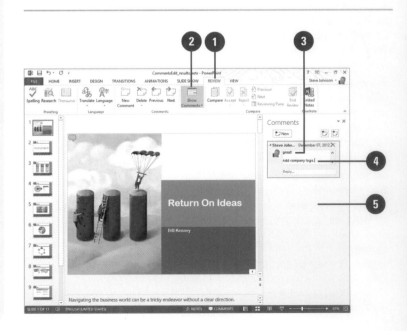

Respond to a Comment

① Click the **Review** tab.

② Click the **Show Comments** button to open the Comments pane.

③ Click in the Reply box (**New!**) in the original comment.

④ Type your reply in the comment box.

If you're a different reviewer, the comment name changes to reflect the reviewer.

⑤ Click outside the comment.

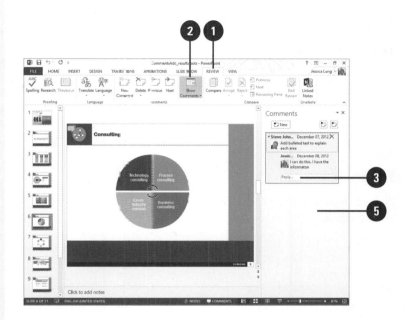

Did You Know?

You can copy comment text. Right-click the comment bubble you want to copy, and then click Copy Text. Paste the comment text where you want.

Delete a Comment

① Click the **Review** tab.

② Click the **Show Comments** button to open the Comments pane.

③ Click the comment you want to remove.

④ Click the **Delete** button (**New!**) in the comment or click the **Delete Comment** button arrow, and then click one of the options:

◆ **Delete** to remove the selected comment.

◆ **Delete All Comments and Ink on This Slide** to remove all comments on the current slide.

◆ **Delete All Comments and Ink in This Presentation** to remove all comments in the presentations.

Delete button

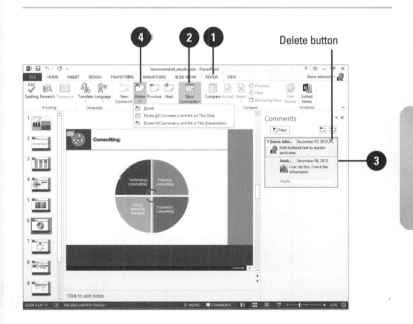

Comparing and Merging Presentations

If you want to compare an earlier version of a presentation with the current version, or if you receive multiple edited versions of the original presentation back from the recipients, you can compare the presentations and merge the changes into one presentation. The changes can be merged into one presentation or viewed for comparison. When you compare or merge presentations, the text that differs between the two versions will be identified by a Change icon and list, and displayed by slide or details in the Reviewing pane.

Compare and Merge Presentations

1. Open the original presentation in which you want to compare and merge.

2. Click the **Review** tab.

3. Click the **Compare** button.

4. Select the presentation to which you want to compare and merge, and then click **Merge**.

    The Reviewing pane opens, displaying the Slides or Details tab with information about the differences between the presentations. A Change icon appears displaying a list of the individual changes.

5. To move between the slide changes, click the **Previous** or **Next** button.

6. To accept or reject a change, select or clear a Change icon check box, or click the **Accept** or **Reject** button arrow, and then click an option to accept or reject an individual change, all changes to the current slide, or all changes to the presentation.

7. To close or open the Reviewing pane, click the **Reviewing Pane** button.

8. To end the review, click the **End Review** button.

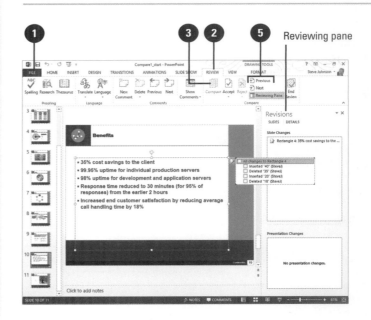

Reviewing pane

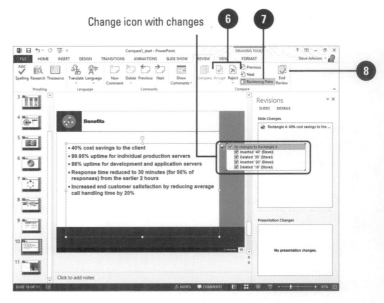

Change icon with changes

Creating and Linking OneNotes

Microsoft OneNote is a digital notebook program you can use to gather, manage, and share notes and information. In PowerPoint and Word, you can create and open notes directly from the Review tab by using the Linked Notes button. OneNote auto-links notes to the Office document you're viewing, which you can disable or change in the Advanced section of OneNote Options. You can open a OneNote note by clicking the Linked Notes button. The Linked Notes button is not available on the Review tab until you start the program and create an initial account, which is quick and easy.

Create and Link Notes with OneNote

1. Open the presentation you want to link notes from OneNote.

2. Click the **Review** tab.

3. Click the **Linked Notes** button.

4. On first document use, select a section or page in which to put the notes, and then click **OK**.

5. In OneNote, enter the notes you want for the page.

6. To work with notes in OneNote, click the **Linked Note** icon, and then click an option:

   ◆ **Linked File(s).** Use to select a linked Office document to view.

   ◆ **Delete Link(s) on This Page.** Use to delete links on the current page.

   ◆ **Linked Notes Options.** Select to open OneNote Options.

7. When you're done, click the **Linked Note** icon in OneNote, and then click **Stop Taking Linked Notes**. To restart it, click **Start Taking Linked Notes** on the File tab.

8. To view linked notes, click the **Linked Notes** button to open OneNote if needed, point to a note, and then click the Office program icon.

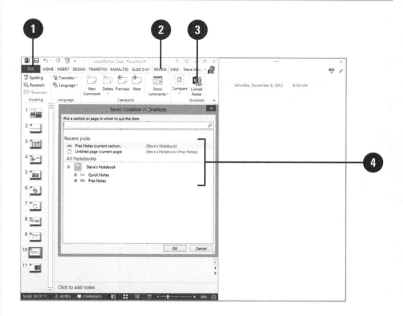

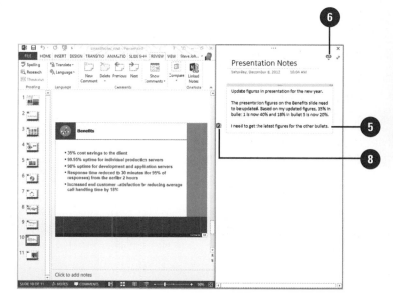

Working with OneNote

Microsoft OneNote can function just like a yellow legal pad. You can take notes, draw pictures, highlight, and scratch out text. However, OneNote is much more. OneNote enables you to flag items within your notes and search for them later. You can create multilevel outlines, gather and paste research information from a variety of sources, insert images or files, move notes around between pages and sections, and create Outlook tasks directly from your notes. With a touch screen, you can draw, erase, and edit using gestures (**New!**). Notes are entered on pages. A page can store pieces of information. Pages are organized into sections. Sections help you organize notes on a particular subject and quickly access them using a section tab. Use folders to group sections together. The notebook is where all your folders, sections, and note pages are stored, which you can save and sync to a SkyDrive (**New!**) for use on other devices. As you work in Office programs, you can use the Send to OneNote tool (**New!**) to take and send notes to OneNote.

Work with OneNote

1. Start **OneNote 2013**.

   - **Windows 8.** Click the tile on the Start screen.

   - **Windows 7.** Click **Start** on the taskbar, point to **All Programs**, and then point to **Microsoft Office**.

2. To create a notebook, click the **File** tab, click **New**, click a store location, specify a name and location, and then click **Create Notebook**.

3. To create a section, click the **Create Section** tab, enter a name, and then press Enter.

4. To create a page, click the **Add Page** button, and then enter a title.

5. To enter text, click and then start typing.

6. To insert other content, click the **Insert** tab, and then use the available buttons.

7. To draw on a page, click the **Draw** tab, and then use the available pens, erasers, and tools, or gestures (**New!**) on a touch screen.

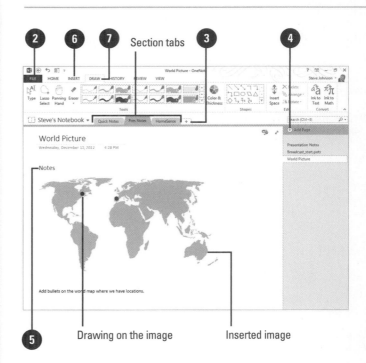

Section tabs

Drawing on the image   Inserted image

Work with Send to OneNote

1 Start PowerPoint and open the document you want to send to OneNote.

2 Start **Send to OneNote 2013**.

- ◆ **Windows 8.** Click the tile on the All Apps screen.

- ◆ **Windows 7.** Click **Start** on the taskbar, point to **All Programs**, point to **Microsoft Office**, and then point to **Office 2013 Tools**.

  The program opens as an app on the taskbar.

3 Click any of the following buttons on the Send To OneNote window:

- ◆ **Screen Clipping.** Drag to select a part of the screen to place in OneNote.

- ◆ **Send to OneNote.** Sends the current document to OneNote; Excel and Visio files are editable (**New!**) in OneNote.

- ◆ **New Quick Note.** Creates a new note in OneNote. Type the notes you want in the small OneNote screen.

  Click the **Normal View** button to open OneNote or click the **Close** button. The note appears on the Quick Notes tab in OneNote.

4 Select the location where you want to place the note in OneNote.

5 Click **OK** or **Send to Selected Location**.

6 Select or clear the **Start with OneNote** check box.

7 Click the **Close** button to close the screen or **Exit** link to quit.

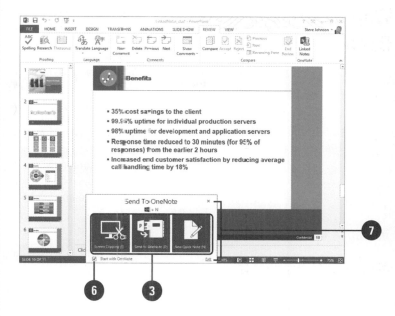

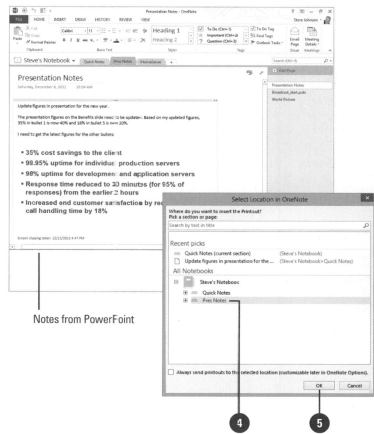

Notes from PowerPoint

Inspecting Documents

While you work on your presentation, PowerPoint automatically saves and manages personal information and hidden data to enable you to collaborate on creating and developing a presentation with other people. The personal information and hidden data includes comments, revision marks, versions, ink annotations, document properties, invisible content, off-slide content, presentation notes, document server properties, custom XML data, and task panes for Office apps (**New!**). The **Document Inspector** uses inspector modules to find and remove any hidden data and personal information specific to each of these modules that you might not want to share with others. If you remove hidden content from your presentation, you might not be able to restore it by using the Undo command, so it's important to make a copy of your presentation before you remove any information.

Inspect a Document

1. Click the **File** tab, click **Save As**, click **Computer**, click **Browse**, type a name to save a copy of the original, specify a folder location, and then click **Save**.

2. Click the **File** tab, and then click **Info**.

3. Click the **Check for Issues** button, and then click **Inspect Document**.

4. Select the check boxes with the content you want to find and remove:

   ◆ **Comments and Annotations.** Includes comments and ink annotations.

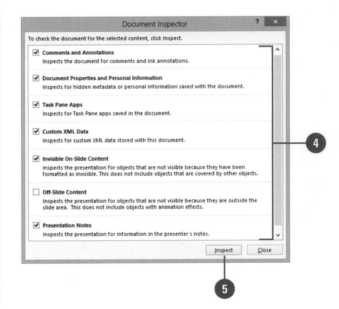

Did You Know?

What is metadata? Metadata is data that describes other data. For example, text in a presentation is data, while the number of slides is metadata.

- **Document Properties and Personal Information.** Includes metadata document Properties (Summary, Statistics, and Custom tabs), the file path for publishing web pages, document server properties, and content type information.

- **Task Pane Apps.** Includes any task pane apps (**New!**) saved in the document.

- **Custom XML Data.** Includes any custom XML data.

- **Invisible On-Slide Content.** Includes objects formatted as invisible. Doesn't include objects covered by other objects.

- **Off-Slide Content.** Includes objects (such as clip art, text boxes, graphics, and table) off the slide area.

- **Presentation Notes.** Includes text entered in the Notes section. Doesn't include pictures in the Notes section.

5 Click **Inspect**.

6 Review the results of the inspection.

7 Click **Remove All** for each inspector module in which you want to remove hidden data and personal information.

TROUBLE? *Before you click Remove All, be sure you want to remove the information. You might not be able to restore it.*

8 Click **Close**.

Adding Password
Protection to
a Presentation

You can assign a password and other security options so that only those who know the password can open the presentation, or to protect the integrity of your presentation as it moves from person to person. At times, you will want the information to be used but not changed; at other times, you will want only specific people to be able to view the presentation. Setting a presentation as read-only is useful when you want a presentation, such as a company-wide bulletin, to be distributed and read, but not changed. Password protection takes effect the next time you open the presentation.

Add Password Protection to a Presentation

1. Open the presentation you want to protect.

2. Click the **File** tab, click **Save As**, click **Computer**, and then click **Browse**.

3. Click **Tools**, and then click **General Options**.

4. Type a password in the Password To Open box (encrypted) or the Password To Modify box (not encrypted).

   IMPORTANT *It's critical that you remember your password. If you forget your password, Microsoft can't retrieve it.*

5. Select or clear the **Remove automatically created personal information from this file on save** check box.

   Personal information includes author, title, subject, manager, company, and other hidden data, such as invisible content, off-slide content, reviewer's names, notes, and custom XML Data.

6. Click **OK**.

7. Type your password again.

8. Click **OK**.

9. Click **Save**, and then click **Yes** to replace existing presentation.

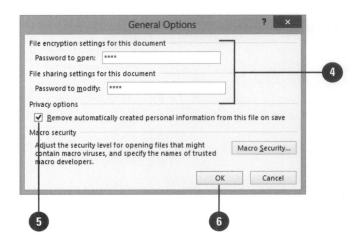

For Your Information

Using a Strong Password

Hackers identify passwords as strong or weak. A strong password is a combination of uppercase and lowercase letters, numbers, and symbols, such as Grea8t!, while a weak one doesn't use different character types, such as Hannah1. Be sure to write down your passwords and place them in a different location.

Open a Presentation with Password Protection

1. Click the **File** tab, click **Open**, navigate to a presentation with password protection, and then click **Open**.

2. Click **Read Only** if you do not wish to modify the presentation, or type the password (test) in the Password dialog box.

3. Click **OK**.

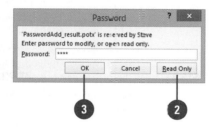

Change or Remove the Password Protection

1. Click the **File** tab, click **Open**, navigate to a presentation with password protection, and then click **Open**.

2. Type the password in the Password dialog box, and then click **OK**.

3. Click the **File** tab, click **Save As**, click **Computer**, click **Browse**, click **Tools**, and then click **General Options**.

4. Select the contents in the Password To Modify box or the Password To Open box.

5. Choose the option you want.

   ◆ **Change password.** Type a new password, click OK, and then retype your password.

   ◆ **Delete password.** Press Delete.

6. Click **OK**.

7. Click **Save**, and then click **Yes** to replace existing presentation.

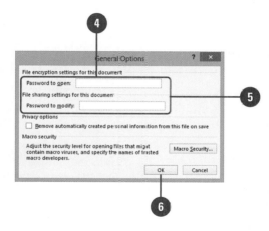

Adding Security Encryption to a Presentation

File encryption is additional security you can apply to a presentation. File encryption scrambles your password to protect your presentation from unauthorized people from breaking into the file. You don't have to worry about the encryption, PowerPoint handles everything. All you need to do is remember the password. If you forget it, you can't open the file. Password protection takes effect the next time you open the presentation. To set password protection using file encryption, use the Protect Presentation button and Encrypt with Password command on the Info screen, enter a password, write it down for safekeeping, and then reenter the password again.

Apply File Encryption

1. Click the **File** tab, and then click **Info**.

2. Click the **Protect Presentation** button, and then click **Encrypt with Password**.

3. Type a password.

4. Click **OK**.

5. Retype the password.

6. Click **OK**.

Did You Know?

You can remove file encryption. Click the File tab, click Info, click the Protect Presentation button, click Encrypt With Password, delete the file encryption password, and then click OK.

Marking a Presentation as Read-Only

As a precaution to prevent readers and reviews from making accidental changes, you can use the Mark as Final command to make a PowerPoint presentation read-only. The Mark as Final command disables or turns off typing, editing commands, and proofing marks, and sets the *Status property* field in the Document Information Panel to Final. The Mark as Final command is not a security option; it only prevents changes to the presentation while it's turned on and it can be turned off by anyone at any time.

Mark a Presentation as Final

1. Click the **File** tab, and then click **Info**.

2. Click the **Protect Presentation** button, and then click **Mark as Final**.

3. Click **OK**.

   The presentation is marked as final and then saved.

4. If necessary, click **OK**.

   The Mark as Final icon appears in the Status bar to indicate the presentation is currently marked as final.

   IMPORTANT *A PowerPoint 2013 presentation marked as final is not read-only when opened in an earlier version of Microsoft PowerPoint.*

Did You Know?

You can enable editing for a presentation marked as final. Click the Edit Anyway button on the Message bar, or File button, click Info, click the Protect Presentation button, and then click Mark As Final again to toggle off the Mark As Final feature.

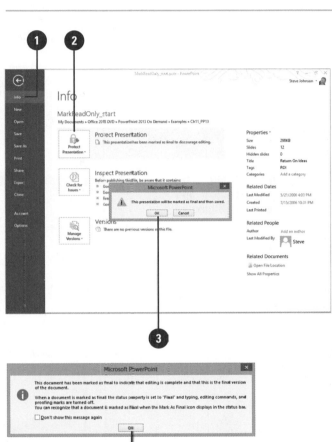

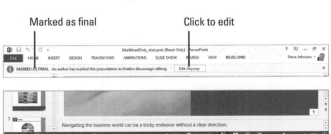

Marked as final   Click to edit

Mark as Final icon

Adding a Digital Signature

After you've finished a document, you might consider adding an invisible digital signature—an electronic, secure stamp of authentication on a document. Before you can add a digital signature, you need to get a **digital ID**, or **digital certificate**, which provides an electronic way to prove your identity. A digital certificate checks a public key to validate a private key associated with a digital signature. To assure a digital signature is authentic, it must have a valid (non expired or revoked) certificate issued by a reputable certification authority (CA), and the signing person must be from a trusted publisher. If you need a verified authenticate digital certificate, you can obtain one from a trusted Microsoft partner CA. If you don't need a verified digital certificate, you can create one of your own. If someone modifies the file, the digital signature is removed and revoked. If you're not sure if a document is digitally signed, you can use the Signatures pane to view or remove valid signatures.

Add a Digital Signature to a Document

1. Click the **File** tab, click **Info**, click the **Protect Document** button, and then click **Add a Digital Signature**.

2. Click the **Commitment Type** list arrow, and then select an option: **None**, **Created and approved this document**, **Approved this document**, or **Created this document**.

3. Enter a purpose for signing this document.

4. Click **Details**.

5. Enter your name or role/title and address.

6. Click **OK**.

7. To change the digital signature, click **Change**, select the one you want, and then click **OK**.

8. Click **Sign**.

9. If prompted, click **Yes** to use the certificate, and then click **OK**.

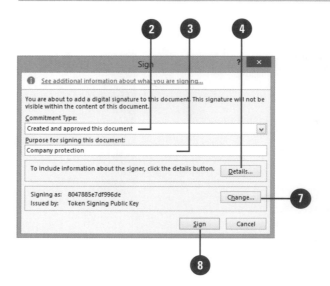

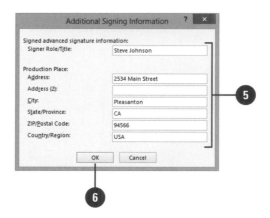

View or Remove Signatures

1 Click the **Signature** icon on the Status bar, or click the **File** tab, click **Info**, and then click the **View Signatures** button.

◆ If you open a presentation with a signature, click **View Signature** on the Message Bar to display the Signatures pane.

The Signatures pane appears, displaying valid signatures in the document. Invalid signatures are no longer automatically removed.

2 Point to a signature, and then click the list arrow.

3 To see signature details, click **Signature Details**, select a signature, click **View**, click **OK** when you're done, and then click **Close**.

4 To remove a signature, point to a signature, click the list arrow, click **Remove Signature**, click **Yes**, and then if necessary click **OK**.

5 Click the **Close** button in the pane.

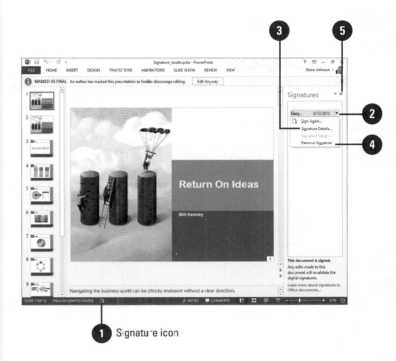

1 Signature icon

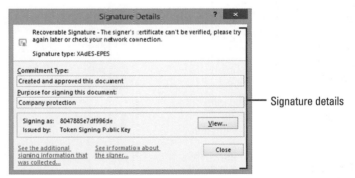

Signature details

Sending a Presentation Using E-Mail

After you finish making changes to a presentation, you can quickly send it to another person for review using e-mail. PowerPoint allows you to send presentations out for review as an attachment, either a presentation, PDF, or XPS document, using e-mail from within the program so that you do not have to open your e-mail program. An e-mail program, such as Microsoft Outlook, needs to be installed on your computer before you begin. When you send your presentation out for review, reviewers can add comments and then send it back to you.

Send a Presentation Using E-Mail

1. Click the **File** tab, click **Share**, and then click **E-mail**.

2. Click the **Send as Attachment** or **Send a Link** button.

3. If the Compatibility Checker appears, click **Continue** or **Cancel** to stop the operation.

   IMPORTANT *To complete the following steps, you need to have an e-mail program installed on your computer and an e-mail account set-up.*

   An e-mail message opens in Microsoft Outlook with your document attached. The subject line contains the file name of the document that you are sending.

4. Enter your recipients and subject (appears with document name by default).

   ◆ To add recipients from your address book or contacts list, click **To**, click the recipient names, click **To**, **Cc**, or **Bcc** until you're done, and then click **OK**.

5. Enter a message for your reviewer with instructions.

6. Click the **Send** button.

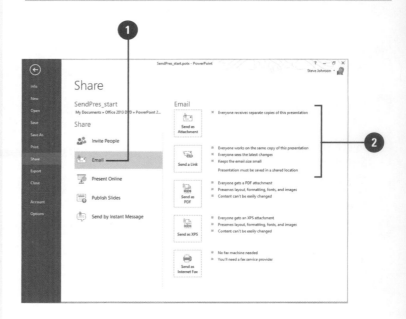

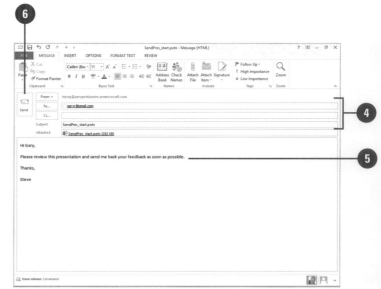

Send a Presentation as a PDF or XPS Using E-mail

1. Click the **File** tab, click **Share**, and then click **E-mail**.

2. Click the **Send as PDF** or **Send as XPS** button.

3. If the Compatibility Checker appears, click **Continue** or **Cancel** to stop the operation.

   IMPORTANT *To complete the following steps, you need to have an e-mail program installed on your computer and an e-mail account set-up.*

   An e-mail message opens in Microsoft Outlook with your document attached. The subject line contains the file name of the document that you are sending.

4. Enter your recipients and subject line (appears with document name by default).

   ◆ To add recipients from your address book or contacts list, click **To**, click the recipient names, click **To**, **Cc**, or **Bcc** until you're done, and then click **OK**.

5. Enter a message for your reviewer with instructions.

6. Click the **Send** button.

See Also

See "Creating a PDF Document" on page 309 or "Creating an XPS Document" on page 310 for information on working with PDF and XPS documents.

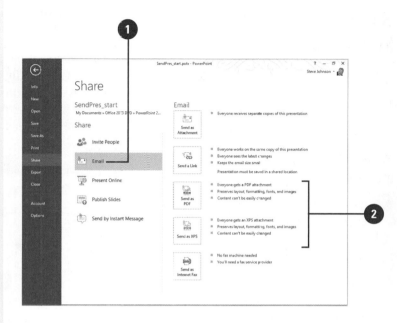

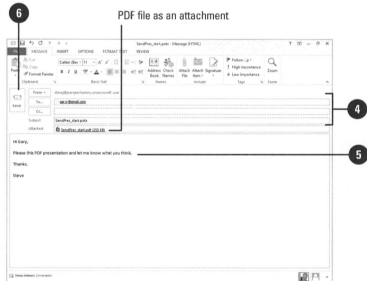

PDF file as an attachment

Sending a Presentation by Internet Fax

If you are a member of an online fax service, such as eFax, InterFAX, MyFax, or Send2Fax, you can use PowerPoint to send and receive faxes over the Internet directly from within your Microsoft Office program. If you're not a member, a web site can help you sign up. You also need to have Microsoft Outlook and Word installed to use the fax service and Outlook must be open to send your fax. If Outlook is not open and you send the fax, it will be stored in your Outbox and not sent until you open Outlook again.

Send a Presentation by Internet Fax

1. Click the **File** tab, click **Share**, and then click **E-mail**.

2. Click the **Send as Internet Fax** button.

3. If you're not signed up with an Internet Fax service, click **OK** to open a web page and sign up for one. When you're done, return to PowerPoint, and then repeat Step 1.

4. If the Compatibility Checker appears, click **Continue** or **Cancel** to stop the operation.

   An e-mail opens in Microsoft Outlook with your document attached as a .tif (image) file.

5. Enter a Fax Recipient, Fax Number and Subject (appears with presentation name by default).

   ◆ You can enter a fax number from your address book. Country codes must begin with a plus sign (+).

   ◆ To send your fax to multiple recipients, click **Add More**, and then enter fax information.

6. In the Fax Service pane, choose the options you want.

7. Complete the cover sheet in the body of the e-mail message.

8. Click the **Send** button.

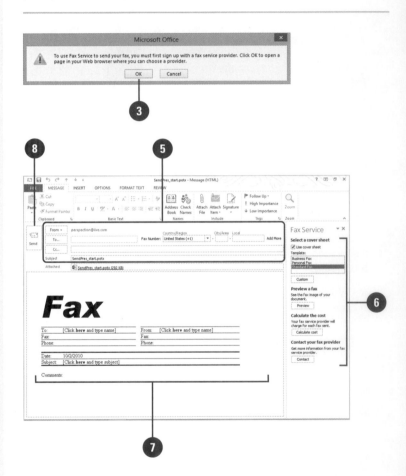

For Your Information

Using Fax Templates

If you want to use an Office fax template, you can download a template from Office.com (**New!**). Click the File tab, click New, type *fax* in the Search for online templates box, press Enter, click an Office app, click the fax template you want, and then click Create.

Sending a Presentation by Instant Message

Microsoft Lync is an instant messaging program that allows you to hold online meetings with an audio and video experience. Lync uses a SharePoint or Office 365 site as the host location for the online meeting. With Lync, you can send an Office document to a participant in an instant message. You can use the Send IM button (**New!**) on the Share screen to start an instant message conversation in Lync and transfer the currently opened document. After the files gets transferred, you can carry on with the instant message conversation by using the action buttons to work with messages, dial pad to call, add video, share presentation content, or work with audience.

Send a Presentation by Instant Message

1. Click the **File** tab, click **Share**, and then click **Send by Instant Message**.

    ◆ If the command is not available on the Share screen, start Microsoft Lync and connect the IM account to your Microsoft account.

2. Enter a contact name or click the Address Book button to select a contact, enter a subject and message for the instant message.

3. Click the **Send IM** button.

    Microsoft Lync opens and then transfers the document in the Conversation window.

4. In the Conversation window, you can continue the session.

5. Use the action buttons to work with messages, dial pad to call, add video, share presentation content, or work with audience.

6. To end the meeting, click the **More Options** button, and then click **End Meeting**.

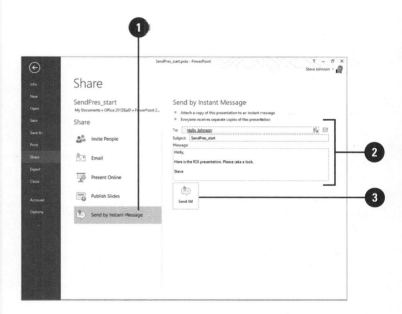

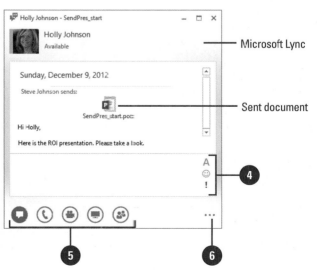

Microsoft Lync

Sent document

Avoiding Harmful Attacks

Spreading Harmful Infections

Many viruses and other harmful attacks spread through file downloads, attachments in e-mail messages, and data files that have macros, ActiveX controls, add-ins, or Visual Basic for Applications (VBA) code attached to them. Virus writers capitalize on people's curiosity and willingness to accept files from people they know or work with, in order to transmit malicious files disguised as or attached to benign files. When you start downloading files to your computer, you must be aware of the potential for catching a computer virus, worm, or Trojan Horse. Typically, you can't catch one from just reading a mail message or downloading a file, but you can catch one from installing, opening, or running an infected program or attached code.

Understanding Harmful Attacks

Phishing is a scam that tries to steal your identity by sending deceptive e-mail asking you for bank and credit card information online. Phishers spoof the domain names of banks and other companies in order to deceive consumers into thinking that they are visiting a familiar web site.

Phishers create a web address that looks like a familiar web address but is actually altered. This is known as a **homograph**. The domain name is created using alphabet characters from different languages, not just English. For example, the web site address "www.microsoft.com" looks legitimate, but what you can't see is that the "i" is a Cyrillic character from the Russian alphabet.

Don't be fooled by spoofed web sites that look like the official site. Never respond to requests for personal information via e-mail; most companies have policies that do not ask

for your personal information through e-mail. If you get a suspicious e-mail, call the institution to investigate and report it.

Spam is unsolicited e-mail, which is often annoying and time-consuming to get rid of. Spammers harvest e-mail addresses from web pages and unsolicited e-mail. To avoid spam, use multiple e-mail addresses (one for web forms and another for private e-mail), opt-out and remove yourself from e-mail lists. See the Microsoft Windows and Microsoft Outlook Help system for specific details.

Spyware is software that collects personal information without your knowledge or permission. Typically, spyware is downloaded and installed on your computer along with free software, such as freeware, games, or music file-sharing programs. Spyware is often associated with **Adware** software that displays advertisements, such as a pop-up ad. Examples of spyware and unauthorized adware include programs that change your home page or search page without your permission. To avoid spyware and adware, read the fine print in license agreements when you install software, scan your computer for spyware and adware with detection and removal software (such as Ad-aware from Lavasoft), and turn on Pop-up Blocker. See the Microsoft Windows Help system for specific details.

Avoiding Harmful Attacks Using Office

There are a few things you can do within any Office program to keep your system safe from the infiltration of harmful attacks.

1) Make sure you activate macro, ActiveX, add-in, and VBA code detection and notification. You can use the Trust Center to help protect you from attached code attacks. The Trust Center checks for trusted publisher and code locations on your computer and provides security options for add-ins, ActiveX controls, and macros to ensure the best possible protection. The Trust Center displays a security alert in the Message Bar when it detects a potentially harmful attack.

2) Make sure you activate web site spoofing detection and notification. You can use the Trust Center to help protect you from homograph attacks. The *Check Office documents that are from or link to suspicious web sites* check box under Privacy Options in the Trust Center is on by default and continually checks for potentially spoofed domain names. The Trust Center displays a security alert in the Message Bar when you have a document open and click a link to a web site with an address that has a potentially spoofed domain name, or you open a file from a web site with an address that has a potentially spoofed domain name.

3) Be very careful of file attachments in e-mail you open. As you receive e-mail, don't open or run an attached file unless you know who sent it and what it contains. If you're not sure, you should delete it. The Attachment Manager provides security information to help you understand more about the file you're opening. See the Microsoft Outlook Help system for specific details.

Avoiding Harmful Attacks Using Windows

There are a few things you can do within Microsoft Windows to keep your system safe from the infiltration of harmful attacks.

1) Make sure Windows Firewall is turned on. Windows Firewall helps block viruses and worms from reaching your computer, but it doesn't detect or disable them if they are already on your computer or come through e-mail. Windows Firewall doesn't block unsolicited e-mail or stop you from opening e-mail with harmful attachments.

2) Make sure Automatic Updates is turned on. Windows Automatic Updates regularly checks the Windows Update web site for important updates that your computer needs, such as security updates, critical updates, and service packs. Each file that you download using Automatic Update has a digital signature from Microsoft to ensure its authenticity and security.

3) Make sure you are using the most up-to-date antivirus software. New viruses and more virulent strains of existing viruses are discovered every day. Unless you update your virus-checking software, new viruses can easily bypass outdated virus checking software. Companies such as McAfee and Symantec offer shareware virus checking programs available for download directly from their web sites. These programs monitor your system, checking each time a file is added to your computer to make sure it's not in some way trying to change or damage valuable system files.

4) Be very careful of the sites from which you download files. Major file repository sites, such as FileZ, Download.com, or TuCows, regularly check the files they receive for viruses before posting them to their web sites. Don't download files from web sites unless you are certain that the sites check their files for viruses. Internet Explorer monitors downloads and warns you about potentially harmful files and gives you the option to block them.

Using the Trust Center

The **Trust Center** is a place where you set security options and find the latest technology information as it relates to document privacy, safety, and security from Microsoft. The Trust Center allows you to set security and privacy settings—Trusted Publishers, Trusted Locations, Trusted Documents, Trusted App Catalogs (**New!**), Add-ins, ActiveX Settings, Macro Settings, Protected view, Message Bar, External Content, File Block Settings, and Privacy Options—and provides links to Microsoft privacy statements, a customer improvement program, and trustworthy computing practices.

View the Trust Center

1. Click the **File** tab, and then click **Options**.

2. In the left pane, click **Trust Center**.

3. Click the links in which you want online information at the Microsoft Online web site.

   ◆ **Show the Microsoft PowerPoint privacy statement.** Opens a Microsoft web site detailing privacy practices.

   ◆ **Office.com privacy statement.** Opens a Microsoft Office.com web site detailing privacy practices.

   ◆ **Customer Experience Improvement Program.** Opens the Microsoft Customer Experience Improvement Program (CEIP) web site.

   ◆ **Microsoft Office Feedback "Send a Smile" Privacy Statement.** Opens a Microsoft web site with information about Microsoft's privacy statement (**New!**).

   ◆ **Microsoft Trustworthy Computing.** Opens a Microsoft web site detailing security and reliability practices.

4. When you're done, close your web browser or dialog box, and return to PowerPoint.

5. Click **OK**.

Selecting Trusted Publishers and Locations

The Trust Center security system continually checks for external potentially unsafe content in your documents. Hackers can hide web beacons in external content—images, linked media, data connections and templates—to gather information about you or cause problems. When the Trust Center detects potentially harmful external content, the Message Bar appears with a security alert and options to enable or block the content. Trusted publishers are reputable developers who create application extensions, such as a macro, ActiveX control, or add-in. The Trust Center uses a set of criteria—valid and current digital signature, and reputable certificate—to make sure publishers' code and source locations are safe and secure. If you are sure that the external content is trustworthy, you can add the content publisher and location to your trusted lists, which allows it to run without being checked by the Trust Center.

Modify Trusted Publishers and Locations

1. Click the **File** tab, and then click **Options**.

2. In the left pane, click **Trust Center**.

3. Click **Trust Center Settings**.

4. In the left pane, click **Trusted Publishers**.

5. Select a publisher, and then use the **View** and **Remove** buttons to make the changes you want.

6. In the left pane, click **Trusted Locations**.

7. Select a location, and then use the **Add new location**, **Remove**, and **Modify** buttons to make the changes you want.

8. Select or clear the **Allow trusted locations on my network (not recommended)** check box.

9. Select or clear the **Disable all Trusted Locations** check box.

10. Click **OK**.

11. Click **OK**.

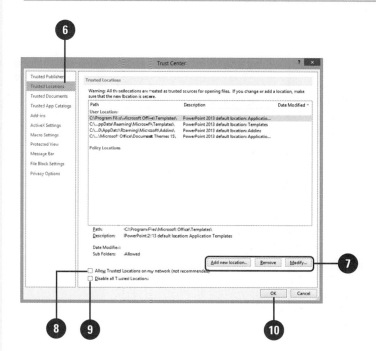

Setting Document Related Security Options

The Trust Center security system allows you to set file-related options to check for potentially unsafe content in your documents. In Trusted Documents, you can set options to open trusted documents without any security prompts for macros, ActiveX controls and other types of active content in the document. For a trusted document, you won't be prompted the next time you open the document even if new active content was added to the document or changes were made to existing active content. You should only trust documents if you trust the source. Protected view provides a place to open potentially dangerous files, without any security prompts, in a restricted mode to help minimize harm to your computer. If you disable Protected view, you could expose your computer to possible harmful threats. In File Block Settings, you can select the Open and Save check boxes to prevent each file type from opening, or just opening in Protected view, and from saving.

Set Options for Trusted Documents

1. Click the **File** tab, and then click **Options**.

2. In the left pane, click **Trust Center**.

3. Click **Trust Center Settings**.

4. In the left pane, click **Trusted Documents**.

5. Select or clear the check boxes you do or don't want.

   ◆ **Allow documents on a network to be trusted.**

   ◆ **Disable Trusted Documents.**

6. To clear all trusted documents so they are no longer trusted, click **Clear**.

7. Click **OK**.

8. Click **OK**.

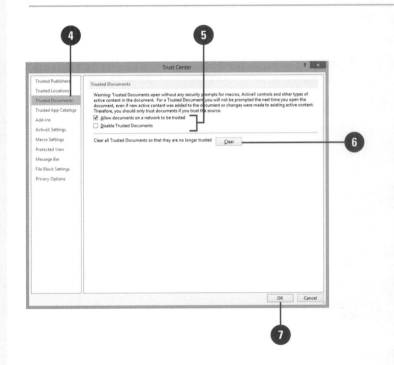

Set Options for Protected View

1. Click the **File** tab, and then click **Options**.

2. In the left pane, click **Trust Center**.

3. Click **Trust Center Settings**.

4. In the left pane, click **Protected View**.

5. Select or clear the check boxes you do or don't want.

   ◆ **Enable Protected View for files originating from the Internet.**

   ◆ **Enable Protected View for files located in potentially unsafe locations.**

   ◆ **Enable Protected View for Outlook attachments.**

6. Click **OK**.

7. Click **OK**.

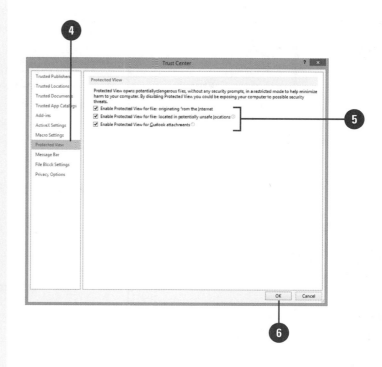

Set Options for File Block Settings

1. Click the **File** tab, and then click **Options**.

2. In the left pane, click **Trust Center**.

3. Click **Trust Center Settings**.

4. In the left pane, click **File Block Settings**.

5. Select the **Open** and **Save** check boxes you want to block for the different file types from opening or saving or clear the ones you don't want.

6. Select the open behavior option you want.

7. Click **OK**.

8. Click **OK**.

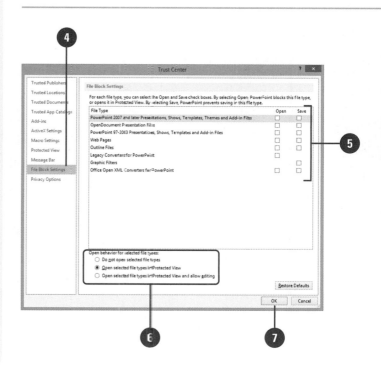

Setting App Catalog Security Options

You can store apps for SharePoint and Office apps for your organization's internal use in an App Catalog site (**New!**). The App Catalog site is a special site collection on a web application. When you create an App Catalog site, you get two libraries for apps: Apps for SharePoint and Apps for Office. App Catalog security options in the Trust Center allow you to set security settings that allow you to specify the trusted app catalogs you want to use.

Set App Catalog Security Options

1. Click the **File** tab, and then click **Options**.

2. In the left pane, click **Trust Center**.

3. Click **Trust Center Settings**.

4. In the left pane, click **Trusted App Catalogs**.

5. Select or clear the check boxes you do or don't want.

   ◆ **Don't allow any apps to start.** Select to not let any apps start.

   ◆ **Don't allow apps from the Office Store to start.** Select to not allow apps from the Office Store to start.

6. Enter a URL for the app catalog, and then click **Add catalog**.

7. To remove or clear a URL, select the URL, and then click **Remove** or **Clear**.

8. Click **OK**, and then click **OK** to save your settings.

   The settings will be applied the next time you start Office.

9. Click **OK**.

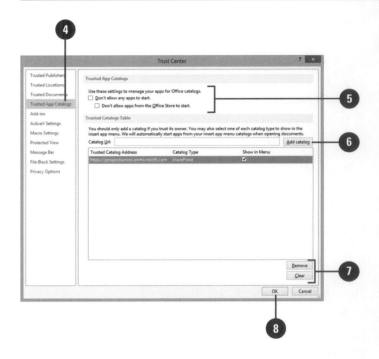

For Your Information

Creating an App Catalog on Office 365

If you have an Office 365 Enterprise team site, you can create an App Catalog site. In your browser, sign-in to your Office 365 Enterprise team site, click Admin, and then click SharePoint. In SharePoint admin center, click App on the left menu, click App Catalog to create a new App Catalog site, and then specify the details you want for your App Catalog site. After you create an App Catalog site, you can add apps to it, such as the ones you create and package from Access 2013.

Setting Add-in Security Options

An add-in extends functionality to Microsoft Office programs. An add-in can add buttons and custom commands to the Ribbon. When an add-in is installed, it appears on the Add-Ins tab of an Office program and includes a special ScreenTip that identifies the developer. Since add-ins are software code added to Microsoft Office programs, hackers can use them to do malicious harm, such as spreading a virus. The Trust Center uses a set of criteria—valid and current digital signature, reputable certificate and a trusted publisher—to make sure add-ins are safe and secure. If it discovers a potentially unsafe add-in, it disables the code and notifies you in the Message Bar. If the add-in security options are not set to the level you need, you can change them in the Trust Center.

Set Add-in Security Options

1. Click the **File** tab, and then click **Options**.

2. In the left pane, click **Trust Center**.

3. Click **Trust Center Settings**.

4. In the left pane, click **Add-ins**.

5. Select or clear the check boxes you do or don't want.

   ◆ **Require Application Add-ins to be signed by Trusted Publisher.** Select to check for a digital signature on the .dll file.

   ◆ **Disable notification for unsigned add-ins (code will remain disabled).** Only available if the above check box is selected. Select to disable unsigned add-ins without notification.

   ◆ **Disable all Application Add-ins (may impair functionality).** Select to disable all add-ins without any notifications.

6. Click **OK**.

7. Click **OK**.

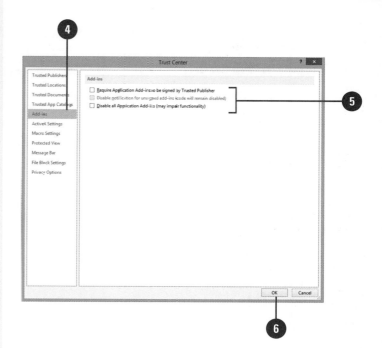

Setting ActiveX Security Options

An ActiveX control provides additional functionality, such as a text box, button, dialog box, or small utility program. ActiveX controls are software code, so hackers can use them to do malicious harm, such as spreading a virus. You can use the Trust Center to prevent ActiveX controls from harming your computer. If the ActiveX security options are not set to the level you want, you can change them in the Trust Center. If you change ActiveX control settings in one Office program, it effects all Microsoft Office programs. The Trust Center uses a set of criteria—checks the kill bit and Safe for Initialization (SFI) settings—to make sure ActiveX controls run safely.

Change ActiveX Security Settings

1 Click the **File** tab, and then click **Options**.

2 In the left pane, click **Trust Center**.

3 Click **Trust Center Settings**.

4 In the left pane, click **ActiveX Settings**.

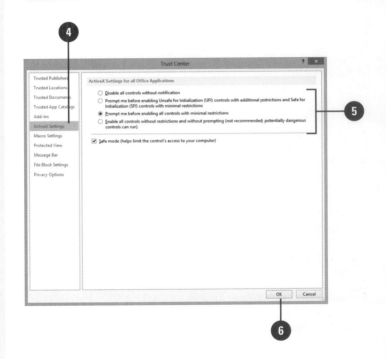

5 Click the option you want for ActiveX in documents not in a trusted location.

◆ Disable all controls without notification.

◆ Prompt me before enabling Unsafe for Initialization controls with additional restrictions and Save for Initialization (SFI) controls with minimal restrictions (default).

◆ Prompt me before enabling all controls with minimal restrictions.

◆ Enable all controls without restrictions and without prompting (not recommended, potentially dangerous controls can run).

6 Click **OK**.

7 Click **OK**.

Setting Macro Security Options

A macro allows you to automate frequently used steps or tasks to save time and work more efficiently. Macros are written using VBA (Visual Basic for Applications) code, which opens the door to hackers to do malicious harm, such as spreading a virus. The Trust Center uses a set of criteria—valid and current digital signature, reputable certificate and a trusted publisher—to make sure macros are safe and secure. If the Trust Center discovers a potentially unsafe macro, it disables the code and notifies you in the Message Bar. You can click Options on the Message Bar to enable it or set other security options. If the macro security options are not set to the level you need, you can change them in the Trust Center.

Change Macro Security Settings

1. Click the **File** tab, and then click **Options**.

2. In the left pane, click **Trust Center**.

3. Click **Trust Center Settings**.

4. In the left pane, click **Macro Settings**.

5. Click the option you want for macros in documents not in a trusted location.

   ◆ Disable all macros without notification.

   ◆ Disable all macros with notification (default).

   ◆ Disable all macros except digitally signed macros.

   ◆ Enable all macros (not recommended, potentially dangerous code can run).

6. If you're a developer, select the **Trust access to the VBA project object model** check box.

7. Click **OK**.

8. Click **OK**.

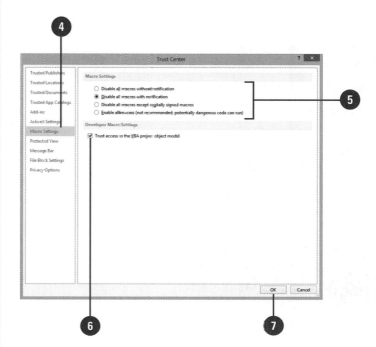

Changing Message Bar Security Options

The Message Bar displays security alerts when Office detects potentially unsafe content in an open document. The Message Bar appears below the Ribbon when a potential problem arises. The Message Bar provides a security warning and options to enable external content or leave it blocked. If you don't want to receive alerts about security issues, you can disable the Message Bar.

Modify Message Bar Security Options

1. Click the **File** tab, and then click **Options**.

2. In the left pane, click **Trust Center**.

3. Click **Trust Center Settings**.

4. In the left pane, click **Message Bar**.

5. Click the option you want for showing the Message bar.

   ◆ Show the Message Bar in all applications when active content, such as ActiveX controls and macros, has been blocked (default).

   This option is not selected if you selected the Disable all macros without notification check box in the Macros pane of the Trust Center.

   ◆ Never show information about blocked content.

6. Click **OK**.

7. Click **OK**.

Setting Privacy Options

Privacy options in the Trust Center allow you to set security settings that protect your personal privacy online. For example, the *Check Office documents that are from or link to suspicious web sites* option checks for spoofed web sites and protects you from phishing schemes. If your kids are doing research online using the Research pane, you can set Privacy Options to enable parental controls and a password to block sites with offensive content.

Set Privacy Options

1. Click the **File** tab, and then click **Options**.

2. In the left pane, click **Trust Center**.

3. Click **Trust Center Settings**.

4. In the left pane, click **Privacy Options**.

5. Select or clear the privacy check boxes you do or don't want.

   The options allow or prevent Office connections to the Internet and suspicious web sites, or install new services for the Research pane.

6. Click **Research Options**.

7. Click **Parental Control**.

8. Select the **Turn on content filtering to make services block offensive results** check box.

9. Select the **Allow users to search only the services that can block offensive results** check box, if necessary.

10. Enter a password, so users cannot change these settings.

11. Click **OK**, retype the password, and then click **OK**.

12. Click **OK**.

13. Click **OK**.

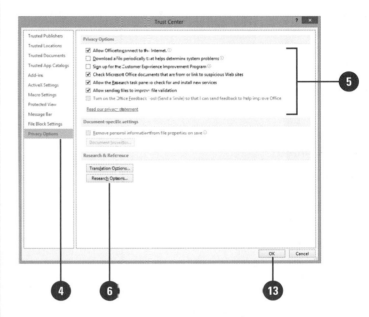

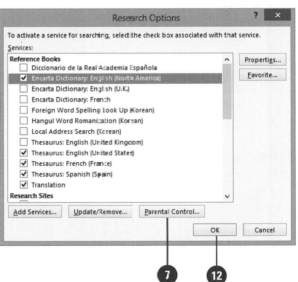

Working with Office Safe Modes

Microsoft Office uses two types of safe modes—Automated and User-Initiated—when it encounters a program problem. When you start an Office program, it automatically checks for problems, such as an extension not properly loading. If the program is not able to start the next time you try, the programs starts in **Automated Safe mode**, which disables extensions—macros, ActiveX controls, and add-ins—and other possible problem areas. If you're having problems and the Office program doesn't start in Automated Safe mode, you can start the program in **User-Initiated Safe mode**. When you start an Office program in Office Safe mode, not all features are available. For instance, templates can't be saved, AutoCorrect list is not loaded, preferences cannot be saved, and all command-line options are ignored (except /a and /n). Before you can use Office Safe mode, you need to enable it in the Trust Center. When you're in safe mode, you can use the Trust Center to find out the disabled items and enable them one at a time to help you pin point the problem.

Enable Safe Mode

1. Click the **File** tab, and then click **Options**.

2. In the left pane, click **Trust Center**.

3. Click **Trust Center Settings**.

4. In the left pane, click **ActiveX Settings**.

5. Select the **Safe Mode (helps limit the control's access to your computer)** check box.

6. Click **OK**.

7. Click **OK**.

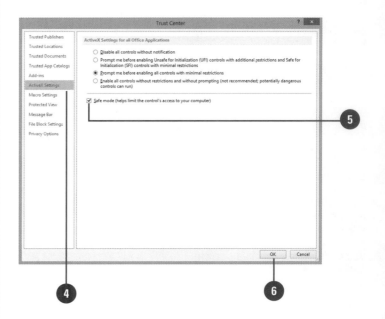

See Also

See "Maintaining and Repairing Office" on page 422 for information on fixing problems with a Microsoft Office program.

View Disabled Items

1 Click the **File** tab, and then click **Options**.

2 In the left pane, click **Add-Ins**.

3 Click the **Manage** list arrow, and then click **Disabled Items**.

4 Click **Go**.

5 In the dialog box, you can select an item, click **Enable** to activate and reload the add-in, and then click **Close**.

6 Click **OK**.

Did You Know?

You can use the Run dialog box to work in Safe mode. At the command prompt, you can use the */safe* parameter at the end of the command-line to start the program.

You can start an Office app in safe mode. In Windows 7, click the Start button on the taskbar, point to All Programs, and then click Microsoft Office. Press and hold Ctrl, and then click Microsoft <Program> 2013.

Customizing the Way You Work

Introduction

Once you've become familiar with Microsoft PowerPoint and all the features it contains, you might want to customize the way you work with PowerPoint. You can customize the performance of many PowerPoint features including its editing, saving, spelling, viewing, printing and security procedures. You can change your view settings so that your PowerPoint window looks the way you want it to. PowerPoint comes with set defaults, such as opening all documents using a certain view, showing the vertical ruler, or how many files you've recently opened, which you can change to a new default.

Some of the other PowerPoint customization features allow you to set a default font and related attributes to use when you are typing text in text boxes. Other defaults might be the color or line style of a shape object that you create. You can change the location of the Ribbon, and the configuration of the Quick Access Toolbar to include commands not available on the Ribbon.

In addition to PowerPoint, Microsoft Office 2013 also comes with other helpful tools including Upload Center, Lync, Lync Recording Manager, SkyDrive Pro, Language Preferences, Spreadsheet or Database Compare, and Telemetry Log or Dashboard. If you want to add or remove Office features, reinstall Office, or remove it entirely, you can use Office Setup's maintenance feature.

What You'll Do

Set Start Up Options

Set Office Options

Set General Options

Set Image Options

Set Chart Options

Set Slide Show Options

Set Display Options

Change Recent Presentation Options

Change Default File Locations

Set Advanced Save Options

Work with Touch Screens

Access Commands Not in the Ribbon

Customize the Way You Create Objects

Work with Office Tools

Maintain and Repair Office

Setting Start Up Options

You can customize several settings in the PowerPoint work environment to suit the way you like to work. You can specify start up options (**New!**) for how you want PowerPoint to start including opening files with specified extensions, detecting if PowerPoint isn't the default program for presentations, and showing the Start screen when PowerPoint starts. Taking a few minutes to change PowerPoint's default setting saves time in the long run.

Change Start Up Options

1. Click the **File** tab, and then click **Options**.

2. In the left pane, click **General**.

3. Select the Start up options for PowerPoint you want:

   ◆ **Default Programs**. Click to select the extensions you wan to open with PowerPoint (**New!**).

   ◆ **Tell me if Microsoft PowerPoint isn't the default program for viewing and editing presentations**. Select to detect if PowerPoint isn't the default presentation program (**New!**).

   ◆ **Show the Start screen when this application starts**. Select to show it or deselect to show a blank presentation (**New!**).

4. Click **OK**.

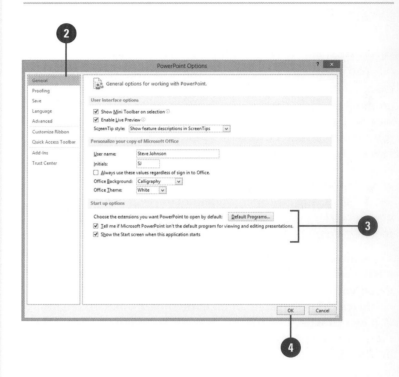

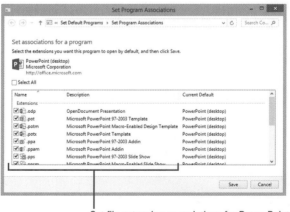

Set file extension associations for PowerPoint

Setting Office Options

PowerPoint Options includes some common settings for all Office programs that allow you to customize your work environment to your personal preferences. You can change general options to personalize the appearance of the PowerPoint window with an Office Background (**New!**) at the top of the program window or Office Theme (**New!**) color scheme. In addition, you can specify if you want to use these settings regardless to whether you are signed in to Office.

Change Office Options

1. Click the **File** tab, and then click **Options**.

2. In the left pane, click **General**.

3. Select Office related options for PowerPoint you want:

   ◆ **Always use these values regardless of sign in to Office**. Select to always use the Office options (**New!**).

   ◆ **Office Background**. Select to apply a background at the top of the program window (**New!**).

   ◆ **Office Theme**. Select to apply a color scheme to the program window (**New!**).

4. Click **OK**.

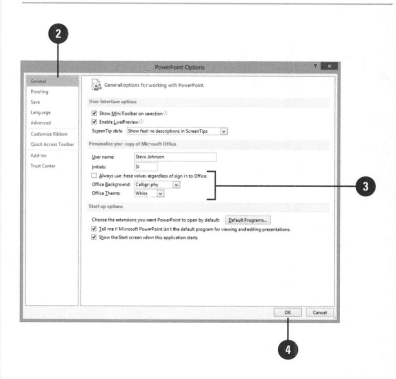

Did You Know?

You can change the appearance of Office programs in Windows. The appearance of the ribbon, toolbars, menus, and dialog boxes in Microsoft Office programs follows the theme or color scheme you set up in the Windows control panel.

Setting General Options

Each person uses PowerPoint in a different way. The General section of PowerPoint Options allows you to change popular options to personalize what appears in the PowerPoint window. For example, you can set options to show the Mini toolbar on selection, enable live preview, change the window background and theme, and show ScreenTips. In the Advanced section, you can set general options to provide error indicators in PowerPoint. When you change these options, PowerPoint uses them for all subsequent PowerPoint sessions until you change them again.

Change General Options

① Click the **File** tab, and then click **Options**.

② In the left pane, click **General**.

③ Select the options for working with PowerPoint you want:

- ◆ **Show Mini Toolbar on Selection**. Select to show a miniature semi-transparent toolbar that helps you work with selected text.

- ◆ **Enable Live Preview**. Select to show preview changes in a presentation.

- ◆ **ScreenTip style**. Click the list arrow to select a ScreenTip option: Show enhanced ScreenTips, Don't show enhanced ScreenTips, or Don't show ScreenTips.

④ Type your name and initials as you want them to appear in Properties, and review comments.

⑤ Click **OK**.

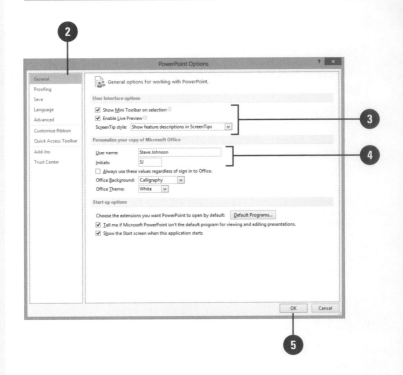

Change Other General Options

1. Click the **File** tab, and then click **Options**.

2. In the left pane, click **Advanced**.

3. Select the general options you want:

    ◆ **Provide feedback with sound**. Select to make a sound when an error occurs.

    ◆ **Show add-in user interface errors**. Select to show errors with an user interface add-in.

4. Click **OK**.

Setting Image Options

PowerPoint Options allows you to set options for images in a presentation. When you insert images into a presentation, the size of the file increases. You can set image options to compress all images to reduce the file size, or don't compress all images to maintain image quality in a larger file size. If you edit an image and don't want to keep the original content for restore purposes, you can discard it. If you want to print high quality images, you can set a print option to do it.

Change Image Options

1. Click the **File** tab, and then click **Options**.

2. In the left pane, click **Advanced**.

3. Select or clear any of the check boxes to change the image size and quality options you want.

   ◆ **Image Size and Quality.** Click the list arrow, and then select the presentation where you want to apply display options.

   ◆ **Discard editing data.** Select to delete data which is used to restore edited pictures to their original state.

   ◆ **Do not compress images in file.** Select to don't compress all images in the file to maintain quality or clear to compress all images to reduce the file size.

   ◆ **Set default target output to.** Specify a resolution output size for graphics in the file.

4. Click **OK**.

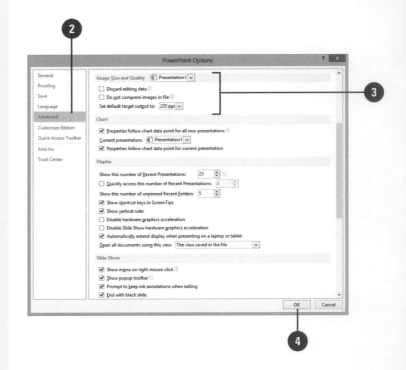

Setting Chart Options

PowerPoint Options allows you to set options for charts in a presentation. When you insert charts into a presentation, you can set options to have custom formatting and chart data labels follow data points as they move or change in the chart for the current presentation or for all new presentations (**New!**).

Change Chart Options

1. Click the **File** tab, and then click **Options**.

2. In the left pane, click **Advanced**.

3. Select or clear any of the check boxes to change the chart options you want.

   ◆ **Properties follow chart data point for all new presentations.** Select to have custom formatting and chart data labels follow data points as they move or change in the chart for all new presentations. (Default on). (**New!**)

   ◆ **Current presentation.** Select the presentation to which you want to apply property chart options. (**New!**)

   ◆ **Properties follow chart data point for current presentation.** Select to have custom formatting and chart data labels follow data points as they move or change in the chart. (Default on). (**New!**)

4. Click **OK**.

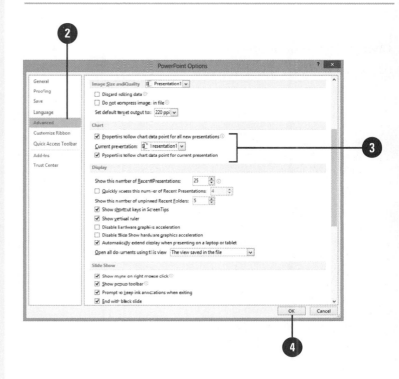

Setting Slide Show Options

When you give a slide show presentation in PowerPoint, you can set options to display options and tools to customize what is available during your slide show. You can set options on the Advanced pane in PowerPoint Options to show or hide a shortcut menu when you right-click a slide during a slide show, show or hide the popup toolbar in a slide show, save your changes when you write on slides during a slide show, and insert a black slide at the end of the presentation.

Change Slide Show Options

1. Click the **File** tab, and then click **Options**.

2. In the left pane, click **Advanced**.

3. Select or clear any of the check boxes to change the display view options you want.

- ◆ **Show menu on right mouse click.** Select to show a shortcut menu when you right-click a slide during a slide show. (Default on).

- ◆ **Show popup toolbar.** Select to show the popup toolbar in a slide show. (Default on).

- ◆ **Prompt to keep ink annotations when exiting.** Select to save your changes when you write on slides during a slide show. (Default on).

- ◆ **End with black slide.** Select to insert a black slide at the end of the presentation. (Default on).

4. Click **OK**.

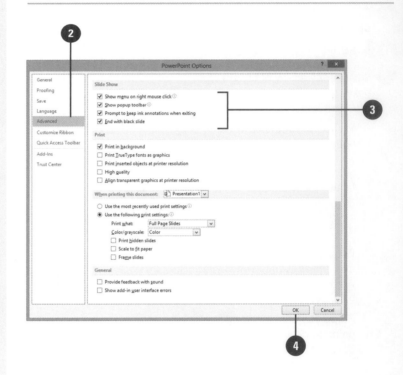

Setting Display Options

You can set options on the Advanced pane in PowerPoint Options to show or hide these elements when you work on a presentation. In addition, you can also show or hide PowerPoint window elements, such as shortcut keys and the vertical ruler. Sometimes hardware graphics accelerators used to speed up graphic displays for games can cause problems displaying content in a PowerPoint or slide show. If this happens, you can disable the hardware graphics acceleration (**New!**). You can specify whether to automatically extend the display monitor when presenting on a laptop or tablet (**New!**). If you prefer opening presentations in a specific view, you can specify the one you want or use the option to use the view saved in the file.

Change Display View Options

① Click the **File** tab, and then click **Options**.

② In the left pane, click **Advanced**.

③ Select or clear any of the check boxes to change the display view options you want.

- ◆ **Show shortcut keys in ScreenTips**. Select to show shortcut keys in ScreenTips.

- ◆ **Show vertical ruler.** Select to show the vertical ruler along with the horizontal ruler.

- ◆ **Disable hardware graphics acceleration**. Select to avoid display problem with media.

- ◆ **Disable Slide Show hardware graphics acceleration.** (Default off). (**New!**)

- ◆ **Automatically extend display when presenting on a laptop or tablet.** (Default off). (**New!**)

- ◆ **Open all documents using this view**. Click the list arrow to select a default view when you open a presentation.

④ Click **OK**.

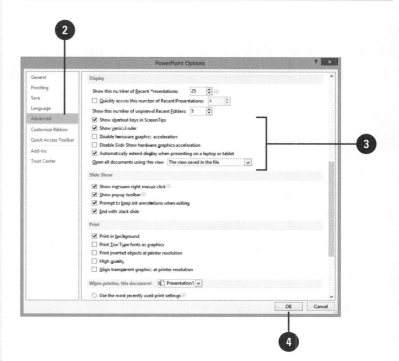

Setting Recent Presentation Options

When you display the Start and Open screens in PowerPoint, you can use the Recent Presentations option to display a list of recently used presentations for easy access when you want to open them again. In the Advanced pane in PowerPoint Options, you can specify the number of recent presentations that you want to display on the screens. If you want to save yourself even more time accessing them, you can add them to the File tab. In options, you can specify the number of presentations that you want to show on the tab. In addition to recent presentations, you can also display recent folders, which is also available in the Save As screen. In options, you can specify the number of unpinned folders that you want to show on the screens (**New!**). A pinned item stays on the screen whenever you need it until you unpin it.

Change Recent Presentation and Folder Display Options

1. Click the **File** tab, and then click **Options**.

2. In the left pane, click **Advanced**.

3. Select or clear any of the check boxes to change the display view options you want.

   ◆ **Show this number of Recent Presentations.** Shows this number of recent presentations on the Start and Open screens.

   Set to 0 to turn off the recent presentations display.

   ◆ **Quickly access this number of Recent Presentations**. Shows this number of recent presentations on the File tab. (Default off).

   ◆ **Show this number of unpinned Recent Folders.** Shows this number of unpinned recent folders on the Start, Open, and Save As screens. (**New!**)

   Set to 0 to turn off the recent folders display.

4. Click **OK**.

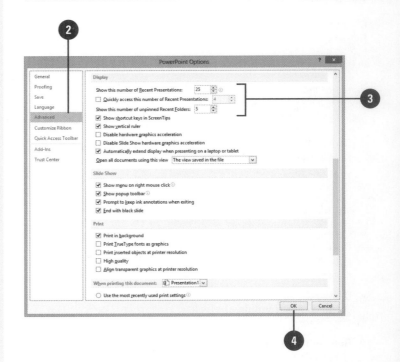

Changing Default File Locations

If you always save presentations in a specific folder, you can change the default location where presentations are saved. You can change the default local folder locations for presentations, images, personal templates (that appear on the Start and New screens) (**New!**), AutoRecover files. PowerPoint startup, Office tools, and offline documents on file management servers, such as SharePoint. PowerPoint specifies default folder locations based typical places where Microsoft stores things. However, if you want to change them to a location better suited for your needs, you can use the Browse button on the Save pane. After you make a change, PowerPoint uses the new setting for all subsequent PowerPoint sessions until you change the setting again.

Change Default File Locations

1. Click the **File** tab, and then click **Options**.

2. In the left pane, click **Save**.

3. Click **Browse**, select a folder location, and then click **OK** or enter a complete folder path location for any of the following:

   ◆ **AutoRecover file location.** Specifies the local folder location where PowerPoint creates and stores files for recovery.

   ◆ **Default local file location.** Specifies the local folder location to open or save files.

   ◆ **Default personal templates location.** Specifies the local folder location for storing and using custom templates. The templates appear on the Custom tab in the Start and New screens (**New!**).

   ◆ **Server drafts location.** Specifies the local folder for storing draft versions of files checked out (offline) from SharePoint and other file servers.

4. Click **OK**.

Setting Advanced Save Options

In addition to the standard save options on the Save pane in PowerPoint Options, you can also set more advanced save options that allow you to by-pass the Backstage screen, always show added places on the Save As screen, save presentations to your computer by default, and edit and share presentations on a document management server, such as SharePoint. If you are using nonstandard fonts to create a presentation, you can embed the fonts you use so they "travel" (are saved) with your presentation, Then, if the computer you use to show or print the presentation does not have all your presentation fonts installed, the embedded fonts appear in the presentation and your presentation quality will not suffer. When you embed fonts, the size of your presentation increases.

Change Advanced Save Options

1. Click the **File** tab, and then click **Options**.

2. In the left pane, click **Save**.

3. Select the save options you want:

   - **Don't show the Backstage when opening or saving files.** Select to display the Open or Save As dialog box when you select Open or Save As on the File tab. (Default off).

   - **Show additional places for saving, even if sign-in may be required.** Select to always show added places on the Save As screen. (Default on).

   - **Save to Computer by default** Select to save presentations to your computer by default (Default off).

4. Select the save options for presentations on a document management server you want:

   - **Save checked-out file to.** Select an option, and then specify a drafts location.

   - **Show detailed merge changes when a merge occurs.** Select to show merge details when sharing presentations online. (Default off).

5. Click **OK**.

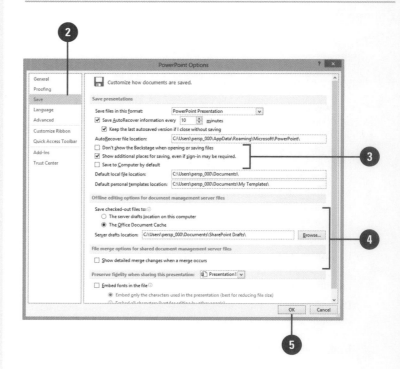

Change Embedding Options

① Click the **File** tab, and then click **Options**.

② In the left pane, click **Save**.

③ Click the **Preserve fidelity when sharing this presentation** list arrow, and then select the presentation you want to specify options.

④ Select the presentation embedding options you want:

◆ **Embed fonts in the file.** Select to save fonts in a file. (Default off).

◆ **Embed only the characters used in the presentation.** Select to save only the fonts you actually use in a presentation. (Default off).

◆ **Do not embed common system fonts.** Select to reduce file size when you use Windows and Office fonts. (Default off).

⑤ Click **OK**.

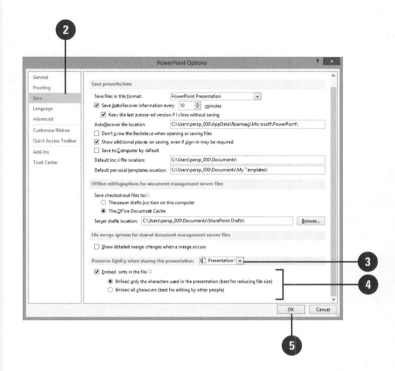

> ### See Also
>
> See "Saving a Presentation" on page 26 for more information on setting save presentation options.

Working with Touch Screens

If you're working with PowerPoint on a touch screen device, all you need is your finger to make gestures (**New!**). A gesture is the movement of one or more fingers on a touch screen or pad. For example, touching the screen is called tapping or dragging your finger with a flicking motion at the end of the movement is called swiping. You can swipe, tap, scroll, zoom, and pan within any PowerPoint view to navigate between and work with slides. To make PowerPoint easier to use with touch screens, the program provides Touch/Mouse Mode (**New!**), which adds or removes more space between commands on the Ribbon.

Use Touch/Mouse Mode

1. Click the **Quick Access Toolbar** list arrow, and then click **Touch/Mouse Mode**.

   This adds the button to the Quick Access Toolbar.

2. Click **Touch/Mouse Mode** button on the Quick Access Toolbar.

3. Click **Mouse** or **Touch**.

Did You Know?

You can use touch commands. In Office, you can use the following touch commands:

Click - Tap in the file.

Double-click - Double-tap in the file.

Drag - Tap and slide.

Zoom - Pinch or stretch two fingers.

Pan - Pinch or stretch two fingers and drag.

Scroll - Touch and slide up or down.

Swipe - Touch and flick right or left.

Select - Tap an object. For multiple objects, select one (tap and hold), and then tap others. For text, tap and drag.

You can make text and objects bigger. In Windows, open the Control Panel, tap Appearance & Personalization, tap Display, and tap Medium - 125% or Larger - 150%, and then tap Apply.

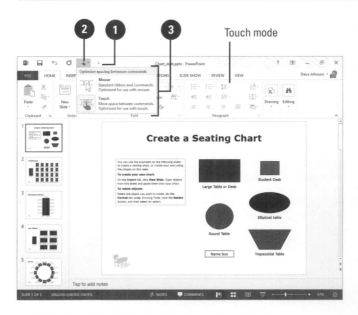

Touch mode

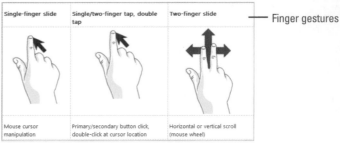

Finger gestures

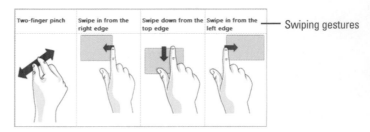

Swiping gestures

Accessing Commands Not in the Ribbon

If you don't see a command in the Ribbon that was available in an earlier version of PowerPoint, you might think Microsoft removed it from the product. To see if a command is available, check out the Customize Ribbon or Quick Access Toolbar section in PowerPoint Options. The Quick Access Toolbar and Custom Ribbon give access to commands not in the Ribbon, which you can add to the toolbar or ribbon. For example, you can add the following commands: Create Microsoft Outlook Task, Replace Fonts, Send to Microsoft Word, and Web Page Preview.

Add Commands Not in the Ribbon to the Quick Access Toolbar or Ribbon

1. Click the **File** tab, click **Options**, and then click **Quick Access Toolbar** or **Customize Ribbon**.

2. Click the **Choose commands from** list arrow, and then click **Commands Not in the Ribbon**.

3. Click the **Customize Quick Access Toolbar** and then click **For all documents (Default)**, or click the **Customize the Ribbon** list arrow, and then click **For All Tabs**.

4. Click the command you want to add (left column).

    TIMESAVER *For the Quick Access Toolbar, click <Separator>, and then click Add to insert a separator line between buttons.*

5. Click **Add**.

6. Click the **Move Up** and **Move Down** arrow buttons to arrange the commands in the order you want them to appear.

7. To reset the Quick Access Toolbar to its original state, click **Reset**, click **Reset only Quick Access Toolbar** or **Reset only selected Ribbon tab**, and then click **Yes**.

8. Click **OK**.

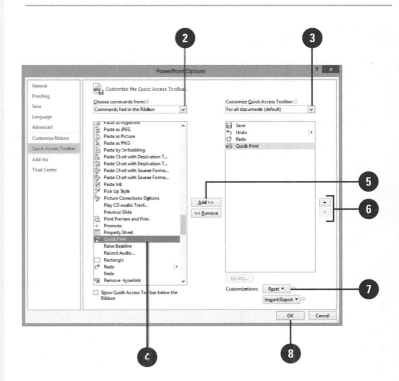

Customizing the Way You Create Objects

When you create a text box, PowerPoint applies a set of default text attributes. Some examples of PowerPoint's font default settings include font style, size, and formatting options, such as bold, italic, and underline. When you draw an object, PowerPoint applies a set of default object attributes. Examples of object default settings include fill color, shadow, and line style. To find out the current default settings for your presentation, you can draw an object, or create a text object and check the object's attributes. If you change a default setting, PowerPoint will use the new setting for all subsequent PowerPoint sessions until you change the setting again.

Customize the Way You Create Text Objects

1. Create a text box.

2. Change the text attributes, including font type, style, and size.

3. Right-click the text box (not the text inside), and then click **Set as Default Text Box**.

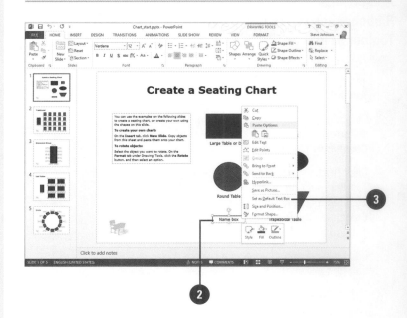

Customize the Way You Create Shape Objects

1. Create a shape.

2. Change the shape attributes, including fill color or effect, text color, outline color and style; and font type, style, and size.

3. Right-click the shape, and then click **Set as Default Shape**.

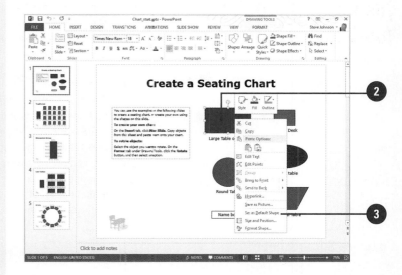

Working with Office Tools

In addition to the main programs, Office 2013 includes some helpful tools including SkyDrive Pro (**New!**), Upload Center, Language Preferences, Spreadsheet or Database Compare (**New!**), and Telemetry Log or Dashboard (**New!**). With SkyDrive Pro, you can connect and synchronize your SkyDrive cloud storage on a SharePoint site with your desktop. As you upload files to a server, like a SharePoint site, you can use the Upload Center to view progress or issues on a transfer. The Upload Center shows you pending uploads, recently uploaded files and all cached files from a server. If you need to compare two Excel spreadsheets, you can use the Spreadsheet Compare tool, a stand-alone app. Telemetry Log records Office events in an Excel spreadsheet to help you troubleshoot problems. Telemetry Dashboard is an Excel spreadsheet that connects to an SQL database to collect client data from other sources in a shared folder.

Compare Spreadsheets

1. Start **Spreadsheet Compare 2013** or **Database Compare 2013**.

   ◆ **Windows 8.** Click the tile on the All Apps screen.

   ◆ **Windows 7.** Click **Start** on the taskbar, point to **All Programs**, point to **Microsoft Office**, and then point to **Office 2013 Tools**.

2. Click the **Browse** folder, and then select the two files you want to compare.

3. Click **OK**.

   The differences appears color coded in the two panes and list.

4. Select or clear option check boxes to show or hide results.

5. Use the Home tab buttons to show results, export results, or copy results to the Clipboard.

6. To exit, click the **Close** button.

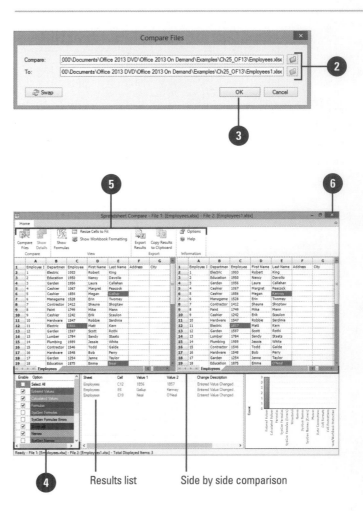

Results list   Side by side comparison

See Also

See "Using Multiple Languages" on page 300 for information on using Language Preferences.

Work with the Upload Center

1. Start **Office 2013 Upload Center**.

   ◆ **Windows 8.** Click the tile on the All Apps screen.

   ◆ **Windows 7.** Click **Start** on the taskbar, point to **All Programs**, point to **Microsoft Office**, and then point to **Office 2013 Tools**.

   ◆ **Desktop taskbar.** Click the **Upload Center** icon on the desktop taskbar, and then click **Open Upload Center**.

2. To display pending uploads, click the **View** list arrow, and then click **Pending Uploads**.

3. Use any of the following options:

   ◆ **Actions.** Use options to open the selected file, open site with the file, save a copy, or discard changes.

   ◆ **Upload All.** Use to upload all files.

   ◆ **Pause Uploads.** Use to pause the selected file.

   ◆ **Settings.** Use to open settings dialog box.

   ◆ **Refresh.** Use to refresh the files in the Upload Center.

4. To resolve issues or take actions, click **Resolve** or **Actions**, and then select an option.

5. To display recent uploads, click the **View** list arrow, and then click **Recently Uploaded**.

6. To exit Upload Center, click the **Close** button.

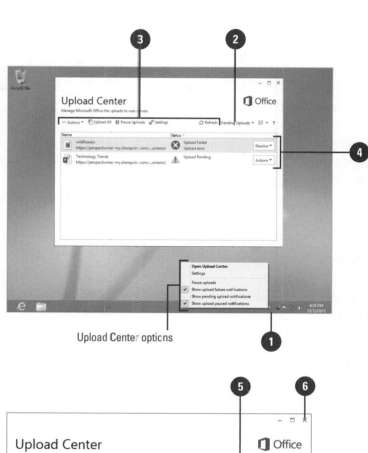

Upload Center options

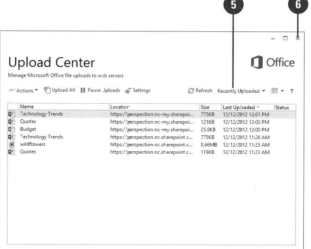

See Also

See "Syncing Documents on SharePoint" on page 460 for information on using SkyDrive Pro.

Maintaining and Repairing Office

At times you may determine that an Office program is not working as efficiently as it once did. This sometimes happens when you install new software or move files into new folders. Office does the work for you with the Repair option, which locates, diagnoses, and fixes any errors in the program itself. Note that this feature does not repair personal files like documents, presentations, or workbooks. If the Repair option does not fix the problem, you might have to reinstall Office. If you want to add or remove features, reinstall Office, or remove it entirely, you can use Office Setup's maintenance feature.

Perform Maintenance on Office Programs

1. Insert the Office disc in your drive or navigate to the folder with the setup program.

2. In File or Windows Explorer, double-click the Setup icon.

3. Click one of the following maintenance buttons.

   ◆ **Add or Remove Features** to change which features are installed or remove specific features.

   ◆ **Remove** to uninstall Microsoft Office 2013 from this computer.

   ◆ **Repair** to repair Microsoft Office 2013 to its original state.

   ◆ **Enter a Product Key** to type the product registration key (located in the product packaging) for Office 2013.

4. Click **Continue**, and then follow the wizard instructions to complete the maintenance.

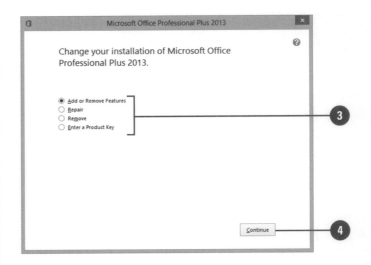

See Also

See "Working with Office Safe Modes" on page 400 for information on fixing problems with a Microsoft Office 2013 program.

For Your Information

Updating Office 2013 along with Windows 8

Microsoft continually improves Office with updates that include bug fixes and feature improvements. With Windows 8, you can automatically get updates to Office 2013 along with the operating system. To set the update option, open the Desktop app, open the Control Panel, click System and Security, click Windows Update, click Change settings in the left pane, select the Give Me Updates For Other Microsoft Products When I Update Window check box, and then click OK. When Windows 8 scans your system and checks for updates, it also checks for Office 2013 updates (**New!**) as well as other Microsoft products.

Expanding PowerPoint Functionality

13

Introduction

An Office App is a third-party software component that adds functionality or extends features in an Office program. For example, you can add an app called Wikipane to search for Wikipedia information directly in an Office program. You can quickly install, insert, and manage apps from the Office Store at Office.com directly from an Office program.

An add-in also extends the functionality of PowerPoint and other Office programs. An add-in is typically a third-party program you can purchase—some are shareware—and download from the web. You can find a list of add-ins for PowerPoint on Office.com. Before you can use an add-in, you need to load it first. After you load an add-in, the feature may add a command to a Ribbon tab.

If you want to customize Microsoft PowerPoint and create advanced presentations, you'll need to learn how to work with the Microsoft Office programming language, **Microsoft Visual Basic for Applications (VBA)**. VBA is powerful and flexible, and you can use it in all major Office applications. To create a VBA application, you have to learn VBA conventions and syntax. Office makes VBA more user-friendly by providing the Visual Basic Editor, an application that includes several tools to help you write error-free VBA applications. The Visual Basic Editor provides extensive online Help to assist you in this task. A practical way to use VBA is to create macros. Macros can automate common repetitive tasks that you use regularly in PowerPoint.

An ActiveX control is a software component that adds functionality to an existing program. An ActiveX control supports a customizable, programmatic interface for you to create your own functionality, such as a form. PowerPoint includes several pre-built ActiveX controls—including a label, text box, command button, and check box—to help you create a user interface.

What You'll Do

Add and Insert Apps for Office

Manage Apps for Office

View and Manage Add-ins

Load and Unload Add-ins

Enhance a Presentation with VBA

View the Visual Basic Editor

Set Developer Options

Simplify Tasks with Macros

Control a Macro

Add a Digital Signature to a Macro Project

Assign a Macro to a Toolbar or Ribbon

Save and Open a Presentation with Macros

Insert ActiveX Controls

Use ActiveX Controls

Set ActiveX Control Properties

Play a Movie Using an ActiveX Control

Change the Document Information Panel

Adding Apps for Office

With the Office Store at Office.com (**New!**), you can add functionality with a third-party app to an Office program, and then use the app to extend features in a presentation. For example, you can add an app called Wikipane to provide an easy way to access Wikipedia directly from any Office program. Some apps are free, while others charge a fee. To use Office.com, you need to have a Microsoft account, and be signed in with your Office program. You can insert an app by using the Apps for Office button (**New!**) on the Insert tab. Apps are designed for specific Office programs and only appear for them.

Add an Office App

1. Click the **Insert** tab.

2. Click the **Apps for Office** button (**New!**), and then click **See All**.

   A list of installed or featured apps appears in the dialog box.

3. Click **FEATURED APPS**.

   A list of available apps appears under FEATURED APPS.

4. To add a featured app, click the app title or the **Add** button.

   The app is added to your account at Office.com and inserts an object or opens a pane. Specify the app options you want to apply.

5. To exit, click the **Close** button in the dialog box or pane.

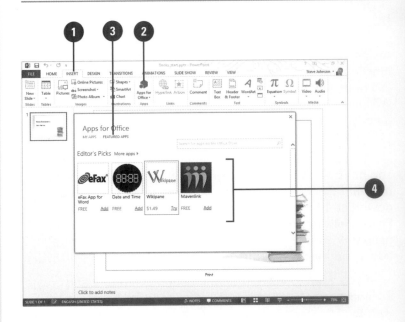

Did You Know?

You can get apps for Office programs. Apps are available for Word, Excel, Outlook, Project, PowerPoint, and SharePoint 2013 from the Office Store at *www.office.com/store*.

See Also

See "Managing Apps for Office" on page 427 for information on showing and hiding installed apps.

MY APPS

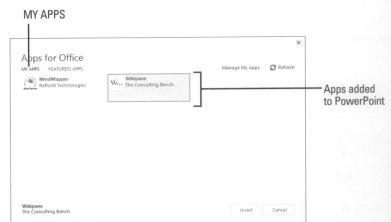

Apps added to PowerPoint

Search for Office Apps at Office.com

1. Click the **Insert** tab.

2. Click the **Apps for Office** button (**New!**), and then click **See All**.

   A list of installed or featured apps appears in the dialog box.

3. Click **FEATURED APPS**.

   A list of available apps appears under FEATURED APPS.

4. Type your search text in the Search box, and then click the **Search** button or press Enter.

   The Office Store opens in your web browser.

5. To add an app, click the app, and then click **Add**.

   ◆ Sign-in to your account, if prompted, or click **Sign in**.

   ◆ **See All Apps.** Click the **See all products** link.

   ◆ **Sort Apps.** Click any of the SORT BY options: **Relevance**, **Price**, or **Rating**.

6. To exit, click the **Close** button in your web browser.

Did You Know?

You can find more apps at the Office Store. Click the Insert tab, click the Apps for Office button, click See All, and then click the Find more apps at the Office Store link. The Office Store web site opens. Sign in, if necessary, and then browse available apps for the Office program you want.

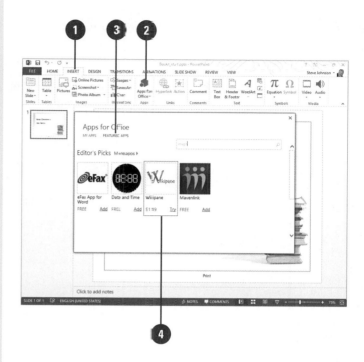

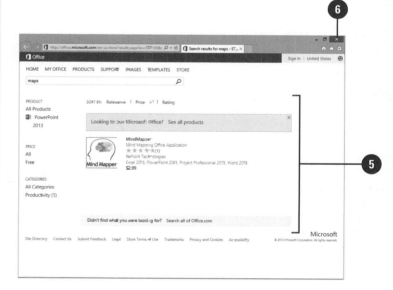

Inserting Apps for Office

After you add an App for Office from the Office Store at Office.com (**New!**), you can use the app in an Office program. Some apps insert an object, while others open a pane. For example, the Dictionary - Merriam app opens in a pane, where you can quickly find a definition. You can insert an app by using the Apps for Office button (**New!**) on the Insert tab. Recently used apps appear on the Apps for Office button menu for easy access. Apps are designed for specific Office programs and only appear for them.

Insert an App for Office

1. Click the **Insert** tab.

2. To insert a recently used app object, click the **Apps for Office** button (**New!**), and then click the recently used app on the menu.

3. To see all apps, click the **Apps for Office** button (**New!**), and then click **See All**.

   A list of installed or featured apps appears in the dialog box.

4. Click **MY APPS**.

   A list of installed apps appears under MY APPS.

5. Click the app tile you want to insert.

6. Click **Insert**.

   The app inserts an object or opens a pane. Specify the app options you want to apply.

See Also

See "Adding Apps for Office" on page 424 for information on finding and adding an Office app to an Office program.

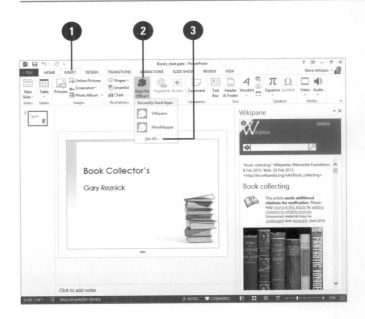

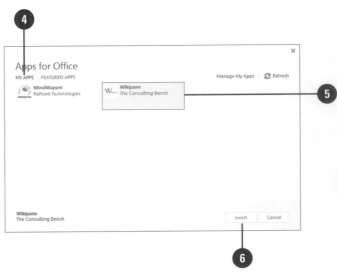

Managing Apps for Office

The apps you add to your Office programs are managed online at Office.com using your web browser. You can access the web site from within your Office program using the Apps for Office button (**New!**) on the Insert tab. To use Office.com, you need to have a Microsoft account, and be signed in with your Office program. At Office.com (**New!**), you can view your Visible and Hidden apps. The Visible list displays the apps available in your Office programs, while the Hidden list displays the apps you've installed and added to your account. In the Visible list, you can hide apps and in the Hidden list, you can retrieve (show) apps. Apps are designed for specific Office programs and only appear for them.

Manage Office Apps

1. Click the **Insert** tab.

2. Click the **Apps for Office** button (**New!**), and then click **See All**.

   A list of installed or featured apps appears in the dialog box.

3. Click **MY APPS**.

   A list of available apps appears under MY APPS.

4. Click **Manage My Apps**, and then wait for your web browser to open.

   ◆ Sign-in to your account, if prompted, or click **Sign in**.

5. To hide an app, click **Visible**, and then click the **Hide** link.

6. To show an app, click **Hidden**, and then click the **Retrieve** link.

7. To exit, click the **Close** button in your web browser.

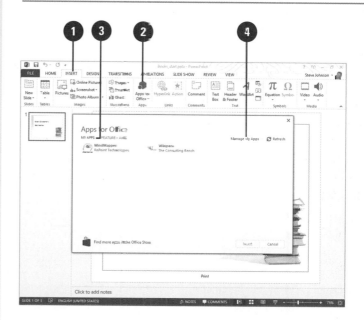

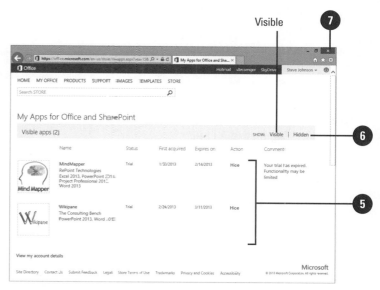

Viewing and Managing Add-ins

An add-in extends functionality to PowerPoint and other Microsoft Office programs. An add-in can add buttons and custom commands to the Ribbon or menu items on the File tab. You can get add-ins for PowerPoint on the Office.com web site, or on third-party vendor web sites. When you download and install an add-in, it appears on the Add-Ins or other tabs depending on functionality, and includes a special ScreenTip that identifies the developer. You can view and manage add-ins from the Add-Ins pane in PowerPoint Options.

View Installed Add-ins

1 Click the **Add-Ins** tab, or click the **File** tab, click **Add-Ins**, point to an add-in menu option, if available, and then select a command.

Add-ins with buttons and controls appear on the Ribbon. To display a ScreenTip, point to a button or control.

2 Click the **File** tab, and then click **Options**.

3 In the left pane, click **Add-Ins**.

The installed add-ins appear in the list by category.

◆ **Active Application Add-ins.** Lists the registered and running add-ins. A selected check box for a COM add-in appears here.

◆ **Inactive Application Add-ins.** Lists the installed add-ins, but not currently loaded. A cleared check box for a COM add-in appears here.

◆ **Document Related Add-ins.** Lists template files currently open in a document.

◆ **Disabled Application Add-ins.** Lists automatically disabled add-ins causing Office programs to crash.

4 Click an add-in to display information about it.

5 Click **OK**.

Add-in

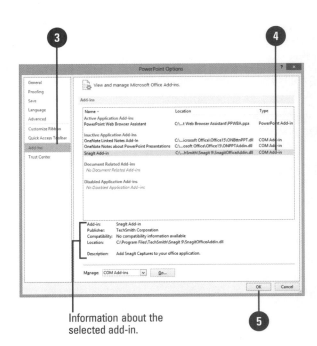

Information about the selected add-in.

Manage Installed Add-ins

① Click the **File** tab, and then click **Options**.

② In the left pane, click **Add-Ins**.

③ Click the **Manage** list arrow, and then click the add-in list you want to display:

◆ **COM Add-ins.** Opens the COM Add-Ins dialog box and lists the Component Object Model (COM) add-ins.

◆ **PowerPoint Add-ins.** Opens the Add-Ins dialog box and lists the currently installed PowerPoint add-ins.

◆ **Actions.** Opens the AutoCorrect dialog with the Actions tab and list the installed actions.

◆ **Disabled Items.** Opens the Disabled Items dialog box and lists the disabled items that prevent PowerPoint from working properly. If you want to try and enable an item, select it, click Enable, click Close, and then restart PowerPoint.

④ Click **Go**.

⑤ Click **OK**.

COM Add-Ins dialog box

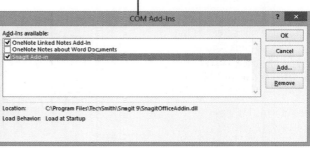

Loading and Unloading Add-ins

Add-ins are additional programs, designed to run seamlessly within PowerPoint or Office. There are two main types of add-ins: PowerPoint and **Component Object Model (COM)**. PowerPoint add-ins are custom controls designed specifically for PowerPoint, while COM add-ins are designed to run in one or more Office programs and use the file name extension .dll or .exe. Some add-ins are installed when you run the Setup program, while others can be downloaded from Microsoft Office Online or purchased from third-party vendors. To load or unload add-ins, PowerPoint provides commands you can access from an added button on the Quick Access Toolbar, Developer tab, or the Add-Ins pane in PowerPoint Options. When you load an add-in, the feature may add a command to a tab or toolbar. You can load one or more add-ins. If you no longer need an add-in, you should unload it to save memory and reduce the number of commands on a tab. When you unload an add-in, you also may need to restart PowerPoint to remove an add-in command from a tab.

Load or Unload a PowerPoint Add-in

1 Click the **Developer** tab.

◆ To display the Developer tab, use the Customize Ribbon pane in PowerPoint Options.

◆ You can also click the File tab, click Options, click Add-ins, click the Manage list arrow, click PowerPoint Add-ins, and then click Go.

2 Click the **Add-Ins** button.

3 Click the add-in you want to load or unload.

TROUBLE? *If the add-in is not available in the list, click Add New, locate and select the add-in you want, and then click OK.*

4 Click **Load** or **Unload**.

5 To remove the selected add-in, click **Remove**.

6 Click **Close**.

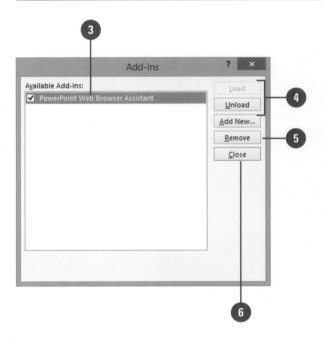

Load or Unload a COM Add-in

1 Click the **Developer** tab.

- ◆ To display the Developer tab, use the Customize Ribbon pane in PowerPoint Options.

- ◆ You can also click the File tab, click Options, click Add-ins, click the Manage list arrow, click COM Add-ins, and then click Go.

2 Click the **COM Add-Ins** button.

3 Select the check box next to the add-in you want to load, or clear the check box you want to unload.

> **TROUBLE?** *If the add-in is not available in the list, click Add, locate and select the add-in you want, and then click OK.*

4 To remove the selected add-in, click **Remove**.

5 Click **OK**.

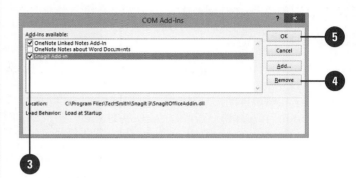

Did You Know?

You can can get more information about COM online. Visit *www.microsoft.com/com.*

You can open an add-in dialog box from PowerPoint Options. Click the File tab, click Options, click Add-ins, click the Manage list arrow, click PowerPoint Add-ins or COM Add-ins, and then click Go.

For Your Information

Dealing with an Add-in Security Alert

When there is a problem with an add-in, PowerPoint disables it to protect the program and your data. When a problem does occur, a security alert dialog box appears, displaying information about the problem and options you can choose to fix or ignore it. You can choose an option to help protect me from unknown content (recommended), enable this add-in for this session only, or enable all code published by this publisher. See "Setting Add-ins Security Options" on page 395 for more information about setting options that trigger the Add-in security alert.

Enhancing a Presentation with VBA

Office applications like PowerPoint, Access, Excel, Word, and Visio share a common programming language: Visual Basic for Applications (VBA). With VBA, you can develop applications that combine tools from these Office products, as well as other programs that support VBA. Because of the language's power and flexibility, programmers often prefer to use VBA to customize their Office applications.

Introducing the Structure of VBA

VBA is an object-oriented programming language because, when you develop a VBA application, you manipulate objects. An object can be anything within your presentation, such as a shape, text box, picture, or table. Even PowerPoint itself is considered an object. Objects can have properties that describe the object's characteristics. Text boxes, for example, have the Font property, which describes the font PowerPoint uses to display the text. A text box also has properties that indicate whether the text is bold or italic.

Objects also have methods, actions that can be done to the object. Deleting and inserting are examples of methods available with a record object. Closely related to methods are events. An event is a specific action that occurs on or with an object. Clicking a button initiates the Click event for the button object. VBA also refers to an event associated with an object as an event property. The form button, for example, has the Click event property. You can use VBA to either respond to an event or to initiate an event.

Writing VBA Code

A VBA programmer types the statements, or **code**, that make up the VBA program. Those statements follow a set of rules, called **syntax**, that govern how commands are formulated. For example, to change the property of a particular object, the command follows the general form:

Object.Property = Expression

Where **Object** is the name of a VBA object, **Property** is the name of a property that object has, and **Expression** is a value that will be assigned to the property. The following statement sets the ViewType property of the ActiveWindow to Slide View:

ActiveWindow.ViewType = ppViewSlide"

You can use Office and VBA's online Help to learn about specific object and property names. If you want to apply a method to an object, the syntax is:

Object.Method arg1, arg2, ...

Where **Object** is the name of a VBA object, **Method** is the name of method that can be applied to that object, and **arg1, arg2**, ... are optional **arguments** that provide additional information for the method operation. For example, to exit all running slide shows, you could use the Exit method as follows:

SlideShowWindows(1).View.Exit

Working with Procedures

You don't run VBA commands individually. Instead they are organized into groups of commands called **procedures**. A procedure either performs an action or calculates a value. Procedures that perform actions are called **Sub procedures**. You can run a Sub procedure directly, or Office can run it for you in response to an event, such as clicking a button or opening a form. A Sub procedure initiated by an event is also called an **event procedure**. Office provides event procedure templates to help you easily create procedures for common events. Event procedures are displayed in each object's event properties list.

A procedure that calculates a value is called a **function procedure**. By creating function procedures you can create your own function library, supplementing the Office collection of built-in functions. You can access these functions from within the Expression Builder, making it easy for them to be used over and over again.

Working with Modules

Procedures are collected and organized within **modules**. Modules generally belong to two types: class modules and standard modules. A **class module** is associated with a specific object. In more advanced VBA programs, the class module can be associated with an object created by the user. **Standard modules** are not associated with specific objects, and they can be run from anywhere within a database. This is usually not the case with class modules. Standard modules are listed in the Database window on the Modules Object list.

Building VBA Projects

A collection of modules is further organized into a **project**. Usually a project has the same

name as a presentation. You can create projects that are not tied into any specific presentation, saving them as PowerPoint add-ins that provide extra functionality to PowerPoint.

Using the Visual Basic Editor

You create VBA commands, procedures, and modules in Office's **Visual Basic Editor**. This is the same editor used by Excel, Word, and other Office programs. Thus, you can apply what you learn about creating programs in PowerPoint to these other applications.

The Project Explorer

One of the fundamental tools in the Visual Basic Editor is the Project Explorer. The **Project Explorer** presents a hierarchical view of all of the projects and modules currently open in PowerPoint, including standard and class modules.

The Modules Window

You write all of your VBA code in the **Modules** window. The Modules window acts as a basic text editor, but it includes several tools to help you write error-free codes. PowerPoint also provides hints as you write your code to help you avoid syntax errors.

The Object Browser

There are hundreds of objects available to you. Each object has a myriad of properties, methods, and events. Trying to keep track of all of them is daunting, but the Visual Basic Editor supplies the **Object Browser**, which helps you examine the complete collection of objects, properties, and methods available for a given object.

Viewing the Visual Basic Editor

The Project Explorer displays a hierarchical list of all open projects and modules.

The Modules window allows you to enter VBA commands.

VBA projects

Currently selected module

The Properties window displays properties for selected objects.

A VBA statement

Method

Properties

Objects

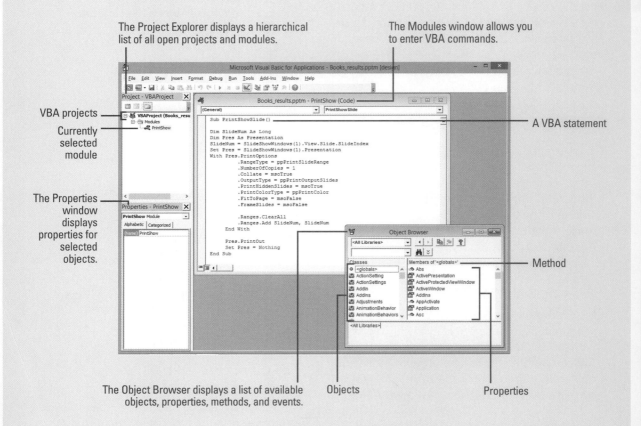

The Object Browser displays a list of available objects, properties, methods, and events.

Setting Developer Options

The Developer tab is a specialized Ribbon that you can use to access developer controls, write code, or create macros. You can set an option in the Customize Ribbon section in PowerPoint Options to show or hide the Developer tab. As a developer, you can also set an option to show errors in your user interface customization code.

Set Developer Options

1. Click the **File** tab, and then click **Options**.

2. In the left pane, click **Customize Ribbon**.

3. Select the **Developer** check box to display the Developer tab.

4. In the left pane, click **Advanced**.

5. Select the **Show add-in user interface errors** check box.

6. Click **OK**.

Simplifying Tasks with Macros

If you find yourself repeating the same set of steps over and over or if you need to add new functionality to PowerPoint, you could create a macro. Macros can run several tasks for you at the click of a button. You create macros using a programming language called Microsoft Visual Basic for Applications (VBA). With VBA, you create a macro by writing a script to replay the actions you want. The macros for a particular presentation are stored in a macro module, which is a collection of Visual Basic codes.

Create a Macro

1. Click the **View** or **Developer** tab.

2. Click the **Macros** button.

3. Type a name for the macro.

4. Click the Macro in list arrow, and then click **All open presentations** or the presentation to which you want the macro stored.

5. If you want, add a macro description in the Description box.

6. Click **Create**.

   The Microsoft Visual Basic window opens.

7. Click the Module window, and then type new Visual Basic commands, or edit existing ones.

8. When you're done, click the **File** menu, and then click **Close and Return to Microsoft PowerPoint**.

Did You Know?

You can use macros from earlier versions of PowerPoint. If you created a macro using the Macro Recorder in an earlier version of PowerPoint (97-2003), you can use VBA to edit the macro. The Macro Recorder actually writes a program in VBA to create a macro.

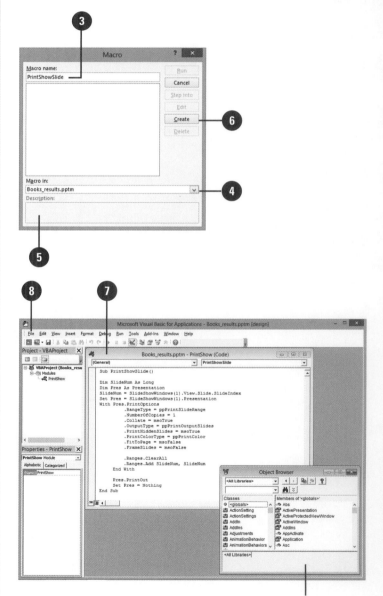

Object Browser helps you insert commands.

Run a Macro

1 Click the **View** or **Developer** tab.

2 Click the **Macros** button.

> **TIMESAVER** *Click the Marcos button on the Status bar.*

3 Click the name of the macro you want to run.

4 Click **Run**.

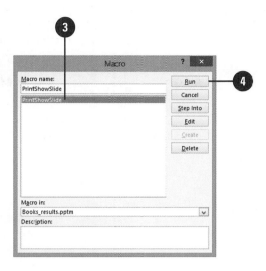

Did You Know?

You can stop a macro. Press Ctrl+Break to stop a macro before it completes its actions.

Delete a Macro

1 Click the **View** or **Developer** tab.

2 Click the **Macros** button.

3 Click the macro name.

4 Click **Delete**.

5 Click **Delete** to confirm the macro deletion.

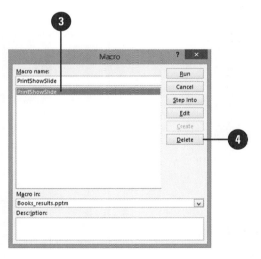

Did You Know?

You can set up a macro to run during a slide show. In Normal view, click the text or object you want to use to run a macro, click the Insert tab, click the Action button, click the Mouse Click tab or the Mouse Over tab, click the Run Macro option, click the list arrow, select the macro you want, and then click OK.

Controlling a Macro

If a macro doesn't work exactly the way you want it to, you can fix the problem using Microsoft Visual Basic for Applications (VBA). VBA allows you to **debug**, or repair, an existing macro so that you change only the actions that aren't working correctly. All macros for a particular presentation are stored in a macro module, a collection of Visual Basic programming codes that you can copy to other presentation files. You can view and edit your Visual Basic modules using the Visual Basic editor. By learning Visual Basic you can greatly increase the scope and power of your programs.

Debug a Macro Using Step Mode

1. Click the **View** or **Developer** tab.

2. Click the **Macros** button.

3. Click the name of the macro you want to debug.

4. Click **Step Into**.

   The Microsoft Visual Basic window opens.

5. Click the **Debug** menu, and then click **Step Into** (or press F8) to proceed through each action.

   ◆ Use other commands like **Step Over** and **Step Out** to debug the code.

6. When you're done, click the **File** menu, and then click **Close and Return to Microsoft PowerPoint**.

7. Click **OK** to stop the debugger.

Did You Know?

You can display the Debug toolbar. In the Visual Basic editor, click the View menu, point to Toolbars, and then click Debug.

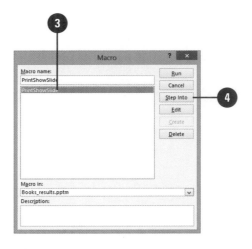

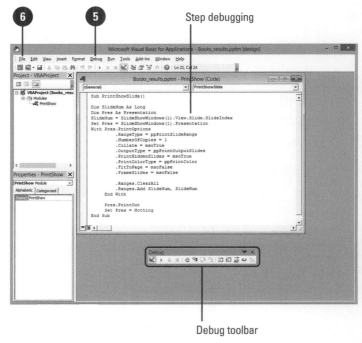

Step debugging

Debug toolbar

Edit a Macro

1. Click the **View** or **Developer** tab.

2. Click the **Macros** button.

3. Click the name of the macro you want to edit, and then click **Edit**.

4. Click the Module window containing the Visual Basic code for your macro.

5. Type new Visual Basic commands, or edit the commands already present.

6. Click the **File** menu, and then click **Close and Return to Microsoft PowerPoint**.

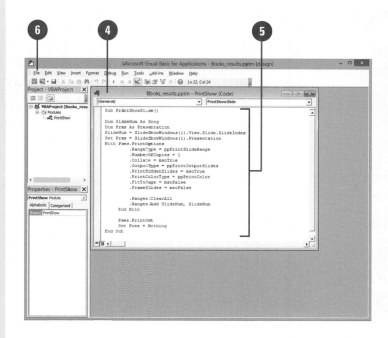

Copy a Macro Module to Another Presentation

1. Open the presentation files you want to copy the macro from and to.

2. Click the **Developer** tab.

3. Click the **Visual Basic** button.

4. Click the **View** menu, and then click **Project Explorer**.

5. Drag the module you want to copy from the source presentation to the destination presentation.

6. Click the **File** menu, and then click **Close and Return to Microsoft PowerPoint**.

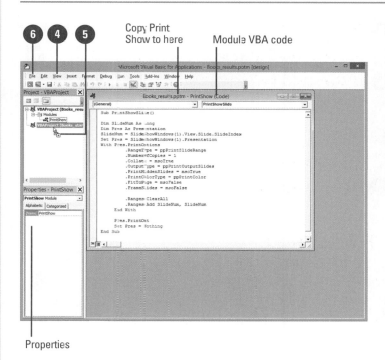

Copy Print Show to here   Module VBA code

Properties

Adding a Digital Signature to a Macro Project

If you want to add a digital signature to a presentation with a macro, you need to add it using the Visual Basic editor. If you open a presentation that contains a signed macro project with a problem, the macro is disabled by default and the Message Bar appears to notify you of the potential problem. You can click Options or Enable Content in the Message Bar to view information about it. For more details, you can click Show Signature Details to view certificate and publisher information. If a digital signature has problems—it's expired, not issued by a trusted publisher, or the presentation has been altered—the certificate information image contains a red X. When there's a problem, contact the signer to have them fix it, or save the presentation to a trusted location, where you can run the macro without security checks.

Sign a Macro Project

1. Open the presentation that contains the macro project, and then click the **Developer** tab.

2. Click the **Visual Basic** button to open the Visual Basic window.

3. Click the **Tools** menu, and then click **Digital Signature**.

4. Click **Choose**.

5. Select a certificate in the list.

6. To view a certificate, click **View Certificate** or a link, and then click **OK**.

7. Click **OK**.

8. Click **OK** again.

9. Click the **Save** and **Close** button in the Visual Basic window.

Assigning a Macro to a Toolbar or Ribbon

After you create a macro, you can add the macro to the Quick Access Toolbar or Ribbon for easy access. When you create a macro, the macro name appears in the list of available commands when you customize the Quick Access Toolbar or Ribbon in PowerPoint Options. When you point to a macro button on the Quick Access Toolbar or Ribbon, a ScreenTip appears, displaying Macro: *presentation name!macro name*.

Assign a Macro to a Toolbar or Ribbon

1. Click the **File** tab, click **Options**, and then click **Quick Access Toolbar** or **Customize Ribbon**.

2. Click the **Choose commands from** list arrow, and then click **Macros**.

3. Click the **Customize Quick Access Toolbar** and then click **For all documents (default)**, or click the **Customize the Ribbon** list arrow, and then click **For All Tabs**.

4. Click the macro you want to add (left column).

5. Click **Add**.

6. Click the **Move Up** and **Move Down** arrow buttons to arrange the commands in the order you want them to appear.

7. Click **Modify** or **Rename**.

8. Type a name for the button.

9. Click an icon in the symbol list.

10. Click **OK**.

11. Click **OK**.

See Also

See "Working with the Ribbon and Toolbars" on page 6 and "Accessing Command Not in the Ribbon" on page 417 for information on using the Quick Access Toolbar.

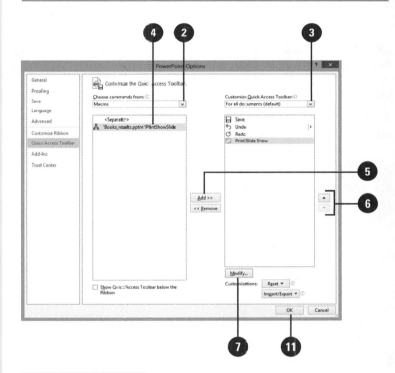

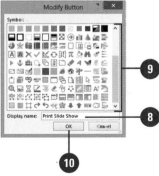

Macro button

Saving a Presentation with Macros

Macros are created using Visual Basic for Applications (VBA) code. If you add a macro to a presentation, you need to save it with a file name extension that ends with an "m", either PowerPoint Macro-Enabled Presentation (.pptm), PowerPoint Macro-Enabled Show (.ppsm), or PowerPoint Macro-Enabled Design Template (.potm). If you try to save a presentation containing a macro with a file name extension that ends with an "x" (such as .pptx, .sldx, or .potx), PowerPoint displays an alert message, restricting the operation. These PowerPoint file types are designated to be VBA code-free.

Save a Presentation with Macros

1. Click the **File** tab, and then click **Save As**.

2. Click the **Save in** list arrow, and then click the drive or folder where you want to save the file.

3. Type a presentation file name.

4. If necessary, click the **Save as type** list arrow, and then click one of the following:

   ◆ **PowerPoint Macro-Enabled Presentation.** A presentation (.pptm) that contains VBA code.

   ◆ **PowerPoint Macro-Enabled Show.** A presentation slide show (.ppsm) that includes preapproved macros.

   ◆ **PowerPoint Macro-Enabled Design Template.** A template (.potm) that includes preapproved macros.

5. Click **Save**.

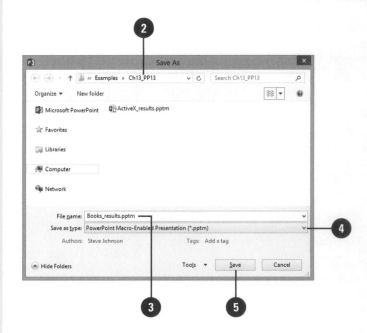

Opening a Presentation with Macros

When you open a presentation with a macro, VBA, or other software code, PowerPoint displays a security warning to let you know the presentation might contain potentially harmful code that may harm your computer. If you know and trust the author of the presentation, you can change security options to enable the macro content and use the presentation normally. If you don't trust the content, you can continue to block and disable the content and use the presentation with limited functionality in Protected view. If you don't want a security alert to appear, you can change security settings in the Trust Center in PowerPoint Options.

Open a Presentation with Macros

1 Click the **File** tab, and then click **Open**.

2 Click the **Files as type** list arrow, and then click one of the following presentation types with macros:

- ◆ **PowerPoint Macro-Enabled Presentation.** A presentation (.pptm) that contains VBA code.

- ◆ **PowerPoint Macro-Enabled Show.** A presentation slide show (.ppsm) that includes preapproved macros.

- ◆ **PowerPoint Macro-Enabled Design Template.** A template (.potm) that includes preapproved macros.

3 If the file is located in another folder, click the **Look in** list arrow, and then navigate to the file.

4 Click the presentation with macros you want to open, and then click **Open**.

5 Click **Options** in the Message Bar.

- ◆ You can also click the **File** tab, click **Info**, click the **Enable Content** button, and then click **Advanced Options**.

6 Click **OK** to enable content or click **Cancel** to keep disabled.

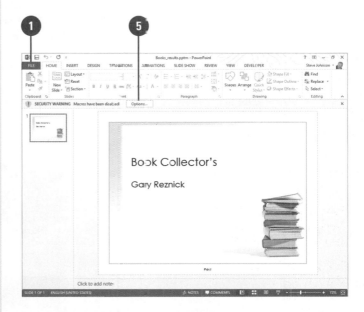

Inserting ActiveX Controls

An ActiveX control is a software component that adds functionality to an existing program. An ActiveX control is really just another term for an OLE (Object Linking and Embedding) object, known as a Component Object Model (COM) object. An ActiveX control supports a customizable, programmatic interface. PowerPoint includes several pre-built ActiveX controls on the Developer tab, including a label, text box, command button, image, scroll bar, check box, option button, combo box, list box, toggle button, and more controls. To create an ActiveX control, click the control you want in the Developer tab, and then drag to insert it with the size you want. If there is a problem with an ActiveX control, PowerPoint disables it to protect the program and your data. When a problem does occur, a security alert dialog box appears, displaying information about the problem and options you can choose to leave it disabled in Protected view or enable it.

Insert ActiveX Controls

1. Click the **Developer** tab.

2. Click the button with the ActiveX control you want to use.

    See the next page for a list and description of each ActiveX control.

3. Display the slide where you want to place the ActiveX control.

4. Drag (pointer changes to a plus sign) to draw the ActiveX control the size you want.

5. To resize the control, drag a resize handle (circles) to the size you want.

Deal with an ActiveX Control Security Alert

1. Click the **File** tab, and then click **Open**.

2. Click the **File as type** list arrow, and then click the presentation type that contains the Active X control.

3. If the file is located in another folder, click the **Look in** list arrow, and then navigate to the file.

4. Click the presentation with the ActiveX control you want to open, and then click **Open**.

5. Click the **File** tab, click **Info**, click the **Enable Content** button, and then click **Advanced Options**. To enable all content (make trusted), click **Enable All Content** on the menu.

   ◆ You can also click **Enable Content** in the Message Bar with the Security Warning.

6. If you trust the document content, click the **Enable content for this session** option to use it. If you don't trust it, click the **Help protect me from unknown content (recommended)** option to block and disable the macros & activeX.

7. Click **OK**.

See Also

See "Setting ActiveX Security Options" on page 379 for more information about setting options that trigger the ActiveX security alert.

Click for more details   Enable Content in the Message Bar

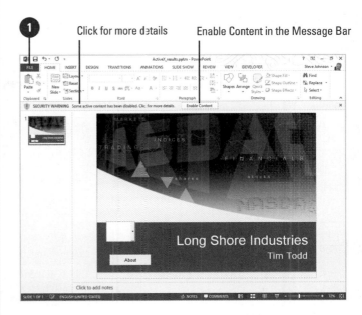

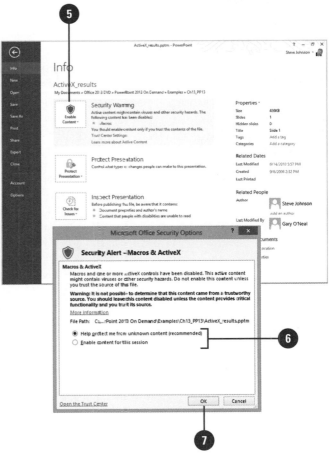

Using ActiveX Controls

ActiveX Controls

Button	Name	Description
A	Label	This button creates a text label. Because the other controls already include a corresponding label, use this button to create labels that are independent of other controls.
abl	Text Box	This button creates a text box in which the user can enter text (or numbers). Use this control for objects assigned to a text or number data type.
⬍	Spin Button	This button creates a box in which the user can click arrows to increase or decrease numbers in a box. Use this control assigned to a number data type.
⬜	Command Button	This button creates a button that runs a macro or Microsoft Visual Basic function when the user clicks the button in the form.
🖼	Image	This button inserts a frame, in which you can insert a graphic in your form. Use this control when you want to insert a graphic, such as clip art or a logo.
⬍	Scroll Bar	This button creates a scroll bar pane in which the user can enter text (or numbers) in a scrollable text box. Use this control or objects assigned to a text or number data type.
☑	Check Box	This button creates a check box that allows a user to make multiple yes or no selections. Use this control for fields assigned to the yes/no data type.
◉	Option Button	This button creates an option button (also known as a radio button) that allows the user to make a single selection from at least two choices. Use this control for fields assigned to the yes/no data type.
▦	Combo Box	This button creates a combo box in which the user has the option to enter text or select from a list of options. You can enter your own options in the list, or you can display options stored in another table.
▤	List Box	This button creates a list box that allows a user to select from a list of options. You can enter your own options in the list, or can have another table provide a list of options.
▭	Toggle Button	This button creates a button that allows the user to make a yes or no selection by clicking the toggle button. Use this control for fields assigned to the yes/no data type.
🛠	More Controls	Click to display other controls, such as Adobe Acrobat Control for ActiveX, Microsoft Forms 2.0, Microsoft InfoPath controls, and Microsoft web Browser.

Setting ActiveX Control Properties

Every ActiveX control has **properties**, or settings, that determine its appearance and function. When you work with a control, you can open a property sheet that displays all the settings for that control in alphabetic or category order. The ActiveX controls appear in the Properties window in two columns: the left column displays the name of the control, and the right column displays the current value or setting for the control. When you select either column, a list arrow appears in the right column, allowing you to select the setting you want. After you set properties, you can add VBA code to a module to make it perform.

Set ActiveX Control Properties

1. Select the control whose properties you want to modify.

2. Click the **Developer** tab.

3. Click the **Properties** button to display the Properties window only, or the **View Code** button to open the Visual Basic Editor.

   If necessary in the Visual Basic Editor, click the **Properties Window** button to show it.

4. To switch controls, click the **Controls** list arrow (at the top), and then select the one you want.

5. Click the **Alphabetic** or **Categorized** tab to display the control properties so you can find the ones you want.

6. Click the property box for the property you want to modify, and then do one of the following.

   ◆ Type the value or information you want to use.

   ◆ If the property box contains a list arrow, click the arrow and then click a value in the list.

   ◆ If a property box contains a dialog button (...), click it to open a dialog box to select options or insert an object, such as a picture.

7. When you're done, click the **Close** button on the Properties window.

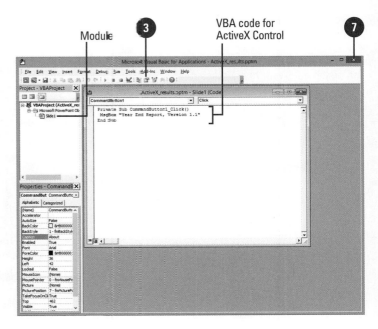

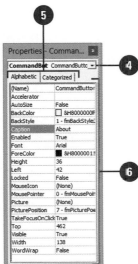

Playing a Movie Using an ActiveX Control

Although you cannot insert a Flash movie into a PowerPoint presentation, you can play one using an ActiveX control and the Flash player. Before you can use the control, the ActiveX control and Flash player need to be installed on your computer. You can get the ActiveX control at *http://activex.microsoft.com/activex/activex/*. To play the Flash (.swf) movie, you add the Shockwave Flash Object ActiveX control to the document and create a link to the file. If a movie doesn't play, check ActiveX security options in the Trust Center in PowerPoint Options.

Play a Flash Movie

1. Save the Flash file to a Flash movie file (.swf) using the Flash software.

2. In Normal view, display the slide on which you want to play the Flash movie.

3. Click the **Developer** tab.

4. Click the **More Controls** button.

5. Click **Shockwave Flash Object**.

6. Click **OK**.

Continue Next Page

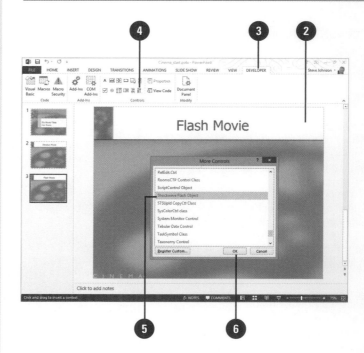

7 Drag to draw the control.

8 Select the Shockwave Flash Object.

9 Click the **Properties** button.

10 Click the **Alphabetic** tab.

11 Click the **Movie** property, click in the value column next to Movie, type full path and file name (c:\MyFolder\Movie.swf), or the URL to the Flash movie file you want.

> **TIMESAVER** *If you place the .dcr file in the same folder as your presentation, you only need to type the file name.*

12 To set specific options, choose any of the following:

- ◆ To play the file automatically when the slide appears, set the Playing property to True.

- ◆ To play the movie once, set the Loop property to False.

- ◆ To embed the Flash file, set the EmbedMovie property to True.

13 When you're done, click the **Close** button.

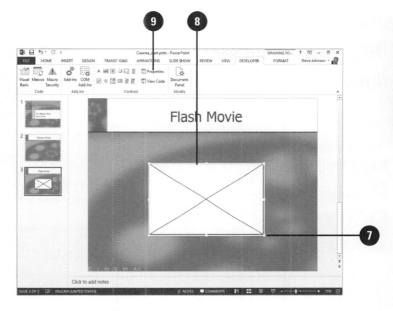

Changing the Document Information Panel

The Document Information Panel helps you manage and track document property information—also known as metadata—such as title, author, subject, keywords, category, and status. The Document Information Panel displays an XML-based mini-form using an InfoPath Form Template (.xsn) file developed in Microsoft InfoPath 2007. By using an XML InfoPath form, you can create your own form templates to edit the document property data and perform data validation.

Select a Document Information Panel Template

1 Click the **Developer** tab.

2 Click the **Document Panel** button.

3 Click **Browse**, locate and select the custom template you want, and then click **Open**.

◆ **URL.** Short for Uniform Resource Locator. The address of resources on the web.

http://www.perspection.com/index.htm

◆ **UNC.** Short for Uniform or Universal Naming Convention. A format for specifying the location of resources on a local-area network (LAN).

\\server-name\shared-resource-pathname

◆ **URN.** Short for Uniform Resource Name.

4 Click the **Display by default** list arrow, and then select the default properties you want.

5 Select the **Always show Document Information Panel on document open and initial save** check box.

6 Click **OK**.

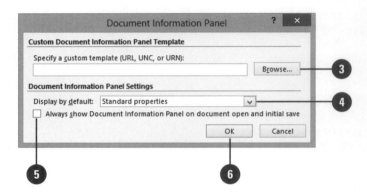

Working Online with Office Documents

14

Introduction

Instead of storing and working on Office documents on your desktop, you can store them on the web and work on them with an Office Web App. An Office Web App allows you to work with an Office document in a web browser. The process of using the web instead of a desktop as a base of operation is known as **cloud computing**. SkyDrive and SharePoint are two types of cloud computing sites, where you can store and share information. SkyDrive is a free service provided by Microsoft, which is available at *www.skydrive.com* with a Microsoft account, while SharePoint is web server software created by Microsoft.

When you store an Office document on SkyDrive or on a Microsoft SharePoint server configured with Office Web Apps, such as Office 365 SharePoint, a subscription-based service provided by Microsoft, you can view or edit the document in a web browser using the same look and feel as an Office 2013 program. To make storing files on SkyDrive or SharePoint quick and easy, Office 2013 programs provide command on the Save As screen on the File tab for you to save Office documents directly to a SkyDrive or SharePoint folder.

If you have a Windows Phone, Apple iOS (iPhone and iPad), BlackBerry, or Android, you can use your web browser or Office Web Apps to work with your Office documents from anywhere. You can view and edit Office documents stored on your phone, sent to you as e-mail attachments, or stored on a SkyDrive or SharePoint site. Since the files are synced online, the changes you make on your mobile device are available on your desktop too.

What You'll Do

Work Online with SharePoint and SkyDrive

Sign in to SharePoint or SkyDrive

Save and Open on SharePoint or SkyDrive

Access Documents on SharePoint

Sync Documents on SharePoint

Publish Slides to a SharePoint Library

Share Documents on SkyDrive

Access Documents on SkyDrive

Manage Documents on SkyDrive

Download or Upload Documents on SkyDrive

Create Office Documents on SkyDrive

Send Links to Documents on SkyDrive

Compare the Office Desktop App to the Web App

Work with Office Web Apps

Save or Print Documents in Office Web Apps

Co-author Documents with Office Web Apps

Block Co-authoring Documents

Working Online with SharePoint and SkyDrive

Office 2013 is integrated to work with online services (**New!**) to make it easier for you to save and open Office documents on other devices and share Office documents with others. Office provides two main online services: SkyDrive and SharePoint. **SkyDrive** is a personal cloud storage and sharing system on the web provided as a free service by Microsoft at *www.skydrive.com* with a Microsoft account. You can store and share information, such as contacts, e-mail (using hotmail), photos, and files. Microsoft **SharePoint** server is an organizational cloud storage, sharing, and tracking system with customizable apps hosted on the web by an organization. Instead of setting up your own SharePoint site, you can use **Office 365**, a subscription-based Microsoft web site with SharePoint services that allows you to take advantage of expanded cloud capabilities.

Connecting to a SkyDrive or SharePoint Site

You can access and connect to a SkyDrive and SharePoint site by using your web browser or any Office 2013 program. For SkyDrive, you can also use a stand-alone app, such as SkyDrive (Win 8) or SkyDrive for Windows (Win 7 or 8)—an app downloaded from the SkyDrive site that allows you to access files from Windows Explorer.

In order to connect to SkyDrive or SharePoint from Office, you need to sign in and connect with your account. When you set up Office 2013, it requests a Microsoft account to work with SkyDrive and other online services. However, you can add other accounts for Office 365 SharePoint and other online services, such as Facebook, Twitter, Linkedin, and Flickr. To access account settings in Office, click the user name (upper-right corner of any Office program), and then click an account option, or click the File tab, and then click Accounts. You can add, switch, or modify accounts or sign out entirely.

SkyDrive or SkyDrive Pro?

When you install Office 2013, you also get a helpful tool called SkyDrive Pro (**New!**). The name is similar to SkyDrive, however it works with SharePoint, not SkyDrive personal. A SharePoint site includes its own SkyDrive as well as other Document Libraries. With SkyDrive Pro, you can connect to and synchronize the contents of a SkyDrive or Document Library on a SharePoint or Office 365 site with a folder on your desktop. SkyDrive Pro performs the same function for SharePoint sites as the stand-alone SkyDrive apps—SkyDrive (Win 8) or SkyDrive for Windows (Win 7 or 8)—do for a personal SkyDrive.

Using a SkyDrive or SharePoint Site from Office

In Office 2013, you can save and open documents directly to a SkyDrive or SharePoint site. With your Office documents on a SkyDrive or SharePoint site, you can do a lot of things. You can sync the files from the SkyDrive or SharePoint site to your desktop or other devices, such as a tablet or mobile phone for easy access from anywhere. You can view or edit Office documents online from an Office program or Office Web App, and get access to files even when you're offline. You can share a document with other people using e-mail or social networks (**New!**) and even work on the same Office document at the same time with more than one person (**New!**).

Using Office 365

Office 365 is a subscription-based Microsoft web site with SharePoint services that provides cloud-based storage and sync capabilities to keep your Office content up-to-date everywhere. Office 365 provides web-based collaboration and sharing that allows you to work with Outlook mail, calendar, people, newsfeed, SkyDrive, and SharePoint Team sites and public web sites. Newsfeed lets you follow documents, sites and people to track what they are doing. You can also collaborate with instant messaging, video/audio conferencing and online meetings with Lync. In Outlook, you can access Site Mailboxes (**New!**) with e-mail and documents in the same place. You can access Office 365 at *www.office365.com*, where you can sign up for a subscription or trial.

Using Office Web Apps

An Office Web App allows you to work with an Office document in a web browser. When you store an Office document on a SkyDrive or SharePoint site, you can view or edit the document in a web browser using the same look and feel as an Office 2013 program, although some what limited in functionality. Office Web Apps provide a web-based version of Word, Excel, PowerPoint, and OneNote (**New!**). For a SharePoint site, Access and Lync are also available. You can view Office documents in a web browser using a Web App or edit the document in the desktop Office program.

Using Office on Mobile Devices

If you have a Windows Phone, Apple iOS (iPhone and iPad), BlackBerry, or Android, you can use your web browser or Office Web Apps to work with your Office documents from any-

where. You can view and edit Office documents stored on your phone, sent to you as e-mail attachments, or stored on a SkyDrive or SharePoint site. Since the files are synced online, the changes you make on your mobile device are available on your desktop too.

Using Office Co-authoring

If you're working on a SharePoint site, you can have multiple authors work on the same Office document from a Document Library at the same time without intruding on one another's work or locking out other users. When multiple authors are working on the same document, you can see who is editing the document and where they are working in the Status bar or on the File tab Info screen. Any changes made by other authors get merged into the main document where you can review and modify them. You can co-author Office documents using Word, Excel, PowerPoint, and Visio Professional (**New!**) as well as Word Web App (**New!**) and PowerPoint App (**New!**), which include support for comments and revision marks (**New!**).

PowerPoint Web App in a web browser

Signing in to SharePoint or SkyDrive

Office provides access to two main online services: SkyDrive and SharePoint. SkyDrive personal is a free storage and sharing service provided by Microsoft. SharePoint is a web-hosted server for storage, sharing, and tracking documents. Instead of setting up your own SharePoint site, you can use Office 365 SharePoint, a subscription-based service provided by Microsoft. Before you can work with Office documents on SkyDrive or SharePoint, you need to create a Microsoft account for SkyDrive or a site account for SharePoint. When you set up Office 2013, it requests a Microsoft account to work with online services, such as SkyDrive. If you already have a Hotmail, Messenger, Windows Live, or Xbox Live account, you can use it as your Microsoft account. To get a SharePoint account, you need to contact your site administrator or sign up for Office 365. After you establish accounts, you need to add them to Office in order to work seamlessly with the online services (**New!**).

Sign in to Office 365 SharePoint

1. Open your web browser, and go to *www.office365.com*.

2. If you don't have an account, click the link to get a free trial. Follow the online instructions to create the account.

3. Click the **Sign in** link.

4. Enter your User ID and Password for your Office 365 account.

5. Select the **Remember me** and/or **Keep me signed in** check boxes to speed up sign in process in the future. However, it allows others who have access to your computer to sign in.

6. Click **Sign in**.

   Your Office 365 SharePoint site appears in your web browser.

7. To sign out, click the Account Name on the toolbar, and then click **Sign out**.

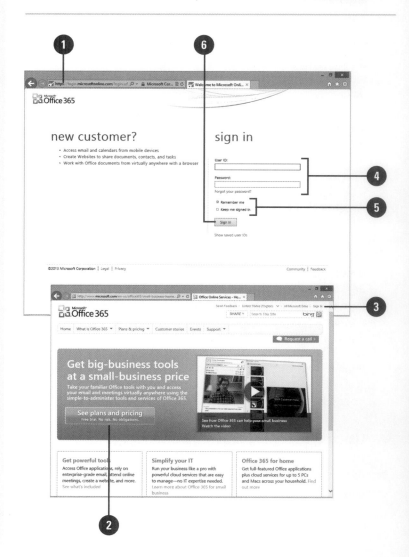

Sign in to SkyDrive

1. Open your web browser, and go to *www.skydrive.com*.

2. If you don't have a Microsoft account, click the link to get a free account. Follow the online instructions to create the account.

3. Enter you Microsoft account user name and password.

4. Select the **Keep me signed in** check box to speed up sign in process in the future. However, it allows others who have access to your computer to sign in.

5. Click **Sign in**.

    Your SkyDrive site appears in your web browser.

6. To sign out, click the Account Name on the toolbar, and then click **Sign out**.

Add Online Storage Services

1. Click the **File** tab, and then click **Account (New!)**.

2. Click **Add a service (New!)**, and then point to **Storage**.

3. Click **Office 365 SharePoint** or **SkyDrive**, and then follow the on-screen connection instructions to sign in and add the service.

4. Click the **Back** button to exit the File tab.

Saving and Opening on SharePoint or SkyDrive

Office is integrated to work with online services (**New!**) to make it easier for you to save and open Office documents on other devices and share Office documents with others. With your Microsoft or SharePoint account, you can save Office documents directly to a SkyDrive (**New!**), a cloud-based online storage system, or Office 365, a Microsoft web site with SharePoint services. When you save documents online, you can have multiple authors work on the same Office document from the server at the same time (**New!**). Before you can use these online services, you need to add (connect) them to Office 2013. During the process, you'll need to provide a user name and password to establish a connection.

Save an Office Document to SharePoint or SkyDrive

1. Create or open an Office document.

2. Click the **File** tab, and then click **Save As**.

3. Click the SkyDrive or SharePoint name.

   ◆ **Sign in.** If prompted, sign-in to your account.

4. Click **Browse** or a recent folder.

5. Navigate to the location where you want to save the file.

6. Type a document file name.

7. Click the **Save as type** list arrow, and then click **<Program> <Document>**, such as PowerPoint Presentation, Word Document, or Excel Workbook.

8. Click **Save**.

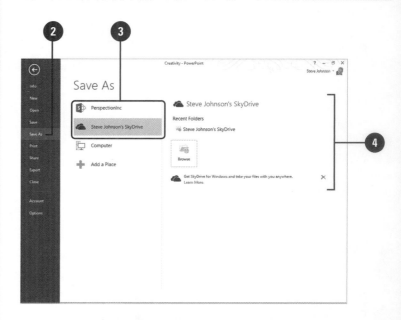

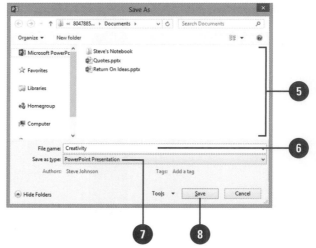

Open an Office Document from SharePoint or SkyDrive

1. Click the **File** tab, and then click **Open**.

2. Click the SkyDrive or SharePoint name.

3. Click **Browse** or a recent folder.

4. Navigate to the location where you want to open the file, and then select the Office file.

5. Click **Open**.

Did You Know?

You can add a place for easy access later. In the Open or Save As screen, click Add a Place, click Office 365 SharePoint or SkyDrive, and then follow the on-screen connection instructions.

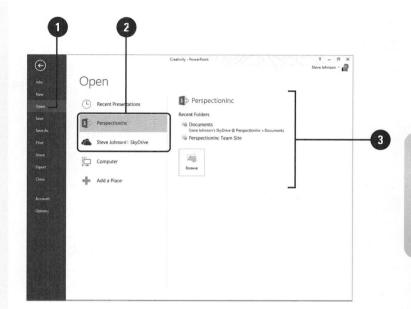

Office 365 SharePoint

Accessing Documents on SharePoint

Any Office document that resides on SharePoint (**New!**) can be accessed from any computer or device that has an Internet connection. You can access Office documents on SharePoint using your web browser or File Explorer on your desktop. In your web browser, you can navigate to a document and then open it in an Office Web App. An Office Web App provides a subset of the features in the desktop version. In your desktop, you can open File Explorer, navigate to a document in a SharePoint Document Library or SkyDrive Pro (**New!**), and then open it in the Office Desktop App. SkyDrive Pro is SkyDrive on SharePoint, which is separate and different from SkyDrive personal.

Access SharePoint in a Web Browser

1. Open your web browser, go to SharePoint Team Site web address or *www.office365.com*, and then sign in.

2. Navigate to the SharePoint or SkyDrive folders:
   - **SharePoint.** Click **Sites**, click **Team Site**, and then click a library.
   - **SkyDrive.** Click **SkyDrive**.

3. Click a folder icon to navigate to the folder with the Office document.

4. To navigate back to a previous location, click a navigation or Home link, or click the Back button.

5. To manage files, select the files or folders you want to work with, click the **Files** tab, and then use the toolbar buttons, such as Create Folder, Delete, Upload Document, Download Copy, or Share.

6. To open an Office document in the Office Web App, click the document name link.
   - To edit the document, click the **Edit <document>** menu, and then click **Edit in <program>** or **Edit in <program> Web App**.
   - To exit and return, click the **File** tab, and then click **Exit**.

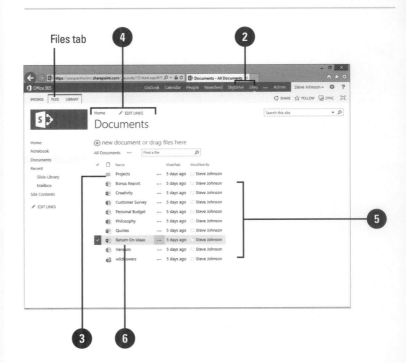

Files tab

Access SharePoint from a Desktop

1. In the Start screen, click the Desktop tile (Win 8).

2. Click the **File Explorer** icon on the taskbar.

3. In the Navigate pane under Favorites, click either of the following:

   ◆ **SharePoint.** Opens the Document Library folders on the SharePoint Team Site.

   ◆ **SkyDrive Pro.** Opens the Documents folder on the SharePoint SkyDrive.

4. Click a folder icon to navigate to the folder with the Office document.

5. To add or remove files, use the following:

   ◆ **Add.** Copy and paste or drag files to the folder.

   ◆ **Remove.** Select the files, and then click the **Delete** button on the Home tab.

   The folders are synchronized for both locations, desktop and site.

6. To open an Office document in the Office Desktop App, double-click the document icon.

   ◆ To exit, click the **Close** button.

See Also

See "Syncing Documents on SharePoint" on page 460 for information on setting up to use SkyDrive Pro for SharePoint.

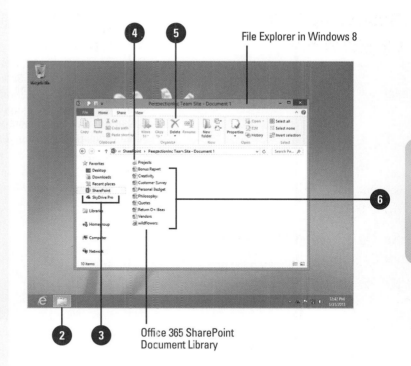

File Explorer in Windows 8

Office 365 SharePoint Document Library

Syncing Documents on SharePoint

With SkyDrive Pro (**New!**), you can connect to and sync the contents of a SkyDrive or Document Library on a SharePoint (Team Site) or Office 365 site with a folder on your desktop. You can set up the sync by entering a site address to the SkyDrive or Document Library or using the SYNC button on the SharePoint or Office 365 site for the open SkyDrive or Document Library. After creating a connection, you'll notice a SkyDrive Pro cloud icon on the notification tray in the taskbar, which you can use to access the desktop folder or modify syncing options. SkyDrive Pro syncs to your user folder by default, though you can change the location. In the Open and Save As dialog boxes in Office programs or in an Explorer window in Windows, you can select the site —SharePoint or SkyDrive Pro—from the Favorites list to access your files.

Set Up or Change SkyDrive Pro for SharePoint

1. Start **SkyDrive Pro 2013**.

   ◆ **Windows 8.** Click the tile on the Start screen.

   ◆ **Windows 7.** Click **Start** on the taskbar, point to **All Programs**, and then point to **Microsoft Office**.

   ◆ **Office 365 Site.** Click **SkyDrive** or **Sites**, display the library to sync, and then click **SYNC** on the toolbar.

   The site is connected to your system or a dialog box opens.

2. Enter the URL address to the SkyDrive or Document library on the SharePoint or Office 365 site.

3. To change the desktop folder, click the **Change** link.

4. Click **Sync Now**.

   After you setup SkyDrive Pro, starting the program opens the folder on your desktop.

Office 365 SharePoint SkyDrive

Click to select a SkyDrive or SharePoint site (Libraries)

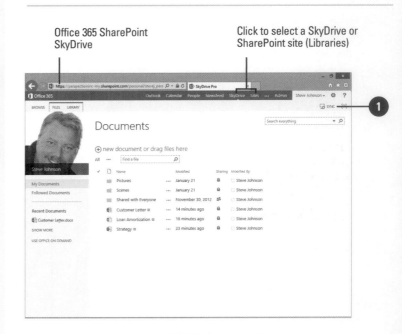

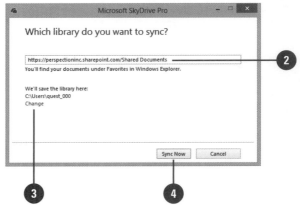

Work with SkyDrive Pro on SharePoint

1 In the desktop, click the **SkyDrive Pro** icon on the desktop taskbar, and then click **Open your SkyDrive Pro folder**.

2 Click **SkyDrive Pro** or **SharePoint** in the Navigate pane under Favorites, and then navigate to the folder you want to use.

3 To add or remove files, use the following:

◆ **Add.** Copy and paste or drag files to the folder.

◆ **Remove.** Select the files, and then click the **Delete** button on the Home tab.

The folders are synchronized for both locations, desktop and site.

4 To change syncing options, click the **SkyDrive Pro** icon on the desktop taskbar, and then click any of the following:

◆ **Sync a new library.** Use to add a new SharePoint site library.

◆ **Sync now.** Use to manually sync files.

◆ **Pause syncing.** Use to pause syncing.

◆ **View sync programs.** Use to open Office Upload Center.

◆ **Stop syncing a folder.** Use to select a folder to stop syncing.

5 To exit SkyDrive Pro, click the **SkyDrive Pro** icon on the desktop taskbar, and then click **Exit**.

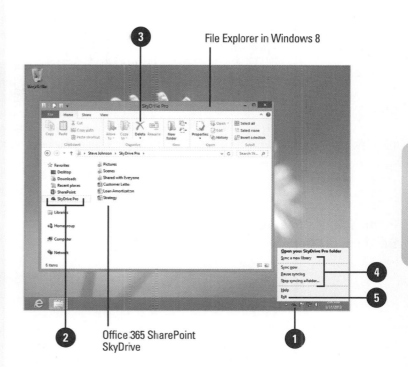

File Explorer in Windows 8

Office 365 SharePoint SkyDrive

See Also

See "Working with Office Tools" on page 420 for information on using Office 2013 Upload Center.

Publishing Slides to a SharePoint Library

You can publish one or more slides directly from PowerPoint to a Slide or Document Library on a network running Microsoft SharePoint Server or to a folder location on your computer or network to store, share, track, and reuse later. Before you can publish slides to a Library, you need to create a Slide or Document Library on the SharePoint or Office 365 site, where you can also identify the online location for the publishing process, which you can copy from from the site. When you publish slides to a Library to a SharePoint or Office 365 site, team members can use the Reuse Slides pane to quickly insert the ones they want into presentations. When you make changes to slides in a Library, the next time you open your presentation locally with the reused slides, PowerPoint notifies you there is a change.

Publish Slides to a SharePoint Document Library

1. Click the **File** tab, click **Share**, click **Publish Slides**, and then click the **Publish Slides** button.

2. Select the check boxes next to the slides you want to publish, or click **Select All** to select all the slides.

   PowerPoint automatically names each slide file by using the presentation name and a unique ID number in sequential order.

3. To show only selected slides, select the **Show Only Selected Slides** check box.

4. To rename a slide file name, click the existing file name, and then type a new name.

5. To include a description, click in the description area, and then type a description.

6. Click the **Publish To** list arrow, click a location, or click **Browse** to select a SharePoint Slide Library location; display the library on the SharePoint site, click Settings, and then click Slide Library Settings.

7. Click **Publish**.

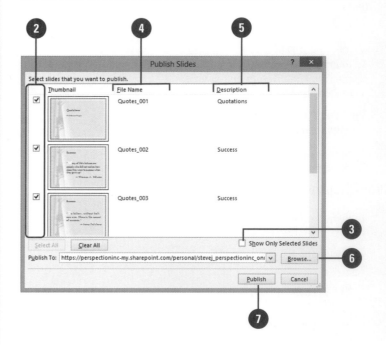

Reuse Published Slides

1. Open the presentation, and then click the **Home** tab.

2. Click the **New Slide** button arrow, and then click **Reuse Slides**.

3. If the presentation you want is not available, click **Browse**, click **Browse Slide Library**, locate and select the shortcut to the library you want, and then click **Select**.

4. Click a slide to insert it, or right-click a slide, and then click **Insert All Slides**.

5. To be notified when a slide change happens, select the slide, and then select the **Tell me when this slide changes** check box.

6. When you're done, click the **Close** button in the pane.

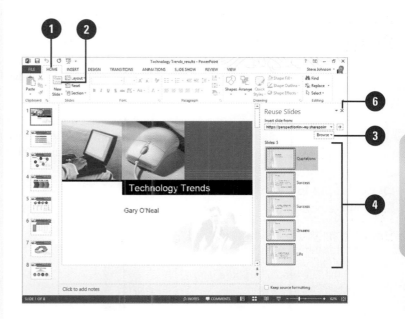

Check Reused Slides for Updates

1. Open the presentation that contains reused slides.

2. In the Alert dialog box, click **Get Updates**.

   If the dialog box doesn't appear, right-click the reused slide in the Slide pane (Normal view), point to **Check for Updates**, and then click **Check This Slide for Changes** or **Check All Slides for Changes**.

3. If no slides in the presentation need to be updated, a message alert appears. Click **OK**.

4. If the Confirm Slide Update dialog box appears, click **Replace** to replace the local slide with the changed slide from the Slide Library, or click **Append** to add the changed slide after the outdated one in your presentation.

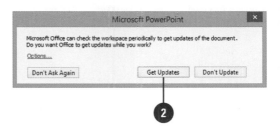

Sharing Documents on SkyDrive

After you save an Office document to a SkyDrive (**New!**), you can share it with others. On the Share screen under the File tab, you can use three related options—Invite People (**New!**), Get a Sharing Link (**New!**), and Post to Social Networks (**New!**)—to allow others to access to a SkyDrive document. The Invite People option allows you to send an invitation for other to access the SkyDrive document. The Get a Sharing Link option lets you create links to the document you can share with others. And finally, the Post to Social Networks option (in Word and Excel) lets you make blog posts on your connected social networks, such as Facebook, Linkedin, Twitter, Flickr, or Google.

Invite People to Share a SkyDrive Document

1 Open the Office document you want to share.

2 Click the **File** tab, click **Share**, and then click **Invite People**.

3 If the document is not saved to a SkyDrive, click the **Save To Cloud** button, and then save it to your SkyDrive. If prompted, sign-in to your account.

4 Enter a contact name or click the Address Book button to select a contact.

5 Click the **Access** list arrow, and then click **Can edit** or **Can view**.

6 Enter a message for the invitation.

7 Select or clear the **Require user to sign in before accessing document** check box.

8 Click **Share**.

An email is sent to the contact with a link to access the SkyDrive document, and contact status appears at the bottom of the Share screen.

You can click the contacts to send mail or instant messages.

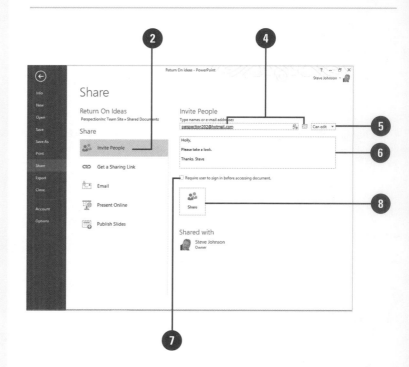

Get a Sharing Link to a SkyDrive Document

1. Open the Office document you want to share.

2. Click the **File** tab, click **Share**, and then click **Get a Sharing Link**.

3. Click the **Create Link** button for View Link or Edit Link.

   A link to the SkyDrive document appears and a status icon appears at the bottom of the Share screen.

4. Select and copy (Ctrl+C) the link, where you can paste it in a place, such as a network, where others can access it.

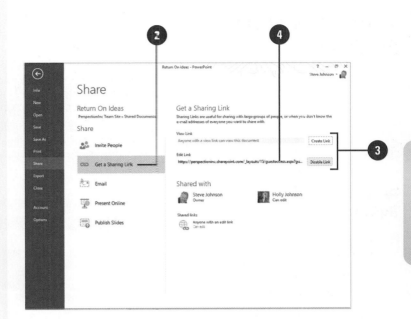

Post a SkyDrive Document Link to a Social Network

1. In Word and Excel, open the Office document you want to share.

2. Click the **File** tab, click **Share**, and then click **Post to Social Networks**.

   If you're not connected to your social networks, click the **Click here to connect social networks** link to make the connections you want, and then click **Refresh** button.

3. Select the check boxes for the connected social networks you want to post.

4. Click the **Access** list arrow, and then click **Can edit** or **Can view**.

5. Enter a message for the post.

   Click the **Post** button.

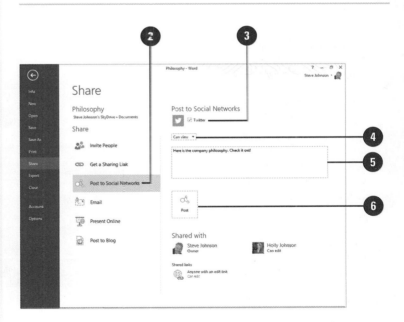

Accessing Documents on SkyDrive

Any Office document that resides on SkyDrive (**New!**) can be accessed from any computer or device that has an Internet connection. You can access Office documents on SkyDrive using your web browser or a SkyDrive app on your desktop or device, including smartphones and tablets. In your web browser, you can navigate to a document and then open it in an Office Web App. An Office Web App provides a subset of the features in the desktop version. In your desktop or device, you can open the SkyDrive app, navigate to a document, and then open it in the Office Desktop App or Office Web App. If you don't have the app on your desktop or device, you can download it at *http://apps.live.com/skydrive*.

Access a SkyDrive in a Web Browser

1. Open your web browser, go to *www.skydrive.com*, and then sign in.

   ◆ You can also go to Windows Live, *www.live.com*, and then click the **SkyDrive** link.

2. Click a folder icon to navigate to the folder with the Office document.

3. To navigate back to a previous location, click a navigation link.

4. To change the view in the current folder, click a view button: **List** or **Tiles**.

5. To sort the documents in the current folder, click the **Sort by:** link, and then click **Name**, **Date modified**, **Date created**, or **Size**.

6. To open an Office document in the Office Web App, click the document icon.

   ◆ To open an Office document in the Office Desktop App, right-click the document, and then click **Open in <program>**.

   ◆ To exit and return, click the **File** tab, and then click **Exit**.

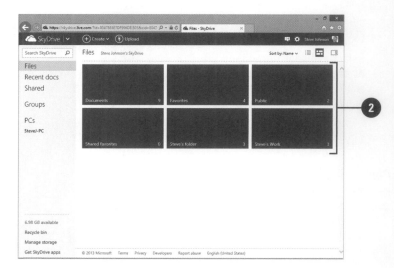

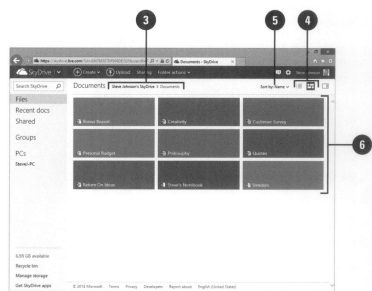

Access a SkyDrive from a Desktop or Device

1 In the Start screen, click the **SkyDrive** tile.

◆ **Download.** You can download the SkyDrive app for devices at *http://apps.live.com/skydrive*.

2 Click a folder icon to navigate to the folder with the Office document.

3 To navigate back to a previous location, click the **Back** button.

4 To change the view in the current folder, click the **Thumbnails** or **Details** button on the App bar.

5 To open an Office document in the Office Desktop App (desktop) or Web App (device), click the document icon.

◆ To exit, click the **Close** button (Desktop App or click the **File** tab, and then click **Exit** (Web App).

Did You Know?

You can manage storage space on a SkyDrive. SkyDrive comes with 7 GB of free space that you can use with your Microsoft account. You can view your storage usage and purchase more space if you want under options. In the SkyDrive app (Win 8), click Settings on the Charm bar, and then click Options. In your web browser, click the Settings button, and then click Options.

SkyDrive app on Windows 8

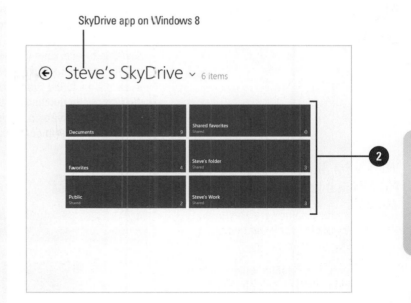

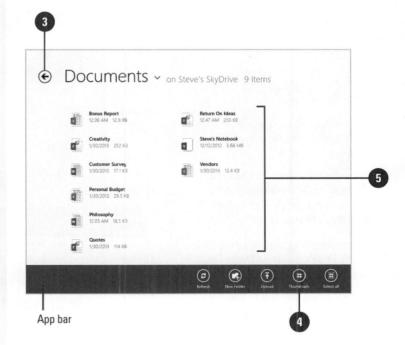

App bar

Managing Documents on SkyDrive

SkyDrive comes with four default folders: Documents, Favorites, Shared Favorites, and Public. The Documents and Favorites folders are private for your eyes only, while the Shared Favorites and Public folders are viewable by everyone in your SkyDrive (Windows Live) network. If you want to share your documents with others, then you need to add, move, or copy them to the Public folder. Instead of using the default folders, you can create and use your own. If you no longer need a file or folder, you can delete it. You cannot rename a default folder, however, you can rename the ones you create.

Work with SkyDrive Files or Folders in a Web browser

1. Open your web browser, go to *www.skydrive.com*, and then sign in.

2. Navigate to the folder where you want to manage files or folders.

3. To create a folder, click the **Create** list arrow, click **Folder**, type a name for the folder, and then press Enter or click outside the box.

4. Point to a file or folder to display a check box, and then click the check box to select it.

   ◆ You can select multiple files or folders to delete, move, or copy them.

5. To manage the selected file(s) or folder(s), click the **Manage** list arrow, and then click any of the following commands:

   ◆ **Rename.** Type a new name for the folder, and then press Enter or click outside the box.

   ◆ **Delete.** Click **Undo** to cancel it or click the **Close** button.

   ◆ **Move to.** Select the destination folder, and then click **Move**.

   ◆ **Copy to.** Select the destination folder, and then click **Copy**.

New folder

Work with SkyDrive Files or Folders from a Desktop

1 In the Start screen, click the **SkyDrive** tile.

♦ **Download.** You can download the SkyDrive app for devices at *http://apps.live.com/skydrive*.

2 Navigate to the folder where you want to manage files or folders.

3 To create a folder, click the **New Folder** on the App bar, type a name for the folder, and then click **Create folder**.

4 Right-click a file or folder to select it.

♦ You can select multiple files or folders to delete or move them.

5 To manage the selected file(s) or folder(s), click the **Manage** button on the App bar, and then click any of the following commands:

♦ **Rename.** Type a new name for the folder, and then click **Rename**.

♦ **Delete.** Click **Delete** to confirm the deletion.

♦ **Move.** Select the destination folder, and then click **Move here** on the Apps bar.

SkyDrive app on Windows 8

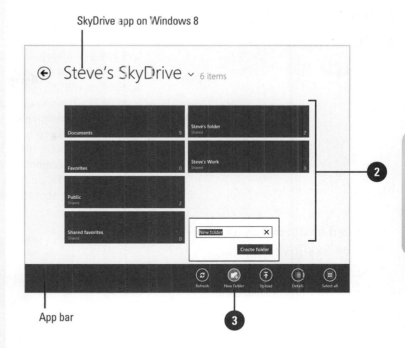

App bar

Downloading or Uploading Documents on SkyDrive

When you no longer want a document or folder of documents on SkyDrive or you want to share them with others, you can download them to your local drive on your computer. You can download individual files one at a time in their native Office file format, such as .pptx, or a multiple selection of documents or an entire folder of documents as a zipped file. The .zip file format compresses all the files in the folder into a single file. You can open a zipped file on Microsoft Windows by double-clicking it and then using an Extract button or by using the Winzip.exe software, which you can download for free from the web at one of many download sites, such as *www.download.com*. If you have one or more documents or entire folder of documents on a local drive, and want to include on your SkyDrive, you can upload them to the cloud site, so you can access them from other computers and devices.

Download or Upload a File or Folder on SkyDrive

1. Open your web browser, go to *www.skydrive.com*, and then sign in.

2. Navigate to the folder where you want to download or upload files or folders.

3. To upload files or folders to the SkyDrive, click the **Upload** button, select the files or folders you want, and then click **Open**.

4. Point to a file or folder to display a check box, and then click the check box to select it. You can select multiple files or folders.

5. To download the selected file(s) or folder(s), click the **Download** button.

6. Click **Save**, navigate to the location where you want to download the file, and then click **Save**.

The document is downloaded to the specified folder.

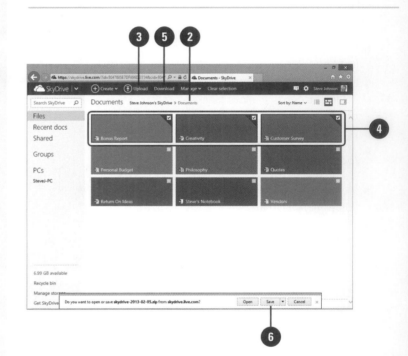

Creating Office Documents on SkyDrive

When you're working on SkyDrive, you create a new Office document. You can create an Excel workbook, a PowerPoint presentation, a Word document, or an OneNote notebook. This option allows you to create a new Office document on a computer that doesn't have the Microsoft Office software. So, if you're working on a different computer while you're on the road that doesn't have the Office programs installed and you need to create a new document to get some work done, you can do it online on SkyDrive.

Create Office Documents on SkyDrive

1. Open your web browser, go to *www.skydrive.com*, and then sign in.

2. Navigate to the folder where you want to create a new Office document.

3. Click the **Create** list arrow, and then click a document option:

   ◆ **Word document.**

   ◆ **Excel workbook.**

   ◆ **PowerPoint presentation.**

   ◆ **OneNote notebook.**

4. Type a name for the document.

5. Click **Create**.

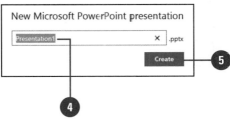

Sending Links to Documents on SkyDrive

After you upload your Office documents to a folder on SkyDrive, you can share access to them with others for review with Office Web Apps. You can share access to individual Office documents or an entire folder on SkyDrive by sending a link in e-mail, posting a link in Twitter, Facebook, LinkedIn or other online services (**New!**), or creating a link (**New!**) and sending it to those you want to access it. In addition, you can also embed a link in a blog or web page, so others can access the folder. The recipients of the link can click it to access the documents on SkyDrive.

Send a Link to a File or Folder

① Open your web browser, go to *www.skydrive.com*, and then sign in.

② Navigate to the folder with the documents you want to share.

③ Point to a file or folder to display a check box, and then click the check box to select it. You can select multiple files or folders.

④ Click the **Sharing** button.

⑤ For a folder, click **Share this folder**. To cancel, click **Don't share this folder**.

⑥ Click **Send email, Post to <service>** (**New!**), or **Get a link** (**New!**) to select a send method.

⑦ Specify the following for the selected method:

◆ **Send email.** Specify recipients, select or clear options to edit or require sign in, and then click **Share**.

◆ **Post to <service>.** Select the check boxes for the services you want, enter a message, select or clear the option to edit, and then click **Post**.

◆ **Get a Link.** Click **Create** for View only or View and edit, or click **Make public** for everyone to access. Press Ctrl+C to copy the link, and then click **Done**. You can paste the link for others to use.

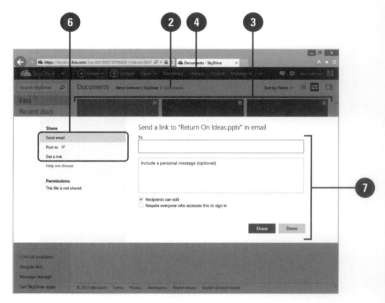

Post to   Twitter   Add more services

Get a link

Embed a Link to a File or Folder in a Blog or Web Page

1. Open your web browser, go to *www.skydrive.com*, and then sign in.

2. Navigate to the folder with the documents you want to share.

3. Point to a file or folder to display a check box, and then click the check box to select it. You can select multiple files or folders.

4. Click the **Embed** button (**New!**).

5. Click **Generate**.

6. Click the **Copy** link to copy the embed code to the Clipboard.

7. Click **Done**.

8. Paste the code into a blog post or web page.

   - **Blog.** Create a blog post in a blogger, such as Windows Live Writer, and then paste the code.

   - **Web Page.** Open a web page in an HTML editor, and then paste the code.

9. Open your web browser, display the blog post or web page, and then click the link to the shared folder or document on SkyDrive.

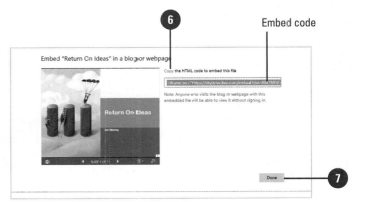

Embed code

Comparing the Office Desktop App to the Web App

An Office Web App provides a subset of the features in the desktop version. Each Office Web App comes with a scaled-down version of the desktop Ribbon and Quick Access Toolbar. The Web Apps Ribbon typically comes with a File tab, Home tab, Insert tab, and View tab. Within each tab, you get a sub-set of commands on the desktop Ribbon. There are no contextual tabs in the Office Web Apps. The Quick Access Toolbar appears above the Ribbon and contains just the Undo and Redo buttons. The content area for each of the Office Web Apps is similar to the desktop version.

Desktop App

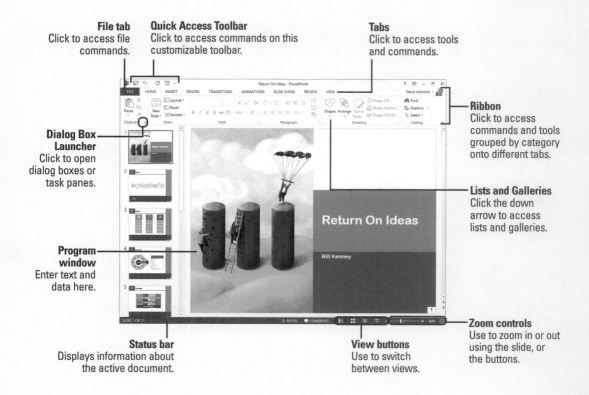

File tab
Click to access file commands.

Quick Access Toolbar
Click to access commands on this customizable toolbar.

Tabs
Click to access tools and commands.

Ribbon
Click to access commands and tools grouped by category onto different tabs.

Dialog Box Launcher
Click to open dialog boxes or task panes.

Lists and Galleries
Click the down arrow to access lists and galleries.

Program window
Enter text and data here.

Status bar
Displays information about the active document.

View buttons
Use to switch between views.

Zoom controls
Use to zoom in or out using the slide, or the buttons.

Web App (Edit in Browser)

Quick Access Toolbar
Click to access commands on a toolbar.

Tabs
Click to access tools and commands.

File tab
Click to access file commands.

Ribbon
Click to access commands and tools grouped by category onto different tabs.

Program window
Enter text and data here.

Web App (View in Browser)

File tab
Click to access file commands.

Menus
Click to access menus and commands.

Program window
View text and data here.

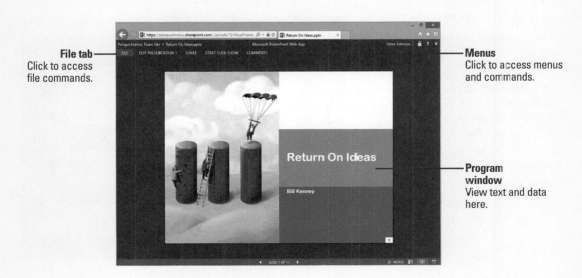

Working with Office Web Apps

An Office Web App allows you to work with an Office document stored on a SkyDrive (**New!**) or SharePoint site in a web browser and on different mobile devices—such as Windows Phones, Apple iOS (iPhones, and iPads), BlackBerry, and Android. Office Web Apps provide a web-based version of Word, Excel, PowerPoint, and OneNote (**New!**). For a SharePoint site, Access and Lync are also available. You can view or edit Office documents in a web browser using a Web App or in the Desktop App. An Office Web App provides a subset of the features in the desktop version.

View an Office Document Using Office Web Apps

1. Open your web browser, and then go to *www.skydrive.com* or SharePoint Team Site web address.

   ◆ **From E-mail or Posts.** If you received an e-mail or a post with a sharing link, click the link to access the document.

2. Navigate to the folder with the document you want to open.

3. Click the Office document you want to view.

   The Web App opens, displaying the document.

4. Use the menus and tools to navigate and view the document.

   ◆ **File management.** You can use the File tab to edit, save as, print, or share the document.

   ◆ **Edit document.** Click the **Edit <document>** menu, and then click **Edit in <program>** or **Edit in <program> Web App.**

5. To exit, click the **File** tab, and then click **Exit** (Web App) or click the **Close** button (desktop program).

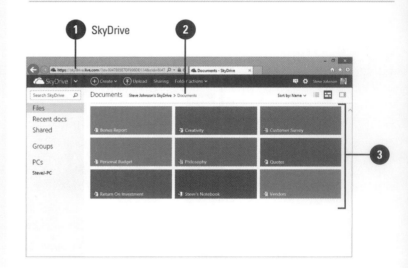

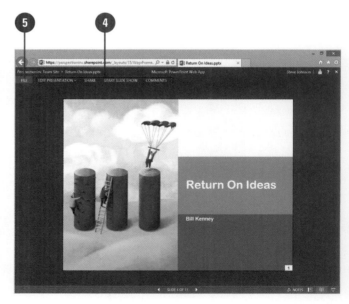

Edit an Office Document Using Office Web Apps

① Open your web browser, and then go to *www.skydrive.com* or SharePoint Team Site web address.

◆ **From E-mail or Posts.** If you received an e-mail or a post with a sharing link, click the link to access the document.

② Navigate to the folder with the document you want to open.

③ Click the Office document you want to edit.

The Web App opens, displaying the document.

④ Click the **Edit <document>** menu, and then click **Edit in <program> Web App.**

◆ **Edit in Desktop App.** Click the **Edit <document>** menu, and then click **Edit in <program>.**

⑤ Use the Ribbon tabs to make changes to the Office document; any changes in a Web App are automatically saved.

◆ **View Document in Reading View.** To view the document in non editing mode, click the **View** tab, and then click the **Reading View** button.

⑥ To close the document and switch to work local in the Desktop App, click the **Open in <program>** button.

⑦ To exit, click the **File** tab, and then click **Exit** (Web App) or click the **Close** button (desktop program).

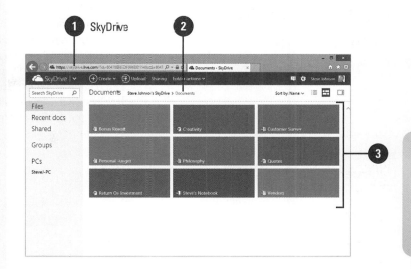

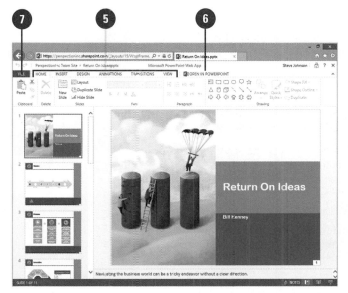

Saving or Printing Documents in Office Web Apps

As you work in an Office document in a web browser, an Office Web App automatically saves your work, so you don't have to do it. However, you might want to download a version to your local computer or network location as a backup or save a copy (in the Excel Web App) of a document in the original location with a different name. Besides saving an Office document, you can also print it to a printer (in the Excel Web App) or create a printable PDF (in the Word Web App and PowerPoint Web App).

Save or Download an Office Document in an Office Web App

1. Open your web browser, and then go to *www.skydrive.com* or SharePoint Team Site web address.

2. Navigate to the folder with the document you want to open.

3. Click the Office document you want to edit.

   The Web App opens, displaying the document.

4. Click the **Edit <document>** menu, and then click **Edit in <program> Web App.**

5. Click the **File** tab, click **Save As**, and then click an option (options vary depending on the Office Web App):

   - **Download.** Downloads the entire document to your computer.

   - **Save a Copy.** In Excel, saves a copy of the workbook in the same online folder as the original.

6. Click **Save**.

7. Navigate to the location where you want to download the file, and then click **Save**.

Download button

Print or PDF an Office Document in an Office Web App

① Open your web browser, and then go to *www.skydrive.com* or SharePoint Team Site web address.

② Navigate to the folder with the document you want to open.

③ Click the Office document you want to edit.

The Web App opens, displaying the document.

④ Click the **Edit <document>** menu, and then click **Edit in <program> Web App.**

⑤ Click the **File** tab, click **Print**, and then click an option (options vary depending on the Office Web App):

◆ **Print to PDF.** In Word and PowerPoint, creates saves a copy of the file in the same online folder as the original. Click a link to view the PDF or click **Close**.

◆ **Print.** In Excel, select an option to print the current selection or entire sheet, click **Print**, and then click **Print** again in the web browser window.

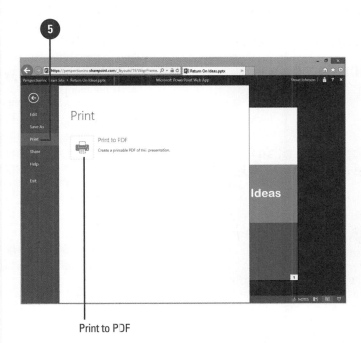

Print to PDF

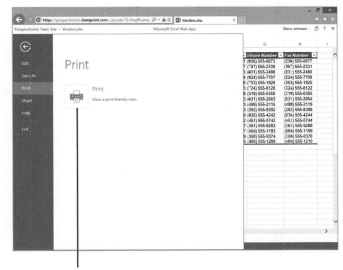

Print to a printer in Excel

Co-authoring Documents with Office Web Apps

If you're working with an Office document stored on a SharePoint site, multiple authors can collaborate on the same document at the same time (**New!**), known as co-authoring. Co-authoring allows you to see who is editing the document and where they are working in the Status bar or on the File tab Info screen. With Office Web Apps you can simultaneously edit documents, known as co-authoring. Co-authoring allows two or more people to work on a document at the same time in real-time without the need to save and reject or accept changes. If two people edit the same thing, each Office Web App deals with differently. Before you can co-author a document, you need to send a link in e-mail, online service post, such as Twitter, Facebook, or LinkedIn, to those you want to share the Office document or embed a link in a blog or web page, so others can access it.

Co-author an Office Document on SharePoint

1. Have each author open the Office document from the library on the SharePoint site.

   ◆ **From Office.** Click the **File** tab, click **Open**, click the SharePoint site, click **Browse**, and then open the document.

   ◆ **From Web browser.** Start your web browser, go to the SharePoint site address, and then open the document.

   ◆ **From E-mail or Posts.** If you received an e-mail or a post with a sharing link, click the link to access the document.

2. If prompted, sign in to the SharePoint site.

   The Web App opens, displaying the document.

3. For a Web App, click the **Edit <document>** menu, and then click **Edit in <program>** or **Edit in <program> Web App.**

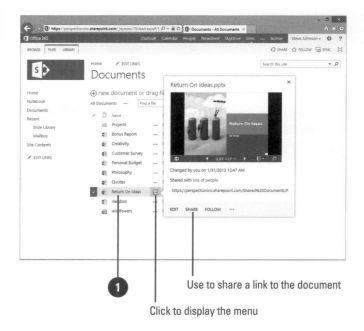

Use to share a link to the document

Click to display the menu

Options to send a link to the document

④ To view who is editing the documents, click the **Authors** button on the Status bar or click the **File** tab, and then click **Info**.

◆ On the Share screen, you can use the **Share with People** button to send a message.

⑤ Each author can edit the document using the program tools.

◆ **Comments and Track Changes.** In Word, PowerPoint, and Excel (desktop), each author can insert and show comments and enable track changes during editing so all the authors can see the changes being made.

⑥ To exit, click the **File** tab, and then click **Exit** (Web App) or click the **Close** button (desktop program).

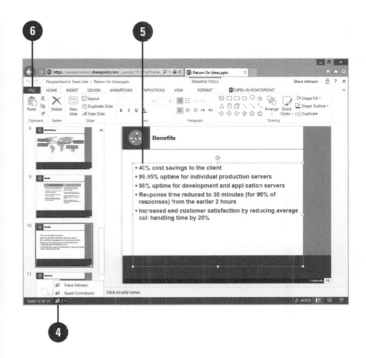

See Also

See "Working with Office Web Apps" on page 476 for more information on using Office Web Apps.

For Your Information

Roundtripping with Office Web Apps

When you edit or view an Office document with an Office Web App, the file format doesn't change or affect the content of the file. In other words, you can upload an Office file to the web, make changes using an Office Web App, download the file back to your desktop, and then make changes to it using your desktop Office App without any problems. This is called **roundtripping**. Any unsupported features in the Office Web App doesn't affect the Office file during a roundtrip.

Blocking Co-authoring Documents

Co-authoring allows multiple people to edit an Office document stored on a SharePoint site. When multiple people open the same Office document from a SharePoint site, the number of authors editing it appears in the Status bar, which you can click to find out who is currently editing it. If the item is not on the Status bar, you can right-click the Status bar to display it. If you don't want to let multiple authors edit all or part of a Word document, all you need to do is select the content in the document and then use the Block Authors button on the Review tab to prevent others from making changes. At any time, you can release all the blocked areas, so others can edit it.

Block Co-authoring of a Document on SharePoint

1 In Word, open the document from the SharePoint site.

   ◆ You can also open a local Word document, and then save it to the SharePoint site.

2 Select the text you want to prevent others from changing.

3 Click the **Review** tab.

4 Click the **Block Authors** button, and then click **Block Authors**.

   The selected area is marked with an icon and dashed outline to let others know the area is blocked.

5 To unlock all blocked areas, click the **Block Authors** button, and then click **Release All of My Blocked Areas**.

6 Click the **File** tab, and then click **Save** to apply the changes.

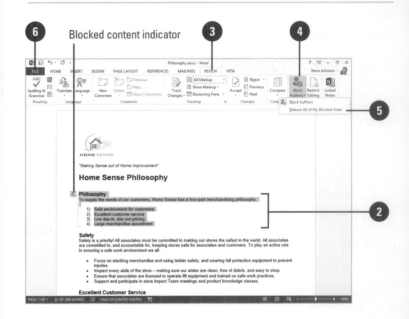

Blocked content indicator

See Also

See "Co-authoring Document with Office Web Apps" on page 480 for more information on co-authoring documents on SharePoint.

New! Features

Microsoft PowerPoint 2013

Microsoft PowerPoint 2013 is a presentation graphics program that helps you create and deliver slide shows either in person or online. With enhancements to the user interface, Backstage, Slide Show view, and Presenter view, and the addition of Start and New screens, theme variations, touch screen navigation, online pictures, motion path animation, and merge shapes, you can create high-impact presentations more easily in PowerPoint 2013.

Only New Features

If you're already familiar with PowerPoint 2010, you can access and download all the tasks in this book with Microsoft PowerPoint 2013 New Features to help make your transition to the new version simple and smooth. The PowerPoint 2013 New Features as well as other 2010 to 2013 transition helpers are available on the web at *www.perspection.com*.

What's New

If you're searching for what's new in PowerPoint 2013, just look for the icon: **New!**. The new icon appears in the table of contents and throughout this book so you can quickly and easily identify a new or improved feature in PowerPoint 2013. The following is a brief description of each new feature and its location in this book.

Office 2013

◆ **Start Screen (p. 2, 10-15, 110)**   Office programs open to a Start Screen where you have options to open an existing document or create a new blank document or one from a template or document theme.

◆ **Ribbon Display Options (p. 4)**   Office includes a Ribbon Display Options button that lets you change the way the Ribbon works. The options include Auto-hide Ribbon, Show Tabs, or Show Tabs and Commands.

◆ **Enhanced Mini-Toolbar (p. 5, 126)**   You can use a Mini-Toolbar to apply styles, fills, outlines, and other options. For example, select text or right-click the object you want to modify, click the Style, Fill, or Outline button, and then select an option.

- **Back Button (p. 5)** The File tab provides a Back button that lets you return back to the main screen for the Office program.

- **New Screen (p. 10-13)** Office programs open to the Start screen or you can open the New screen where you have options to open an existing document or create a new blank document or one from a template or document theme.

- **Personal Templates (p. 11-13, 110-112)** You can specify a default folder, such as My Templates, in Save Options for your own custom personal templates, which you can access from the Start and New screens.

- **Pin Recent Files or Folders (p. 14-15)** If you frequently open a specific file or folder, you can pin the recently used file or folder to the Start, Open, or Save As screens. If you frequently use a template, you can pin the template to the Start or New screens.

- **Strict Open XML (p. 14, 28-29)** You can open documents in the Strict Open XML format to resolve leap year issues with 1900.

- **SkyDrive (p. 14-15, 26-27, 30, 130-131, 164, 192-193, 452-457, 464-473)** SkyDrive is a cloud-based online storage system that requires a Microsoft account to access. You can open and save files from a SkyDrive directly from Office, and share them with others. In addition, you can use three related options—Invite People, Get a Sharing Link, and Post to Social Networks—to allow others to access to a SkyDrive document.

- **Office 365 and SharePoint (p. 14-15, 26-27, 30, 130-131, 164, 452-463)** SharePoint server is an organizational cloud storage, sharing, and tracking system with customizable apps on the web. Office 365 is a subscription-based Microsoft web site with SharePoint services that allows you to take advantage of expanded cloud and sharing capabilities.

- **Document Windows (p. 16)** Office documents open in their own program window instead of one program window and a collection of individual windows to make it easier to display several windows at once.

- **Options Pane (p. 17)** Office changes many dialog boxes—including Format Shape, Format Picture, Format Text, and Format Background—to task panes that appear on the right side of the screen.

- **Windows Help (p. 24-25)** The web browser-like Help Viewer allows you to browse a catalog of topics to locate information, use popular searches, or enter your own phrases to search for information.

- **Save Options (p. 26-27)** Office adds new save options, which include Don't Show the Backstage when opening or saving files, Show additional places for saving, even if sign-in may be required, and Save to Computer by default.

- **Online Services (p. 30-31, 130-131, 162-163, 192-193)** You can connect to and integrate online services into Office programs. The online services include SkyDrive and Office 365 SharePoint for storage, Flickr and YouTube for images and video, and Facebook, LinkedIn, and Twitter for sharing and messaging.

- **User Account (p. 31, 455)** Office integrates a user account that lets you connect to online services, such as SkyDrive, Office 365 SharePoint, YouTube, Facebook, Linkedin, Twitter, and Flickr. Within any Office 2013 program, you can add, modify or switch accounts or sign out entirely.

- **No Exit Command (p. 34)** Except for Outlook, the File tab doesn't have an Exit command. Since each document opens in its own program window, it's not needed. To exit, you click the Close button on the program window.

- **Online Pictures (p. 37, 160-164, 248-249)** If you need a picture to insert into a document and don't have one, you can search for and insert clip art from Office.com, a picture from the web using Bing Image Search, a picture from your SkyDrive, or a picture from an online service, such as Flickr.

- **Live Layout Preview (p. 38-39, 114-115, 124)** As you resize or move an object, a live layout preview appears for the object on the screen.

- **Apps for Office (p. 293, 297, 376-377, 424-427)** With Office.com, you can add functionality with a third-party app to an Office program, and then use the app to extend features in a document. If you have an App for Office dictionary installed from the Office Store, a definition appears in the Spelling pane and Thesaurus pane.

- **Touch/Mouse Mode (p. 346-347, 416)** To make Office easier to use with a touch screen, each program provides Touch/Mouse Mode, which adds or removes more space between commands on the Ribbon.

- **Office Presentation Service (p. 358-359)** The Office Presentation Service (OPS) allows you to deliver an Office document as a presentation over the Internet. OPS is a free public service provided by Microsoft for use with your Microsoft account ID.

- **Send Documents by Instant Message (p. 387)** With Lync, you can send an Office document to a participant in an instant message.

- **Trusted Apps Catalog (p. 390, 394)** An App Catalog site is a special site collection on a web application. You can store apps for SharePoint and Office apps for your organization's internal use in an App Catalog site.

- **Office Background and Theme (p. 405)** You can select an Office program background and theme in General Options.

- **Office Web Apps (p. 474-482)** An Office Web App allows you to work with an Office document stored on a SkyDrive or SharePoint site in a web browser or on different mobile devices. Office Web Apps provide a web-based version of Word, Excel, PowerPoint, and OneNote. If you're working with an Office document stored on a SharePoint site, multiple authors can collaborate on the same document at the same time.

Office Tools

- **OneNote (p. 358, 373-375)** In an Office program, you can use Send To Notes to send a screen clip, document, or note to OneNote. With Microsoft Lync, you can participate in an online meeting and share notes with OneNote. With Office Presentation Service, you can give an online document presentation and share notes with OneNote.

- **Lync (p. 360-363)** Microsoft Lync is an instant messaging program that allows you to send and receive instant messages, hold video chats, present meetings, and share files. Lync uses a SharePoint or Office 365 site as the meeting or conversation host.

◆ **Lync Recording Manager (p. 362-363)** If not everyone is able to attend an online Lync meeting, you can record the session to play it back later. You can manage the recording with the Lync Recording Manager tool.

◆ **Spreadsheet or Database Compare (p. 420-421)** If you need to compare two Excel spreadsheets or Access databases, you can use the Spreadsheet Compare or Database Compare tools.

◆ **Upload Center (p. 420-421)** The Upload Center shows you pending uploads, recently uploaded files and all cached files from a server in one location, which includes working with SkyDrive and SharePoint sites.

◆ **Telemetry Log or Dashboard (p. 420-421)** Telemetry Log records Office events in an Excel spreadsheet to help you troubleshoot problems. Telemetry Database is an Excel spreadsheet that connects to an SQL database to collect client data from other sources in a shared folder.

◆ **SkyDrive Pro (p. 420-421)** With SkyDrive Pro, you can connect and synchronize your SkyDrive cloud storage on a SharePoint site with your desktop.

◆ **Update Office (p. 422)** With Windows 8, you can automatically get updates to Office 2013 along with the operating system.

PowerPoint 2013

◆ **New Presentation (p. 2, 10-11, 12-13)** You can use the Start and New screens to create a presentation. Instead of starting from a blank presentation, you can start a presentation from a template, theme, or presentation.

◆ **Status Bar (p. 9)** The Status bar allows you to check the on/off status of certain features and add/remove options, including Notes and Comments. You can click an item on the Status bar to open or enable a command.

◆ **Slides and Outline Panes (p. 18-19, 21, 40-41)** You can switch between the Slides and Outline panes by clicking the Normal view button on the Status bar.

◆ **Notes Pane (p. 18-19)** You can click the Notes button on the View tab to show or hide the Notes pane.

◆ **Touch Screen Navigation (p. 20-21, 346-347)** You can use typical touch screen gestures, such as swipe, tap, scroll, zoom, and pan, to navigate in the PowerPoint window or Slide Show.

◆ **Improved PowerPoint Options (p. 45, 409, 411, 412)** PowerPoint includes some new options that include the following: Properties follow chart data point for all new presentations, Properties follow chart data point for current presentation, Disable Slide Show hardware graphics acceleration, Automatically extend display when presenting on a laptop or tablet, and Do not automatically hyperlink.

◆ **Theme Variations (p. 98-99)** Instead of changing individual theme attributes, such as color and fonts, you can apply a set of variations to a theme.

◆ **Eyedropper (p. 128, 174, 189)** You can use an eyedropper to apply a color from an object on the screen.

- **Smart Guides (p. 144-145, 148)** As you drag objects, Smart Guides automatically appear so you can adjust the spacing and alignment the selection to other objects.

- **Merge Shapes (p. 156)** You can merge two or more shapes to create new shapes. The merge options include Union, Combine, Fragment, Intersect, and Subtract.

- **Insert Video and Audio (p. 192-193, 198-199, 204)** You can insert a video from a file, SkyDrive, Bing Video Search, or a social media web site, such as YouTube, using an embed code. PowerPoint supports MP4 and MOV with H.264 video and Advanced Audio Coding (AAC) audio. You can also play audio in the background.

- **Optimize Media Compatibility (p. 204)** When you have audio or video media in a presentation that could present compatibility issues, you can optimize the media in the presentation for use on different devices.

- **Embed Excel Charts (p. 222-226)** PowerPoint uses Microsoft Excel 2013 to embed a chart, which you can access and work with chart data from within a worksheet in PowerPoint or Excel 2013.

- **Chart Buttons (p. 232-233, 237, 240-241)** When you create or select a chart, buttons—Chart Styles, Chart Elements, and Chart Filters—appear on the document for easy access to format the chart, modify chart elements, and filter chart data.

- **Chart Labels (p. 239)** You can have data labels appears as callouts or just about any shape, and even add leader lines to them.

- **Slide Size (p. 280-281)** You can set the proportions of your presentation slides to standard (4:3) or widescreen (16:9).

- **Check Grammar and Spelling (p. 288, 292-293)** You can select an option to check grammar when you check spelling in a presentation. When you check spelling, the Spelling pane appears. In the pane, you can also specify the language you want to use as you check spelling. If you have an App for Office dictionary installed from the Office Store, a definition appears in the pane.

- **Thesaurus Pane (p. 297)** If you have an App for Office dictionary installed from the Office Store, a definition appears in the Thesaurus pane. You can also access Foreign languages at the bottom of the pane.

- **Motion Paths (p. 322)** When you create a motion path an mation, the original object stays put, and PowerPoint displays a ghost image as it moves along the path to the end.

- **Hardware Graphics Acceleration (p. 334)** If your system includes a hardware graphics accelerator for gaming, it may create problems in the PowerPoint window or slide show. You can disable hardware graphics acceleration to fix the problem.

- **Multiple Monitor Support (p. 334, 350-351)** When you setup a slide show, you can specify the monitor you want to use and the resolution to display it.

- **Slide Show Toolbar (p. 342)** The Slide Show Toolbar includes buttons to see all slides using the Slide Navigator and zoom in and out.

- ◆ **Slide Navigator (p. 344, 346)**   You can use Slide Navigator to access slides or sections, and navigation commands on the shortcut menu to access slides in custom slide shows.

- ◆ **Laser Tool (p. 348)**   When you are presenting a slide show, you can turn your mouse pointer into a pen tool to highlight and circle your key points or a laser tool to point to areas on the screen.

- ◆ **Presenter View (p. 352-353)**   With Presenter view, you can deliver a slide show on one monitor while you control it from another. You can use Presenter view with one monitor to practice or two monitors to deliver it. In Presenter view, you can view the presentation time, current slide, speaker notes, and next slide, and use slide show view options.

- ◆ **Comments Pane (p. 368-371)**   When you insert a comment, PowerPoint creates a comment bubble icon and opens the Comments pane, where you enter your comments and reply to comments.

- ◆ **Start Up Options (p. 404)**   You can specify start up options for how you want PowerPoint to start including opening files with specified extensions, detecting if PowerPoint isn't the default program for presentations, and showing the Start screen when PowerPoint starts.

What Happened To . . .

- ◆ **Exit Command (p. 34)**   The command has been removed from the File tab. Since each document opens in its own program window, it's not needed. To exit, you click the Close button on the program window.

- ◆ **Fax Templates (p. 386)**   Fax templates are not included in the Office 2013 installation to reduce the size of the installation. However, you can still download them. Click the File tab, click New, and then type fax in the Search for online templates.

- ◆ **Microsoft Office Picture Manager**   Picture Manager has been replaced by Windows Photo Gallery.

- ◆ **Microsoft Clip Organizer**   Clip Organizer has been replaced by Online Pictures, which allows you to insert content from the Office.com Clip Art collection and other resources, such as Bing Image/Video search, Flickr, and your SkyDrive or Facebook page.

Microsoft Office Specialist

About the MOS Program

The Microsoft Office Specialist (MOS) certification is the globally recognized standard for validating expertise with the Microsoft Office suite of business productivity programs. Earning an MOS certificate acknowledges you have the expertise to work with Microsoft Office programs. To earn the MOS certification, you must pass a certification exam for the Microsoft Office desktop applications of Microsoft Word, Excel, PowerPoint, Outlook, Access, OneNote, SharePoint, or Office 365. (The availability of Microsoft Office Specialist certification exams varies by program, program version, and language. Visit *www.microsoft.com* and search on *MOS* or *Microsoft Office Specialist* for exam availability and more information about the program.) The Microsoft Office Specialist program is the only Microsoft-approved program in the world for certifying proficiency with Microsoft Office programs.

What Does This Logo Mean?

It means this book has been approved by the Microsoft Office Specialist program to be certified courseware for learning Microsoft PowerPoint 2013 and preparing for the certification exam. This book will prepare you for the Microsoft Office Specialist exam for Microsoft PowerPoint 2013. Each certification level, either Core or Expert, has a set of objectives, which are organized into broader skill sets. Content that pertains to a Microsoft Office Specialist objective is identified with the following objective number and the specific pages throughout this book:

PP13C-1.1
PP13C-2.2

Preparing for a MOS Exam

Every Microsoft Office Specialist certification exam is developed from a list of objectives based on how Microsoft Office programs are actually used in the workplace. The list of objectives determine the scope of each exam, so they provide you with the information you need to prepare for MOS certification. Microsoft Office Specialist Approved Courseware, including the On Demand series, is reviewed and approved on the basis of its coverage of the objectives. To prepare for the certification exam, you

should review and perform each task identified with a MOS objective to confirm that you can meet the requirements for the exam.

Taking a MOS Exam

The Microsoft Office Specialist certification exams are not written exams. Instead, the exams are performance-based examinations that allow you to interact with a "live"

Office program as you complete a series of objective-based tasks. All the standard ribbons, tabs, toolbars, and keyboard shortcuts are available during the exam. Microsoft Office Specialist exams for Office 2013 programs consist of 25 to 35 questions, each of which requires you to complete one or more tasks using the Office program for which you are seeking certification. A typical exam takes from 45 to 60 minutes. Passing percentages range from 70 to 80 percent correct.

The Exam Experience

After you fill out a series of information screens, the testing software starts the exam and the Office program. The test questions appear in the exam dialog box in the lower right corner of the screen.

◆ The timer starts when the first question appears and displays the remaining exam time at the top of the exam dialog box. If the timer and the counter are distracting, you can click the timer to remove the display.

◆ The counter at the top of the exam dialog box tracks how many questions you have completed and how many remain.

◆ If you think you have made a mistake, you can click the Reset button to restart the question. The Reset button does not restart the entire exam or extend the exam time limit.

◆ When you complete a question, click the Next button to move to the next question. It is not possible to move back to a previous question on the exam.

◆ If the exam dialog box gets in your way, you can click the Minimize button in the upper right corner of the exam dialog box to hide it, or you can drag the title bar to another part of the screen to move it.

Tips for Taking an Exam

◆ Carefully read and follow all instructions provided in each question.

◆ Make sure all steps in a task are completed before proceeding to the next exam question.

◆ Enter requested information as it appears in the instructions without formatting unless you are explicitly requested otherwise.

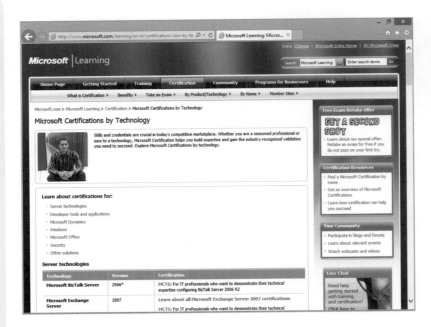

- ◆ Close all dialog boxes before proceeding to the next exam question unless you are specifically instructed otherwise.

- ◆ Do not leave tables, boxes, or cells "active" unless instructed otherwise.

- ◆ Do not cut and paste information from the exam interface into the program.

- ◆ When you print a document from an Office program during the exam, nothing actually gets printed.

- ◆ Errant keystrokes or mouse clicks do not count against your score as long as you achieve the correct end result. You are scored based on the end result, not the method you use to achieve it. However, if a specific method is explicitly requested, you need to use it to get credit for the results.

- ◆ The overall exam is timed, so taking too long on individual questions may leave you without enough time to complete the entire exam.

- ◆ If you experience computer problems during the exam, immediately notify a testing center administrator to restart your exam where you were interrupted.

Exam Results

At the end of the exam, a score report appears indicating whether you passed or failed the exam. An official certificate is mailed to successful candidates in approximately two to three weeks.

Getting More Information

To learn more about the Microsoft Office Specialist program, read a list of frequently asked questions, and locate the nearest testing center, visit:

www.microsoft.com

For a more detailed list of Microsoft Office Specialist program objectives, visit:

www.perspection.com

Index

eyedropper, 128, 174, 189

F

Facebook
    adding account to Office, 31
    sharing with, 464-465, 472-473, 480-481
fading out effects, 318
fax, sending presentations by, 386
Featuring categories
    for blank presentations, 10
    list of, 10
    for templates, 11
File Block settings, 392-393
file encryption, 380
file extensions, 275
    for macros, 442
    showing/hiding, 23
files. *See also* movies/videos; SharePoint; synchronizing files; specific formats
    audio file formats, 192
    hyperlinks to, 266
    movies/videos from file, inserting, 192-193
    OLE (object linking and embedding) for, 254
    pictures from file, inserting, 165
    sounds/audio from file, inserting, 192-193
Files of Type list, 14-15
File tab, 3, 5
FileZ, 389
fills. *See also* color fills; gradient fills; textures
    table, adding fill to, 251
    WordArt, text fills for, 188-189
filtering chart data, 241
finding and replacing text, 75
first-line indents, 66
Fit To Window button, 9
Flash movies, 192
    playing, 448-449
Flickr
    adding account to Office, 31
    inserting picture from, 162-163, 130-131
    sharing with, 464-465, 472-473, 480-481
flipping. *See* rotating

folders
    for presentations, 356-357
Font Color button, 97, 101, 106
fonts. *See also* characters; TrueType fonts
    CDs, slide shows on, 356-357
    differences between, 340
    embedding fonts, 340
    entire presentation, replacing fonts for, 65
    formatting text fonts, 65
    for headers and footers, 93
    for hyperlinks, 271
    kerning with, 62
    printing options, 311
    Ribbon, changing font with, 64
    in slide shows, 340
    for symbols, 71
    for text boxes, 72
    theme fonts, 102, 103
Footer placeholder, 90
footers. *See* headers and footers
foreign languages
    adding to programs, 300
    designating, 290
    French spellings, 288-289
    keyboard switch languages, 291
    marking text as language, 290
    Mini Translator, 298-299
    spelling, 292-293
    Spanish spelling, 288-289
    thesauruses, 297
    translating text to, 298
Format Painter, 70
    slides, applying themes to, 97
Format Shape pane
    for color fills, 128
    for effects, 136
    for gradient fills, 134
    for texture fills, 132
    undoing changes in, 128, 130, 132
formatting. *See also* charts; formatting text; SmartArt graphics
    connector lines, 151
    curves, 121
    freeforms, 121
    Handout Master, 282
    hyperlinks, 271
    movies/videos, 197

keyboard *(continued)*
    grid settings, overriding, 145
    nudging drawing object with, 125
    objects, moving, 39
    switch languages, 291
    window panes, resizing, 17
KeyTips, 4
keywords for online pictures, 161

L

Label
    ActiveX control, 446
labels in chart, changing, 239
landscape orientation, 280-281
languages. *See also* foreign languages
    adding to programs, 300
    Office tool, 420-421
    using, 300
LAN (local-area network), 450
laser pointer, 335, 344
layouts. *See also* charts; slide layouts
    organization chart layout, changing, 220-221
    SmartArt graphic layout, changing, 213
left indents, 66
legend series. *See* charts
letter paper slide size, 280
libraries
    SharePoint libraries, 462-463
lines or arrows
    in charts, 237
    connector lines, 150-151
    Counterbalance Arrows, 208
    customizing attributes, 418-419
    editing, 119
    modifying, 119
    Quick Style to line, adding, 118
    straight lines or arrows, drawing, 118
line spacing, 60
Linkedin
    adding account to Office, 31
    sharing with, 464-465, 472-473, 480-481
linking. *See also* hyperlinks; OLE (object linking and embedding)
    defined, 253

list boxes, 8
    ActiveX control, 446
list purpose, SmartArt, 207
lists. *See* bulleted lists; numbered lists
Lists and Galleries, 3
live preview, 4. *See also* tables
    general options, setting, 406
    of organization charts, 220
    with Picture Shape gallery, 173
    for SmartArt graphics, 215
    themes, 96
    of transitions, 318
Lock Aspect Ratio check box, 246
luminosity, 100, 101
Lync. *See* Microsoft Lync

M

Macintosh PICT, 167
Macro-Enabled Design Template, 29
Macro-Enabled Show, 29
macros, 436-437, 423. *See also* Trust Center
    controlling, 438-439
    copying to other presentations, 439
    creating, 436-437
    debugging, 438
    deleting, 437
    digital signatures on, 440
    earlier versions, macros from, 436
    editing, 439
    file extensions for, 275, 442
    harmful attack sand, 266-267
    ribbon, assigning macro to, 441
    running, 437
    saving presentations with, 442
    security settings, 397
    self-signing certificates for, 440
    stopping macros, 437
    toolbar, assigning macro to, 441
    VBA macros, 432-433
maintenance, performing, 422
margins
    tables, changing cell margins in, 246
    for text boxes, 72
    wrapping and adjusting, 73
Margins button, 246
Marks as Final command, 381
Master Layout, 88